Readings in Contemporary Criminological Theory

Advisor in Criminal Justice to Northeastern University Press
GILBERT GEIS

Readings in

CONTEMPORARY
CRIMINOLOGICAL
THEORY

Edited by

Peter Cordella
& Larry Siegel

Northeastern University Press
BOSTON

Northeastern University Press

Library of Congress Cataloging-in-Publication Data

Readings in contemporary criminological theory / edited by Peter
  Cordella and Larry Siegel.
        p. cm.
    Includes bibliographical references and index.
    ISBN 1–55553–223–3 (cl : alk. paper). — ISBN 1–55553–224–1 (pa :
alk. paper)
        1. Criminology. 2. Crime. I. Cordella, Peter. II. Siegel,
Larry J.
HV6018.R35   1996
364—dc20   96–19387

Designed by Diane Levy

Composed in Palatino by Coghill Composition Company in Richmond, Virginia.

Printed and bound by The Maple Press Company in York, Pennsylvania. The paper is Sebago Antique, an acid-free sheet.

MANUFACTURED IN THE UNITED STATES OF AMERICA
99 98 97 96   4 3 2 1

Contents

    Kathleen Daly and Meda Chesney-Lind

23 An Assensus Model of Justice   365
    Herman Bianchi

24 A Communitarian Theory of Social Order   379
    Peter Cordella

    Contributors   393

    Acknowledgments   397

    Index   401

Readings in Contemporary Criminological Theory

Introduction

Criminology is an evolving field of study, one that has been undergoing change and development for more than two hundred years. During this period, the various schools of criminological thought have displayed a great deal of vitality and longevity. Rather than becoming outdated and eventually abandoned by the scholarly community, early schools of thought have been modified and updated as more knowledge becomes available.

This theoretical robustness may be troubling to some who complain that "old theories never die" but are resurrected time and again in slightly different formats. As current and more popular views lose favor, they are replaced with newer versions of the theory that they themselves replaced. The longevity of criminological theories may be due to the fact that at their core lie axioms that are difficult to ignore or refute: Criminals are greedy; criminals are psychologically abnormal; criminals live in a bad environment; criminals had a rough childhood; criminals are rebels and outcasts, and so on. The reason it is difficult to refute any of these core beliefs is that their converse seems outlandish. Could we ever believe that criminals are well-adjusted overachievers born to supportive families in affluent neighborhoods?

Although the core concepts upon which criminological theories are built seem immutable, their link to crime is often complex, rendering them ineffective as singular explanations of criminal behavior. Because scientific parsimony is a necessary requirement of effective social theory, the complexity of criminal behavior has proved a challenge for criminologists searching for the single "holy grail" of criminological theory.

An example of this complexity can be seen in theories based on the view that poverty and privation are the cause of most criminal activity. This view is supported because there are strong links between poverty and crime. Aggregate statistics show that the most serious and violent crime occurs in disorganized, poverty-stricken, urban neighborhoods. The prisons are filled not with the affluent but with the children of poverty and want. This prima facie link between poverty and crime is problematic, however. First, there is little evidence that crime rates increase during periods of high unemployment; in fact the opposite may be true. Crime rates decline when people are unemployed because there are fewer suitable targets and more capable guardians at home to protect them. Teenagers, among whom the crime rate is high, are much less affected by job losses, since many are still in school. Their activities may be curtailed because parents are now at home and better able to supervise their after-school activities. It is also unlikely that a law-abiding businessperson who is suddenly laid off will begin to steal cars and commit burglaries. Therefore, the unemployment rate, though an indicator of economic well-being, has generally not been useful in predicting crime rates.

Second, national data show that the United States, one of the world's most affluent nations, has one of the highest crime rates in the world. If poverty was a direct cause of crime, then rates in less developed nations, which have much lower standards of living than the United States, would be higher. This is not the case. Finally, self-report surveys do not indicate that lower-class youth are significantly more delinquent or criminal than middle-class adolescents.

Despite this conflicting evidence, there is little question that known criminals are members of the lower class, that prisons are populated by the poor and uneducated, and that lower-class environments contain a significant portion of all predatory criminals.

The relationship between poverty and crime is a prime example of the ecological fallacy: What applies to the individual case may not apply to society as a whole. The reason a particular person commits a crime may not hold up as an explanation of crime trends and patterns. Nonetheless, a theory that predicts criminality on an individual level of analysis but fails to explain or predict highly correlated social and economic trends will surely be a target for criticism.

Because they need to explain both micro-level individual traits and macro-level social behavior patterns, it is not surprising that over the field's history of more than two hundred years, criminologists have developed numerous and varied visions of why people commit crime and why crime rates change. What are these visions, and how have they evolved?

Classical Criminology

During the mid-eighteenth century, influenced by the social and philosophical changes that were sweeping Europe, utilitarian social philosophers began to advocate rethinking the prevailing concepts of law and justice. They argued that because human behavior is designed to be useful, purposeful, and reasonable, a rational approach to punishment was needed. The founder of what is today known as the classical school, Cesare Beccaria

(1738–1794), suggested that the drive motivating human behavior is the desire for pleasure and the avoidance of pain. Because crimes must provide some pleasure to the criminal, it follows that to deter crime, one must administer pain in an appropriate amount to counterbalance the pleasure obtained from crime. Beccaria summarized his famous theorem as follows:

> In order for punishment not to be in every instance, an act of violence of one or many against a private citizen, it must be essentially public, prompt, necessary, the least possible in the given circumstances, proportionate to the crimes, dictated by the laws.[1]

British philosopher Jeremy Bentham (1748–1833) helped popularize Beccaria's views in his writings on *utilitarianism*. According to his theory, actions are evaluated by their tendency to produce advantage, pleasure, and happiness and to avoid or prevent mischief, pain, evil, or unhappiness. "Nature has placed mankind under the governance of two sovereign masters, pain and pleasure," declared Bentham, ". . . they govern us in all we do, in all we say, in all we think: every effort we can make to throw off our subjection will serve but to demonstrate and confirm it."[2]

Bentham believed that the purpose of all law is to produce and support the greatest possible happiness of the community it serves. Since punishment is in itself harmful, its existence is justified only if it promises to prevent greater evil than it creates. The writings of Beccaria and Bentham form the core of what today is referred to as *classical criminology*. As originally conceived in the eighteenth century, classical theory included several core elements: (1) People in society have free will to choose criminal or conventional solutions to meet their needs or settle their problems; (2) criminal solutions may be more attractive than conventional ones, because they usually require less effort for a greater payoff (profit without work, sex without commitment, vengeance without legal process); (3) illegal actions are limited by the fear of detection and punishment; (4) the more severe, certain, and swift legal punishment is, the better it can control criminal behavior.

The classical perspective influenced judicial and legal philosophy during much of the late eighteenth and nineteenth centuries. At Beccaria's urging, the routine torture of prisoners was abandoned. Prison sentences in proportion to the seriousness of the crime replaced physical punishments. Capital punishment was still widely used, but slowly it began to be implemented only for the most serious crimes. The vision of the rational criminal who could be swayed by the fear of punishment dominated legal thought for almost one hundred years.

The classical approach fell into disfavor among criminologists during the mid-nineteenth century, when the core doctrine that human behavior was self-directed and a product of rational choice was challenged by a group of social scientists calling themselves positivists. This group was developing a vision of human behavior, in contradistinction to the established view.

Nineteenth-Century Positivism

The *positivist* tradition developed as the scientific method began to take hold in Europe. This movement was inspired by new discoveries in biology, astronomy, and chemistry. If the scientific method could be applied to the study of nature, then why not use it to study human behavior? Auguste Comte (1798–1857), who is considered the founder of sociology, applied scientific methods to the study of society. According to Comte, societies pass through stages that can be organized on the basis of how their members try to understand the world in which they live. People in primitive societies consider inanimate objects as having life (e.g., the sun is a god); in later social stages people embrace a rational, scientific view of the world. Comte called this final stage the positive stage, and those who followed his writings became known as *positivists*.

As we understand it today, the positivist tradition has two main elements. The first is the belief that human behavior is a function of external forces that are beyond individual control. Some of these forces are social, such as the effect of wealth and class; others are political and historical, such as war and famine. Still other forces are more personal and psychological, such as an individual's brain structure, biological makeup, and mental ability. Each of these forces operates to influence human behavior.

The second aspect of positivism is its embrace of the scientific method to solve problems. Positivists rely on the strict use of empirical methods to test hypotheses. That is, they believe in the factual, firsthand observation and measurement of conditions and events. Positivists would agree that an abstract concept such as intelligence exists, because it can be measured by an IQ test. They would challenge a concept such as "the soul," however, because it is a condition that cannot be verified by the scientific method. The positivist tradition was spurred on by Charles Darwin (1809–1882), whose work on the evolution of man encouraged a nineteenth-century "cult of science" based on the conviction that all human activity could be verified by scientific principles.

Positivist Criminology

If the scientific method could be used to explain all behavior, then it was to be expected that by the nineteenth century, it would be applied to understanding criminality. The earliest of these "scientific" studies were biologically oriented. Physiognomists, such as J. K. Lavater (1741–1801), studied the facial features of criminals to determine whether the shape of ears, nose, and eyes and the distance between them were associated with antisocial behavior. Phrenologists, such as Franz Joseph Gall (1758–1828) and Johann K. Spurzheim (1776–1832), studied the shape of the skull and bumps on the head to determine whether these physical attributes were linked to criminal behavior. These phrenologists believed that external cranial characteristics dictate which areas of the brain control physical activity. Though their primitive techniques and quasi-scientific methods have been thoroughly discredited, these efforts were an early attempt to use a "scientific" method to study crime.

Cesare Lombroso and Criminal Man

In nineteenth-century Italy Cesare Lombroso studied the cadavers of executed criminals in an effort to determine scientifically whether law violators were physically different from people of conventional values and behavior. Lombroso (1835–1909), known as the "father of criminology," was a physician who served in the Italian army for much of his career. That experience gave him ample opportunity to study the physical characteristics of soldiers convicted and executed for criminal offenses. Later, he studied inmates at institutes for the criminally insane at Pavia, Pesaro, and Reggio Emilia.

Lombrosian theory, which helped spur interest in *criminal anthropology* (see the article by Nicole Hahn Rafter), can be outlined in a few simple statements.[3] First, Lombroso believed that serious offenders, those who engaged in repeated assault or theft, inherit their criminal traits. According to this view, these "born criminals" inherit physical problems that impel them to a life of crime. Second, born criminals suffer from *atavistic anomalies*; physically, they are throwbacks to more primitive times when people were savages. For example, criminals were believed to have the enormous jaws and strong canine teeth common to carnivores and savages who devour raw flesh. In addition, Lombroso compared the behavior of criminals with that of the mentally ill and those suffering some forms of epilepsy. According to Lombrosian theory, criminogenic traits can be acquired through indirect heredity, from a "degenerate family with frequent cases of insanity, deafness, syphilis, epilepsy, and alcoholism among its members." Direct heredity—being related to a family of criminals—is the second primary cause of crime.

Lombroso's version of criminal anthropology was introduced to the United States via articles and textbooks that adopted his ideas. He attracted a circle of followers who expanded upon his vision of biological determinism. His work was actually more popular in the United States than it was in Europe. By the beginning of the twentieth century, American authors were discussing the "science of penology" and the "science of criminology."[4] Chapter 5 discusses the theories of criminology that have their roots in Lombroso's biological determinism and view individual characteristics as the cause of crime.

The Development of Sociological Criminology

At the same time that biological views were dominating criminology, another group of thinkers was developing the science of sociology as a way of scientifically studying the major social changes that were then taking place in nineteenth-century society.

Sociology seemed an ideal perspective from which to study society. After thousands of years of stability, the world was undergoing a "population explosion"; the population estimated at 600 million in 1700 had risen to 900 million by 1800. People were flocking to cities in ever-increasing numbers. Manchester, England, had 12,000 inhabitants in 1760 and 400,000 in 1850; during the same period, the population of Glasgow, Scotland, rose from 30,000 to 300,000. The development of machinery such as power looms had doomed cottage industries and given rise to a factory system in which large numbers of people toiled for extremely low wages. The spread of agricultural machines increased the food supply while reducing the need for a large rural work force; the excess laborers further swelled the cities' populations. Political, religious, and social traditions continued to be challenged by the scientific method.

Foundations of Sociological Criminology

The foundations of sociological criminology can be traced to the works of L. A. J. (Adolphe) Quetelet (1796–1874) and Emile Durkheim (1858–1917). Quetelet was a Belgian mathematician who—along with a Frenchman, André-Michel Guerry—established what is known as the cartographic school of criminology.[5] Quetelet, who made use of statistics developed in France in the early nineteenth century (called the comptes généraux de l'administration de la justice), was one of the first social scientists to use objective mathematical techniques to investigate the influence of social factors—such as season, climate, sex, and age—on the propensity to commit crime. Quetelet's most important finding was that these social forces correlated significantly with crime rates. In addition to finding that age and sex had a strong influence on crime, Quetelet also uncovered evidence that season, climate, population composition, and poverty were also related to criminality. More specifically, he found that crime rates were greatest in the summer, in southern areas, among heterogenous populations, and among the poor and uneducated; they were also influenced by drinking habits.[6] Quetelet was a pioneer of sociologically oriented criminology. He identified many of the relationships between crime and social phenomena that still serve as a basis for criminological study today.

Emile Durkheim

(David) Emile Durkheim (1858–1917) was one of the founders of sociology and a significant contributor to criminology.[7] His definition of crime as a "normal" and necessary social phenomenon has influenced modern criminology more than any other.

Durkheim was a positivist with a sociological rather than a biological orientation. According to his vision of social positivism, crime is part of human nature because it has existed in every age, in both poverty and prosperity.[8] Crime is normal because it is virtually impossible to imagine a society in which criminal behavior is totally absent. Such a society would almost demand that all people be and act exactly alike. The inevitability of crime is linked to the differences (heterogeneity) within society. Since people are so different from one another and employ such a variety of methods and forms of behavior to meet their needs, it is not surprising that some will resort to criminality. Even if "real" crimes were eliminated, human weaknesses and petty vices would be elevated to the status of crime. As long as human differences exist, then, crime is inevitable and one of the fundamental conditions of social life.

Crime, argued Durkheim, can also be useful and, on occasion, even "healthy" for a society to experience. The existence of crime implies that a way is open for social change and that the social structure is not rigid or inflexible. Put another way, if crime did not exist, it would mean that everyone behaved the same way and was in complete agreement concerning what is right and wrong. Such universal conformity would stifle creativity and independent thinking. To illustrate this concept, Durkheim offered the example of the Greek philosopher Socrates, who was considered a criminal and put to death for corrupting the morals of youth.

Durkheim distinguished this altruistic criminal type from the common criminal by analyzing the motivation and reason behind the deviant behavior of each. The common criminal rejects all discipline, makes destruction or violation of law an end unto itself, and manifests little interest in moral conduct. The altruistic criminal is offended by the rules of society and seeks social change and an improved moral climate through his or her acts. In addition, Durkheim argued, crime is beneficial because it calls attention to social ills. A rising crime rate can signal the need for social change and promote a variety of programs designed to relieve the human suffering that may have caused crime in the first place.

In *The Division of Labor in Society*, Durkheim described the consequences of the shift from a small, rural society—which he labeled mechanical—to the more modern "organic" society with a large urban population, division of labor, and personal isolation. From this shift flowed *anomie*, or norm and role confusion, a powerful sociological concept that helps to explain the chaos and disarray accompanying the loss of traditional values in modern society. Durkheim's research on suicide indicated that anomic societies maintain high suicide rates; by implication, anomie could cause other forms of deviance to develop.

The Chicago School

The primacy of sociological positivism was secured by research begun in the early twentieth century by Robert Ezra Park (1864–1944), Ernest W. Burgess

(1886–1966), Louis Wirth (1897–1952), and their colleagues in the Sociology Department at the University of Chicago. Known as the Chicago School, their pioneering research on the social ecology of the city inspired a generation of scholars to study the social forces operating in urban areas that create criminal interactions; some neighborhoods become "natural areas" for crime.[9] These urban neighborhoods maintain such a high level of poverty that there is a breakdown of critical social institutions, such as the school and the family. Their ability to control behavior is thus reduced, and the resulting social disorganization leads to a high crime rate.

The Chicago School sociologists and their contemporaries focused on the functions of social institutions and how their breakdown influences behavior. They pioneered the ecological study of crime; crime was a function of where one lived. However, beginning as early as the 1930s, another group of sociologists, influenced by psychology, added an interpersonal component to criminological theory. They concluded that the individual's relationship to important social processes—such as education, family life, and peer relations—was the key to understanding human behavior. In any social milieu, children who grow up in a home racked by conflict, attend an inadequate school, and associate with deviant peers become exposed to procrime forces. Some of these theorists held that people *learn* criminal attitudes from older, more experienced law violators and that the learning of attitudes in support of criminality precedes entry into a criminal career. Others believed, in contrast, that crime occurs when social forces are insufficient to control and regulate behavior. Some criminologists focused on the internal self-controls that people develop through socialization in their family, school, and peer group. Others examined the behavioral constraints that were a by-product of socialization. People were forced to control their behavior if they wished to maintain attachments to their family and community, or if they were involved in behavior that would one day pay off in social advancement. Failure to conform would mean rejection, alienation, and ties to peer groups that supported criminal behavior and substance abuse. Each of these views linked criminality to the failure of socialization.

By mid-century, most criminologists had embraced either the ecological or socialization view of crime. However, these were not the only views of how social institutions influence human behavior. In Europe, the writings of another social thinker, Karl Marx (1818–1883), pushed the understanding of social interaction in another direction and sowed the seeds for a new direction in criminology.[10]

Conflict Criminology

Oppressive labor conditions prevalent during the rise of industrial capitalism convinced Marx that the character of every civilization is determined by its mode of production, that is, the way its people develop and produce material goods (materialism). The most important relationship in industrial culture, he argued, is between the owners of the means of production, the capitalist *bourgeoisie,* and the people who do the actual labor, the *proletariat.* According to Marx, the economic system controls all facets of human life; consequently, people's lives revolve around the means of production. The exploitation of the working class would, he believed, eventually lead to class conflict and the end of the capitalist system.

Although Marx did not attempt to develop a theory of crime and justice, his writings were applied to legal studies by a few social thinkers, including Ralf Dahrendorf, George Vold, and Willem Bonger.[11] These writings laid the foundation for a Marxist criminology, but decades passed before Marxist theory had an important impact on criminology. In the United States during the 1960s, social and political upheaval were fueled by the Vietnam War, the development of an anti-establishment counterculture movement, the civil rights movement, and the women's movement. Young sociologists who became interested in applying Marxist principles to the study of crime began to analyze the social conditions in the United States that promoted class conflict and crime. What emerged from this intellectual ferment was a Marxist-based radical criminology that held the economic system responsible for creating the conditions conducive to a high crime rate. This conflict tradition has played a significant role in criminology ever since.

Criminology Today

As noted above, the various schools of criminology developed over a period of two hundred years. Though they have undergone great change and innovation, each continues to have an impact on the field. The classical theory that developed from the writings of Beccaria and his eighteenth-century contemporaries is now manifested in rational choice theory. This idea rests on the premise of a thinking, reasoning criminal who weighs the costs and benefits of crime before choosing a line of action and whose final choice is structured by the fear of punishment. According to this view, then, the rational criminal can be thwarted or frightened off by an array of legal deterrents ranging from the threat of harsh punishment to the implementation of security systems and alarms.

Criminal anthropology has also undergone considerable evolution. Although few criminologists still believe that a single trait present at birth or developed soon after can explain a predisposition toward crime, some are convinced that biological and mental traits interact with environmental factors to influence all human behavior, including criminality. Criminologists interested in the biological and neurological basis of crime, sometimes referred to as biosocial theorists, study the association between criminal behavior and such traits as diet, hormonal makeup, personality, and intelligence.

Sociological theories, as developed first by Quetelet and Durkheim and the Chicago School sociologists, still play a prominent role in criminological theory. There are a number of schools of thought within contemporary sociological criminology. One view focuses on the social environment and how it influences both individual and group behavior. Borrowing heavily from the Chicago School, these ecological theorists maintain that individuals' lifestyles and living conditions directly control their criminal behavior. Those at the bottom of the social structure, residing in deteriorated, disorganized areas, cannot achieve success and experience instead anomie, strain, failure, and frustration. Their life circumstances encourage both drug abuse and gang membership.

The writings of Marx and his followers also continue to be influential. Social conflict models still view economic and political imbalance as the root cause of crime. The highly competitive economic structure of the United States and other advanced capitalist countries, which remains structurally biased and inherently inequitable, is the engine that supports the high crime rate. If anything, conflict views have become richer and more complex, especially as they now include feminist and humanist perspectives.

The latest trend in criminological theory is to integrate these various theoretical visions into a complex and all-inclusive vision of crime, borrowing from psychological, biological, and sociological theories. Consolidating these individual factors into complex, *multifactor theories* allows criminologists to derive more powerful and robust explanations of crime.

The selections in this book, which is divided into five parts, present some of the most important works of contemporary criminological theory. Part I reviews important contributions to the choice theory perspective, Part II is devoted to modern biosocial theory, Part III covers recent advances in sociological criminology, and Parts IV and V contain papers on conflict and integrated theory.

Notes

1. Cesare Beccaria, *On Crimes and Punishments*, 6th ed., trans. Henry Paolucci (Indianapolis: Bobbs-Merrill, 1977), 99; see also Edward Devine, "Cesare Beccaria and the Theoretical Foundations of Modern Penal Jurisprudence," *New England Journal on Prison Law* 7 (1982): 8–21.

2. Jeremy Bentham, *A Fragment on Government and an Introduction to the Principle of Morals and Legislation*, ed. Wilfred Harrison (Oxford: Basil Blackwell, 1967), 21.

3. Nicole Hahn Rafter, "Criminal Anthropology in the United States," *Criminology* 30 (1992): 525–547.

4. Rafter 535.

5. L. A. J. Quetelet, *A Treatise on Man and the Development of His Faculties* (Gainesville, Fla.: Scholars' Facsimiles and Reprints, 1969), 82–96.

6. Quetelet 85.

7. See, generally, Robert Nisbet, *The Sociology of Emile Durkheim* (New York: Oxford University Press, 1974), 209.

8. Emile Durkheim, *Rules of the Sociological Method*, trans. S. A. Solvay and J. H. Mueller, ed. G. Catlin (New York: Free Press, 1966), 65–73; Emile Durkheim, *De la division de travail social: Etude sur l'organisation des sociétiés supérieures* (Paris: Felix Alcan, 1893); idem, *The Division of Labor in Society* (New York: Free Press, 1964). *Suicide: A Study in Sociology* (Glencoe, Ill.: Free Press, 1951).

9. Robert Park and Ernest Burgess, *The City* (Chicago: University of Chicago Press, 1925).

10. Karl Marx and Friedrich Engels, *Capital: A Critique of Political Economy*, trans. E. Aveling (Chicago: Charles Kern, 1906); Karl Marx, *Selected Writings in Sociology and Social Philosophy*, trans. P. B. Bottomore (New York: McGraw Hill, 1956). For a general discussion of Marxist thought, see Michael Lynch and W. Byron Groves, *A Primer in Radical Criminology* (New York: Harrow & Heston, 1986), 6–26.

11. Willem Bonger, *Criminality and Economic Conditions* (1916, abridged ed., Bloomington: Indiana University Press, 1969).

PART I
RATIONAL CHOICE THEORIES

Introduction

Contemporary classical theory, referred to here as rational choice theory, began to emerge in the mid-1970s. There were a number of reasons for its development and resulting popularity. The rehabilitation of known criminals was a cornerstone of liberal criminology at that time. But the idea that if crime was caused by some social or psychological problem such as poverty, it could be reduced simply by providing known and potential criminals with good jobs and economic opportunities was widely considered to have failed. A number of national surveys (the best known being Robert Martinson's "What Works?") had failed to uncover examples of rehabilitation programs that prevented future criminal activity.[1] And a well-publicized book, *Beyond Probation*, by Charles Murray and Louis Cox, went as far as suggesting that punishment-oriented programs could "suppress" future criminality much more effectively than those that relied on rehabilitation and treatment efforts.[2] The so-called failure of rehabilitation implied that criminals might not be motivated by their life circumstances, since efforts to improve them seemed to have little effect on their behavior. A reasonable, alternative view was that law violators were greedy, callous people who responded better to the closed fist than the open hand.

A significant increase in the reported crime rate, as well as serious disturbances in the nation's prisons, frightened the general public. To many criminologists it made more sense to revive the classical concepts of social control and punishment than to make futile attempts to improve entrenched social conditions and/or rehabilitate criminals using ineffectual methodologies.[3] In *Thinking About Crime*, a 1975 book that came to symbolize renewed interest in classical views, political scientist James Q. Wilson debunked the positivist view that crime is a function of external forces such as poverty, which can be altered by government programs. Instead, he argued, efforts should be made to reduce criminal opportunity by deterring would-be offenders and incarcerating known criminals. According to Wilson, persons who are at risk of committing crime lack inhibition against misconduct, value the excitement and thrills of breaking the law, have a low stake in conformity, and are willing to take greater chances than the average person. If they were convinced that their actions would bring severe punishment, only the totally irrational would be willing to engage in crime.[4]

Wilson's views coincided with a conservative shift in U.S. public policy following the election of Ronald Reagan in 1980. Political decision makers embraced his ideas as a means to reduce the crime rate. Wilson's views helped shape criminal justice policy for the next two decades. From these roots a newer version of classical theory evolved, based on intelligent thought processes and criminal decision making; it is today referred to as the *rational choice* approach to crime causation.[5]

The readings that follow represent both the core ideas of rational choice theory and some observations on where this vision of crime may be heading. Marcus Felson briefly and succinctly summarizes two of the key components of rational choice theory: routine activities and situational crime prevention. The first concept holds that the likelihood of crime occurring hangs on three factors: motivated (rational) offenders, the presence of suitable targets, and the absence of capable guardians. A rational offender will desist from crime if there is nothing worth taking or if whatever there is is well guarded and the risks are too high. The latter concept, situational crime prevention, suggests that crime can be reduced or eliminated by convincing rational criminals that the opportunity to commit crime has been reduced. Dovetailing with the routine activity concept, situational crime prevention assumes that even the most motivated criminal can be deterred by a commonsense approach to crime control, which stresses either making targets tougher to penetrate and/or increasing the threat of capture by vigilant guardians.

The chapter by Mark Stafford and Mark Warr is important because it helps explain two other key concepts of choice theory, general and specific deterrence. General deterrence strategies are aimed at making potential criminals fear the consequences of crime. The threat of punishment is aimed at convincing rational criminals that "crime does not pay." The concept of general deterrence holds that crime rates will be influenced and controlled by the threat of criminal punishment. If people fear apprehension and punishment, they will not risk breaking the law. An inverse relationship should thus exist between crime rates and the severity, certainty, and celerity (speed) of legal sanctions. If, for example, the punishment for a crime is increased and at the same time the effectiveness and efficiency of the justice system in enforcing the law prohibiting it is improved, then the number of people engaging in that act should decline.

In contrast, specific deterrence refers to punishing known criminals severely so that they will never be tempted to repeat their offenses. If crime is rational, then painful punishments should reduce its future incidence. If criminal sanctions are sufficiently severe, known criminals will never repeat their criminal acts. For example, burglars who spend five years in a tough, maximum security prison should find their enthusiasm for theft dampened upon release. In principle, punishment works if a connection can be established between the planned action and memories of its consequence; if these recollections are intense enough, the action will be prevented or reduced in frequency. Stafford and Warr show how these concepts are linked and then propose some alternative ways of thinking about deterrence.

In "Crime, Shame, and Reintegration," John Braithwaite bases his concepts on his observation that countries in which a criminal conviction brings an inordinate amount of shame and humiliation have extremely low crime rates. In Japan, for example, prosecution for a criminal offense proceeds only when the normal process of public apology, compensation, and forgiveness by the victim breaks down. Shame, then, can become a powerful tool of informal social control. In contrast, citizens in cultures in which crime is not "shameful" view themselves merely as "victims" of the justice system; their punishment comes at the hands of neutral strangers being paid to act. Braithwaite's theory provides an interesting twist on the rational choice approach: The rational criminal might be swayed not so much by the fear of punishment as the fear of exposure and humiliation. However, Braithwaite argues that the shaming experience must be reintegrative: it must ultimately bring offenders closer to society rather than isolating them from the mainstream.

Notes

1. Robert Martinson, "What Works?—Questions and Answers about Prison Reform," *Public Interest* 35 (1974):22–54.
2. Charles Murray and Louis Cox, *Beyond Probation* (Beverly Hills, Calif.: Sage Publications, 1979).
3. Ronald Bayer, "Crime, Punishment and the Decline of Liberal Optimism," *Crime and Delinquency* 27 (1981):190.
4. James Q. Wilson, *Thinking About Crime* (New York: Basic Books, 1975).
5. See, generally, Derek Cornish and Ronald Clarke, eds. *The Reasoning Criminal: Rational Choice Perspectives on Offending* (New York: Springer-Verlag, 1986).

1
Routine Activity Approach

MARCUS FELSON

For most of its history, criminology has assumed that criminals were its primary focus and criminal acts were of secondary interest. But in recent decades some criminologists have begun to argue that the tail was wagging the dog. Criminal incidents themselves became the focus of study, moving from sideshow to center stage. Evidence began to accumulate that burgeoning opportunities to carry out illegal acts draw more people into crime and make those already involved much more efficient at their illegal actions. This interest in criminal opportunities has led criminologists to pay much more attention to the settings and situations in which opportunities for illegal behavior arise and to the specific makeup of illegal incidents.

The routine activity approach (Cohen and Felson, 1979) is part of this recent trend. It began by studying predatory crimes, namely, those offenses in which at least one person attacks the person or property of another. Limiting itself to predatory offenses involving direct physical contact, the routine activity approach specified three minimal elements for such offenses: a likely offender, a suitable target of crime, and the absence of a capable guardian against a crime. A likely offender might be anybody but was more often than not a young male.

A suitable *target* for crime could be a personal or property target. Its suitability for crime was driven by four attributes summed up in the acronym VIVA: value, inertia, visibility, and access. Value is calculated from the offender's viewpoint. Inertia refers to physical aspects of the person or property that interfere with its suitability as a target. A target that is visible to more people is more likely to draw their attention for illegal attack. A target that is also accessible to more people is subject to greater risk of such attack. In sum, the most suitable property for illegal predation is high in value, low in weight, highly visible, and extremely accessible. For example, money has high value per pound; when placed in a high-traffic area, it is very likely to be stolen. Similar principles apply to the suitability of a victim for violent crime.

A capable *guardian* against a crime is less likely to be a police officer or security guard than an individual looking after a household or family. Guardianship is the most subtle of the three minimal elements of predatory crime, since it occurs inadvertently when people engage in daily routines together or when people are close to their possessions.

The essential feature of the routine activity approach is the physical convergence of its three minimal elements. Thus, a predatory crime is most likely to occur when an offender converges in time and space with a target of crime in the absence of a guardian. This convergence is made possible by the routine structure of everyday life. Illegal acts thus feed upon the legal behaviors of life, such as work, school, and family life. The routine activity approach therefore broadens criminology to consider not only offenders but also nonoffenders as crucial participants in crime production and prevention.

Although the routine activity approach began with predatory crimes, it has been expanded (Felson, 1983, 1987) to include fights, illegal sales, and illegal consumption. For example, at least two combatants must converge to produce a fight; at least one buyer and one seller must converge for an illegal sale to occur. Even predatory crimes often involve co-offenders. What Tremblay (1993) calls the "search for suitable co-offenders" is an important feature of many illegal routines.

The routine activity approach also considers the more general supervision of youths. The proximity of adults to youths becomes important for their supervision, to prevent not only their victimization but also their offending (see Felson, 1986; Felson and Gottfredson, 1984). As with guardianship of people and property to block victimization, supervision of youths to discourage their illegal activities may occur quietly and inadvertently.

Perhaps the main contribution of the routine activity approach is that it explores tangible links between criminal events and larger social change. It explains how a crime wave can far exceed any increase in the number of offenders. Indeed, crime can rise as long as offenders are more likely than before to find targets with guardians absent. Whether offenders evade supervision by parents, suitable targets are more numerous, or guardianship of these targets is lax, the opportunity for crime will rise.

The routine activity approach demonstrates its success by explaining the crime wave in the United States since 1963 with a few simple facts. During this period, American society experienced (1) the proliferation of lightweight, durable goods and (2) a dispersion of activities away from family and household settings (Cohen and Felson, 1979; Felson and Cohen, 1981). Thus, youths could more readily escape parental supervision (Felson and Gottfredson, 1984), becoming both offenders and victims of crime, while people of all ages were subject to greater risk of illegal attack in nonfamily, nonhousehold settings. The routine activity approach draws upon the basic activities of everyday life in providing the background to a crime wave.

References

Cohen, L. E., & Felson, M. (1979). Social change and crime rate trends: A routine activity approach. *American Sociological Review, 44,* 588–608.

Felson, M., & Cohen, L. E. (1982). Modeling crime rate trends—A criminal opportunity perspective. *Journal of Research in Crime and Delinquency, 18,* 138–164, as corrected 1982, *19,* 1.

Felson, M., & Gottfredson, M. R. (1984, August). Adolescent activities near peers and parents. *Journal of Marriage and the Family, 46,* 709–714.

Felson, M. Ecology of crime. (1983). In *Encyclopedia of crime and justice.* New York: Macmillan.

Felson, M. (1987). Routine activities and crime prevention in the developing metropolis. *Criminology, 25,* 911–931.

Felson, M. Routine activities, social controls, rational decisions and criminal outcomes. (1986). In D. Cornish & R. V. Clarke (Eds.), *The reasoning criminal.* New York: Springer-Verlag.

Tremblay, P. Searching for suitable co-offenders. (1993). In R. V. Clarke & M. Felson (Eds.), *Advances in criminological theory,* vol. 5. New Brunswick, N.J.: Transaction Press.

2
Situational Crime Prevention

MARCUS FELSON

Situational crime prevention refers to a set of techniques for preventing crime by reducing the opportunity offenders have to carry out illegal acts. Such prevention does not attempt to alter offenders' personalities or directly threaten them with police action. The goal instead is to use a variety of very simple and practical methods to induce people to avoid committing illegal acts.

Situational crime prevention was invented and named by Ronald V. Clarke while he was a senior civil service research officer at the British Home Office in London. Clarke had been trained as a clinical psychologist and had found traditional efforts to work with offenders as individuals to be ineffective. In 1973 he was assigned the task of finding out why boys absconded (ran away) from borstals (reform schools). In the course of his research he found that absconding was attributable not to individual traits but rather to situational features. For example, absconding occurred on weekends when fewer staff members were present, not because staff during the week were using force but rather because simple supervision served to discourage the offense.

After discovering this fact, Clarke began to think of crime in general as the result of human situations and opportunities. In 1976 the Home Office published a book called *Crime as Opportunity*, and Clarke later became head of its Research and Planning Unit. Under his leadership, several British researchers inside and outside the government devised numerous real-life crime prevention experiments, based on the following policy:

- ♦ Avoid academic theories. Gather facts about everyday crime from nature itself.

- Focus on very specific slices of crime, such as vandalism against telephones or soccer violence.
- Develop practical, natural, and simple crime prevention ideas and try to test them at minimal cost.

In *Situational Crime Prevention: Successful Case Studies,* Clarke reviewed over seventy-five examples of situational prevention and presented twenty-two research papers offering examples of situational prevention from various nations. Table 2.1 presents seven of these examples, which deal with crimes ranging from graffiti to robberies of convenience stores to disorderly behavior in Disney World. Proposed solutions range from the simple device of removing telephone booths and redesigning telephones to the more complex planning used by Disney World to keep its crowds under control. A thin line divides situational prevention from crime prevention through environmental design (CPTED); the former is generally simpler and targeted to specific problems, whereas the latter considers more variables in planning the environment so as to channel potential offenders away from criminal behavior.

Table 2.1 Examples of Situational Crime Prevention from Clarke (1992)

Specific Crime Problem	Situational Prevention Effort
Phone vandalism	Redesign phones, remove phone booths
Subway graffiti	Set up efficient subway car cleaning project
Cruising-related crime on weekends	Establish large parking lot as legal cruising area for teenagers
Obscene phone calls	Market special type of telephone with caller identification
Thefts from parking structure	Control pedestrian access to parking structure
Vandalism in upper deck of British school buses	Install video cameras on upper deck, screen for bus driver
Convenience store robberies	Move cash register to front of store and remove advertising from windows
Disorderly behavior in Disney World	Channel movements and clustering of crowds to minimize misbehavior

Examples drawn from Ronald V. Clarke, editor; *Situational Crime Prevention: Successful Case Studies.* New York: Harrow and Heston, 1992.

The diversity of situational crime prevention measures can be summed up in two general categories: working on targets and working on places (see Table 2.2). Working on targets of crime (see column A) includes five subcategories of methods, ranging from direct to indirect. One can directly eliminate targets (ending cash transactions on buses to prevent theft) or spoil targets (attaching ink tags that explode when removed by an unauthorized person, ruining the garment that is a target of theft). A target can be modified (for example, by removing the motor from a small kitchen appliance on display); targets can also be hardened (as when one bolts a computer to the table) or tagged for identification (as in vehicle licensing). Alternatives can be used to deflect offenders from targets (graffiti blackboards in tavern washrooms to distract offenders from less desirable behaviors).

Situational prevention can also work on places (column B of Table 2.2), again ranging from direct to indirect efforts. Access can be eliminated, for example by using guards, construction, or bars on windows; but more modest controls are also feasible, such as locating classrooms on first floors of academic buildings and keeping offices on upper floors with less traffic flow and, hence, less chance of theft. Entry has to be permitted into stores, but employee surveillance can reduce shoplifting, especially when shelves are not so high that surveillance is difficult. Natural surveillance by ordinary citizens can be fostered by, for example, designing spaces with sufficient pedestrian traffic to discourage personal attacks. Access can also be deflected by planting briar bushes to channel traffic away from the grass and onto the sidewalk.

Clearly a great variety of situational prevention methods are available, providing great potential for reducing crime at low cost in monetary and human terms.

Table 2.2 Ten Basic Types of Situational Crime Prevention

	A Working on Targets	B Working on Places
DIRECT	1. Eliminate, spoil targets	Eliminate access
	2. Modify targets	Dilute, modify access
	3. Harden targets	Employee surveillance
	4. Tag targets	Natural surveillance
INDIRECT	5. Provide alternatives	Deflect access

References

Clarke, R. V. (Ed.). (1992). *Situational crime prevention: Successful case studies*. New York: Harrow & Heston.

Mayhew, P., Clarke, R. V., Sturman, A., & Hough, J. M. (1976). *Crime as opportunity*. London: Her Majesty's Stationery Office.

3

A Reconceptualization of General and Specific Deterrence

MARK C. STAFFORD

MARK WARR

A key element of crime prevention is the distinction between general and specific deterrence. Virtually all definitions of those phenomena point in one way or another to this distinction: Whereas general deterrence refers to the effects of legal punishment on the general public (i.e., potential offenders), specific deterrence pertains to the effects of legal punishment on those who have suffered it (i.e., punished offenders; for a review, see Gibbs, 1975:32–39). For example, Nagin (1978) defined general deterrence as the "imposition of sanctions on one person [in order to] demonstrate to the rest of the public the expected costs of a criminal act, and thereby discourage criminal behavior in the general population" (p. 96). In contrast, Andenaes (1968) stated that if persons are "deterred by the actual experience of punishment, we speak of *special* [specific] *deterrence*" (p. 78).

Both definitions recognize the importance of some kind of experience of legal punishment in deterring persons from committing crimes. But for members of the general public (general deterrence) it is indirect experience of punishment (observing or otherwise having knowledge of the punishment of others) that deters, whereas for punished offenders (specific deterrence) it is direct (personal) experience (Meier and Johnson, 1977:294–95).

This conception of general and specific deterrence is widely recognized and accepted by criminologists, but it has serious shortcomings. Put briefly, it will be argued in this chapter that the conventional distinction between general and specific deterrence rests on faulty logic and that it has done little to clarify the deterrence process. After these arguments are presented,

This is a revised version of a paper presented at the 1989 annual meetings of the American Society of Criminology in Reno.

a reconceptualization of general and specific deterrence will be proposed and applied to some current controversies in the deterrence literature.

Distinguishing General and Specific Deterrence

Deterrence studies are classified commonly as bearing on one type of deterrence or the other, with most purportedly involving general rather than specific deterrence (see reviews by Gibbs, 1975:ch. 5; Tittle, 1980:ch. 1; Zimring and Hawkins, 1973:ch. 4). However, the rationale for such classification is not entirely clear.

Consider a hypothetical study of what is likely to be regarded as general deterrence. In such a case, investigators might focus on persons who have never suffered any legal punishment for any crime, on the grounds that such persons have knowledge of punishment, if at all, only indirectly from the experiences of others (Gibbs, 1975:34, 37). However, there are two kinds of people who have never suffered a legal punishment: (1) those who have never committed any crime (ignoring the possibility that innocent persons can be punished) and (2) those who have committed crimes but have avoided punishment. Only the first kind of person can be said to have no direct experience of legal punishment. Although the second kind of person has not suffered a legal punishment, he or she has by definition acquired experience of *avoiding punishment,* and that experience is likely to affect the chances of committing crimes again. In particular, experience of avoiding punishment is likely to affect perceptions of the certainty and severity of punishment, the two principal variables in recent deterrence studies. Of these two variables, perceptions of certainty should be affected more strongly by punishment avoidance, because getting away with a crime provides little information about the legal consequences of being caught (Paternoster, 1987:189; Paternoster, Saltzman, Waldo, and Chiricos, 1983a:281, 1983b:458).

Like the concept of deterrence, which involves the omission of legally proscribed acts (Gibbs, 1975:3; Meier and Johnson, 1977), the notion of punishment avoidance may be somewhat difficult to imagine because it refers to events that did *not* happen. However, unlike deterrence, punishment avoidance is also contingent on events that did occur, that is, the commission of crimes. Hence, in contrast to deterrence, punishment avoidance is not inherently unobservable. For example, everyone who drives in urban America has observed another person driving in a reckless manner but receiving no legal punishment, or has witnessed a criminal event such as a person driving while intoxicated that did not even come to the attention of the police.

To some, the concept of punishment avoidance may appear to add little to deterrence theory, because punishment avoidance is simply the opposite of punishment itself. The distinction may be logically banal, but it is potentially critical for empirical reasons. To illustrate, it is possible that punishment avoidance does more to encourage crime than punishment does to discourage it. Offenders whose experience is limited largely to avoiding punishment may come to believe that they are immune from punishment, even in the face of occasional evidence to the contrary. Perhaps the greatest value of the concept is that it underscores the fundamental principle that no criminal act is without consequences. In the wake of a crime, offenders will always experience punishment or punishment avoidance, and it is dubious to argue that only the former affects subsequent behavior.

The immediate point is that what is usually taken to be general deterrence is not limited necessarily to persons who have no direct experience of legal punishment. The point is crucial because, if self-report data are to be believed, there are few persons (at least among young males) who have never avoided punishment, especially for minor offenses (for a review, see Empey and Stafford, 1991:ch. 6). Consequently, the conventional distinction between general and specific deterrence rests more on the *nature* of prior direct experience of legal punishment than on the mere presence of such experience.

Direct and Indirect Experience of Punishment

Now consider a related problem with specific deterrence. Studies of specific deterrence typically focus on punished offenders (or comparisons of punished and unpunished offenders) and examine the frequency of postpunishment offending for evidence of deterrence (e.g., Murray and Cox, 1979; Schneider and Ervin, 1990; Smith and Gartin, 1989). There is nothing intrinsically wrong with this procedure, but investigators commonly assume that an offender's direct experience of suffering a punishment is the only operative variable when it comes to predicting future behavior. In addition to ignoring the offender's experience of avoiding punishment, such an assumption overlooks the possibility that one can suffer a legal punishment and at the same time have knowledge of punishment from the experiences of others (i.e., have indirect experience of punishment).

Suppose that an individual is caught and fined after shoplifting and that this is his or her first offense of any type. The direct experience of being fined is likely to be salient, but surely its deterrent efficacy will depend on whether the individual believes or knows that other persons (particularly others like him or her) have a similar certainty and severity of punishment, or whether he or she believes that in this particular instance the punishment was ill-fated and others would have gotten away with the crime, or that they would have received a less (or more) severe punishment (Ward, Menke, Gray, and Stafford, 1986:502–3).

The point to be emphasized is that in most populations—whether members of the general public or punished offenders—people are likely to have a *mixture* of indirect and direct experience of punishment and punishment avoidance. That point is not lost on all deterrence researchers. For example, Lempert (1982:532), in a study of enforcement of child-support orders, observes that men who have been jailed for nonpayment often meet or hear of others who are in jail for the same offense. Hence, these men gain both direct and indirect experience of legal punishment (p. 549). However, by adopting the conventional distinction between general and specific deterrence, investigators perpetuate the notion that the two forms of deterrence occur among distinct populations.

The problem with such a notion becomes clearer when one considers that offenders often commit more than one type of crime, and that they may or may not suffer a legal punishment for each type. Consider a person who is caught and punished after committing his or her first burglary but has also committed other crimes (e.g., drug use, robbery, auto theft) and avoided punishment in each case. To claim that the direct experience of being punished for the burglary is the only relevant consideration in predicting the offender's future behavior is to ignore what has been said about the potential effects of punishment avoidance, not to mention the potential effects of indirect experience of punishment. To put it more carefully, there are four relevant considerations in the example at hand: (1) the direct experience of suffering the punishment for the burglary, (2) the direct experience of punishment avoidance for the other crimes, (3) indirect experience of punishment and punishment avoidance for the burglary, and (4) indirect experience of punishment and punishment avoidance for the other crimes.

One possibility is that the direct experience of punishment for the burglary could reduce the offender's likelihood of repeating the other crimes (e.g., by increasing the perceived certainty of punishment for these offenses). However, it could also work in reverse—the direct experience of getting away with the other crimes could increase the chances of committing further burglaries. And when one considers *indirect* experience of punishment and punishment avoidance for all of the offenses, there are still other possibilities. For example, the arrest of fellow offenders for the same crime(s) might lead to the conclusion that the odds of arrest have increased substantially.

An underlying assumption in all such possibilities is that people may estimate the certainty and severity of punishment for a particular type of crime by reference to crimes in general, or at least similar types of offenses (e.g., all property crimes), rather than from information that is "crime-specific" (Gibbs, 1975:35; Erickson and Gibbs, 1975; Paternoster, 1986). If so, it will almost certainly be true that a mixture of indirect and direct experiences of legal punishment and punishment avoidance will be relevant for most persons. Even if people estimate certainty and severity entirely from crime-specific information, a mixture of punishment experiences is likely to be relevant, and research is needed on such questions as whether direct experience of punishment and punishment avoidance affects the deterrent efficacy of indirect experience (Zimring and Hawkins, 1973:224–29).

A Reconceptualization

The conceptual problems outlined above appear to stem from the manner in which general and specific deterrence are commonly defined. That is, the practice of distinguishing general and specific deterrence by reference to distinct populations (either the general public or punished offenders) tends to obfuscate critical issues. Instead, the distinction between the two types of deterrence should be limited to contrasting kinds of experience of legal punishment. If deterrence is defined as the omission or curtailment of a criminal act out of fear of legal punishment (Gibbs, 1975:39), then general deterrence refers to the deterrent effect of *indirect experience of punishment and punishment avoidance* and specific deterrence refers to the deterrent effect of *direct experience of punishment and punishment avoidance.*

The proposed reconceptualization has several advantages over that currently in use. First, it recognizes the possibility that *both* general and specific deterrence can operate for any given person or in any population. Second, it treats punishment avoidance as analytically distinct from the experience of suffering a punishment.

A third advantage of the proposed reconceptualization of general and specific deterrence is its compatibility with contemporary learning theory, particularly the distinction between observational/vicarious learning and experiential learning (for discussions of the connection between deterrence concepts/principles and learning theory, see Akers, 1990; Cavender, 1979; Moffitt, 1983). Bandura (1977), for example, argued that experiential learning

> results from the positive and negative effects that actions produce. When people deal with everyday events, some of their responses prove successful, while others have no effect or result in punishing outcomes. Through this process of differential reinforcement, successful forms of behavior are eventually selected and ineffectual ones are discarded (p. 17).

As for observational or vicarious learning, Bandura (1977) noted that

> people can profit from the successes and mistakes of others as well as from their own experiences. In everyday situations numerous opportunities exist to observe the actions of others and the occasions on which they are rewarded, ignored, or punished. . . . Observed outcomes can alter behavior in their own right in much the same way as directly experienced consequences (p. 117).

Just as recent versions of learning theory suggest that any behavior is likely to be a consequence of both observational/vicarious learning and experiential learning (e.g., Akers, Krohn, Lanza-Kaduce, and Radosevich, 1979:638; Bandura, 1977:ch. 2), the basic premise of the proposed reconceptualization is that the rate of crime in virtually any population will be a function of both general and specific deterrence. This is not to say that the two types of deterrence will be equally important from one population to the next (Gray, Ward, Stafford, and Menke, 1985:83–84). Among persons with limited direct experience of punishment and/or punishment avoidance, the rate of crime is more likely to be a function of general deterrence (indirect experience of punishment and punishment avoidance). Indeed, in the special case of persons who have *no* direct experience of punishment or punishment avoidance—those who have never committed any crimes at all—the only possibly relevant consideration is general deterrence. However, among persons who have been punished many times and/or have avoided punishment repeatedly (i.e., habitual offenders), criminal behavior should be largely a function of specific deterrence (direct experience of punishment and punishment avoidance). The implication is that individuals can be viewed as falling along a continuum characterized by general deterrence at one extreme and specific deterrence at the other.

The reconceptualization of general and specific deterrence proposed here is of little value unless it helps to clarify existing research and stimulates new theoretical questions. Rather, a single theory is possible that centers on indirect experience of legal punishment and punishment avoidance and direct experience of legal punishment and punishment avoidance. Recognizing that people may think of punishment for crimes in general rather than in crime-specific terms, such a theory would need to consider indirect and direct experience of punishment and punishment avoidance for crimes other than those that individuals actually have committed.

Unfortunately, if the proposed reconceptualization is accepted, tests of the deterrence doctrine will necessarily become more complex. For example, tests based on survey data would need to include, at a minimum, measures of (1) persons' perceptions of their own certainty and severity of legal punishment for crimes; (2) persons' perceptions of the certainty and severity of legal punishment for others (presumably those within their immediate social network); (3) self-reported criminal behavior, including self-reports of direct experience of punishment and punishment avoidance; and (4) estimates of peers' criminal behavior, including their experiences of punishment and punishment avoidance.

Of course, there are alternatives to a survey methodology, such as an experimental design. Indeed, an experimental design might facilitate an assessment of the separate effects of indirect and direct experience of legal punishment and punishment avoidance on crime (see, e.g., Sherman and Berk, 1984). However, only a very complex experimental design can facilitate an examination of the *relative* effects of indirect and direct experience of punishment and punishment avoidance, which may be the more important issue as far as a theory of deterrence is concerned.

References

Akers, R. L. (1990). Rational choice, deterrence, and social learning theory in criminology: The path not taken. *Journal of Criminal Law and Criminology, 81,* 653–76.

Akers, R. L., Krohn, M. D., Lanza-Kaduce, L., & Radosevich, M. (1979). Social learning and deviant behavior: A specific test of a general theory. *American Sociological Review, 44,* 636–55.

Andenaes, J. (1968). Does punishment deter crime? *Criminal Law Quarterly, 11,* 76–93.

Bandura, A. (1977). *Social learning theory.* Englewood Cliffs, N.J.: Prentice-Hall.

Cavender, G. (1979). Special deterrence: An operant learning evaluation. *Law and Human Behavior, 3,* 203–15.

Empey, L. T., & Stafford, M. C. (1991). *American delinquency: Its meaning and construction.* Belmont, Calif.: Wadsworth.

Erickson, M. L., & Gibbs, J. P. (1975). Specific versus general properties of legal punishments and deterrence. *Social Science Quarterly, 56,* 390–97.

Gibbs, J. P. (1975). *Crime, punishment, and deterrence.* New York: Elsevier.

Gray, L. N., Ward, D. A., Stafford, M. C., & Menke, B. A. (1985). Observational and experiential effects in probability learning: The case of a deviant behavior. *Social Psychology Quarterly, 48,* 78–85.

Lempert, R. (1982). Organizing for deterrence: Lessons from a study of child support. *Law and Society Review, 16,* 513–68.

Meier, R. F., & Johnson, W. T. (1977). Deterrence as social control: The legal and extralegal production of conformity. *American Sociological Review, 42,* 292–304.

Moffitt, T. E. (1983). The learning theory model of punishment: Implications for delinquency deterrence. *Criminal Justice and Behavior, 10,* 131–58.

Murray, C.A., & Cox, L. A., Jr. (1979). *Beyond probation: Juvenile corrections and the chronic delinquent.* Beverly Hills, Calif.: Sage.

Nagin, D. (1978). General deterrence: A review of the empirical evidence. In A. Blumstein, J. Cohen, & D. Nagin (Eds.), *Deterrence and incapacitation: Estimating the effects of criminal sanctions on crime rates* (pp. 95–139). Washington, D.C.: National Academy of Sciences.

Paternoster, R. (1986). The use of composite scales in perceptual deterrence research: A cautionary note. *Journal of Research in Crime and Delinquency, 23,* 128–68.

Paternoster, R. (1987). The deterrent effect of the perceived certainty and severity of punishment: A review of the evidence and issues. *Justice Quarterly, 4,* 173–217.

Paternoster, R., Saltzman, L. E., Waldo, G. P., & Chiricos, T. G. (1983a). Estimating perceptual stability and deterrent effects: The role of perceived legal punishment in the inhibition of criminal involvement. *Journal of Criminal Law and Criminology, 74,* 270–97.

Paternoster, R., Saltzman, L. E., Waldo, G. P., & Chiricos, T. G. (1983b). Perceived risk and social control: Do sanctions really deter? *Law and Society Review, 17,* 457–79.

Schneider, A. L., & Ervin, L. (1990). Specific deterrence, rational choice, and decision heuristics: Applications in juvenile justice. *Social Science Quarterly, 71,* 585–601.

Sherman, L. W., & Berk, R. A. (1984). The specific deterrent effects of arrest for domestic assault. *American Sociological Review, 49,* 261–72.

Smith, D. A., & Gartin, P. R. (1989). Specifying specific deterrence: The influence of arrest on future criminal activity. *American Sociological Review, 54,* 94–106.

Tittle, C. R. (1980). *Sanctions and social deviance: The question of deterrence.* New York: Praeger.

Ward, D. A., Menke, B. A., Gray, L. N., & Stafford, M. C. (1986). Sanctions, modeling, and deviant behavior. *Journal of Criminal Justice, 14,* 501–8.

Zimring, F. E., & Hawkins, G. J. (1973). *Deterrence: The legal threat in crime control.* Chicago: University of Chicago Press.

4

Crime, Shame, and Reintegration

JOHN BRAITHWAITE

Summary of the Theory

In the first part of this chapter clear definitions are attempted for the key concepts in Figure 4.1, which provides a schematic summary of the theory of reintegrative shaming. The cluster of six variables around interdependency at the top left of Figure 4.1 are characteristics of individuals; the three at the top right are characteristics of societies; while high levels of crime and shaming are variables that apply to both individuals and societies. The theory as summarized in Figure 4.1 thus gives an account of why both some kinds of individuals and some kinds of societies exhibit more crime.

A more parsimonious theory could be obtained by collapsing the similar constructs of interdependency (an individual-level variable) and communitarianism (a societal variable) into a single construct, but then there would no longer be a framework to predict both which individuals and which societies will have more crime. On the desirability of being able to do this Cressey expressed it best:

> A theory explaining social behavior in general, or any specific kind of social behavior, should have two distinct but consistent aspects. First, there must be a statement that explains the statistical distribution of the behavior in time and space (epidemiology), and from which predictive statements about unknown statistical distributions can be derived. Second, there must be a statement that identifies, at least by implication, the process by which individuals come to exhibit the behavior in question, and from which can be derived predictive statements about the behavior of individuals (Cressey 1960:47).

Key Concepts

Interdependency is a condition of individuals. It means the extent to which individuals participate in networks wherein they are dependent on others

Figure 4.1 Summary of the Theory of Reintegrative Shaming

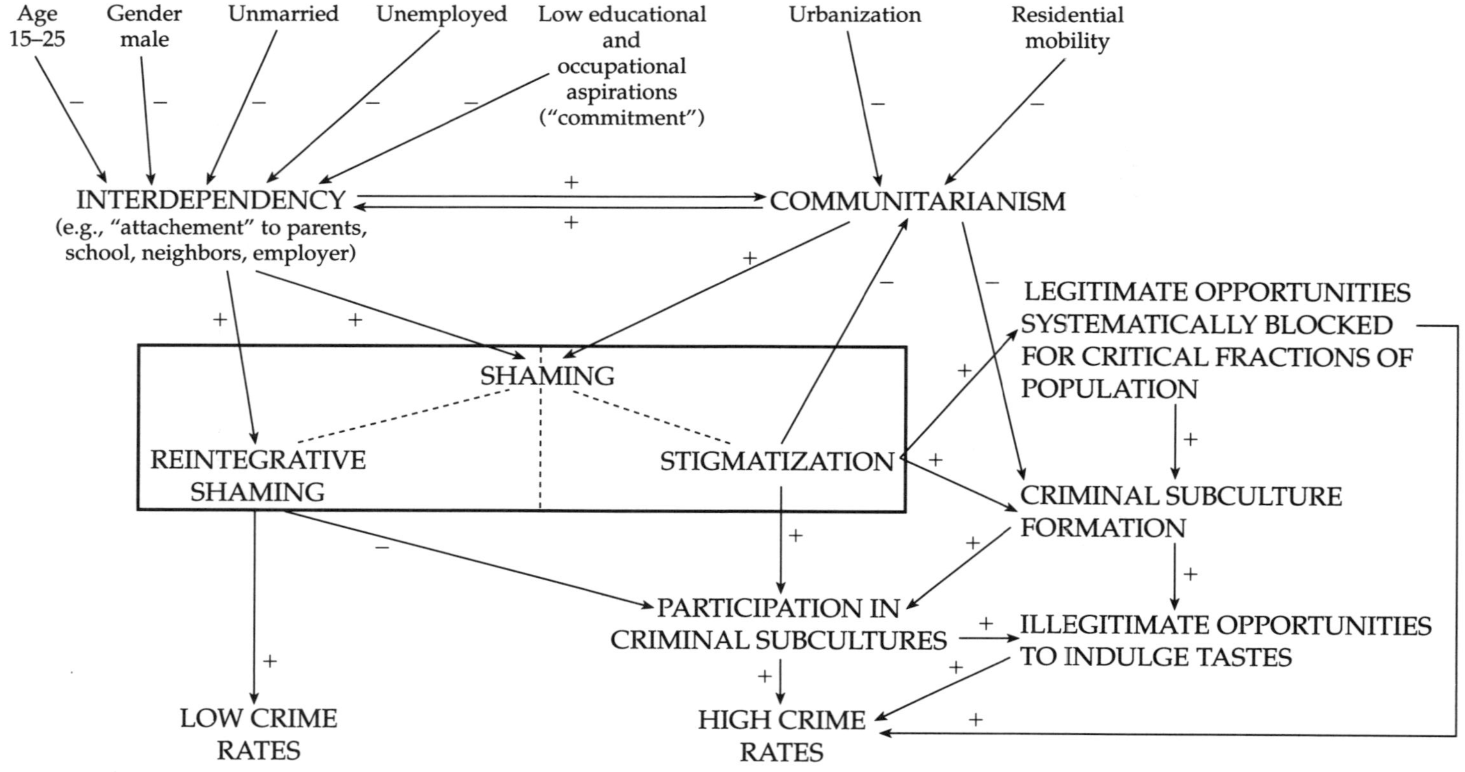

to achieve valued ends and others are dependent on them. We could describe an individual as in a state of interdependency even if the individuals who are dependent on him or her are different from the individuals on whom he or she is dependent. Interdependency is approximately equivalent to the social bonding, attachment, and commitment of control theory.

Communitarianism is a condition of societies. In communitarian societies individuals are densely enmeshed in interdependencies that have the special qualities of mutual help and trust. The interdependencies have symbolic significance in the culture as group loyalties, which take precedence over individual interests. The interdependencies also have symbolic significance as attachments that invoke personal obligation to others in a community of concern, rather than simply interdependencies of convenience as between a bank and a small depositor. A communitarian culture rejects any pejorative connotation of dependency as threatening individual autonomy. Communitarian cultures resist interpretations of dependency as weakness and emphasize the need for mutuality of obligation in interdependency (to be both dependent and dependable). The Japanese are said to be socialized not only to *amaeru* (to be succored by others) but also to *amayakasu* (to be nurturing to others) (Wagatsuma and Rosett, 1986).

Shaming means all social processes of expressing disapproval that have the intention or effect of invoking remorse in the person being shamed and/ or condemnation by others who become aware of the shaming. When associated with appropriate symbols, formal punishment often shames. But societies vary enormously in the extent to which formal punishment is associated with shaming and in the extent to which the social meaning of punishment is no more than to inflict pain to tip reward-cost calculations in favor of certain outcomes. Shaming, unlike purely deterrent punishment, sets out to moralize with the offender to communicate reasons for the evil of his or her actions. Most shaming is neither associated with formal punishment nor perpetrated by the state, though both shaming by the state and shaming with punishment are important types of shaming. Most shaming is by individuals within interdependent communities of concern.

Reintegrative shaming is shaming followed by efforts to reintegrate the offender back into the community of law-abiding or respectable citizens through words or gestures of forgiveness or ceremonies to decertify the offender as deviant. Shaming and reintegration do not occur simultaneously but sequentially, with reintegration occurring before deviance becomes a master status. It is shaming that labels the act as evil while striving to preserve the identity of the offender as essentially good. It is directed at signifying evil deeds rather than evil persons in the Christian tradition of "hate the sin and love the sinner." Specific disapproval is expressed within relationships characterized by general social approval; shaming criminal behavior is complemented by ongoing social rewarding of alternative behavior patterns. Reintegrative shaming is not necessarily weak; it can be cruel, even vicious.

It is distinguished from stigmatization not by its potency but by (1) a finite rather than open-ended duration, which is terminated by forgiveness, and (2) efforts to maintain bonds of love or respect throughout the finite period of suffering shame.

Stigmatization is disintegrative shaming in which no effort is made to reconcile the offender with the community. The offender is outcast, his or her deviance is allowed to become a master status, degradation ceremonies are not followed by ceremonies to decertify deviance.

Criminal subcultures are sets of rationalizations and conduct norms that cluster together to support criminal behavior. The clustering is usually facilitated by subcultural groups that provide systematic social support for crime in any one of a number of ways—supplying members with criminal opportunities, criminal values, attitudes that weaken conventional values of law-abidingness, or techniques of neutralizing conventional values.

Short Summary of the Theory

The following might serve as the briefest possible summary of the theory. A variety of life circumstances increase the chances that individuals will be in situations of greater interdependency, the most important of which are being of a certain age (under fifteen and over twenty-five), married, female, employed, and with high employment and educational aspirations. Interdependent persons are more susceptible to shaming. More important, societies in which individuals are subject to extensive interdependencies are more likely to be communitarian, and shaming is much more widespread and potent in communitarian societies. Urbanization and high residential mobility are societal characteristics that undermine communitarianism.

The shaming produced by interdependency and communitarianism can be either of two types: shaming that becomes stigmatization or shaming that is followed by reintegration. The shaming engendered is more likely to become reintegrative in societies that are communitarian. In societies where shaming does become reintegrative, low crime rates are the result because disapproval is dispensed without eliciting a rejection of the disapprovers, so that the potentialities for future disapproval are not dismantled. Moreover, reintegrative shaming is superior even to stigmatization for conscience building.

Shaming that is stigmatizing, in contrast, makes criminal subcultures more attractive because these are in some sense subcultures that reject one's rejectors. Thus, when shaming is allowed to become stigmatization for want of reintegrative gestures or ceremonies that decertify deviance, the deviant is both attracted to criminal subcultures and cut off from other interdependencies (with family, neighbors, church, etc.). Participation in subcultural groups supplies criminal role models and training in techniques of crime and techniques of neutralizing crime (or other forms of social support) that make choices to engage in crime more attractive. Thus, to the extent that shaming is of the stigmatizing rather than the reintegrative sort, and to the extent that criminal subcultures are widespread and accessible in the society, higher crime rates will be the result. While societies characterized by high levels of stigmatization will have higher crime rates than societies characterized by reintegrative shaming, the former will have higher or lower crime rates than societies with little shaming at all, depending largely on the availability of criminal subcultures.

Yet a high level of stigmatization in the society is one of the very factors that encourages criminal subculture formation by creating populations of outcasts with no stake in conformity, no chance of self-esteem within the terms of conventional society—individuals in search of an alternative culture that allows them self-esteem. A communitarian culture, on the other hand, nurtures deviants within a network of attachments to conventional society, thus inhibiting the widespread outcasting that is the stuff of subculture formation.

For clarity of exposition, the two types of shaming have been presented as a stark dichotomy. In reality, for any society some deviants are dealt with in ways that are more stigmatic, whereas others receive more reintegrative shaming. Indeed, a single deviant will be responded to more stigmatically by some, more reintegratively by others. To the extent that the greater weight of shaming tends to stigmatization, the crime-producing processes on the right of Figure 4.1 are more likely to be triggered; to the extent that the balance of shaming tips toward reintegration, informal processes of crime control are more likely to prevail over these crime-producing processes.

The other major societal variable that fosters criminal subculture formation is systematic blockage of legitimate opportunities for critical fractions of the population. If black slum dwellers are systematically denied economic opportunities because of the stigma of their race and neighborhood, then criminal subcultures will form in those outcast neighborhoods. It can be seen that stigmatization (as opposed to social integration) as a cultural disposition may contribute to the systematic blockage of these economic opportunities; but cultural variables like stigmatization will be of rather minor importance compared with structural economic variables in determining opportunities. It has been argued here that the blockages in this part of the theory are not restricted to closed opportunities to climb out of poverty; systematically blocked opportunities for ever greater wealth accumulation by the most affluent of corporations often lead to corporate criminal subculture formation.

Criminal subcultures are the main mechanism for constituting illegitimate opportunity structures—knowledge on how to offend, social support for offending or communication of rationalizations for offending, criminal role models, subcultural groups that assist with the avoidance of detection and organize collective criminal enterprises. However, illegitimate opportunities are greater in some societies than others, for a variety of further reasons that are not incorporated within the theory. Although the effects of legitimate and illegitimate opportunities on crime are mostly mediated by participation in criminal subcultures, the blockage of legitimate opportunities, combined with the availability of illegitimate opportunities, can independently increase crime. Whether illegitimate opportunities to engage in crime are supplied by participation in criminal subcultures or otherwise, they must be opportunities that appeal to the tastes of tempted individuals for them to result in crime.

This summary is crudely simple because it ignores what goes on within the shaming box in Figure 4.1. That is, it ignores the social processes that combine individual acts of shaming into cultural processes of shaming that are more or less integrative: gossip, media coverage of shaming incidents, children's stories, etc. In turn, the summary has neglected how these macro-level processes of shaming feed back to ensure that micro-level practices of shaming cover the curriculum of crimes.

Ecological Fallacies?

In a theory that simultaneously provides an account of individual behavior and societal behavior, one can slip variables across from one level of analysis to the other. Thus, when testing the theory at the individual level of analysis, one can code individuals according to whether they live in large cities or whether they have been residentially mobile. That is, the two societal variables at the top right of Figure 4.1 can be translated into individual-level variables.

Equally, an individual-level variable like "age 15–25" can become a societal variable—percentage of the population of the society aged fifteen to twenty-five. However, in making these shifts it is possible to perpetrate the ecological fallacy—to assume glibly that what is true at the individual level of analysis will be true at the societal level. A society is more than the sum of its individual parts. Thus, when a society accumulates unusually high numbers of young people, the behavior of *older* people may change in response—they might vote for increased investment in education or police juvenile aid bureaus, for example. There is some evidence, for example, that while unemployment is a strong predictor of individual criminality, societies with high unemployment rates do not necessarily have high crime rates (Braithwaite, 1979; but see Chiricos, 1987). Gender is another variable that does not usefully shift from the individual to the societal level of analysis, because societies do not vary in what proportion of their population is female.

Apart from these two, there is no sound theoretical or empirical reason that the variables in Figure 4.1 cannot move between both the individual and societal levels of analysis.

Capacity of the Theory to Explain What We Know About Crime

What is the capacity of the theory to explain the correlates of crime? Some indeterminacy arises over the different effects of reintegrative shaming versus stigmatization. For example, what does the theory predict should be the association between gender and crime? Figure 4.1 shows that being female increases interdependency, which in turn fosters shaming. If the extra shaming produced is reintegrative, being female is associated with low crime rates. However, if the extra shaming amounts to stigmatization, higher crime rates become possible where subcultural support is found for the outcast status.

This problem can be solved by making a rather modest assumption. This assumption, as argued earlier, is that in most societies criminal subcultures are minority phenomena—narrowly diffused—so that stigmatization will in only a minority of cases be followed by an opportunity to participate in a subculture that is attractive to the individual. It follows that the level of shaming should be unambiguously negatively related to the crime rate, because most shaming will be either reintegrative shaming or stigmatic shaming, which does not lead to subcultural attachments, and both of these options will reduce crime. In any case, as is clear from Figure 4.1, variables (like gender) that increase interdependency have their effect on shaming partly through increasing communitarianism, and shaming that is a product of communitarianism is most likely to be reintegrative. Interdependency both increases the prospects of shaming and decreases the chances that such shaming as occurs will be stigmatic.

Thus, the characteristics associated with low interdependency—being male, between fifteen and twenty-five years of age, unmarried, unemployed, and with low educational and vocational aspirations—should all be associated with high involvement in crime. Urbanization and high residential mobility are also predicted by the theory as correlates of crime. All of these characteristics are strong and consistent correlates of crime.

In establishing the relationship between communitarianism and crime, there is far too much reliance on qualitative evidence from Japan and more doubtful qualitative evidence from a handful of other societies. The association between interdependency as a characteristic of individuals and crime, on the other hand, is well established. Control theory has spawned impressive evidence that young people who are "attached" to their parents and to the school are less likely to engage in delinquency.

There is no such impressive and unambiguous literature on "attachment" to neighbors and crime. The recent review of sixty-five studies of religiosity and deviance by Tittle and Welch (1983) suggested the possibility—contrary to some conventional wisdom in criminology—that interdependency via church affiliation may reduce crime. Tittle and Welch concluded that "the evidence seems remarkably consistent in suggesting that religion is related to deviant behavior. Indeed, only a few variables in social science (possibly gender and age) have proven to be better predictors of rule breaking."

The theory offers a convincing explanation of why crime rates have been increasing in most Western societies since World War II. The recent development of Western societies has been associated with a decline in interdependency and communitarianism and a progressive uncoupling of punishment and shaming. This has been a period when urbanization, residential mobility, delayed marriage and marriage breakdown, and an explosion of the population between the ages of fifteen and twenty-five have occurred in most countries.

References

Anderson, L. S., Chiricos, T. G., & Waldo, G. P. (1977). Formal and informal sanctions: A comparison of deterrent effects. *Social Problems, 25*, 103–14.

Baumrind, D. (1978). Parental disciplinary patterns and social competence in children. *Youth and Society, 9*, 239–76.

Bayley, D. H. (1976). *Forces of order: Police behavior in Japan and the United States.* Berkeley: University of California Press.

Black, D. J. (1976). *The behavior of law.* New York: Academic Press.

Braithwaite, J. (1979). *Inequality, crime and public policy.* London: Routledge & Kegan Paul.

Braithwaite, J. (1980). The political economy of punishment. In E. L. Wheelwright & K. Buckley (Eds.), *Essays in the political economy of Australian capitalism,* vol. IV. Sydney: ANZ Books.

Braithwaite, J. (1982). The limits of economism in controlling harmful corporate conduct. *Law and Society Review, 16*, 481–506.

Braithwaite, J. (1985a). *To punish or persuade: Enforcement of coal mine safety.* Albany: State University of New York Press.

Braithwaite, J., & Braithwaite, V. (1981). Delinquency and the question of values. *International Journal of Offender Therapy and Comparative Criminology, 25*, 273–89.

Chiricos, T. G. (1987). Rates of crime and unemployment: An analysis of aggregate research evidence. *Social Problems, 34*, 187–212.

Christie, N. (1981). *Limits to pain.* Oslo: Universitetsforlaget.

Clinard, M. B. (1978). *Cities with little crime.* Cambridge, England: Cambridge University Press.

Fisher, S. (1972). Stigma and deviant careers in schools. *Social Problems, 20*, 78–83.

Goffman, E. (1968). *Stigma: Notes on the management of spoiled identity.* Harmondsworth: Pelican.

Griffiths, J. (1970). Ideology in criminal procedure or a third "model" of the criminal process. *Yale Law Journal, 79*, 359–417.

Jensen, G. F., & Erickson, M. (1978). The social meaning of sanctions. In M. Krohn & R. Akers (Eds.), *Crime, law and sanctions: Theoretical perspectives.* Beverly Hills, Calif.: Sage.

Lynd, H. M. (1958). *On shame and the search for identity.* London: Routledge & Kegan Paul.

Newman, G. (1976). *Comparative deviance: Perception and law in six cultures*. New York: Elsevier.

Tannenbaum, F. (1938). *Crime and the community*. New York: Columbia University Press.

Tittle, C. R., & Welch, M. R. (1983). Religiosity and deviance: Toward a contingency theory of constraining effects. *Social Forces, 61,* 653–82.

Wagatsuma, H., & Rosett, A. (1986). The implications of apology: Law and culture in Japan and the United States. *Law and Society Review, 20,* 461–98.

PART II
BIOSOCIAL AND PSYCHOLOGICAL THEORIES

Introduction

Biosocial and psychological theories of crime belong to a larger category of positivist theories of human behavior. The basis of the positivist approach to behavior is a search for individual causation. The positivist school bases its understanding of crime on a multifactorial approach that integrates biological, psychological, and social factors. For the positivist, social reality consists of events and phenomena just as the natural world consists of objects and processes. The positivist likens social reality to an organism that is made up of interrelated parts that are both determinable and determinate. Unlike other organisms in nature, however, human beings possess "inner states," consisting of motives, emotions, beliefs, and attitudes that intervene between the stimulus and the response (Wilson, 1983). Because of the presence of such "inner states," the study of social realities such as a crime cannot be considered purely positivistic. These inner states can be incorporated into a scientific study as intervening variables that help to explain connections between the stimulus and the response. For example, to help explain why young males are much more highly represented in crime statistics than young females, it could be inferred that differences between the world views of males (competitive, aggressive, and conflict-oriented) and those of females (generous, cooperative, and conciliatory) make males more likely to take more risks and use unconventional means to try to achieve their goals, thereby increasing the likelihood of their participation in criminal activity. The presence of these inner states does not necessarily invalidate the deterministic assumption of positivistic analysis. Positivists assert that while human behavior appears to be free, it is actually determined by the combined effect of numerous factors. The challenge for positivist analysis is the accurate measurement of the relative importance of each of these factors to the response (in this case, crime).

Much of the earliest positivist work involved the study of crime as a distinct social phenomenon. Beginning with Cesare Lombroso's *L'uomo delin-*

quente (*Criminal Man*) in 1876, which suggested that criminals were evolutionary throwbacks and thus less civilized than their noncriminal neighbors, criminology has been at the center of positivistic debate. While criminal anthropologists like Lombroso, Benedikt, and MacDonald emphasized direct observation and data collection, they did not define positivism in the same structured terms as do modern practitioners of positivistic criminology. For example, Gottfredson and Hirschi (1990:10) have defined positivism as "the scientific approach to the study of crime where science is characterized by methods, techniques or rules of procedure rather than substantive theory." Despite the failure of the earliest criminal anthropologists to meet such a standard, Nicole Hahn Rafter's chapter, "Criminal Anthropology in United States," which serves as the lead selection in this section, asserts that their work framed the key issues of a debate that still persists among criminologists. Rafter argues that even though the doctrine of the criminal as a physically anomalous human type has long been discredited, the search for deterministic causes of crime continues. The remaining chapters in this section represent the major lines of positivistic inquiry into crime. Lee Ellis's discussion of arousal theory is a definitive example of the biosocial approach to crime, while Terrie Moffitt's neuropsychological analysis of conduct disorder is representative of a primarily psychiatric understanding of conduct that often heralds the onset of criminal behavior. David Farrington's psychosocial analysis of antisocial personality identifies the interconnectedness of psychological and social factors as the crucial variable in understanding the antisocial personality as predisposed to crime.

Nicole Hahn Rafter uses a sociology of knowledge perspective to trace the influence of criminal anthropology on the major developments and controversies in American criminology, including the connection between the criminal's physical being and ethical behavior, heredity as a determinant of criminal activity, and intelligence level as a variable of crime. Although others soon discredited the specific findings of the early criminal anthropologists—such as Lombroso's theses connecting bad heredity and primitive nature, Isaac Ray's alienist theory linking mental disorders and crime, and E. W. Farnham's phrenology theory attributing crime to organic causes—it was they who established criminology as a distinct profession separate from jurisprudence and penology. Despite their failed methodologies, these early criminological investigations established the primacy of positivistic theories of crime causation. Rafter suggests that while modern positivists such as James Q. Wilson, Richard Herrnstein, Michael Gottfredson, and Travis Hirschi acknowledge the influence of social factors such as poverty on crime rates, they inevitably return to what they consider the more fundamental question of what inherent traits contribute to the delinquency of some persons living in poverty but not others. Rafter then describes the transformation of positivistic criminology from the rudimentary study of physical traits and heredity to the more sophisticated study of the influence of specific physiological and psychological phenomena on human behavior that may predispose individuals to criminality.

Lee Ellis's construction of an arousal theory of crime ("Arousal Theory and the Religiosity-Criminality Relationship") is a prime example of a biosocial positivist theory of crime. Ellis identifies "brain stimulation" as a primary variable in determining predisposition toward criminality. Ellis argues that individuals react differently to novel and intense stimuli (e.g., deviant opportunities) based on the physiological composition of their brains. Ellis begins his theory construction by establishing three distinct arousal levels. The type I level includes those individuals who are "superoptimally aroused." These individuals have such a low threshold of arousal that just contemplating deviance or crime creates an unbearable level of arousal. Ellis describes type II individuals as being "normally aroused." The mere thought of committing a crime would not raise their arousal to unbearable levels, but actually to commit a crime would do so, especially if there was a significant risk of being caught. The type III, or "suboptimally aroused," individual, according to Ellis, needs to engage in sensation-seeking behavior such as crime in order to reach normal levels of arousal. As a way of demonstrating the arousal potential of criminal participation, Ellis juxtaposes it against participation in religious activities. In the case of the superoptimally aroused individual, religious services, with their familiar rituals and friends and family in attendance, provide predictability and comfort. Regular worship attendance provides numerous opportunities for the type I individual to internalize a standard set of religious doctrines directed toward social conformity. For the normally aroused individual, attendance varies according to the nature of the services. Religious services with sufficient variety and new social contacts would sufficiently arouse the type II individual, whereas more orthodox services would not. Suboptimally aroused individuals are unlikely to go to services voluntarily because the services would likely bore them and make them restless. Lower worship attendance by these type III individuals in turn reduces their commitment to the very religious doctrines that are directed toward social conformity. For Ellis, the simultaneous push away from conventional activities such as religious practice and the pull toward sensation-seeking activities such as crime combine to predispose the suboptimally aroused individual toward criminality. Ellis supports his thesis with positivistic evidence measuring brain activity, physiological symptoms of stress, and hyperactivity.

Following in the tradition of theories that have either directly or indirectly linked intelligence (specifically, low IQ scores) with delinquency (Gordon, 1976; Hirschi and Hindelang, 1977), Terrie Moffitt's chapter, "The Neuropsychology of Conduct Disorder," attempts to clarify the link by identifying which neurological defects lead to the specific psychological deficits that are responsible for a set of behaviors that constitute conduct disorder. Moffitt begins her theoretical analysis by distinguishing between conduct disorders, which she describes as "a variety of antisocial acts committed over a period of time beginning early in childhood" and juvenile delinquency, which she describes as a legal status that may or may not include those who suffer from conduct disorders. Moffitt argues that it is important to distinguish between young persons who are temporarily experimenting with mild delinquent acts and those children whose antisocial behaviors are more serious, persistent, and physically aggressive. Moffitt points out that an IQ deficit of one standard deviation (or about 8 points) separates delinquents from nondelinquents; a closer inspection, however, reveals a mean deficit of 1 point for the temporarily experimenting delinquent and 17 points for delinquents who have been aggressive since early childhood. Moffitt suggests that compromised neurological health may be only one factor for this small, albeit serious, subgroup of antisocial juveniles.

In her review of forty-seven studies of conduct disorders, Moffitt identifies two specific mental domains as being primarily responsible for conduct functions: (1) language-based verbal skills and (2) executive self-control skills. Moffitt's review shows a strong correlation between conduct disorder and measurable deficits in these two functions. The importance of language skills for self-control, according to Moffitt, is related to how parents' instructions and admonitions are converted into verbally based social control skills. Language-based mechanisms of social control include both simple skills (e.g., the ability to understand a simple "no") and complex skills (e.g., the ability to comprehend the social repercussions of one's behavior). Moffitt points out that those young persons who have a verbal skill deficit do not necessarily benefit (as other young persons generally do) from parents labeling a class of behaviors as incurring punishment, thereby increasing the likelihood of the children experiencing more frequent punishments. The greater frequency of punishment in turn generates stronger and stronger oppositional behavior in the young person. This cycle of punitive/oppositional interaction short-circuits the typical prosocial child-parent interaction that is the foundation of successful socialization.

Using the same organic basis of neuropsychological deficits (the underdevelopment of the frontal lobes of the brain) that she used to explain verbal skills development, Moffitt then examines the role of executive dysfunction in conduct disorders. Moffitt identifies a series of mental functions, described as executive functions, that enable a person to inhibit unsuccessful and inappropriate behaviors. Among the executive functions Moffitt identifies as crucial to developing self-control are sustaining attention and concentration, reasoning abstractly, forming concepts, initiating purposive behavior, self monitoring and being self aware. As with her review of studies on verbal skills deficits, Moffitt establishes a correlation between measurable deficits in these executive functions and conduct disorder.

The final chapter on positivistic theory, David Farrington's "The Development of Offending and Antisocial Behavior from Childhood to Adulthood," demonstrates how social phenomena such as poverty and social processes such as child rearing affect the personality development of the individual. Farrington bases his psychosocial theory of criminal offending on evidence gathered from a longitudinal study of criminal careers. Farrington's Cambridge Study of Delinquency Development found a consistency among career offenders; an equal number of offenses were committed as juveniles, young adults, and adults. Farrington suggests that such consistency can be explained in terms of an antisocial personality. Criminal offending, according to Farrington, is one aspect of a larger pattern of antisocial behavior that helps to explain the early onset and persistence of criminal behavior. Farrington points out that among career criminals criminal offending is preceded by other antisocial behaviors (e.g., troublesomeness, physical aggression, etc.) that are not present in the early years of nonoffenders. Farrington identifies six types of variables that correlate strongly with career criminality. Three of these variables are more biosocial in nature: (1) impaired social control functions leading to dishonesty, aggression, etc.; (2) psychomotor deficiencies leading to hyperactivity, impulsiveness, and attention deficit disorder; and (3) low intelligence, leading to frustration and poor reasoning. The remaining three variables are more sociological in nature: (4) family criminality; (5) family poverty; and (6) poor child rearing. Farrington's multifactorial analysis of crime shows that the more of these variables that are present, the greater the likelihood that an individual will become a career criminal.

Using these variables as his empirical base, Farrington constructs a four-stage theory of criminality. Criminal offending, according to Farrington, is dependent on motives, methods, internalized beliefs, and decision making. Motives represent the desire for material goods and status among intimate friends. There are long-term differences among individuals, as well as short-term fluctuations within individuals, that affect the strength of their motives. Farrington argues that such motives will produce antisocial tendencies only if illegal methods for satisfying them are habitually chosen. Poor children, for example, because they are less able to satisfy these material desires or achieve status through legal or socially accepted methods, become more likely to choose alternative methods that violate social norms. Such antisocial behavior is not inevitable. According to Farrington, antisocial behavior is either inhibited or facilitated by internalized beliefs or attitudes about lawbreaking. Working in the tradition of differential association theory, Farrington provides evidence showing that parents who exercise close supervision and consistently punish socially disapproved behavior through love-oriented discipline are more succesful in inhibiting antisocial behavior. Conversely, Farrington shows that through a process of modeling, parents who are themselves criminogenic expose their children to attitudes favoring criminal offending. Whether a person actually commits a crime in a given situation is dependent on the availability of criminal opportunities and the perceived probabilities of the costs and benefits of different possible outcomes. In this final stage of Farrington's theory, the perceived direct (e.g., arrest) and indirect (e.g., parental disapproval) costs are weighed against the perceived direct (e.g., money) and indirect (e.g., increased social status among peers) benefits of a particular criminal behavior such as the sale of drugs. Farrington concludes his analysis by pointing out that the development of an antisocial personality can be affected by specific events. For example, data from the Cambridge study lend support to the labeling thesis by showing an increase in self-reported offending after an adjudication of delinquency.

References

Gottfredson, M., & Hirschi, T. (1990). *A general theory of crime.* Stanford, Calif.: Stanford University Press.

Wilson, J. (1983). *Social theory.* Englewood Cliffs, N.J.: Prentice-Hall.

5

Criminal Anthropology in the United States

NICOLE HAHN RAFTER

As criminologists, we have to deal with a number of unsettling issues about the nature of our field. We debate our disciplinary status—some claim a distinct disciplinary identity, others consider themselves specialists within sociology, and yet others view criminology as an area to which biologists, economists, lawyers, policymakers, psychologists, sociologists, and others can all contribute. We contend over methods and whether our field can or should even try to qualify as a science. We also argue about our goals—is our purpose to help control crime or to produce disinterested knowledge?[1]

These issues have been present since criminal anthropologists founded U.S. criminology one hundred years ago.[2] Because criminal anthropologists' doctrine of the criminal as a physically anomalous human type has long been discredited, we tend to ignore their work, at the same time overlooking the legacy of professional issues that they, as the first criminologists, bequeathed to us. If we are to resolve those issues, or even come to grips with and accept them as unavoidable aspects of our field, we must know how we acquired them.

This chapter examines an almost unrecognized phenomenon, the U.S. experience with criminal anthropology, in order to expose the roots of key debates within American criminology. I argue that by investigating the interplay between U.S. criminal anthropologists' professionalization of criminology and the kinds of information they produced, criminologists can better grasp the origins of three persistent problems: criminology's difficulties in (1) establishing a clear-cut disciplinary identity; (2) defining its meth-

I am grateful to Kathleen Daly and John H. Laub for comments on an earlier draft of this chapter and to Jeanne K. Siraco, of Northeastern University's library, for her bibliographical help.

ods; and (3) distinguishing its role as a knowledge enterprise from its contributions to crime control.

This study covers the production and substance of criminal anthropology in the United States over three decades, from 1881, when the first book on the topic (a German translation) appeared, to 1911, by which time leading theorists had rejected the doctrine (e.g., Parmelee, 1911) and had begun to favor another biological theory, defective delinquency theory, which equated criminality with mental retardation (for one of the earliest statements, see Fernald, 1909). After defining my terms and describing my basic procedure, I trace the diffusion of criminal anthropology in the United States and suggest why this process sowed confusion about criminology's disciplinary identity. Next I summarize the substance of U.S. criminal anthropology and show that its promulgators were uncertain about their doctrine's scientific status.

Terms and Method

In what follows I use the term *criminal anthropologists* to refer to writers who held that the worst ("born," "congenital," "incorrigible," or "instinctive") criminals deviate from ethical and biological normality because they are atavisms, reversions to a more primitive evolutionary state. I distinguish between *criminal anthropology in the United States*, defined as all writings endorsing the doctrine published in the United States through 1911, irrespective of the author's nativity or the language in which the work initially appeared, and *U.S. criminal anthropology*, the subset of works authored by U.S. citizens (also called "Americans" for convenience). I do not attempt to improve on criminal anthropologists' loose definitions of *criminals* and *the criminal*, terms they used variously to denote lawbreakers, prisoners, recidivists, and all "degenerates," including the poor and mentally impaired. When I speak of criminology as a discipline or field, I mean only that it is a branch of knowledge and am concerned not with its organization but with its practitioners' claims to be producers of knowledge about crime and criminals.[3] I use the term *professionalization of criminology* to describe criminal anthropologists' establishment of the field as a new specialty.

It is necessary to say a few words about *positivism*, which criminal anthropologists interpreted somewhat differently than we do. Gottfredson and Hirschi (1987:10) have recently defined positivism as "the scientific approach to the study of crime where science is characterized by methods, techniques, or rules of procedure rather than by substantive theory." Most contemporary positivists would probably agree that their approach is empirical, often but not necessarily quantitative, inductive, and grounded in "belief in an objective external reality" (Gottfredson and Hirschi, 1987:19). Criminal anthropologists, too, emphasized the importance of direct observation and data collection, but as data they accepted folk wisdom, anecdotes derived from creative literature, and analogies between criminals and "lower" forms of life that would no longer be considered "empirical." When they dealt with the "born" criminal, moreover, they equated positivism with materialism (or naturalism), the philosophical position according to which all phenomena can be explained in terms of physical laws; and they espoused an absolute determinism, denying any role whatsoever to free will.

Instead of critiquing criminal anthropologists' methods, this chapter emphasizes the methodological assumptions about materialism and determinism that they considered crucial to positivism and that led to their conclusions. When I observe that criminal anthropologists failed to differentiate between their procedures and conclusions, I do so to indicate an aspect of their work that has, as Gottfredson and Hirschi (1987) more generally point out, left the discipline confused about the nature of its science. My interest, in short, lies in criminal anthropology as a discourse rather than the accuracy of its findings. I am concerned with documenting not its methodological sins but the ways in which it laid the basis for some of criminology's ongoing debates.

My central methodological problem was identifying the major U.S. criminal anthropologists. First, I defined them as American authors of book-length works published through 1911 who endorsed the concept of the criminal as a physically distinct, savage human being and who were frequently cited in the primary and secondary U.S. literature on criminal anthropology. I next listed all criminal anthropological books mentioned in the relevant chapters of three important secondary sources: Fink's *Causes of Crime: Biological Theories in the United States, 1800–1915* (1938), Haller's *Eugenics: Hereditarian Attitudes in American Thought* (1963), and Zeman's dissertation on the American criminological tradition (1981). When I excluded books on juvenile crime and general sociology and reduced Arthur MacDonald's many criminal anthropological works to one, his *Criminology,*[4] my list consisted of nine books by eight authors, most of them mentioned in at least two of the secondary sources. I read the nine books to discover whether they frequently cited other works that fit my definition. They did not; rather, they referred (within my definition's confines) mainly to previously published books already on my list. This made me confident that the nine books had indeed been primary vehicles for the doctrine's dissemination and that their authors had been major U.S. proponents of criminal anthropology.

The Diffusion of Criminal Anthropology in the United States

To follow the diffusion of criminal anthropology in the United States, one must distinguish among three groups of producers: the Europeans who generated the theory in the first place ("originators"); those who initially gave Americans access to the originators' work ("channelers"); and the Americans who then elaborated on the channelers' materials ("U.S. criminal anthropologists"). Analysis of the diffusion process reveals that few U.S. criminal anthropologists had firsthand contact with the work of Lombroso, the originator on whom they depended most heavily, and that although most were professionals of one sort or another, they had little expertise in social science. As a result, U.S. criminology began without a well-defined research agenda or sense of its disciplinary boundaries.

Originators

The first book on criminal anthropology published in the United States, Moriz Benedikt's *Anatomical Studies upon Brains of Criminals,* appeared in 1881, well in advance of any work by Lombroso. A Hungarian who taught in Vienna, Benedikt was inspired to study the cranium and brain of criminals by the work of Franz Joseph Gall, the founder of phrenology; he was also aware of Lombroso's investigations (p. vii). Dissections led Benedikt to conclude that

> THE BRAINS OF CRIMINALS EXHIBIT A DEVIATION FROM THE NORMAL TYPE, AND CRIMINALS ARE TO BE VIEWED AS AN ANTHROPOLOGICAL VARIETY OF THEIR SPECIES, AT LEAST AMONGST THE CULTURED RACES (p. 157, capitalization as in original).

This finding excited some debate, especially among physicans (Fink, 1938:107–109), on the existence of an anatomically distinct criminal type. But Benedikt's book was too abstruse to have much impact on mainstream U.S. thinking about the causes of crime, and its methodology—brain dissection— was not one that social scientists could easily adopt. In addition, this was Benedikt's only book to be translated into English. Thus, *Anatomical Studies* became little more than a footnote in the work of U.S. criminal anthropologists.

The other originator, Lombroso,[5] exercised far greater influence, but for years Americans knew his work mainly through secondary sources. Lombroso's own writings appeared slowly in English and at first in the form of his introductions to books by U.S. followers and articles. MacDonald's *Criminology* carried one of these introductions; August Drahms's *The Criminal* (1900) another. Subscribers to the journal *The Forum* could read Lombroso's "Criminal Anthropology: Its Origin and Application," an 1895 survey of the field. Portions of one of his major studies also appeared in English in 1895 as *The Female Offender* (Lombroso and Ferrero, 1895), just two years after its initial Italian publication, and this work was reprinted six times before 1911. But Americans who knew only English had to wait another sixteen years before they could read a digest of Lombroso's key work, *L'Uomo Delinquente,* the first Italian edition of which had appeared in 1876. This summary, compiled by Lombroso's daughter with his assistance and carrying yet another of his introductions, was published in 1911 as *Criminal*

Man (Lombroso–Ferrero, 1911).[6] His *Crime: Its Causes and Remedies* appeared the same year (Lombroso, 1911).

Americans who could not read Lombroso's *oeuvre* in Italian or French translation, then, lacked direct access to it until criminal anthropology's heyday had passed. This meant that those who built on his research usually worked at some distance from their source material. Their own writings were often doubly derivative, dependent on both Lombroso's research and the channelers who gave them access to it.

Channelers

Among the channelers who provided access to the originators' works, translators played an important role by determining, through their initiatives, which European works would reach U.S. audiences. Americans might never have heard of Benedikt, for example, had E. P. Fowler, a New York physician, not translated his *Anatomical Studies* from German—a task he undertook, he tells us, to establish "a scientific basis for the prevention of crime" (in Benedikt, 1881:xi). Henry P. Horton, who translated Lombroso's *Crime: Its Causes and Remedies* from French and German sources, helped introduce Americans to Italian criminal anthropology.[7] Horton's significance as a channeler is eclipsed, however, by that of the organization that arranged this translation, the American Institute of Criminal Law and Criminology. Although this professional association was not founded until enthusiasm for criminal anthropology had begun to wane, it immediately evinced a deep and relatively sophisticated interest in biological theories of crime. Criminological historian Leonard Savitz suggests that the organization's publication policies contributed to Lombroso's American "triumph": "the powerful American Institute of Criminal Law and Criminology, very fierce adherents to the Positivist School, translated Lombroso, Garofalo and Ferri, but, of the French environmentalists, only Tarde." Thus, "the monoglot American criminologist" had less access than Europeans to alternative theoretical traditions (Savitz, 1972:xix).

European criminal anthropology further flowed to the United States through a group of writers who, by summarizing the originators' work in English, first alerted Americans to it. Of these, far and away the most influential was Havelock Ellis, author of *The Criminal* (1890). The multilingual Ellis, an English eugenicist, wrote on an enormous range of subjects, from art to sexology. Although *The Criminal* was his only foray into criminal anthropology, it proved to be an extended foray. By 1911 the book was in its fourth edition and had gone through nine printings. For it, Ellis relied on numerous sources, but primarily Lombroso's work. *The Criminal* became the well into which many U.S. Lombrosians dipped for data on born criminals.

Very early American reports on Lombroso's research, while much briefer than *The Criminal*, formed yet another channel through which the doctrine passed into the United States. Joseph Jastrow, a psychology professor, produced one of the first articles of this type, "A Theory of Criminality," for the journal *Science* in 1886. Observing that "a change in our view of crime and criminals seems about to take place," Jastrow uncritically outlines Lombroso's theory of criminality as "a morbid phenomenon . . . a defect" (pp. 22, 20), deriving his information from a French review by Lombroso. An 1887 paper on "The Criminal Type," published in the *American Journal of Social Science* by William Noyes, a physician at New York's Bloomingdale Asylum, emphasizes the criminal's bad heredity and primitive nature; based on a French edition of *L'Uomo Delinquente* (p. 32), it too is undilutedly Lombrosian.

Criminal anthropology is better digested in two presentations by Hamilton Wey (1888, 1890), the physician at New York's Elmira Reformatory, that introduced members of the National Prison Association to criminal anthropology. Citing Benedikt, the influential English hereditarian Francis Galton, and Ellis as well as Lombroso, Wey supplements his outline of criminal anthropology with data gathered through his own research at Elmira. Wey's relatively critical attitude toward Lombroso's ideas and the fact that he went beyond his European sources make him a transitional figure between the channelers and the first generation of U.S. criminal anthropologists.

U.S. Criminal Anthropologists

As news of Lombroso's theory spread, many Americans began writing about it. Thus, the third group of producers, U.S. elaborators of criminal anthropology, outnumbered the other two. This group, however, had core members, identified through procedures described earlier; they and their books are listed in Table 5.1.

The initial book in this series, MacDonald's *Criminology* (1893), was the first U.S. treatise to identify its subject as "criminology" and its author as a specialist in the area.[8] MacDonald asserts expertise by listing his credentials and claiming that his findings have scientific status; he also dedicates his book to Lombroso, "the founder of criminology," who wrote its introduction.[9] For these reasons, *Criminology's* 1893 appearance may be taken as the U.S. field's starting point. However, as other titles in Table 5.1 indicate, for some time to come the study of crime and criminals remained intertwined with investigations of other "degenerate" types.

These major American books on criminal anthropology addressed somewhat different audiences but on the whole were directed toward educated laypeople, especially the growing body of social welfare workers. Henderson designed his *Introduction to the Study of the Dependent, Defective and Delinquent Classes* (1893) as a textbook for college students and welfare workers (p. ix); Parsons' *Responsibility for Crime* (1909), originally a Columbia Univer-

Table 5.1   Major U.S. Books on Criminal Anthropology Published 1893–1911

Author	Title	First Date of Publication	Other Dates of U.S. Publication
MacDonald, A.	*Criminology*	1893*	—
Boies, H.	*Prisoners and Paupers*	1893	—
Henderson, C. R.	*An Introduction to the Study of the Dependent, Defective and Delinquent Classes*	1893	1901, 1908, 1909
Talbot, E.	*Degeneracy*	1898	1904
Drahms, A.	*The Criminal: His Personnel and Environment*	1900	—
McKim, W. D.	*Heredity and Human Progress*	1900	1901
Boies, H.	*The Science of Penology*	1901	—
Lydston, G. F.	*The Diseases of Society*	1904	1905, 1906, 1908
Parsons, P.	*Responsibility for Crime*	1909	—

Source: Library of Congress, *National Union Catalog* (Washington, D.C.) for all except Drahms.
*This book, copyrighted in 1892, is labeled "second edition." However, the first edition seems to have been an 1892 pamphlet that reprinted an article MacDonald published earlier the same year. The *National Union Catalog* lists no third edition. It does refer to a fourth edition, for which it gives a copyright date of 1892 but no publication date. I have been unable to confirm this edition's publication.

sity dissertation, also seems to have been written for classroom use.[10] Lydston intended *The Diseases of Society* "primarily for professional readers" but hoped it would do "a little missionary work" among "the reading public" as well (1904:9). The other works were written to inform—usually to alarm—the general public. None of the nine books was aimed chiefly at scholars.

The major U.S. criminal anthropologists were all well-educated, male professionals;[11] those commonalities aside, the group was occupationally diverse. Some were social welfare workers (Boies, Drahms, and Henderson), some educators (Henderson, Lydston, MacDonald, and Talbot),[12] some physicians (Lydston, McKim, and Talbot), and some ministers (Drahms and Henderson; MacDonald, too, had studied theology). Professional heterogeneity characterized most of them as individuals as well. McKim held both Ph.D. and M.D. degrees; Lydston, a physician, was a university professor and successful writer; Henderson, a minister heavily involved in welfare work, taught sociology at the University of Chicago; MacDonald, a psychologist and specialist in the education of "the abnormal and weakling classes," had studied theology, medicine, psychiatry, and criminology (MacDonald, 1893:title page and unnumbered next page); and Talbot, a professor of dental and oral surgery, held both M.D. and D.D.S. degrees.

This multiplicity of professional backgrounds among the first U.S. criminologists affected the field negatively in the long run. Like Lombroso, who trained as a physician, the Americans came to criminology from the outside, as amateur specialists. This situation was inevitable: Like social science in general, criminology was still in its "formative period" (MacDonald, 1893:271). As yet the field had no "inside," no training program (Kellor, 1901:5) that could give its practitioners a common set of skills or foster consensus on research goals. MacDonald's European studies had included some formal training in criminology, and four of the other authors had had extensive contact with prisoners; but otherwise American advocates of the "new science" (Lombroso–Ferrero, 1911:5) had few qualifications other than an ability to digest their sources and speak knowledgeably. Although they present masses of data, they did no experimental work (also see Garland, 1985:97). Thus, the field they founded initially had no clearly defined kernel of skills or even goals, other than to broadcast versions of criminal anthropology. Nor did they themselves have a uniform professional identity. The result was a discipline that lacked boundaries and continues into the present to overlap with others, such as psychology and sociology.

The Substance of U.S. Criminal Anthropology

U.S. criminal anthropologists wrote in a context in which the primary experts on criminal matters were legal authorities and penologists. Their own work was not as unprecedented as they claimed, for a tradition of positivist criminological research had been accumulating throughout the nineteenth century, built up by alienists who analyzed the connections between mental disorders and crime (e.g., Ray, 1838), phrenologists who investigated the organic causes of crime (e.g., Farnham, 1846; also see Davies, 1955:ch. 8; Savitz et al., 1977), and degenerationists, such as Richard Dugdale (1877), who associated criminal behavior with bad heredity. But these forerunners did not present their work as "criminology" nor themselves as "criminologists." Lombroso's followers had to identify a new jurisdiction (Abbott, 1988)—to stake out professional territory, separate from jurisprudence and penology—over which criminologists would have authority. To accomplish this task they used two tactics, first claiming that their approach constituted an entirely new science and then producing information on criminal types that confirmed that claim.

Criminal Anthropology as a Science

Echoing Lombroso, the Americans insisted that criminal anthropology had for the first time carried the study of crime across the divide between idle speculation and true science. Noyes's (1887:32) early article heralded the advent of a "new science, which considers the criminal rather than the crime"; Drahms, calling crime a "social disease," claimed that "Criminology . . . reaches the dignity of a science by the same right of necessity that gives to the medical profession its place" (1900:xxi–xxii). They did not always label this science "criminology," however. Because the field was just beginning to emerge, through their work, they sometimes preferred to fold the study of criminal man into better accepted sciences—"scientific sociology" (MacDonald, 1893:173), "the science of penology" (Boies, 1901), or the "scientific" investigation of degeneracy (Talbot, 1898:viii). But all considered their work "scientific," by which they meant that unlike earlier commentators on crime, who had included God and free will in the causational picture, they would be materialists, examining only phenomena anchored in the natural world of matter.

Benedikt had made this materialist position explicit by writing that "man thinks, feels, desires, and acts according to the anatomical construction and physiological development of his brain" (1881:vii). A decade later Wey observed, "Of criminologists there are, generally speaking, two schools, the theological or spiritualistic and the material or anthropological" (1890:275; also see Drahms, 1900:22). Lydston (1904:18) contrasted the work of "the sentimental, nonscientific moralist" and that of "the scientific criminologist," whose job was "to reduce the subject to a material, scientific, and, so far as possible, evolutionary basis." With such remarks, criminal anthropologists voiced their determination to uncover the physical determinants of crime.

From their materialism, two methodological conclusions followed. First, criminal anthropologists would use only empirical methods, starting with direct observation instead of theory or metaphysics. They would report on measurements of criminals' bodies made with scientific equipment, such as callipers, the dynanometer, and the aesthesiometer; they would collect information on criminal jargon and tattoos, excerpt passages from confessions, and gather "proverbs expressing distrust of the criminal type" (Lombroso–Ferrero, 1911:50). All such data would be recorded dispassionately. "A large part of the most rigid science," one learns on the first textual page of MacDonald's (1893:17) *Criminology*, "consists in simple and exact description, which should be given, of course, without regard to any views that one may consciously or unconsciously hold." Materialism implied, second, that criminal anthropologists would use induction to formulate natural laws. Like other scientists, they would build up to whatever theory the facts indicated.

Materialism led criminal anthropologists to their central assumption— that the body must mirror moral capacity. They took for granted a one-to-one correspondence between the criminal's physical being and ethical behavior. Criminals, wrote Boies (1893:265–266), are "the imperfect, knotty, knurly, worm-eaten, half-rotten fruit of the human race," their bodies illustrating "the truth of the reverse Latin adage, *'insana mens insano corpore.'* " Nature had made the investigator's task relatively simple: To detect born criminals, one needed only the appropriate apparatus. Degree of criminality could be determined by charting the offender's deformities. The assumption that offenders literally embody their criminality led in turn to criminal anthropology's distinctive collapse of methods and findings. The doctrine's adherents believed that, just as moral worth could be directly read from the body, so too could the body be unmediatedly charted by their documents (see, esp., Green, 1985; Sekula, 1986). Theoretical assumptions did not intervene in either case, for theirs were the methods of science.

The Born Criminal

At criminal anthropology's heart lay Lombroso's perception of "the congenital criminal as an anomaly, partly pathological and partly atavistic, a revival of the primitive savage" (Lombroso–Ferrero, 1911:xxii). All nine of the U.S. books in Table 5.1 reiterate this message. "Criminals," Talbot (1898:18) writes in a typical passage,

> form a variety of the human family quite distinct from law-abiding men. A low type of physique indicating a deteriorated character gives a family likeness due to the fact that they form a community which retrogrades from generation to generation.

Most of the U.S. criminal anthropologists repeat Lombroso's descriptions of the born criminal's physical anomalies—his pointed head, heavy jaw, receding brow, scanty beard, long arms, and so on. They also adhere closely to Lombroso by enumerating the criminal's "psychical" anomalies—his laziness and frivolity, his use of argot and tendency to inscribe both his cell and his body with hieroglyphics, his moral insensibility and emotional instability. Seemingly the most scientific aspect of criminal anthropology, these were also its most sensational findings.

But five of the eight American authors express doubts about the born criminal's existence even while devoting entire chapters to his stigmata. Apparently unable to resist reporting Lombroso's galvanizing findings, these five simultaneously qualify their reports, often without reconciling their enthusiasm for the "new science" with their uneasiness about it. After filling many pages with such statements as "Flesch, out of 50 brains of criminals, did not find one without anomalies," MacDonald (1893:58, 65) confess that little is known about the relation of "psychical" to organic peculiarities. Henderson (1893:113) lauds Lombroso while warning that his views "are by no means universally accepted as final." Lydston (1904:25–26) masks his ambivalence by mocking the "ultra-materialism" of "so-called criminal anthropologists" and aligning himself with the doctrine's true practitioners.

But Drahms (1900) and Parsons (1909) completely fail to harmonize their misgivings about born-criminal theory with their desire to advance it. These first criminologists lacked confidence in the scientific centerpiece of their doctrine. They endorsed a science that even to them seemed shaky.

Insofar as they deviated from Lombroso's teachings about born criminals, the Americans did so not by rejecting his theory but by supplementing it, particularly by placing greater emphasis on the criminal's weak intelligence. In *Criminal Man*, Lombroso pays little attention to the criminal's mentality aside from stating that "*Intelligence* is feeble in some and exaggerated in others" (Lombroso–Ferrero, 1911:41 [emphasis in original]; also see Lombroso and Ferrero, 1895:170–171). Four of the eight U.S. criminal anthropologists, in contrast, carry Lombroso's implications to their logical conclusion by finding that criminals are intellectually as well as ethically weak, mental as well as moral imbeciles. Talbot (1898:18), for example, draws on evolutionism to explain that "there is truly a brute brain within the man's, and when the latter stops short of its characteristic development, it is natural that it should manifest only its most primitive functions." Lydston (1904:946), noting that "a defective moral sense is most likely to be associated with defective development of the brain in general," concludes that it is "not surprising that the typic or born criminal should lack intelligence" (see also MacDonald, 1893:ch. 4; Drahms, 1900:72–75). The American concern with the criminal's poor intelligence formed the bridge between criminal anthropology and its successor, defective delinquency theory, which identified criminality with "feeble-mindedness."

The U.S. authors further supplemented Lombroso's work by thoroughly integrating criminal anthropology with degeneration theory. Popular on both sides of the Atlantic, degenerationism attributed the genesis of socially problematic groups—paupers and the insane and feeble-minded, as well as the criminalistic—to an inherited tendency toward organic devolution ("degeneracy," "depraved heredity," "innate viciousness," and other synonyms). (On degenerationism, see, generally, Chamberlin and Gilman, 1985; Pick, 1989.) Lombroso did not immediately realize that degeneration could explain the criminal's bad heredity; at first he relied on the notion of atavism (Parmelee, 1911:xxix; Wolfgang, 1972:247, 249). His American followers, writing after degeneration theory had had more time to mature, made it the basis for their hereditarianism. Aside from MacDonald (who depends most heavily on European sources), the U.S. authors emphasize that the born criminal comes "of a degenerate line, and that if he have offspring some measure of his innate viciousness will be transmitted" (McKim, 1900:23).

American criminal anthropologists stressed the close connections among degenerate types; poverty, mental disease, and crime were but interchangeable symptoms of the underlying organic malaise. "The Degenerate Stock," Henderson (1893:114) explained, "has three main branches, organically united,—Dependents, Defectives and Delinquents. They are one blood." It followed that "vice, crime, and insanity may be regarded as merely different phases of degeneracy which so resemble one another that we are often at a loss when we would distinguish between them" (McKim, 1900:64). The term "criminal anthropology," Haller (1963:16) has pointed out, was "in a sense . . . a misnomer," for the doctrine "was concerned with the nature and causes of all classes of human defects." This was especially true of U.S. criminal anthropology. Wedded to degenerationism, the first American criminologists had no interest in defining the study of crime as a field apart from the study of other social problems.

Notes

1. We also debate whether any knowledge can in fact be "disinterested." For a review of this issue that relates closely to the production of the type of information discussed here, see MacKenzie (1981:esp. ch. 2).
2. As a field of inquiry, American criminology is about to reach its centennial; the first U.S. book in the area, a criminal anthropological tract by Arthur MacDonald titled *Criminology*, appeared in 1893. Although copyrighted in 1892 and labeled "second edition," this 1893 publication seems to have been the first book-length version of the work; the 1892 "first" edition was a pamphlet reprint of an article published earlier that year.

    Unless otherwise noted, all of this chapter's information on publications was derived from the Library of Congress's *National Union Catalog*.
3. This conceptualization of *discipline* draws on discussions of the relationship between professions and knowledge production that appear in Abbott, 1988; Bledstein, 1976; Larson, 1977; and MacKenzie, 1981.
4. MacDonald's other substantial works on adult criminals aimed at persuading Congress to establish laboratories for the study of degenerate types and were published by the Government Printing Office, not as trade books.
5. I do not deal here with the work of Lombroso's colleagues Enrico Ferri and Raffaele Garofalo, in part because they were so closely associated with him and in part because I could not confidently gauge their impact in the United States. Some U.S. criminal anthropologists cite Ferri (e.g., McKim, 1900), but most were poor footnoters, and I concluded from internal evidence that they had sometimes used secondary sources instead of the Italian originals and French translations that they cite.

    Ferri's work became available in the United States relatively early: his *Criminal Sociology* appeared in 1896 and was reprinted frequently thereafter, and *The Positive School of Criminology* was published in 1906 and reprinted in 1910. None of Garofalo's books appeared until 1914, after this study's cut-off point.
6. A French translation, *L'homme Criminel*, became available considerably earlier (1887, 1895). Several U.S. criminal anthropologists cite this translation as their source on Lombroso's work.
7. I have not been able to identify the translators of *The Female Offender* or *Criminal Man*.
8. Although two other titles listed in Table 5.1 also appeared in 1893, I give MacDonald's book priority due to its 1892 copyright; see note 2, above.

9. This was apparently Lombroso's first U.S. publication.
10. Parsons subsequently published two works clearly designed as textbooks (in 1924 and 1926) and authored no other books.
11. That they were all men helps explain why, despite the popularity of Lombroso's *Female Offender*, "the" criminal whom they described was nearly always male.
12. Parsons, too, may have been an educator, to judge from details in the *National Union Catalog*'s listing of his writings, but I was unable to confirm this.

References

Abbott, A. (1988). *The system of professions*. Chicago: University of Chicago Press.

Benedikt, M. (1881). *Anatomical studies upon brains of criminals*. New York: William Wood.

Bledstein, B. J. (1976). *The culture of professionalism*. New York: W. W. Norton.

Boies, H. M. (1893). *Prisoners and paupers*. New York: G. P. Putnam's.

Boies, H. M. (1901). *The science of penology: The defence of society against crime*. New York: G. P. Putnam's.

Chamberlin, J. E., & Gilman, S. L. (Eds.). (1985). *Degeneration: The dark side of progress*. New York: Columbia University Press.

Davies, J. D. (1955). *Phrenology: Fad and science*. New Haven: Yale University Press.

Drahms, A. (1900). *The criminal: His personnel and environment—A scientific study, with an introduction by Cesare Lombroso*. (1971). Montclair, N.J.: Patterson Smith.

Dugdale, R. L. (1877). *"The Jukes": A study in crime, pauperism, disease and heredity; also Further studies of criminals*. New York: G. P. Putnam's.

Ellis, H. (1890). *The criminal*. London: Walter Scott.

Farnham, E. W. (1846). Introductory preface. In M. B. Sampson, *Rationale of crime*. New York: D. Appleton.

Fernald, W. E. (1909). The imbecile with criminal instincts. *American Journal of Insanity, 65*, 731–749.

Fink, A. E. (1938). *Causes of crime: Biological theories in the United States, 1800–1915*. Philadelphia: University of Pennsylvania Press.

Garland, D. (1985). *Punishment and welfare: A history of penal strategies*. Brookfield, Vt.: Gower.

Gottfredson, M. R., & Hirschi, T. (1987). The positivist tradition. In M. R. Gottfredson & T. Hirschi (Eds.), *Positive criminology*. Newbury Park, Calif.: Sage.

Gould, S. J. (1981). *The mismeasure of man*. New York: W. W. Norton.

Green, D. (1985). Veins of resemblance: Photography and eugenics. *Oxford Art Review, 7*, 3–16.

Haller, M. (1963). *Eugenics: Hereditarian attitudes in American thought*. New Brunswick, N.J.: Rutgers University Press.

Henderson, C. R. (1893). *An introduction to the study of the dependent, defective and delinquent classes*. Boston: D. C. Heath.

Jastrow, J. (1886). A theory of criminality. *Science, 8*, 20–22.

Kellor, F. A. (1901). *Experimental sociology. Descriptive and analytical. Delinquents*. New York: Macmillan.

Lombroso, C. (1895). Criminal anthropology: Its origin and application. *The Forum, 20*, 33–49.

Lombroso, C. (1911). *Crime: Its causes and remedies*. 1918. Boston: Little, Brown.

Lombroso, C., & Ferrero, W. (1895). *The female offender*. 1915. New York: D. Appleton.

Lombroso–Ferrero, G. (1911). *Criminal man according to the classification of Cesare Lombroso*. 1972. Montclair, N.J.: Patterson Smith.

Lydston, G. F. (1904). *The diseases of society (the vice and crime problem)*. 1905. Philadelphia: J. B. Lippincott.

MacDonald, A. (1893). *Criminology, with an introduction by Dr. Cesare Lombroso*. New York: Funk & Wagnalls.

MacKenzie, D. A. (1981). *Statistics in Britain, 1865–1930*. Edinburgh: Edinburgh University Press.

McKim, W. D. (1900). *Heredity and human progress*. New York: G. P. Putnam's.

Noyes, W. (1887). The criminal type. *American Journal of Social Science, 24*, 31–42.

Parmelee, M. (1911). Introduction to the English version of Cesare Lombroso, *Crime: Its causes and remedies* (1918). Boston: Little, Brown.

Parsons, P. A. (1909). *Responsibility for crime*. New York: Columbia University; Longmans, Green, agents.

Parsons, P. A. (1924). *Introduction to modern social problems*. New York: Knopf.

Parsons, P. A. (1926). *Crime and the criminal: An introduction to criminology*. New York: Knopf.

Pick, D. (1989). *Faces of degeneration: A European disorder, c.1848–c.1918*. New York: Cambridge University Press.

Ray, I. (1838). *A treatise on the medical jurisprudence of insanity*. 1983. New York: Da Capo.

Savitz, L. D. (1972). *Introduction to the reprint edition of Gina Lombroso-Ferrero, Criminal Man* (1911). Montclair, N.J.: Patterson Smith.

Savitz, L. D., Turner, S. H., & Dickman, T. (1977). The origin of scientific criminology: Franz Joseph Gall as the first criminologist. In R. F. Meier (Ed.), *Theory in criminology: Contemporary views*. Beverly Hills: Sage.

Talbot, E. S. (1898). *Degeneracy: Its causes, signs, and results*. New York and London: Walter Scott.

Wey, H. D. (1888). A plea for physical training of youthful criminals. National Prison Association, Proceedings, 181–93.

Wey, H. D. (1890). Criminal anthropology. National Prison Association, Proceedings, 274–90.

Wolfgang, M. E. (1972). Cesare Lombroso. In Herman Mannheim (Ed.), *Pioneers in criminology*. Montclair, N.J.: Patterson Smith.

Zeman, T. E. (1981). Order, crime, and punishment: The American criminological tradition. Ph.D. dissertation, University of California, Santa Cruz.

6

Arousal Theory and the Religiosity-Criminality Relationship

LEE ELLIS

Biosocial theories share the assumption that it is not simply the social environment that causes variations in criminal behavior but rather interactions between biological and environmental factors (Ellis, 1990). As one of several expressions of the biosocial perspective, arousal theory maintains that due to both genetic and environmental factors, people's brains function differently, and some of these differences influence the probabilities of criminal behavior (Raine, 1993:180). Here the theory will be extended to argue that these same differences in brain functioning can account for the fact that religious people are somewhat less criminal than nonreligious people (Ellis, 1987a). People's varying degrees of religiosity may be defined in terms of being a member of a particular religion, holding various religious beliefs, or participating in church (or mosque or synagogue) services.

While nearly all criminologists recognize that the brain is the direct controller of behavior, few believe that there is enough individual variation in brain functioning to explain why some people engage in crime more than others. Arousal theory assumes that variations in brain functioning do account for significant variations in criminal behavior. In particular, some brains are exceedingly sensitive to incoming stimuli, whereas others are very insensitive. The latter group seems to have a higher probability than the former of frequently engaging in law-violating behavior.

Even more controversial is the possibility that these same aspects of brain functioning may affect people's involvement in religious activities. This chapter will maintain that the reason religiosity and criminality covary is that both are influenced by brain functioning as it relates to environmental

I thank Katharine Hoyenga, Myrna Nelson, Anthony Walsh, and Cherie Martin for their helpful comments on drafts of this chapter.

sensitivity. Before considering this proposal, let us look at what research has found regarding the relationship between religiosity and criminality.

The Religiosity-Criminality Relationship

Surveys conducted among the general public both in the United States (Jensen, 1981) and in Britain (Banks, Maloney, and Wittrock, 1975) have revealed that at least one-third of adults in both countries believe that religion can have a significant deterrent impact on crime. Stated simply, if people were more religious, crime would be less prevalent.

What do criminologists believe about this possibility? If criminology textbooks are any indication, criminologists are largely dubious that religion has any effect on crime. In a recent survey of eighteen criminology texts published since 1990 sixteen of them did not even contain the words *religion*, *religious*, or *religiosity*. In the two texts where the word *religion* did appear, less than one page was devoted to the possibility of a relationship between religiosity and criminality.

If a sizable minority of the general public believe that religion has significant bearing on crime, why is there so little coverage of the topic in criminology texts? Part of the answer may lie in the controversial and divisive nature of religion. If religion correlates with reduced crime, an inevitable question is, Are some religions linked more strongly to lower crime than others? In fact, over twenty studies have already addressed this question, although no textbook mentions the findings. These studies generally have shown that among the main Western religions, Jews have the lowest crime rates and Catholics the highest (at least when all Protestant denominations are considered as a single group) (reviewed by Ellis, 1985:509). Given how emotional most people are about their religious faiths, it is not hard to understand why criminologists would avoid discussing the issue.

Despite the minimal textbook coverage of religiosity and criminality, numerous scientific reports on the topic have been published. By the mid-1980s, over fifty studies had appeared in the research literature (Ellis, 1985), and at least a dozen more reports have been published since then.

Besides denominational differences, what has the research on religiosity and criminality revealed? The most consistently documented relationship between religiosity and crime involves the link between attendance at religious services and the commission of crime. As of 1985, thirty-one studies had investigated this link, and twenty-seven of them concluded that people who attend services most often were significantly less involved in crime than those who attended least often. This *inverse correlation* was also found in the remaining five studies, but the magnitude of the differences relative to the number of subjects studied did not warrant considering the relationship significant from a statistical standpoint (reviewed by Ellis, 1985:506; see also Gartner, Larson, and Allen, 1991). Since 1985 five additional studies have been published, all confirming that attendance at relgous services and criminality are inversely correlated (Sloane and Potvin, 1986:91; Ellis and Thompson, 1989; Mitchell et al., 1990:492; Nagin and Paternoster, 1991:580; Cochran et al., 1994).

It is also important to note that the inverse relationship between attendance at services and crime appears to be stronger than the relationship between any specific religious belief and crime (reviewed by Ellis, 1985; Gartner et al., 1991:9). In other words, a person's belief in a particular type of God or in immortality seems to have less bearing on criminal behavior than does the frequency with which that person attends religious services. In addition, the worship attendance–crime relationship appears to be stronger in the case of victimless offenses, especially drug offenses, than in the case of violent and property crimes (Burkett and White, 1974; Albrecht et al., 1977; Sloane and Potvin, 1986:91; Ellis and Thompson, 1989). Let us now consider the theory of criminal behavior that may best explain why such behavior is inversely associated with attendance at religious services.

A Brief Description of Arousal Theory

Arousal theory maintains that much of what motivates human behavior boils down to an attempt to maintain a preferred (or optimal) level of arousal. If people experience too much novel and intense stimulation all at once, they feel *anxiety* and *stress*. At the other extreme, if too little is happening in their environment, they feel *bored.* An assumption made by arousal theorists is that differences in how individual brains work cause people to vary a great deal in their response to whether novel and intense stimuli are "too much" or "too little." Some people "naturally" prefer much more environmental stimulation than others. These people have come to be called "sensation seekers" (Zuckerman, 1979; Raine, 1993:179).

Figure 6.1 presents a diagram to illustrate the theory (the overlapping curves at the extreme right will be discussed later in this chapter). The diagram identifies three hypothetical persons and illustrates what will be called their *resting levels of arousal,* that is, the level of arousal an individual's brain will exhibit under more or less "normal" environmental conditions.

Person A is shown feeling superoptimally aroused under ordinary environmental conditions. Such a person would almost never attempt to supplement his or her level of environmental input; in other words, this person would almost never become a sensation seeker. In fact, most of the time this person would be actively trying to reduce the amount of excitement in his or her life. Were such an individual seriously to contemplate committing a major crime, the thought of any adverse consequences (e.g., being caught) would elevate his or her arousal levels to unbearable levels. Consequently, Person A would find it very unpleasant to dwell on such thoughts. With regard to religion, Person A would probably find comfort in attending quiet

Figure 6.1 Arousal Theory and the Religiosity—Criminality Relationship

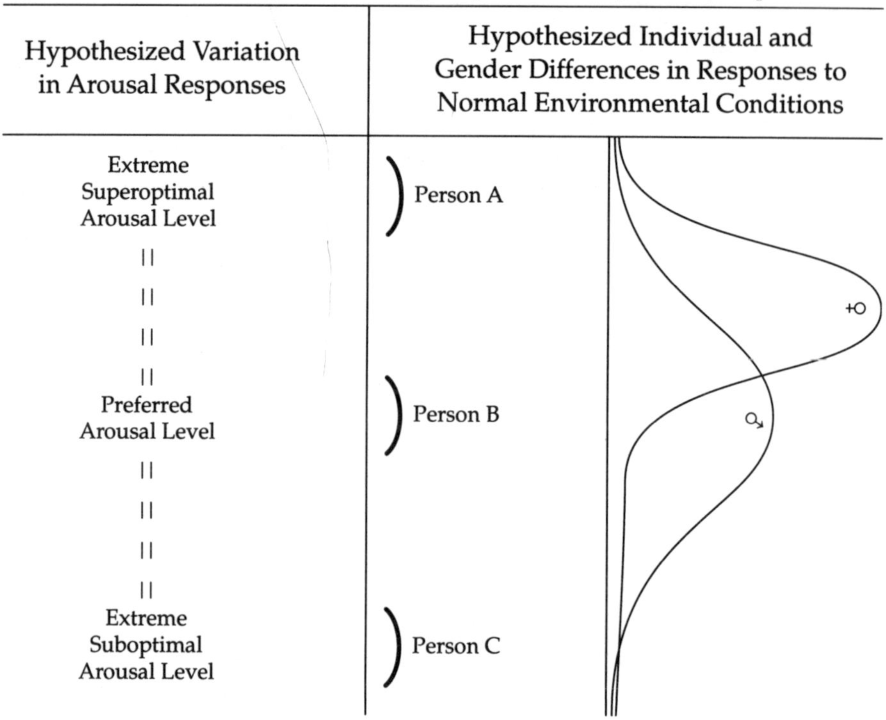

Hypothesized Variation in Arousal Responses	Hypothesized Individual and Gender Differences in Responses to Normal Environmental Conditions	
Extreme Superoptimal Arousal Level	) Person A	
||		
||		
||		+♂
||		
Preferred Arousal Level	) Person B	♀
||		
||		
||		
||		
Extreme Suboptimal Arousal Level	) Person C	

services filled with familiar rituals, especially if friends and relatives also attended and the tone of the sermons was reassuring. As a result of regular worship attendance, Person A would have numerous opportunities to internalize a standard set of religious doctrines.

Person B, according to arousal theory, represents roughly where the majority of people are situated. While the mere thought of committing a crime might not cause Person B's arousal levels to rise into the superoptimal range, *actually* committing a crime probably would do so, especially if the risks of being apprehended seemed to be significant. Consequently, Person B might commit a few offenses over a lifetime but would be an unlikely career criminal. As far as religiosity is concerned, Person B would probably be moderately involved. Religious services containing a reasonable amount of variety and new social contacts would probably have some appeal, but Person B would probably not be drawn to regular attendance as much as Person A. Person B would therefore be less likely than Person A to subscribe to a set of orthodox religious beliefs.

Finally, arousal theory postulates that Person C should exhibit sensation-seeking behavior to an unusually high degree, because such a person is suboptimally aroused under normal environmental conditions. In terms of criminal behavior, Person C should not only have a relatively high probability of experiencing pleasurable excitement while contemplating the commission of a crime but should actually enjoy committing crimes. Sometimes even experiencing moderate physical pain might be preferable to remaining suboptimally aroused. Were Person C to attend a typical religious service, he or she would be unlikely to return, at least voluntarily. The only services that could possibly appeal to Person C would be those that are unusually provocative (e.g., ones with gruesome, "fire and brimstone" sermons or detailed depictions of sex and violence). Due to low attendance at religious services, Person C's religious beliefs should be relatively unorthodox.

Using Arousal Theory to Explain Variations in Criminal Behavior

Is there actually evidence to support the theory just outlined? If arousal theory can account for varying tendencies to commit crimes, there should be at least subtle differences in brain functioning that correlate with actual degree of involvement in crime. Of course, these relationships will not be perfect, partly because of the difficulty in measuring both brain functioning and criminal behavior. In addition, the theory does not deny the involvement of other factors such as peer relationships, parental guidance and supervision, and mere opportunities for crime. Arousal theory is concerned only with varying neurological *propensities* to engage in crime.

At least five lines of evidence support the view that the brains of those who are most criminally prone function suboptimally compared with the brains of persons who are least criminally prone.

First, studies have shown that criminals have slower EEG brain wave patterns than occur in the general population (reviewed by Elliott, 1978; Syndulko et al., 1975; Syndulko, 1978; Mednick et al., 1981; Volavka, 1987). Criminally prone persons also have lower resting heart rates and skin conductance activity than persons who are not criminally prone (reviewed by Raine, 1993:166). Although other factors are involved, both heart rate and skin conductivity (sweating of the palms) increase when the brain is alert and aroused.

Second, persons with extensive criminal histories are more likely than those without such histories to have been diagnosed as children as suffering from attentional deficit disorders with hyperactivity (ADHD) (reviewed by Ellis, 1987a:911; Satterfield, 1987). The relationship between childhood ADHD and later delinquency and criminality is well established (reviewed by Ellis, 1988; see also Mannuzza et al., 1989; Loeber, 1990; Satterfield et al., 1994). Arousal theory predicts this relationship as reflecting a nervous system seeking greater-than-normal levels of environmental stimulation.

Third, persons with extensive criminal histories are not as likely as other people to exhibit symptoms of stress when threatened with impending pain (e.g., electric shock) (Hare, 1978, 1982; Hinton and O'Neill, 1978; Woodman, 1979). Arousal theory would characterize this relative indifference to pain as another reflection of suboptimal arousal. If so, it is predictable that criminally prone persons will be slow to learn how to avoid irritating others.

Fourth, when they are subjected to stress, persons with extensive criminal histories tend to recover more slowly than most people to a baseline level of arousal (Mednick, 1975; Siddle et al., 1976). This slow recovery to baseline may mean that criminally prone persons find it less rewarding to withdraw from punishment than people who recover quickly to baseline after withdrawing from a stressful situation (Mednick, 1975, 1977). This line of reasoning suggests, therefore, that persons with extensive crime histories are more likely than people in general to have had numerous accidental injuries (Douglas et al., 1968; Shanok and Lewis, 1981:237; Lewis et al., 1985; Miller et al., 1985).

Fifth, studies have shown that low levels of *monoamine oxidase* (MAO), an enzyme in the blood, are inversely associated with criminal behavior (Haire et al., 1980:341; Davis et al., 1983:534; Von Knorring, Oreland, and Winblad, 1984; Yu et al., 1984). Low MAO levels have also been associated with impulsivity and monotony avoidance, childhood ADHD, poor academic performance relative to ability, sensation seeking, and recreational drug use (especially excessive use of alcohol) (reviewed by Ellis, 1991:235). Exactly how MAO in the blood relates to MAO activity in the brain is still being investigated, but it seems to reflect how active *serotonin*, an important neurotransmitter, has been inside the brain (Oreland, Wiberg, and Fowler, 1981). More will be said about serotonin and arousal shortly.

Applying Arousal Theory to Explain Variations in Religiosity

Most religious services are structured around a familiar set of rituals, and neither these rituals nor the sermons are what most people would describe as exciting. Therefore, persons who are suboptimally aroused would be unlikely to participate regularly in such services, at least voluntarily. As a result of infrequent attendance (and probably paying little attention to sermons when they did attend), suboptimally aroused persons would thus be unlikely to internalize the doctrines of any particular religion.

Unfortunately, at the present time there is little evidence directly linking religiosity to any of the measures of arousal that were just reviewed with reference to crime. However, two studies have looked at the effects of suboptimal arousal on the inverse relationship between religiosity and criminality. Their results are encouraging.

In one study over 350 college students in North Dakota were asked to self-report their religiosity and delinquency on an anonymous questionnaire (Ellis and Thompson, 1989). In addition, the students were asked how readily they became bored when attending religious services and how comforting they found such services. Arousal theory led the researchers to expect an inverse correlation between religiosity and criminality, which was found. The theory also suggested the following hypothesis: If the disparity in the degree to which students were bored versus comforted by attending religious services was eliminated, the inverse relationship between religion and crime would disappear. This hypothesis was tested with a mathematical procedure called *partialing*, which allows a researcher to make subjects statistically equal with respect to one or more characteristics (in this case, regarding "boredom" and "comfort" at religious services). After equalizing the subjects for these two traits, the researchers found that, as arousal theory predicted, almost all of the correlations between religiosity and criminality disappeared.

Recently, this study was replicated and extended to a large sample of high school students in Oklahoma (Cochran, Wood, and Arneklev, 1994). Suboptimal arousal was measured by asking subjects questions about thrill seeking, impulsivity, and preference for energetic physical activity. The findings from this study largely agreed with those of the earlier study that suboptimal arousal accounted for most of the inverse relationship between religiosity and criminality. Nonetheless, the Oklahoma researchers appropriately noted that one other criminological theory, called *control theory*, also predicts that religiosity and criminality will be inversely correlated (see also Arnold and Brungardt, 1983:154). This later point will be discussed near the end of the chapter.

What Causes Variations in Arousal?

What is it about one person's brain that makes him or her suboptimally aroused relative to someone else? The areas of the brain that appear to have the greatest influence on arousal control start at the base of the brain in a region called the *reticular formation*. This dense bundle of nerve cells extends upward and forward from the brain stem through the limbic system (an emotion control center), and terminates in a region just above the eyes, called the *frontal lobes* (Longo, 1972:23; Warm and Dember, 1986:49; Graham, 1990:404; Ellis and Coontz, 1990:168).

There are at least two neurotransmitter systems in this neurological region that seem to be responsible for arousal regulation, although a third system may also be involved (Cloninger, 1986, 1987). One system involves three chemically similar neurotransmitters known as *catecholamines (dopamine, epinephrine,* and *norepinephrine)* and the other system involves the neurotransmitter *serotonin* (Soubrie, 1986).

The neurochemistry of arousal control is complex and still not fully deciphered. Part of its complexity lies in the fact that one cannot simply equate arousal with the amount of any one neurotransmitter, or even with a combination of neurotransmitters. Besides the number of different neurotransmitters, the number of receptor sites on the nerve cells for each neurotransmitter must also be taken into consideration. Some people's brains have nerve cells with many more receptor sites for the various neurotransmitters involved than do other people's brains.

Nonetheless, studies have suggested that at least modest associations exist between low levels of catecholamines (especially norepinephrine or dopamine) and suboptimal arousal (Cools and van Rossum, 1970; Iversen, 1977; Shekim et al., 1982). For instance, low levels of norepinephrine activity have been linked to hyperactivity (Carter & Pycock, 1980; Robinson & Stitt, 1981; Duterte-Boucher et al., 1988) and to impulsivity and resistance to punishment (Rogeness et al., 1990).

Various stimulant drugs, such as amphetamines and methylphenidate (Ritalin), have been shown either to facilitate catecholamine activity or to mimic these neurotransmitters (Buchsbaum et al., 1981; Nurnberger et al., 1981; Hernandes et al., 1994). Consequently, stimulant drugs can alleviate the symptoms of ADHD (Sprague et al., 1970; Weiss et al., 1971), presumably by making the brain more responsive to incoming stimuli (Ellis, 1987c:502; Russo et al., 1991:400).

Low levels of serotonin appear to be associated with suboptimal arousal. Several studies have associated low functioning of this neurotransmitter system with ADHD (Wender, 1969; Coleman, 1971; Greenberg and Coleman, 1973; Brase and Loh, 1975) as well as with conduct disorders (Pliszka et al., 1988) and aggressive-impulsive behavior (Brown et al., 1982; Pucilowski and Kostowaski, 1983).

Studies have shown that reductions in serotonin turnover rates in the brains of laboratory animals cause them to be overly reactive to a wide variety of stimuli (Carlton and Advokat, 1973; Harvey and Yunger, 1973; Weissman, 1973). Such animals also appear to respond to prolonged isolation with unusually aggressive behavior (Garattini et al., 1969; Valzelli, 1974).

Accounting for Sex and Age Variations in Religiosity and Criminality

In addition to providing an explanation for the inverse correlation between religiosity and criminality, arousal theory may help to explain sex and age variations in both aspects of behavior. The nature of these relationships is as follows: Regarding sex and religion, in many parts of the world females have been shown to be more religious than males by every reasonable measure used (Gannon, 1970:502; Wilson and Lee, 1974; Alzate, 1978; Sidanius and Ekehammar, 1980; Shiels, 1981; Francis, Pearson, and Kay, 1982; Brown, 1987; de Vaus and McAllister, 1987; Francis, 1987; Ellison, Gay, and Glass, 1989:115; Francis and Greer, 1990; Greer and Francis, 1992).

In the case of sex and crime, over one hundred studies have been conducted, some extending back more than three hundred years into European history. Without exception, these studies have shown males to be more involved in crime than females, especially in the case of serious offenses (reviewed by Ellis, 1988:535).

Concerning age and religiosity, studies have found people to be least religious during the second and third decades of life (Hoge, 1979; Harding and Phillips, 1986:40; Willits and Crider, 1989; Francis and Greer, 1990). It is also the case that most crimes throughout the world are committed by people in these same two decades of their life (reviewed by Ellis, 1988:534).

Could sex and age variations in suboptimal arousal be responsible for these worldwide patterns? In fact, there is evidence to suggest that males are more suboptimally aroused than females, and that both sexes are most likely to be suboptimally aroused during their second and third decades.

Regarding sex, studies have found males to be more prone to sensation seeking than females (Zuckerman et al., 1978; Zuckerman, 1979; Ball et al., 1984; Simo et al., 1991; Torki, 1993) although some studies have concluded that the differences are too slight to be considered statistically significant (reviewed by Torki, 1993). The aspect of sensation seeking to which males are significantly more prone than females involves risk taking (Cohen et al., 1955; Jamieson, 1977; Hudgens and Fatkin, 1985; Verma, 1991; Moore & Rosenthal, 1993). Even in the first year of life, infant boys exhibit stronger desires for novel stimuli that do infant girls (Goldberg & Lewis, 1969; McCall & Kagan, 1970). This same sex difference was also found to be true of monkeys (Rosenblum, 1974:138).

Second, males are also more likely than females to describe their lives as boring (Farmer and Sundberg, 1986; Vodanovich and Kass, 1990; Sundberg et al., 1991).

Third, in all countries where studies have been conducted, ADHD has been shown to be more prevalent among males than among females (Weiss and Hechtman, 1979:1350; Richman et al., 1982; Salili and Hoosain, 1985; Szatmari et al., 1989).

Fourth, despite popular opinion to the contrary, males have been shown to be less sensitive to pain than females (reviewed by Ellis, 1986:530; see also Feine et al., 1991; Fowler-Kerry and Lander, 1991; Mogil et al., 1993).

Fifth, males have been shown to exhibit lower MAO activity levels than females, especially after puberty (reviewed by Ellis, 1991:236). As noted earlier, low MAO activity has been repeatedly associated with suboptimal arousal.

Regarding age, the evidence is less extensive, but still largely consistent with the view that it is during the second and third decades of life that suboptimal arousal is most common. For example, studies have found sensation seeking to be more common among teenagers and those in early adulthood (Kish and Busse, 1968; Zuckerman, 1974:125; Zuckerman et al., 1978; Adams, 1980; Ball et al., 1984). The same is true for risk taking (Hensley,

1977; Zuckerman et al., 1978; Ball et al., 1984; Blaszczynski et al., 1986:115). Likewise, during their teens and twenties people appear to tolerate pain at its greatest intensity (Anonymous, 1972), and this is also the period when MAO activity levels are the lowest (reviewed by Ellis, 1991:237).

What causes these sex and age differences? If arousal theory is correct, biology has a lot to do not only with sex and age differences in crime but also with sex and age differences in sensation seeking, risk taking, hyperactivity, and pain tolerance. Following is some of the evidence implicating biology.

First, some of the differences in behavior just cited parallel what has been found in other animals. For example, in several nonhuman species males tolerate pain at higher intensities than females do (reviewed by Ellis, 1986:530). Also, studies have shown that in other species of primates, males are more likely than females to suffer both accidental injuries and injuries inflicted by others (Strum, 1982:195; Kano, 1984; Crockett and Pope, 1988), suggesting greater risk taking. Furthermore, as noted earlier, studies of infant monkeys have found males preferring greater novelty than do females, just as in infant humans.

Second, studies in both rodents and monkeys have indicated that low MAO activity is associated with high motor activity (Catravas et al., 1977:213; Redmond and Murphy, 1975; Redmond et al., 1979; Zuckerman et al., 1980:200). These studies have also shown that sex hormones have a major effect on variations in MAO activity. Basically, the "male" hormone testosterone and the "female" hormone estradiol (which is also a metabolite of testosterone) reduce MAO activity, whereas progesterone (another "female" hormone) increases MAO activity (reviewed by Ellis, 1991:231).

The above generalizations do not mean that by simply measuring the amount of the various hormones present in the body at a given point in time one can arrive at a fair estimate of the amount of MAO activity that has recently occurred. Rather, both MAO activity and brain functioning are affected by the presence of various sex hormones, primarily during two key stages in life. The first stage, called the *perinatal stage,* occurs prior to birth and for a few months following birth. The second stage, called the *postpubertal stage,* occurs following the onset of puberty. In other words, the most permanent and irreversible effects of sex hormones on brain functioning and, probably, on MAO activity, occur perinatally, whereas postpubertal levels of sex hormones simply modify brain functioning and MAO activity within the limits laid down by perinatal sex hormone exposure (Ellis and Coontz, 1990:168).

Because the brains of nearly all males during the perinatal stage have higher levels of testosterone (and its metabolite estradiol) than do female brains, the brains of males and females are compelled to function differently. Especially after the onset of puberty, when male brains are deluged with testosterone, the sex differences in brain functioning are almost certain to be at their greatest extreme. It is now established beyond doubt that male brains and female brains are both structurally and functionally different, both in humans (for reviews see Booth, 1979; Harlan, 1979; Gorski, 1987; Kimura, 1992; Swaab et al., 1992; Charles et al., 1994) and in other animals (reviewed by Ellis, 1982; Breedlove, 1994; Goldberg et al., 1994). The differences appear to include those having to do with the catecholamine system (Camp et al., 1986:494; Vadasz et al., 1988:537; Melrose et al., 1990) and the serotonin system (Meyerson, 1964; Everitt, 1984). As illustrated in Figure 6.1, these differences lend support to the idea that one of the reasons males are much more criminal and less religious than females is that their brains tend to be more suboptimally aroused.

References

Adams, G. R. (1980). Social psychology of beauty: Effects of age, height, and weight on self-reported personality traits and social behavior. *Journal of Social Psychology, 112,* 287–293.

Agren, H., Mefford, I. N., Rodorfer, M. V., Linnoila, M., & Potter, W. Z. (1986). Interacting neurotransmitter systems: A non-experimental approach to 5HIAA-HVA correlation in human CSF. *Journal of Psychiatric Research, 20,* 175–193.

Albrecht, S. L., Charwick, B. A., & Alcorn, D. S. (1977). Religiosity and deviance: Application of an attitude-behavior contingent consistency model. *Journal for the Scientific Study of Religion, 16,* 263–274.

Alzate, H. (1978). Sexual behavior of Colombian female university students. *Archives of Sexual Behavior, 7,* 43–53.

Anonymous. (1972). Withstanding pain. *Newsweek, 79* (May 15), 72.

Arnold, W. R., & Brungardt, T. M. (1983). Juvenile misconduct and delinquency. Boston: Houghton Mifflin.

Arrindell, W. A., Kolk, A. M., Pickersgill, M. J., & Hageman, W. J. J. M. (1993). Biological sex, sex role orientation, masculine sex role stress, dissimulation and self-reported fears. *Advanced Behavioural Research Theory, 15,* 103–146.

Bainbridge, W. S. (1989). The religious ecology of deviance. *American Sociological Review, 54,* 288–295.

Ball, I. L., Farnill, D., & Wangeman, J. F. (1984). Sex and age differences in sensation seeking: Some national comparisons. *British Journal of Psychology, 75,* 257–265.

Banks, C., Maloney, E., & Wittrock, H. (1975). Public attitudes toward crime and the penal system. *British Journal of Criminology, 15,* 228–240.

Barraclough, C. A., & Wise, P. M. (1982). The role of catecholamines in the regulation of pituitary luteinizing hormone and follicle-stimulating-hormone secretion. *Endocrinology Review, 3,* 91–119.

Ben-Zur, H., & Zeidner, M. (1988). Sex differences in anxiety, curiosity, and anger: A cross-cultural study. *Sex Roles, 19,* 335–347.

Blaszczynski, A. P., Wilson, A. C., & McConaghy, N. (1986). Sensation seeking and pathological gambling. *British Journal of Addiction, 81,* 113–117.

Block, J. H. (1976). Issues, problems, and pitfalls in assessing sex differences: A critical review of the psychology of sex differences. *Merrill-Palmer Quarterly, 22,* 283–308.

Booth, J. E. (Ed.). (1979). *Sexual differentiation of the brain.* Oxford, England: Clarendon.

Brase, D. A., & Loh, H. H. (1975). Possible role of 5-hydroxytryptamine in minimal brain dysfunction. *Life Sciences, 16,* 1005–1016.

Breedlove, S. M. (1994). Sexual differentiation of the human nervous system. *Annual Review of Psychology, 45,* 389–418.

Brown, L. B. (1987). *The psychology of religious belief.* New York: Academic Press.

Brown, A. M., & Crawford, H. J. (1988). Fear survey schedule-III: Oblique and orthogonal factorial structures in an American college population. *Personality and Individual Differences, 9,* 401–410.

Brown, G. L., Goodwin, F. K., & Bunney, W. E. J. (1982). Human aggression and suicide: Their relationship to neuropsychiatric diagnoses and serotonin metabolism. In B. T. Ho, J. C. Schoolar, & E. Usdin (Eds.), *Serotonin in biological psychiatry* (pp. 287–307). New York: Raven Press.

Brunner, H. G., Nelson, M., Breakefield, X. O., Ropers, H. H., & van Oost, B. A. (1993). Abnormal behavior associated with a point mutation in the structural gene for monoamine oxidase A. *Science, 262,* 578–580.

Buchsbaum, M. S., Davis, G. C., Coppola, R., & Dieter, N. (1981a). Opiate pharmacology and individual differences. I. Psychophysical pain measurement. *Pain, 10,* 357–366.

Buchsbaum, M. S., Davis, G. C., Coppola, R., & Dieter, N. (1981b). Opiate pharmacology and individual differences. II. Somatosensory evoked potentials. *Pain, 10,* 367–377.

Burkett, S. R., & White, W. (1974). Hellfire and delinquency: Another look. *Journal for the Scientific Study of Religion, 13,* 455–462.

Camp, D. M., Becker, J. B., & Robinson, T. E. (1986). Sex differences in the effects of gonadectomy on amphetamine-induced rotational behavior in rats. *Behavioral and Neural Biology, 46,* 491–495.

Carlton, P. L., & Advokat, C. (1973). Attenuated habituation due to parachlorophenylalanine. *Pharmacology Biochemistry and Behavior, 1,* 657–663.

Carter, C. J., & Pycock, C. J. (1980). Behavioural and biochemical effects of dopamine and noradrenaline depletion within the medial prefrontal cortex of the rat. *Brain Research, 192,* 163–176.

Catravas, G. N., Takenage, J., & McHale, C. G. (1977). Effect of chronic administration of morphine on monoamine oxidase activity in discrete regions of the brain of rats. *Biochemical Pharmacology, 26,* 211–214.

Chadwick, B. A., & Top, B. L. (1993). Religiosity and delinquency among LDS adolescents. *Journal for the Scientific Study of Religion, 32,* 51–67.

Charles, H. C., Lazeyras, F., Krishnan, K. R., Boyko, O. B., Patterson, L. J., Doraiswamy, P. M., & McDonald, W. M. (1994). Proton spectroscopy of human brain: Effects of age and sex. *Progress in Neuropsychopharmacology and Biological Psychiatry, 18,* 995–1004.

Cloninger, C. R. (1986). A unified biosocial theory of personality and its role in the development of anxiety states. *Psychiatric Developments, 3,* 167–226.

Cloninger, C. R. (1987). A systematic method for clinical descriptions and classification of personality variants: A proposal. *Archives of General Psychiatry, 44,* 573–588.

Coccaro, E. F. (1989). Central serotonin and impulsive aggression. *British Journal of Psychiatry, 155*(S-8), 52–62.

Cochran, J. K., Wood, P. B., & Arneklev, B. J. (1994). Is the religiosity-delinquency relationship spurious? A test of arousal and social control theories. *Journal of Research in Crime and Delinquency, 31*, 92–123.

Cohen, J., Dearnaley, E. J., & Hansel, C. E. M. (1955). The risk taken in crossing a road. *Operational Research Quarterly, 6*, 120–128.

Coleman, M. (1971). Serotonin concentrations in whole blood of hyperactive children. *Journal of Pediatrics, 78*, 985–990.

Comings, D. E. (1990). Blood serotonin and tryptophan in Tourette syndrome. *American Journal of Medical Genetics, 36*, 418–430.

Cools, A. R., & van Rossum, J. M. (1970). Caudal dopamine and stereotype behavior of cats. *Archives of International Pharmacodynamics, 187*, 163–173.

Cornish, D., & Clarke, R. (1986). *The reasoning criminal: Rational choice perspectives on offending*. New York: Springer-Verlag.

Crockett, C. M., & Pope, T. (1988). Inferring patterns of aggression from red howler monkey injuries. *American Journal of Primatology, 15*, 289–308.

Davis, B. A., Yu, P. H., Boulton, A. A., Wormith, J. S., & Addington, D. (1983). Correlative relationship between biochemical activity and aggressive behavior. *Progress in Neuropsychopharmacology and Biological Psychiatry, 7*, 29–35.

De Vaus, D., & McAllister, I. (1987). Gender differences in religion: A test of the structural location theory. *American Sociological Review, 52*, 472–481.

Denno, D. W. (1990). *Biology and violence from birth to adulthood*. Cambridge, England: Cambridge University Press.

Douglas, J. W. B., & Ross, J. M. (1968). Characteristics of delinquent boys and their homes. In J. M. Thoday & A. S. Parkes (Eds.), *Genetic and environmental influences on behavior*. Edinburgh: Oliver and Boyd.

Dubey, D. R. (1976). Organic factors in hyperkinesis: A critical evaluation. *American Journal of Orthopsychiatry, 46*, 353–366.

Duterte-Boucher, D., Leclere, J. F., Panissaud, C., & Coustntin, J. (1988). Acute effects of direct dopamine agonistis in the mouse behavioral despair test. *European Journal of Pharmacology, 154*, 185–190.

Eaves, L. J., Martin, N. G., & Heath, A. C. (1990). Religious affiliation in twins and their parents: Testing a model of cultural inheritance. *Behavior Genetics, 20*, 1–22.

Elliott, F. A. (1978). Neurological aspects of antisocial behavior. In W. H. Reid (Ed.), *The psychopath: A comprehensive study of antisocial disorders and behaviors* (pp. 146–189). New York: Brunner/Mazel.

Ellis, L. (1982). Developmental androgen fluctuations and the five dimensions of mammalian sex (with emphasis upon the behavioral dimension and the human species). *Ethology and Sociobiology, 3*, 171–197.

Ellis, L. (1985). Religiosity and criminality: Evidence and explanations surrounding complex relationships. *Sociological Perspective, 28*, 501–520.

Ellis, L. (1986). Evidence of neuroandrogenic etiology of sex roles from a combined analysis of human, nonhuman primate and nonprimate mammalian studies. *Personality and Individual Differences, 7*, 519–552.

Ellis, L. (1987a). Religiosity and criminality from the perspective of the arousal theory. *Journal of Research on Crime and Delinquency, 24*, 215–232.

Ellis, L. (1987b). Relationships of criminality and psychopathy with eight other apparent behavioral manifestations of sub-optimal arousal. *Personality and Individual Differences, 8*, 905–925.

Ellis, L. (1987c). Neurohormonal bases of varying tendencies to learn delinquent and criminal behavior. In E. K. Morris & C. J. Braukmann (Eds.), *Behavioral approaches to crime and delinquency* (pp. 499–518). New York: Plenum.

Ellis, L. (1988). The victimful-victimless crime distinction, and seven universal demographic correlates of victimful criminal behavior. *Personality and Individual Differences, 9*, 525–548.

Ellis, L. (1989/90). Sex differences in criminality: An explanation based on the concept of r/K selection. *Mankind Quarterly, 30*, 17–37.

Ellis, L. (1991). Monoamine oxidase and criminality: Identifying an apparent biological marker for antisocial behavior. *Journal of Research on Crime and Delinquency, 28*, 227–251.

Ellis, L., & Coontz, P. D. (1990). Androgens, brain functioning, and criminality: The neurohormonal foundations of antisociality. In L. Ellis & H. Hoffman (Eds.), *Crime in biological, social, and moral contexts* (pp. 162–193). New York: Praeger.

Ellis, L., & Thompson, R. (1989). Relating religion, crime, arousal and boredom. *Sociology and Social Research, 73*, 132–139.

Ellison, C. G., Gay, D. A., & Glass, T. A. (1989). Does religious commitment contribute to individual life satisfaction? *Social Forces, 68*, 99–123.

Everitt, B. J. (1984). Monoamines and the control of sexual behaviour. In M. Sheperd (Ed.), *The spectrum of psychiatric research* (pp. 26–32). Cambridge, England: Cambridge University Press.

Eysenck, H. J., & Gudjonsson, G. H. (1989). *The causes and cures of criminality*. New York and London: Plenum Press.

Farmer, R., & Sundberg, N. D. (1986). Boredom proneness—The development and correlates of a new scale. *Journal of Personality Assessment, 50*, 4–17.

Feine, J. S., Miron, D., & Duncan, G. H. (1991). Sex differences in the perception of noxious heat stimuli. *Pain, 44*, 255–262.

Ferguson, H. B., Pappas, B. A., Trites, R. L., Peters, D. A. V., & Taub, H. (1981). Plasma free and total tryptophan, blood serotonin, and the hyperactivity syndrome: No evidence for the serotonin deficiency hypothesis. *Biological Psychiatry, 16*, 231–238.

Fischette, C. T., Biegon, A., & McEwen, B. S. (1983). Sex differences in serotonin 1 receptor binding in rat brain. *Science, 222*, 333–335.

Fowler-Kerry, S., & Lander, J. (1991). Assessment of sex differences in children's and adolescents' self-reported pain from venipuncture. *Journal of Pediatric Psychology, 16*, 783–793.

Francis, L., Pearson, P. R., & Kay, W. K. (1982). Eysenck's personality quadrants and religiosity. *British Journal of Psychology, 21*, 262–264.

Francis, L. J. (1987). The decline in attitudes towards religion among 8–15 year olds. *Educational Studies, 13*, 125–134.

Francis, L. J., & Greer, J. E. (1990). Measuring attitudes towards Christianity among pupils in Protestant secondary schools in Northern Ireland. *Personality and Individual Differences, 8*, 853–856.

Free, M. D. J. (1992). Religious affiliation, religiosity, and impulsive and intentional deviance. *Sociological Focus, 25*, 77–91.

Gannon, T. M. (1970). Religious control and delinquent behavior. In M. E. Wolfgang, L. Savitz, & N. Johnston (Eds.), *The sociology of crime and delinquency* (pp. 499–508). New York: Wiley.

Garattini, S., Giacolone, E., & Valzelli, L. (1969). Biochemical changes during isolation-induced aggressiveness in mice. In S. Garattini & E. Sigg (Eds.), *Aggressive behavior*. New York: Wiley.

Gartner, J., Larson, D. B., & Allen, G. D. (1991). Religious commitment and mental health: A review of the empirical literature. *Journal of Psychology and Theology, 19*, 6–25.

Goldberg, E., Harner, R., Lovell, M., Podell, K., & Riggio, S. (1994). Cognitive bias, functional cortical geometry, and the frontal lobes: Laterality, sex, and handedness. *Journal of Cognitive Neuroscience, 6*, 276–296.

Goldberg, S. & Lewis, M. (1969). Play behavior in the year-old infant: Early sex differences. *Child Development, 40*, 21–31.

Gordon, H. W., & Lee, P. A. (1986). A relationship between gonadotropins and visuospatial function. *Neuropsychologia, 24*, 563–576.

Gorski, R. A. (Ed.). (1987). *Sex differences in the rodent brain: Their nature and origins*. New York: Oxford University Press.

Graham, R. B. (1990). *Physiological psychology*. Belmont, Calif.: Wadsworth.

Greenberg, A., & Coleman, M. (1973). Use of blood serotonin levels for the classification and treatment of hyperkinetic behavior disorders. *Neurology, 23*, 428.

Greer, J. E., & Francis, L. J. (1992). Religious experience and attitude toward Christianity among secondary school children in Northern Ireland. *Journal of Social Psychology, 132*, 277–279.

Haier, R. J., Buchsbaum, M. S., Murphy, D. L., Gottesman, I. I., & Corsey, R. D. (1980). Psychiatric vulnerability, monoamine oxidase, and the average evoked potential. *Archives of General Psychiatry, 37*, 340–347.

Harding, S., & Phillips, D. (1986). *Contrasting values in Western Europe: Unity, diversity and change*. London: Macmillan.

Hare, R. D. (1978). Psychopathy and electrodermal responses to nonsignal stimulation. *Biological Psychology, 6*, 237–246.

Hare, R. D. (1982). Psychopathy and the personality dimensions of psychoticism, extraversion and neuroticism. *Personality and Individual Differences, 3*, 35–42.

Harlan, R. E., Gordon, J. H., & Gorski, R. A. (1979). Sexual differentiation of the brain: Implications for neuroscience. *Reviews of Neuroscience, 4*, 31–71.

Harvey, J. A., & Yunger, L. M. (1973). Relationship between telecephalic content of serotonin and pain sensitivity. In J. Barchas & E. Usdin (Eds.), *Serotonin and behavior* (pp. 179–189). New York: Academic Press.

Hensley, W. E. (1977). Probability, personality, age, and risk taking. *Journal of Psychology, 95*, 139–145.

Hernandez, L., Gonzalez, L., Murzi, E., Paez, X., Gottberg, E., & Baptista, T. (1994). Testosterone modulates mesolimbic dopaminergic activity in male rats. *Neuroscience Letters, 171*, 172–174.

Hinton, J., & O'Neill, M. (1978). Pilot research on psychophysiological response profiles of maximum security hospital patients. *British Journal of Social and Clinical Psychology, 17*, 103.

Hirschi, T. (1969). *Causes of delinquency*. Berkeley: University of California Press.

Hirschi, T., & Stark, R. (1969). Hellfire and delinquency. *Social Problems, 17*, 202–213.

Hoge, D. R. (1979). National contextual factors influencing church trends. In D. R. Hoge & D. A. Roozen (Eds.), *Understanding church growth and decline*. New York: Pilgrim Press.

Hudgens, G. A., & Torsani Fatkin, L. (1985). Sex differences in risk taking: Repeated sessions on a computer-simulated task. *Journal of Psychology, 199,* 197.

Iversen, S. D. (1977). Brain dopamine systems and behavior. In L. L. Iverson, S. D. Iverson, & S. H. Snyder (Eds.), *Drugs, neurotransmitters, and behavior: Vol. 8. Handbook of psychopharmacology.* New York: Plenum.

Jamieson, B. D. (1977). Sex differences among drivers in yielding right-of-way. *Psychological Reports, 41,* 1243–1248.

Jensen, G. (1981). *Sociology of delinquency: Current issues.* London: Sage.

Joubert, C. E. (1994). Religious nonaffiliation in relation to suicide, murder, rape, and illegitimacy. *Psychological Reports, 75,* 10.

Kano, T. (1984). Observations of physical abnormalities among the wild bonobos (Pan paniscus) of Wamba, Zaire. *American Journal of Physical Anthropology, 63,* 1–11.

Kimura, D. (1992, September). Sex differences in the brain. *Scientific American, 267,* 119–125.

Kish, G. B., & Busse, W. (1968). Correlates of stimulus seeking: Age, education, intelligence and aptitudes. *Journal of Consulting and Clinical Psychology, 32,* 633–637.

Lester, D. (1988). Religion and personal violence (homicide and suicide) in the USA. *Psychological Reports, 62,* 618.

Lewis, D. O., Feldman, M., & Barrengos, A. (1985). Race, health, and delinquency. *Journal of the American Academy of Child Psychiatry, 24,* 161–167.

Linnoila, M., Virkunnen, M., & Scheinin, M. (1983). Low cerebrospinal fluid 5-hydroxy-indoleacetic acid concentration differentiates impulsive from nonimpulsive violent behavior. *Life Sciences, 33,* 2609–2614.

Loeber, R. (1990). Development and risk factors of juvenile antisocial behavior and delinquency. *Clinical Psychology Review, 10,* 1–41.

Longo, V. G. (1972). *Neuropharmacology and behavior.* San Francisco: W. H. Freeman.

Mannuzza, S., Gittelman Klein, R., Horowitz Konig, P., & Giampino, T. L. (1989). Hyperactive boys almost grown up. *Archives of General Psychiatry, 46,* 1073–1079.

McCall, R. B., & Kagan, J. (1970). Individual differences in the infant's distribution of attention to stimulus discrepancy. *Developmental Psychology, 2,* 90–98.

Mealey, L., & Segal, N. L. (1993). Heritable and environmental variables affect reproduction-related behaviors, but not ultimate reproductive success. *Personality and Individual Differences, 14,* 783–794.

Mednick, S. A. (1975). Autonomic nervous system recovery and psychopathy. *Scandinavian Journal of Behavior Therapy, 4,* 55–68.

Mednick, S. A., (1977). Preface. In S. A. Mednick & K. O. Christiansen (Eds.), *Biosocial bases of criminal behavior.* New York: Gardner.

Mednick, S. A., Kirkegaard-Sorense, L., Hutchings, B., Knop, J., Rosenberg, R., & Schulsinger, F. (1977). An example of biosocial interaction research: The interplay of socioenvironmental and individual factors in the etiology of criminal behavior. In S. A. Mednick & K. O. Christiansen (Eds.), *Biosocial bases of criminal behavior* (pp. 9–24). New York: Gardner Press.

Mednick, S. A., Volavka, J., Gabrielli, W. F. J., & Itil, T. M. (1981). EEG as a predictor of antisocial behavior. *Criminology, 19,* 219–229.

Melrose, S. A., & Hutchings, B. (1990). Dopamine in the cerebrospinal fluid of prepubertal and adult horses. *Brain, Behavior and Evolution, 35,* 98–106.

Meyerson, B. J. (1964). Central nervous system monoamines and hormone-induced oestrous behavior in the spayed rat. *Acta Physiologica Scandinavica*, Supplement, *241*, 1–32.

Miller, F. J. W., Kolvin, I., & Fells, H. (1985). Becoming deprived: A cross-generation study based on the Newcastle-upon-Tyne 1000-Family Survey. In A. R. Nicol (Ed.), *Longitudinal studies in child psychology and psychiatry* (pp. 223–240). New York: Wiley.

Mitchell, J., Dodder, R. A., & Norris, T. D. (1990). Neutralization and delinquency: A comparison by sex and ethnicity. *Adolescence, 25,* 487–492.

Mogil, J. S., Sternberg, W. F., Kest, B., Marek, M., & Liebeskind, J. C. (1993). Sex differences in the antagonism of swim stress-induced analgesia: Effects of gonadectomy and estrogen replacement. *Pain, 53,* 17–25.

Moore, S. M., & Rosenthal, D. A. (1993). Venturesomeness, impulsiveness, and risky behavior among older adolescents. *Perceptual and Motor Skills, 76,* 98.

Morell, V. (1993). Evidence found for a possible "aggression gene." *Science, 260,* 1722–1723.

Nagin, D., & Paternoster, R. (1991). The preventative effects of the perceived risk of arrest: Testing an expanded conception of deterrence. *Criminology, 29,* 561–587.

Nakazato, K., & Shimonaka, Y. (1989). The Japanese state-trait anxiety inventory: Age and sex differences. *Perceptual and Motor Skills, 69,* 611–617.

Nurnberger, J. I., Gershon, E. S., Jimerson, D. C., Buchsbaum, M. S., Gold, P., Brown, G., & Ebert, M. (1981). Pharmacogenetics of d-amphetamine response in man. In E. S. Gershon, S. Matthysse, X. O. Breakefield, & R. D. Ciaranello (Eds.), *Genetic research strategies for psychobiology and psychiatry* (pp. 257–268). Pacific Grove, Calif.: Boxwood Press.

Oreland, L., Wiberg, A., & Fowler, C. J. (1981). Monoamine oxidase activity in platelets as related to monoamine oxidase activity and monoaminergic function in the brain. In A. Angrist, M. Burrows, M. Lader, O. Ligjaerde, & S. G. Wheatley (Eds.), *Recent advances in neuropsychopharmacology* (pp. 195–201). New York: Pergamon.

Plaznik, A., Kostowski, W., & Archer, T. (1989). Serotonin and depression: Old problems and new data. *Progress in Neuropsychopharmacology and Biochemical Psychiatry, 13,* 623–633.

Pliszka, S. R., Rogeness, G. A., & Renner, P. (1988). Plasma neurochemistry in juvenile offenders. *Journal of the American Academy of Child and Adolescent Psychiatry, 27,* 588–594.

Pucilowski, O., & Kostowski, W. (1983). Aggressive behavior and the central serotonergic systems. *Behavioural Brain Research, 9,* 33–48.

Raine, A. (1993). *The psychopathology of crime: Criminal behavior as a clinical disorder.* San Diego, Calif.: Academic Press.

Redmond, D. E., & Murphy, D. L. (1975). Behavioral correlates of platelet monoamine oxidase in rhesus monkeys. *Psychosomatic Medicine, 37,* 80–86.

Redmond, D. E., Murphy, D. L., & Baulu, J. (1979). Platelet monoamine oxidase activity correlates with social affiliative and agonistic behaviors in normal rhesus monkeys. *Psychosomatic Medicine, 41,* 87–100.

Richman, N., Stevenson, J., & Graham, P. J. (1982). *Pre-school to school: A behavioural study.* London: Academic Press.

Robinson, R. G., & Stitt, G. (1981). Intracortical 6-hydroxydopamine induces an asymmetrical behavioral response in the rat. *Brain Research, 213,* 387–395.

Rogeness, G. A., Javors, M. A., Maas, J. W., & Macedo, C. A. (1990). Catecholamines and diagnosis in children. *Journal of the American Academy of Child and Adolescent Psychiatry, 29,* 234–241.

Rosenblum, L. A. (1974). Sex differences in mother-infant attachment in monkeys. In R. C. Friedman, R. M. Richart, & R. L. Van de Wiele (Eds.), *Sex differences in behavior* (pp. 123–141). New York: Wiley.

Russo, M. F., Lahey, B. B., Christ, M. A., Frick, P. J., McBurnett, K., Walker, J. L., Loeber, R., Stouthamer-Loeber, M., & Green, S. (1991). Preliminary development of a sensation seeking scale for children. *Personality and Individual Differences, 12,* 399–405.

Salili, F., & Hoosain, R. (1985). Hyperactivity among Hong Kong Chinese children. *International Journal of Intercultural Relations, 9,* 177–185.

Sanderson, S. K., & Ellis, L. (1992). Theoretical and political perspectives of American sociologists in the 1990s. *American Sociologist, 23,* 26–42.

Satterfield, J. H. (1978). The hyperactive child syndrome: A precursor of adult psychopathy? In R. D. Hare & D. Schalling (Eds.), *Psychopathic behavior* (pp. 329–346). New York: Wiley.

Satterfield, J., Swanson, J., Schell, A., & Lee, F. (1994). Prediction of antisocial behavior in attention-deficit hyperactivity disorder boys from aggression/defiance scores. *Journal of the American Academy of Child and Adolescent Psychiatry, 33,* 185–190.

Shanok, S. S., & Otnow Lewis, D. (1981). Medical histories of delinquent children. In D. Otnow Lewis (Ed.), *Vulnerabilities to delinquency* (pp. 221–239). New York: Spectrum Publications.

Shekim, W. O., Javaid, J., Dekirmenjian, H., Chapel, J. L., Davis, J. M. (1982). Effects of d-amphetamine on urinary metabolites of dopamine and norepinephrine in hyperactive boys. *American Journal of Psychiatry, 139,* 485–488.

Shiels, R. D. (1981). The feminization of American congregationalism, 1730–1835. *American Quarterly, 33,* 46–62.

Sidanius, S. T., & Ekehammar, J. (1980). Sex-related differences in sociopolitical ideology. *Scandinavian Journal of Psychology, 21,* 17–26.

Siddle, D. A., Mednick, S. A., Nicol, A. R., Foggitt, R. H. (1976). Skin conductance recovery in antisocial adolescents. *British Journal of Social and Clinical Psychology, 15,* 425–428.

Simo, S., Santana, G., Perez, J. (1991). A French junior sensation seeking scale (J-SSS). *Personality and Individual Differences, 12,* 669–670.

Sloane, D. M., & Potvin, R. H. (1986). Religion and delinquency: Cutting through the maze. *Social Forces, 65,* 87–105.

Soubrie, P. (1986). Reconciling the role of central serotonin neurons in human and animal behavior. *Behavioral and Brain Sciences, 9,* 319–364.

Sprague, R., Barnes, K., & Werry, J. (1970). Methyphenidate and thioridazine: Learning, activity, and behavior in emotionally disturbed boys. *American Journal of Orthopsychiatry, 40,* 615–628.

Strum, S. C. (1982). Agonistic dominance in male baboons: An alternative view. *International Journal of Primatology, 3,* 175–202.

Stuss, D., & Benson, D. F. (1984). Neuropsychological studies of the frontal lobes. *Psychological Bulletin, 95,* 3–28.

Sundberg, N. D., Latkin, C. A., Farmer, R. F., & Saoud, J. (1991). Boredom in young adults. *Journal of Cross-Cultural Psychology, 22,* 209–223.

Swaab, D. F., Gooren, L. J. G., & Hofman, M. A. (1992). The human hypothalamus in relation to gender and sexual orientation. *Progress in Brain Research, 93,* 205–219.

Syndulko, K. (1978). Electrocortical investigations of sociopathy. In R. D. Hare & D. Schalling (Eds.), *Psychopathic behavior* (pp. 145–156). New York: Wiley.

Syndulko, K., Parker, D. A., Jens, R., Maltzman, I., & Ziskind, E. (1975). Psychophysiology and sociopathy: Electrocortical measures. *Biological Psychology, 3,* 185–200.

Szatmart, P., Offord, D. R., & Boyle, M. H. (1989). Ontario child health study: Prevalence of attention deficit disorder with hyperactivity. *Journal of Child Psychology and Psychiatry, 30,* 219–230.

Tellegen, A., Lykken, D. T., Bouchard, T. J. J., Wilcox, K. J., Segal, N. L., & Rich, S. (1988). Personality similarity in twins reared apart and together. *Journal of Personality and Social Psychology, 54,* 1031–1039.

Tolor, A. (1989). Boredom as related to alienation, assertiveness, internal-external expectancy, and sleep patterns. *Journal of Clinical Psychology, 45,* 260–265.

Torki, M. A. (1993). Sex differences in sensation seeking in Kuwait. *Personality and Individual Differences, 14,* 861–863.

Vadasz, C., Kobor, G., Kabai, P., Sziraki, I., Vadasz, I., & Lajtha, A. (1988). Perinatal anti-androgen treatment and genotype affect the mesotelencephalic dopamine system and behavior in mice. *Hormones and Behavior, 22,* 528–539.

Valzelli, L. (1974). 5-Hydroxytryptamine in aggressiveness. In E. Costa, G. Gessa, & M. Sandler (Eds.), *Advances in biochemical psychopharmacology.* New York: Raven Press.

Verma, B. P. (1991). An investigation into the risk-taking behaviour of male and female adolescents. *Indian Psychological Review, 36,* 1–4.

Vodanovich, S. J., & Kass, S. J. (1990). Age and gender differences in boredom proneness. *Journal of Social Behavior and Personality, 5,* 297–307.

Volavka, J. (Ed.). (1987). *Electroencephalogram among criminals.* Cambridge, England: Cambridge University Press.

von Knorring, L., Oreland, L., & Winblad, B. (1984). Personality traits related to monoamine oxidase activity in platelets. *Psychiatric Research, 12,* 11–26.

Waller, N. G., Kojetin, B. A., Bouchard, T. J. J., Lykken, D. T., & Tellegen, A. (1990). Genetic and environmental influences on religious interests, attitudes, and values: A study of twins reared apart and together. *Psychological Science, 1,* 138–143.

Walsh, A. (1991). *Intellectual imbalance, love deprivation and violent delinquency: A biosocial perspective.* Springfield, Ill.: Charles C. Thomas.

Warm, J. S., & Dember, W. (1986). Awake at the switch. *Psychology Today, 20,* 46–53.

Watt, J. D., & Vodanovich, S. J. (1992). An examination of race and gender differences in boredom proneness. *Journal of Social Behavior and Personality, 7,* 169–175.

Watt, J. D., & Blanchard, M. J. (1994). Boredom proneness and the need for cognition. *Journal of Research in Personality, 28,* 44–51.

Weiss, G., & Hechtman, L. (1979). The hyperactive child syndrome. *Science, 205,* 1348–1354.

Weiss, G., Minde, K., Werry, J. S., Douglas, V. I., & Nemeth, E. (1971). Studies on the hyperactive child, VIII. *Archives of General Psychiatry, 24,* 409–414.

Weissman, A. (1973). Behavioral pharmacology of p-chlorophenylalanine (PCPA). In J. Barchas & E. Usdin (Eds.), *Serotonin and behavior* (pp. 235–248). New York: Academic Press.

Wender, P. H. (1969). Platelet-serotonin level in children with "minimal brain dysfunction." *Lancet, 2,* 1012.

Willitts, F. K., & Crider, D. M. (1989). Church attendance and transitional religious beliefs in adolescence and young adulthood: A panel study. *Review of Religious Research, 31,* 68–81.

Wilson, G. D., & Lee, H. S. (1974). Social attitude patterns in Korea. *Journal of Social Psychology, 94,* 27–30.

Wilson, J. Q., & Herrnstein, R. J. (1985). *Crime and human nature.* New York: Simon & Schuster.

Woodman, D. (1979). Biochemistry of psychopathy. *Journal of Psychosomatic Research, 23,* 342–360.

Yu, P. H., Davis, B. A., Bowen, R. C., Wormith, R. C., Addington, D., Boulton, A. (1984). Platelet monamine oxidase activity and plasma trace acid levels in agrophobic patients and violent offenders. In K. F. Tipton, P. Dosert, & M. Strolin-Benedeti (Eds.), *Monamine oxidase and disease.* London: Academic Press.

Zigmond, M. J., Heffner, T. G., Striker, E. M. (1980). The effect of altered dopaminergic activity on food intake in the rat: Evidence for an optimal level of dopaminergic activity for behavior. *Progress in Neuropsychopharmacology, 4,* 351–362.

Zuckerman, M. (1978). The search for high sensation. *Psychology Today, 11,* 38–43, 46, 96, 99.

Zuckerman, M. (1979). *Sensation seeking: Beyond the optimal level of arousal.* Hillsdale, N.J.: Lawrence Erlbaum.

Zuckerman, M., Eysenck, S., Eysenck, H. J. (1978). Sensation seeking in England and America: Cross-cultural, age, and sex comparisons. *Journal of Consulting and Clinical Psychology, 26,* 139–149.

Zuckerman, M., Buchsbaum, M. S., Monte, S., Murphy, D. L. (1980). Sensation seeking and its biological correlates. *Psychological Bulletin, 88,* 187–214.

7

The Neuropsychology of Conduct Disorder

TERRIE E. MOFFITT

Introduction

The belief that neuropsychological factors are among the causes of antisocial behavior is a very old one. For example, Benjamin Rush (1812, cited in Elliott, 1978:147) referred to the "total perversion of the moral faculties" in people who displayed "innate preternatural moral depravity." Rush proposed that, "there is probably an original defective organization in those parts of the body which are occupied by the moral faculties of the mind." Since Benjamin Rush's day, quite a bit of research has been done to put his "hypothesis" to the scientific test. Modern research methods have improved our ability to understand the role of neuropsychological factors in the antisocial behavior problems of children and adults. Neuropsychological researchers have labored to understand whether youngsters with antisocial behavior problems do differ in "faculties of the mind." The progress that has been made will be described in this chapter.

The Importance of Neuropsychological Health in the Study of Children's Conduct Disorder

Although the neuropsychological hypothesis is old, the scientific evidence for it is relatively new. Thus, it is worth beginning by documenting the strength of the association between antisocial behavior and neuropsychology. This task is easily accomplished by citing data on one of the best measures of *overall* neuropsychological health, scores on tests of intelligence.

How strong is the relation between IQ and conduct problems of the young? A critical mass of research has shown that IQ scores relate to juvenile delinquency about as strongly as measures of class or race do (Hirschi and

Hindelang, 1977). One of the most robust findings in the study of antisocial behavior is an IQ deficit of one-half standard deviation, or about 8 IQ points, between juvenile delinquents and their nondelinquent peers (Hirschi and Hindelang, 1977; Wilson and Herrnstein, 1985). When we evaluate the size of this statistical effect, it is important to remember that almost all studies have lumped together youngsters who are temporarily experimenting with mild delinquent acts and youngsters whose antisocial symptom behaviors are more serious, persistent, or physically aggressive. It is children in the latter group who are most likely to meet diagnostic criteria for conduct disorder. For example, in a representative sample of 536 New Zealand boys, the 8-point IQ difference between delinquents and nondelinquents obtained, but it was discovered to be the pooled result of a 1-point mean deficit for temporary delinquents and a 17-point mean deficit for delinquents who were aggressive since childhood and met diagnostic criteria for an externalizing disorder (Moffitt, 1990a). These findings suggest that compromised neuropsychological health may apply only to a small, albeit serious, subgroup of antisocial youngsters. For that subgroup, the strength of the connection may be stronger than previously thought.

It is important to ask whether or not the relation between neuropsychological variables and antisocial behavior survives after appropriate scientific controls are applied. The link between delinquency and IQ holds when IQ is assessed prospectively, well before the development of illegal behavior (Denno, 1989; Moffitt, 1990a; Moffitt, Gabrielli, and Mednick, 1981). IQ and delinquency share significant variance after controlling for socioeconomic status (Moffitt et al., 1981; Reiss and Rhodes, 1961; Wolfgang, Figlio, and Sellin, 1972), race (Lynam, Moffitt, and Stouthamer-Loeber, 1993; Short and Strodtbeck, 1965; Wolfgang et al., 1972), academic attainment (Denno, 1989; Lynam et al., 1993), and each child's motivation during the IQ test (Lynam et al., 1993). The connection between IQ and antisocial behavior is not an artifact of slow-witted delinquents being more easily detected by police; undetected delinquents who are identified by interview have low IQ scores too (Moffitt and Silva, 1988a). Delinquent siblings have been shown to have lower IQs than nondelinquent siblings within the same family (Healy and Bronner, 1936; Shulman, 1929). Finally, the stability of individual children's low IQ scores has been shown to parallel the stability of their severe antisocial conduct problems when the same children are examined repeatedly from preschool through adolescence (Moffitt, 1990a).

Given the robustness of the IQ deficit, it may come as a surprise to learn that we still do not know *why* or *how* low IQ influences the development of antisocial behavior. One way to approach those questions is to look beyond IQ. Neuropsychologists know that individuals with identical omnibus IQ scores may have very different patterns of mental strengths and weaknesses. Such patterns can be measured with a battery of neuropsychological tests. Two children with identical low IQ scores might suffer from different and relatively isolated problems such as impaired social judgment, weak language processing, poor auditory memory, or failure to integrate spatial information with motor responses (Lezak, 1988). Each deficit type could conceivably be better than the overall IQ at predicting conduct problems, but each would contribute to the development of conduct problems through a different theoretical causal chain. Thus, findings from neuropsychological research can offer keys to the theoretical problem of why cognitive deficit is linked to conduct disorder.

This chapter reviews studies of antisocial youngsters' scores on neuropsychological tests. In all, forty-seven published reports were reviewed. The reports were identified through exhaustive computerized searches of the literature in psychology and medicine from 1965 to 1992, checks of cross-references, reviews of program abstracts of the annual meetings of the International Neuropsychological Society from 1980 to 1992, and a mail survey of selected researchers working in the area.

Only one published neuropsychological study addressed children with *diagnoses* of conduct disorder (Frost, Moffitt, and McGee, 1989). Most of the research linking antisocial behavior with neuropsychological variables has used mid-adolescent juvenile delinquents as research subjects. Conduct disorder (CD) and juvenile delinquency (JD) bear many resemblances to each other: Many of the behaviors that are symptoms of CD are illegal, incarcerated delinquents are often given CD diagnoses, and a diagnosis of CD may be made up to the age of eighteen, which is past the peak age for delinquency. Thus, it is possible to draw some inferences about CD from the neuropsychological studies of delinquents, if some important ways in which CD and JD differ are kept in mind.

Important differences between CD and JD stem from the designation of CD as a mental disorder and JD as a legal status. (1) JD is more prevalent than CD: 25 percent of male youths are arrested by police and 65 percent self-report breaking a law, whereas the prevalence rate of CD among boys ranges from about 3 percent to 12 percent (American Psychiatric Association, 1987; Farrington, Ohlin, and Wilson, 1986). (2) A single adjudicated act is sufficient for legal designation as JD, whereas the diagnosis of CD requires evidence that the youth has committed a variety of antisocial acts over a period of time. (3) The "onset" of JD is truncated arbitrarily at an age beneath which youths may not be charged with crimes, whereas the onset of CD may occur very early in childhood. (4) There has been little concern among delinquency researchers about "comorbidity," whereas many of the poorest CD outcomes are for youngsters who have dual diagnoses of CD and attention deficit disorder with hyperactivity (ADHD). Therefore, it is important to sift the literature on neuropsychology and delinquency for evidence that neuropsychological variables are related to the variety, continuity, age of onset, and comorbidity of antisocial symptom behaviors. Moreover, greater variety, longer continuity, earlier age of onset, and comorbidity with ADHD are known to be the strongest predictors of adult crime and antisocial personality disorder (Farrington, Loeber, and VanKammen, 1990; Robins, 1978). Although it is difficult to estimate the percentage of CD cases with clinically significant levels of neuropsychological impairment, the research reviewed here shows that neuropsychological measures covary significantly with these four indicators of poor outcome for CD children.

The forty-seven studies reviewed here used a wide variety of neuropsychological tests and employed many different methods of ascertaining antisocial behavior. Despite this diversity, and despite the methodological problems in this literature,* the findings were fairly consistent. Across studies, antisocial youngsters were impaired in two specific mental domains: language-based verbal skills and "executive" self-control functions.

This chapter is organized according to the following format: First, it presents an overview of developmental psychopathology perspectives on the neuropsychology of conduct disorder. Second, some specific hypotheses about verbal and executive dysfunctions are extracted from the literature, along with findings from a selection of empirical studies. The chapter concludes with some directions for future research.

Developmental Psychopathology Perspectives

Many explanations for the ways in which neuropsychological deficits might be related to CD are so proximal as to be determinant at the moment of each symptom behavior. For example, it has been said that children with verbal deficits will rely more on physical modes of self-expression, resorting to hitting rather than discussion when disagreements arise. Alternatively, it has been said that children with attentional deficits will neglect to reflect upon the consequences of each bad behavior before rushing into it. Such explanations are not concerned with development; they apply as well to a thirty-year-old adult as to a five-year-old child. However, certain considerations suggest that such direct and immediate links should not be our only explanations for the association between neuropsychological deficit and antisocial behavior.

First, there is a seeming contradiction between the developmental courses of antisocial behavior and neurological damage: Antisocial behavior often grows worse with increasing physical maturity (Loeber, 1988), whereas a frequent progression for neurological damage is improvement, if not recovery. Childhood brain damage is often compensated for by remarkable plasticity of brain development (Rutter, 1983). Second, there is a seeming

---

*Elsewhere, I have critiqued the many and serious methodological problems with the early literature on the neuropsychology of antisocial behavior (Moffitt & Silva, 1988a; Moffitt, 1990b). Because recent studies have corrected most of the early problems, that critique is not repeated here.

disparity between the mildness of antisocial youngsters' neuropsychological deficits and the severity of their behavior problems. Childhood antisocial behavior that is severe enough to attract a DSM-IIIR diagnosis of CD is often subsequently characterized by a high degree of stability over the life course, from childhood into mid-life (Robins, 1966). Brain dysfunction that is severe enough to yield such continuity of maladaptive behavior for years ought to be readily detectable from neuropsychological tests. However, the test score deficits of antisocial samples are generally statistically significant but clinically mild. Few, if any, children with CD are identifiable as "brain damaged" by such clear signs as aphasia, sensory loss, or gait disturbance.

By the age when testing for neuropsychological deficits is done (adolescence, in most studies) the deficits seem to be too mild to account for the severity or persistence of the disorder. This observation suggests that neuropsychological problems may wreak their effects earlier in the life course. Perhaps the effects of early neuropsychological vulnerabilities are amplified over time as children interact with their environments, later culminating in CD. For example, a preschooler who has difficulty understanding language may resist his mother's efforts to read to him, which delays his school readiness. When he enters school, the modal curriculum may not allow for teaching that is tailored to his readiness level, especially if the school is crowded and resources are poor. After a few years of school failure, he will be chronologically older than his classmates, and thus socially rejected. He may be tracked into a remedial class containing pupils with behavioral disorders as well as learning disabilities. Daily association with CD pupils brings familiarity with delinquent behaviors, and he adopts delinquent ways to gain acceptance by peers. In this way, a relatively mild neuropsychological deficit might initiate an invidious downward spiral of interactions between individual characteristics and social contexts, culminating in a diagnosis of CD. As developmental psychopathologists, we must ask how dysfunction in the infant nervous system might negatively influence behavior during infancy and very early childhood causing children to "get off on the wrong foot."

Beginnings: Neuropsychological Risk for Difficult Temperament and Behavioral Problems

It is possible that one etiological chain to CD begins with some factor capable of producing individual differences in the neuropsychological functions of the infant nervous system. Such factors are myriad, and many have been empirically linked to antisocial outcomes.

One possible source of neuropsychological variation that is linked to problem behavior is disruption in the ontogenesis of the fetal brain. Such disruption may be caused by maternal drug abuse, poor prenatal nutrition, or pre- or postnatal exposure to toxic agents (Needleman and Bellinger, 1981; Rodning, Beckwith, and Howard, 1989; Stewart, 1983). Minor physical anomalies, which are thought to be observable markers for hidden anomalies in neutral development, have been found at elevated rates in antisocial samples (Fogel, Mednick, and Michelson, 1985; Kandel, Brennan, and Mednick, 1989; Paulhus and Martin, 1986). Neural development may also be disrupted after birth by neonatal deprivation of nutrition, stimulation, and even affection (Cravioto and Arrieta, 1983; Kraemer, 1988; Meany et al., 1988). Some studies have pointed to child abuse and neglect as possible sources of brain injury in the histories of delinquents with neuropsychological impairment (Lewis, Shanok, Pincus, and Glaser, 1979; Milner and McCanne, 1991; Tarter, Hegedus, Winsten, and Alterman, 1984). In carefully designed longitudinal studies even brain insult suffered due to complications during birth has been empirically linked to later antisocial behavior (Kandel and Mednick, 1991; Szatmari, Reitsma-Street, and Offord, 1986). Finally, some individual differences in neuropsychological health are heritable in origin (Borecki and Ashton, 1984; Martin, Jardine, and Eaves, 1984; Plomin, Nitz, and Rowe, 1990; Tambs, Sundet, and Magnus, 1984; Vandenberg, 1969). Just as parents and children share facial resemblances, they may share some structural similarities within their nervous systems.

Compromised neuropsychological functions are associated with a variety of consequences for cognitive and motor development, as well as for personality development (Rothbart and Derryberry, 1981). Toddlers with subtle neuropsychological deficits may be clumsy and awkward, overactive, inattentive, hard to keep on schedule, late in reaching developmental milestones, poor at verbal comprehension, deficient at expressing themselves, or slow at learning new things. Among the commonly reported behavioral sequelae of compromised neurological health are poor motor coordination, attention deficit disorder, hyperactivity, impulsive self-control problems, language impairments, and learning disabilities (Rutter, 1977; Rutter, 1983; Thomas and Chess, 1977; Wender, 1971).

Hertzig (1983) has described an empirical test of the proposed relation between neurological damage and "difficult temperament" in infancy. She studied a sample of sixty-six low-birth-weight infants from intact middle-class families. Symptoms of brain dysfunction detected during neurological examinations correlated significantly with an index of difficult temperament taken at ages one, two, and three. The parents of the children with neurological impairment and difficult temperament more often sought help from child psychiatrists as their children grew up, and the most frequent presenting complaints were immaturity, overactivity, temper tantrums, poor attention, and poor school performance. Each of these childhood problems has been linked by research to antisocial outcomes (cf. Moffitt, 1990a; 1990b). Significantly, the impairments of the children with neural damage were not massive; their mean IQ score was 96 (only 4 points below the population mean). Hertzig's study showed that even subtle neurological deficits can influence an infant's temperament, increase the difficulty of rearing the baby, and lead to behavioral problems in later childhood.

Elaborating upon Early Risk

Granted that neuropsychological deficits characterize many children who show difficult behavior, how might neuropsychological risk initiate a chain of events that culminates in CD? One possibility is that such behavioral deficits evoke a chain of failed parent-child encounters. The notion that children exert important evocative effects upon their social environments is useful in understanding this hypothetical process (Caspi and Bem, 1990).

Children with such psychological problems pose a challenge to even the most resourceful, loving, and patient families. For example, Waters, Vaughan, and Egeland (1980) found that aspects of neonatal adaptation that are typically included in infant neuropsychological examinations, such as orientation and motor maturity, predicted the quality of later infant-mother attachment. Many parents of preterm infants hold unrealistic expectations about their children's attainment of developmental milestones, and these may contribute to later dysfunctional parent-child relationships (Tinsley and Parke, 1983). More disturbing, neurological health problems in infants have been shown to be related to risk for parental maltreatment and neglect (Friedrich and Boriskin, 1976; Frodi et al., 1978; Hunter, Kilstrom, Kraybill, and Loda, 1978; Milowe and Lowrie, 1964; Sandgrund, Gaines, and Green, 1974).

Numerous studies have shown that a toddler's problem behaviors may affect his parents' disciplinary strategies, as well as subsequent interactions with peers and other adults (Bell and Chapman, 1986; Chess and Thomas, 1987; Lytton, 1990). For example, children characterized by a "difficult" temperament in infancy are more likely to resist their mothers' efforts to control them in early childhood (Lee and Bates, 1985). Similarly, mothers of boys with a "difficult" temperament experience more problems in their efforts to socialize their children. Maccoby and Jacklin (1983) showed that over time these mothers reduce their efforts to guide and direct their children's behavior actively and become less and less involved in the teaching process. In another study, parents of highly active three-year-old children, followed up two years later, had become impatient and hostile with their children and frequently got into power struggles with them (Buss, 1981). Moreover, when the children were seven years old, they were described by their teachers as aggressive, manipulative, noncompliant, and more likely to push limits and stretch the rules in many social encounters (Buss, Block, and Block, 1980).

Research on aggressive children at the Oregon Social Learning Center has shown in elegant detail how interactions between children and their families can create and sustain destructive and aversive patterns of behavior (Patterson, 1982, 1986a; Patterson and Bank, 1990). By recording moment-to-moment interactions in families of antisocial boys, Patterson and his colleagues showed that children's oppositional behaviors often provoke and force adult family members to counter with highly punitive and angry responses, which often intensify into an ever-widening gulf of irritation until these parents eventually withdraw from aversive interactions with their children.

One outcome of such negative reinforcements is that children who coerce parents into providing short-term payoffs in a given situation may thereby learn an interactional style that continues to "work" in similar ways in later social encounters and with different interaction partners. The immediate re-inforcement not only short-circuits the learning of more prosocial interac-tional styles that might have greater adaptability in the long run, it also increases the likelihood that coercive behaviors perfected at home will be extended to other people at other times. For example, children who coerce with one family member are likely to coerce with other family members (Patterson, 1986b). Analyses of sibling interactions show that here, too, nega-tive reinforcement contingencies serve to strengthen the antisocial child's style (Snyder, 1977). An early start to the coercive cycle increases the risk that it will generalize to other relationships (Eron, Heusmann, and Zelli, 1991). The child with neuropsychological problems and difficult behavior may learn early to rely on offensive interpersonal tactics. If the child general-izes antisocial tactics to other settings, his or her style may consolidate into a syndrome of CD.

Early Risk and Environmental Context

The elaboration of early neuropsychological risk into later conduct disorder is, of course, dependent upon each child's environmental context. The long-term behavioral outcomes of children with perinatal health and neurological problems have repeatedly been shown to vary in relation to the supportive-ness of their home environments (cf. Werner, Simonian, Bierman, and French, 1967). The implications for antisocial outcomes are profound: In the New Zealand study of the Dunedin Multidisciplinary Health and Develop-ment cohort, there was an interaction effect between family adversity and neuropsychological deficit on aggressive confrontations with a victim or ad-versary. Among the 536 boys in the sample, the 75 boys who had *both* low neuropsychological scores and adverse home environments earned a mean aggression score more than four times greater than that of boys with either neuropsychological problems or adverse homes (Moffitt, 1990b). Neuropsy-chological problems may render children more vulnerable to pathogenic en-vironments.

Unfortunately, children with neuropsychological disadvantages are not generally born into supportive environments, nor do they even get a fair chance of being randomly assigned to good or bad environments. Unlike the aforementioned infants in Hertzig's (1983) study of temperament and neurological symptoms, most low-birth-weight infants are not born into in-tact, middle-class families; vulnerable infants are disproportionately found in disadvantaged environments. Indeed, because some characteristics of parents and children tend to be connected, parents of children who are at risk for antisocial behavior often inadvertently provide their children with pathogenic environments (Sameroff and Chandler, 1975). Vulnerable children are often subject to adverse homes and neighborhoods because their parents are vulnerable to problems too (cf. Lahey et al., 1988). Parents and children also covary on temperament and personality (Plomin, Chipuer, and Loehlin, 1990). Thus, parents of children who are difficult to manage often lack the necessary psychological and physical resources to cope constructively with a difficult child (Snyder and Patterson, 1987; Scarr and McCartney, 1983). These findings suggest that children whose impulsivity and angry outbursts might be curbed by firm discipline will tend to have parents who are inconsistent disciplinarians; the parents may be impatient and irritable too.

Parents and children also covary on cognitive abilities (Plomin, 1990; Loehlin, 1989); the implication of this finding is that children who are most in need of remedial cognitive stimulation will have parents who may be least able to provide it. Moreover, parents' cognitive abilities can limit their own educational and occupational attainment (Barrett and Depinet, 1991). As one consequence, families whose children have below-average cognitive capacities will often be least able financially to obtain professional interventions or optimal remedial schooling for their at-risk children. Families with low occupational attainment often have to live in neighborhoods with low-cost housing, where their children will be exposed to high normative rates of peer delinquency.

The formulation described in this section has made the assumption that the child's complement of neuropsychological strengths and weaknesses is present very early in life and influences personality and behavioral development from his or her earliest social interactions. The thesis is that children with neuropsychological difficulties may evoke dysfunctional reactions from parents, especially under conditions of family adversity. When adult-child interactions become dysfunctional, important developmental tasks that must be negotiated jointly by small children and their caretakers (such as social skills and school readiness) risk failure. At this point, it is immaterial whether parent-child similarities arise from shared genes or shared homes. A home environment in which prenatal care is haphazard, drugs are used during pregnancy, and infants' basic needs are neglected is a setting where sources of children's neuropsychological dysfunction that are clearly environmental coexist with a social environment that is more likely to exacerbate behavior problems than ameliorate them. If the child who "gets off on the wrong foot" remains on this ill-starred path, subsequent links in a causal chain may culminate in a diagnosis of CD. This condition may thus reflect early individual differences that are perpetuated or exacerbated by interactions with the social environment, with adults and peers, at home, and in school.

Verbal Deficits and Risk for Conduct Disorder

Several theorists have described ways in which verbal neuropsychological deficits might produce children whose behavior poses a challenge to parenting. A. R. Luria (1961; Luria and Hamskaya, 1964) outlined a comprehensive theory of the importance of normal language for the self-control of behavior. Luria tied the very young child's capacity for following verbal instructions to maturational development of the neuronal structures of the frontal lobes and left hemisphere of the brain. He also outlined the developmental process through which parents' instructions and admonishments are converted to internal, verbally based self-control tools. According to Luria, normal auditory verbal memory and verbal abstract reasoning are essential abilities in the development of self-control, and they influence the success of socialization beginning with the earliest parent-child interactions. Language-based mechanisms of self-control range from virtually automatic motor programming for inhibiting simple childhood behaviors (e.g., "No!") to "thinking things through" before embarking upon a course of complex adult behavior such as a robbery. Luria did not discuss conduct disorder in his writings, but the notion that deficient verbal mediation of behavior characterizes aggressive children has received some empirical support (Camp, 1977; Kopp, 1982).

Other writers have also commented on the influence of childhood language deficits on the development of antisocial behavior. Wilson and Herrnstein (1985) suggested that low verbal intelligence contributes to a present-oriented cognitive style, which in turn fosters irresponsible and exploitative behavior. Humans use language as the medium for abstract reasoning; we can keep things that are "out of sight" from also becoming "out of mind" by mentally representing them with words. Normal language development is thus an essential ingredient in prosocial processes such as delaying gratification, anticipating consequences, and linking belated punishments with earlier transgressions.

Eysenck (1977), in his autonomic conditioning theory of antisocial personality disorder, stated that stimulus generalization should be enhanced when parents verbally label their children's various misbehaviors as "naughty," "bad," or "wicked." But children with verbal skill deficits might not profit from the labeling of a class of behaviors as punishment-attracting; they may have to learn by trial and error that each individual act is wrong. Verbally impaired children should thus experience more frequent punishments than verbally adept children, but with proportionately less effect in curbing their problem behaviors. Consistent with Eysenck's prediction, Kaler and Kopp (1990) have demonstrated that much of problem toddlers' noncompliance can be explained by their poor verbal comprehension.

In yet another account, Savitsky and Czyzewski (1978) speculated that a deficit in verbal skills may preclude children's ability to label their perceptions of the emotions expressed by others (victims or adversaries). Such deficits might also limit children's response options in threatening or ambiguous social situations, predisposing them to quick physical reactions rather than more laborious verbal ones. As such, children who feel uncomfortable or inept with verbal modes of communication may be more likely to strike out than to attempt to talk their way out of an altercation. If hitting gets them what they want, then they may enter the cycle of negative reinforcement for coercive behavior (Patterson, 1986a).

Tarter and his colleagues (Tarter, Hegedus, Alterman, and Katz-Harris, 1984; Tarter et al., 1984) mentioned the intriguing notion that children with poor communication skills may elicit less positive interaction and more physical punishment from their parents, especially if the family is distressed. Consistent with Tarter's prediction, McDermott and Rourke (cited in Rourke and Fiske, 1981) found fathers to be more negative, rejecting, and derogatory with their sons who had mild language deficits than with those boys' more verbal brothers. It follows from Tarter's speculation that poor verbal abilities may hinder the development of the healthy parent-child relationships that might forestall conduct problems.

The perspectives introduced in this section have emphasized neuropsychological effects on early parent-child interactions. Other theorists point to the limits neuropsychological impairment places on school achievement. For example, Hirschi's (1969) version of social control theory predicts that differences in intellectual capacity will have implications for how children experience school, a crucial agency in facilitating the transfer of children's respect and obedience from their parents to society's laws. Cognitively able children are likely to receive many rewards at school and to develop bonds to this social institution as a consequence. Less able children may experience school as stressful and hence fail to form the social ties that are thought to prevent conduct problems. Children with neuropsychological deficits have difficulty learning basic academic skills (Rourke, 1985; Knights and Baker, 1976), and the formative educational experience of many children with even subtle mild cognitive impairments includes frustration, humiliation, and failure (Maloney and Ward, 1976).

Empirical Evidence for a Verbal Deficit

Ever since Wechsler (1944) remarked upon the diagnostic utility of a Performance IQ (PIQ) score greater than a Verbal IQ (VIQ) score to identify delinquents, a plethora of studies has been published on the "PIQ > VIQ" sign of delinquency. All of the subtests used to calculate the VIQ score are administered orally, require an oral response, and are solved using language-based processing skills. "Performance" subtests, on the other hand, are administered and solved in the visuospatial mode without the necessary use of language, and they require a manual, not oral, response. Prentice and

Kelly (1963) reviewed twenty-four reports that PIQ was greater than VIQ in delinquents, West and Farrington (1973) reviewed still more studies, and the hypothesis is still finding support (e.g., Haynes and Bensch, 1981; Lynam et al., 1992; Walsh, Petee, and Beyer, 1987). Indeed, in all of the neuropsychological studies reviewed for this chapter that administered the Wechsler IQ scales, delinquents' PIQs exceeded their VIQs. This impressively replicable finding has been taken as strongly supporting the view that delinquents have a specific deficit in language manipulation. Because language functions are subserved by the left cerebral hemisphere in almost all individuals (see Benson and Zaidel, 1985), the PIQ > VIQ findings have also been interpreted as evidence confirming dysfunction of the left cerebral hemisphere in the etiology of antisocial behavior.

Almost all of the neuropsychological studies reviewed for this chapter provided some evidence of deficit on language-based tests for delinquents. The following five studies were selected for detailed review because they measured a representative sample of neuropsychological abilities, allowing for comparision of verbal and nonverbal functions.

Wolff et al. (1982) examined fifty-six adolescent males detained in a low-security facility (30 percent of approached inmates refused to participate). Comparison subjects were high school boys selected by guidance counselors (and therefore subject to unknown selection biases). Delinquents scored significantly worse than comparison subjects on tests of reading, naming, vocabulary, and receptive language. Delinquents did not differ from comparison subjects on spatial or perceptual measures in this study.

Karniski, Levine, Clarke, Palfrey, and Meltzer (1982) tested fifty-four incarcerated teenage boys using twenty-nine tasks that were collapsed on a rational basis into six composite measures of "neuromaturation, gross motor function, temporal-sequential organization, visual processing, and auditory-language function." A comparison group consisted of fifty-one boys from schools in a predominantly blue-collar community. (Comparison subjects were screened for official delinquency, but 70 percent of the comparison families approached declined to participate.) Notable mean group differences were obtained for two of the composite measures, visual processing and auditory language function, but differences were greatest for the auditory language area. When the tails of the distributions were examined, 29.6 percent of delinquents, but only 2 percent of comparison boys, scored two or more standard deviations below the comparison group's mean score on language skills.

Berman and Siegal (1976) administered the Halstead-Reitan Neuropsychological Battery (including the VIQ and PIQ tests) to forty-five boys within one week of their first incarceration. The timing of the testing was selected to avoid the effects of institutionalization upon test scores, but it is possible that reactive depression may have compromised the performance of newly incarcerated subjects. The Halstead-Reitan Battery contains tests of abstract reasoning, rhythmic sequencing, perception of speech sounds, sensory perception, motor response inhibition, and language skills to evaluate the functional integrity of the brain as a whole. It also includes several tests of sensory and manual functions that are repeated on the body's two sides (nonvisual manual problem solving, finger-tapping speed, grip strength, and sensory sensitivity to touch and sound) in order to reveal dysfunction in the brain's two hemispheres. The battery yielded twenty-nine scores, which were analyzed using multiple t tests. If, in order to reduce the likelihood of type 1 error, only those t values statistically significant beyond $p = .001$ are considered, delinquents were deficient on six of seven tests tapping verbal skills.

Sobotowicz, Evans, and Laughlin (1987) compared fifty incarcerated delinquents with fifty high school comparison subjects matched for age, race, and social class. Within each group, half the subjects were learning disabled (LD) and half were normal learners, yielding four groups: Normal, JD, LD, and JD + LD. On tests of verbal language skills, abstract verbal concept formation, and semantic and sequential memory, all three problem groups differed significantly from the comparison group. That the non-LD delinquents differed neuropsychologically from nondelinquents was unexpected, because the two groups were equal on mean full-scale IQ. In this study the three problem groups scored slightly *better* than nondelinquents on PIQ and other measures of nonverbal visuospatial skills. In a replication of the Sobotowicz et al. (1987) study, Henry, Moffitt, and Silva (1992) found that verbal deficits were evident in delinquents and LD subjects but were especially severe in adolescents who were both delinquent and LD.

Language-based measures were found to be more strongly associated with self-reported delinquency than were nonlanguage measures in our own longitudinal study in New Zealand. The New Zealand project is an important one for this field, because it was designed to correct many of the flaws in earlier research and to provide an "acid test" for the hypothesis that children with neuropsychological impairment are at risk for delinquency (Moffitt, 1988). The neuropsychological findings from this prospective longitudinal study have been reported in several papers to date (Frost, Moffitt, and McGee, 1989; Henry, Moffitt, and Silva, 1992; Moffitt, 1990a,b; Moffitt and Henry, 1989; Moffitt and Silva, 1988a,b,c; White, Moffitt, Earls, Robins, and Silva, 1990; White, Moffitt, and Silva, 1989 & 1991).

In the New Zealand project, reduction of the full battery of individual test scores to five composites was accomplished by principal components analysis, and the reduction model was cross-validated using maximum-likelihood confirmatory factor analysis (Moffitt and Heimer, 1988). Delinquent versus nondelinquent group differences were substantially greater for the verbal and auditory verbal memory factors than for factors representing visual-motor integration, visuospatial, and mental flexibility functions. Specific language-based measures on which delinquents scored poorly relative to the sample norm were the Rey Auditory Verbal Learning Test (memorization of a word list), Verbal Fluency (rapid generation of a class of words), and the WISC-R VIQ subtests of Information, Similarities, Arithmetic, and Vocabulary.

A subgroup of delinquents with past histories of ADHD showed especially poor performance on the verbal and verbal memory factors, scoring one full standard deviation below nondelinquents. The comorbid cases had histories of extreme antisocial behavior that remained stable from age three to age fifteen. Apparently, their neuropsychological deficits were as long-standing as their antisocial behavior; at ages three and five these boys had scored more than one standard deviation below the age norm for boys both on the Bayley and McCarthy tests of motor coordination and on the Stanford Binet test of cognitive performance. Contrast groups of boys with single diagnoses of either CD or ADHD showed neither neuropsychological deficits nor cognitive/motor problems; nor were their behavior problems stable over time.

A longitudinal study of the lives of these CD/ADHD boys from age three to fifteen (Moffitt, 1990a) showed that their conduct problems were exacerbated soon after they entered school. These boys had difficulty learning basic academic skills such as reading and spelling. They also had many indicators of poor self-control, such as impulsivity and inattention, that may have interfered with their academic achievement (Hinshaw, 1992). In later years, these same boys were especially ill-prepared for the transition to high school; between ages seven and thirteen, they fell farther and farther behind their peers on repeated tests of reading attainment. As adolescents, their acts of lawbreaking were more aggressive than the acts of other delinquents who did not have a history of neuropsychological deficits and school failure.

Executive Dysfunctions and Risk for Conduct Disorder

Verbal deficits are not the only neuropsychological sources of children's difficult behavior. Children's antisocial behavior may also be associated with deficiencies in the brain's self-control functions. These mental functions, which neuropsychologists commonly refer to as "executive" functions, include sustaining attention and concentration; reasoning abstractly and forming concepts; formulating goals; anticipating and planning; programming and initiating purposive sequences of behavior; self-monitoring and self-awareness; inhibiting unsuccessful, inappropriate, or impulsive behaviors; and interrupting ongoing behavior patterns in order to shift to a more adaptive alternative behavior.

Three separate lines of research have now established that these various executive functions are primarily subserved by the frontal lobes of the brain and by connective pathways between the frontal lobes and other brain systems. Links between self-control of behavior and frontal brain structures have been found in research with animals whose brains have been experimentally lesioned, in clinical case studies of brain-damaged humans, and with *in vivo* neural imaging studies of the brains of children who have behavior disorders (Cohen et al., 1988; Lou, Henriksen, and Bruhn, 1984; Stamm and Kreder, 1979; Stuss and Benson, 1986). One historical rationale for neuropsychological research with delinquents was the apparent resemblance between criminal behavior and the disinhibited antisocial symptoms of patients with injury to the frontal lobes of the brain (Elliott, 1978). Pontius (1972), Gorenstein (1982), and Yeudall (1980) have developed theories based on the observed similarity between the behavior of delinquents and "pseudopsychopathic" patients with frontal lobe brain injuries. Gorenstein and Newman (1980) also described *functional* similarities between disinhibited antisocial human behavior and experimental animal models of damage to the structures of the frontal lobes and limbic system of the brain.

According to these neuropsychological theories, executive dysfunctions should interfere with a child's ability to control his or her own behavior, producing an inattentive, impulsive child who is handicapped in considering the future implications of his or her acts. Such a child should have difficulty understanding the negative impact these behaviors have on others, fail to hold in mind abstract ideas of ethical values and future rewards, and fail to inhibit inappropriate behavior or adapt behavior to changing social circumstances. Executive deficits may thus give rise to early childhood behavior problems that in turn set the stage for emerging antisocial behavior as the child grows physically older, although not necessarily more cognitively mature.

References

American Psychiatric Association (1987). *Diagnostic and statistical manual of mental disorders (DSM-III-R)* (3rd ed., rev. ed.). Washington, D.C.: APA.

Barrett, G. V., & Depinet, R. L. (1991). A reconsideration of testing for competence rather than for intelligence. *American Psychologist, 46,* 1012–1024.

Bell, R. Q., & Chapman, M. (1986). Child effects in studies using experimental or brief longitudinal approaches to socialization. *Developmental Psychology, 22,* 596–603.

Benson, D. F., & Zaidel, E. (1985). *The dual brain.* New York: Guilford Press.

Berman, A., & Siegal, A. W. (1976). Adaptive and learning skills in juvenile delinquents: A neuropsychological analysis. *Journal of Learning Disabilities, 9,* 51–58.

Borecki, I. B., & Ashton, G. C. (1984). Evidence for a major gene influencing performance on a vocabulary test. *Behavior Genetics, 14,* 63–80.

Buss, D. M. (1981). Predicting parent-child interactions from children's activity level. *Developmental Psychology, 17,* 59–65.

Buss, D. M., Block, J. H., & Block, J. (1980). Preschool activity level: Personality correlates and developmental implications. *Child Development, 51,* 401–408.

Camp, B. (1977). Verbal mediation in young aggressive boys. *Journal of Abnormal Psychology, 86*, 145–153.

Caspi, A., & Bem, D. J. (1990). Personality continuity and change across the life course. In L. Pervin (Ed.), *Handbook of personality theory and research* (pp. 549–575). New York: Guilford Press.

Chess, S., & Thomas, A. (1987). *Origins and evolution of behavior disorders: From infancy to early adult life.* Camridge, Mass.: Harvard University Press.

Cohen, R. M., Semple, W. E., Gross, M., Holcomb, H. H., Dowling, M. S., & Nordahl, T. E. (1988). Functional localization of sustained attention: Comparison to sensory stimulation in the absence of instruction. *Neuropsychiatry, Neuropsychology and Behavioral Neurology, 1*, 3–20.

Cravioto, J., & Arrieta, R. (1983). Malnutrition in childhood. In M. Rutter (Ed.), *Developmental Neuropsychiatry* (pp. 32–51). New York: Guilford Press.

Denno, D. J. (1989). *Biology, crime and violence: New evidence.* Cambridge, England: Cambridge University Press.

Elliott, F. A. (1978). Neurological aspects of antisocial behavior. In W. H. Reid (Ed.), *The psychopath* (pp. 146–189). New York: Brunner/Mazel.

Eron, L. D., Huesmann, L. R., & Zelli, A. (1991). The role of parental variables in the learning of aggression. In D. Pepler & K. Rubin (Eds.), *The development and treatment of childhood aggression* (pp. 171–188). Hillsdale, N.J.: Erlbaum.

Eysenck, H. J. (1977). *Crime and personality.* London: Routledge & Kegan Paul.

Farrington, D. P., Loeber, R., & Van Kammen, W. B. (1990). Long-term criminal outcomes of hyperactivity-impulsivity-attention deficit and conduct problems in childhood. In L. N. Robins & M. R. Rutter (Eds.), *Straight and devious pathways from childhood to adulthood* (pp. 62–81). New York: Cambridge University Press.

Farrington, D., Ohlin, L., & Wilson, J. Q. (1986). *Understanding and controlling crime.* New York: Springer-Verlag.

Fogel, C. A., Mednick, S. A., & Michelson, N. (1985). Minor physical anomalies and hyperactivity. *Acta Psychiatrica Scandinavica, 72*, 551–556.

Friedrich, W. N., & Boriskin, J. A. (1976). The role of the child in abuse. *American Journal of Orthopsychiatry, 46*, 580–590.

Frodi, A. M., Laub, M. E., Leavitt, L. E., Donovan, W. L., Neff, C., & Sherry, D. (1978). Fathers' and mothers' responses to the faces and cries of normal and premature infants. *Developmental Psychology, 14*, 490–498.

Frost, L. A., Moffitt, T. E., & McGee, R. (1989). Neuropsychological function and psychopathology in an unselected cohort of young adolescents. *Journal of Abnormal Psychology, 98*, 307–313.

Gorenstein, E. E. (1982). Frontal lobe functions in psychopaths. *Journal of Abnormal Psychology, 91*, 368–379.

Gorenstein, E. E., & Newman, J. P. (1980). Disinhibitory psychopathology: A new perspective and a model for research. *Psychological Review, 87*, 301–315.

Haynes, J. P., & Bensch, M. (1981). The P > V sign of the WISC-R and recidivism in delinquents. *Journal of Consulting and Clinical Psychology, 49*, 480–481.

Healy, W., & Bronner, A. F. (1936). *New light on delinquency and its treatment.* New Haven: Yale University Press.

Henry, B., Moffitt, T. E., & Silva, P. A. (1992). Disentangling delinquency and learning disability: Neuropsychological function and social support. *The International Journal of Clinical Neuropsychology, 13*, 1–6.

Hertzig, M. (1983). Temperament and neurological status. In M. Rutter (Ed.), *Developmental neuropsychiatry* (pp. 164–180). New York: Guilford Press.

Hinshaw, S. P. (1992). Externalizing behavior problems and academic underachievement in childhood and adolescence: Causal relationships and underlying mechanisms. *Psychological Bulletin, 111,* 127–155.

Hirschi, T. (1969). *Causes of delinquency.* Berkeley: University of California Press.

Hirschi, T., & Hindelang, M. J. (1977). Intelligence and delinquency: A revisionist review. *American Sociological Review, 42,* 571–587.

Hunter, R. S., Kilstrom, N., Kraybill, E. N., & Loda, F. (1978). Antecedents of child abuse and neglect in premature infants: A prospective study in a newborn intensive care unit. *Pediatrics, 61,* 629–635.

Kaler, S. R., & Kopp, C. B. (1990). Compliance and comprehension in very young toddlers. *Child Development, 61,* 1997–2003.

Karniski, W. M., Levine, M. D., Clarke, S., Palfrey, J. S., & Meltzer, L. J. (1982). A study of neurodevelopmental findings in early adolescent delinquents. *Journal of Adolescent Health Care, 3,* 151–159.

Kandel, E., Brennan, P., & Mednick, S. A. (1989). Minor physical anomalies and parental modeling of aggression predict to violent offending. *Journal of Consulting and Clinical Psychology, 78,* 1–5.

Kandel, E., & Mednick, S. A. (1991). Perinatal complications predict violent offending. *Criminology, 29,* 519–530.

Knights, R. M., & Bakker, D. J. (Eds.). (1976). *The neuropsychology of learning disorders.* Baltimore: University Park Press.

Kopp, C. (1982). Antecedents of self-regulation: A developmental perspective. *Developmental Psychology, 18,* 199–214.

Kraemer, G. W. (1988). Speculations on the developmental neurobiology of protest and despair. In P. Simon, P. Soubrie, & D. Widlocher (Eds.), *Inquiry into schizophrenia and depression: Animal models of psychiatric disorders* (pp. 101–147). Basel: Karger.

Krynicki, V. E. (1978). Cerebral dysfunction in repetitively assaultive offenders. *Journal of Nervous and Mental Disease, 166,* 59–67.

Lee, C. L., & Bates, J. E. (1985). Mother-child interaction at age two years and perceived difficult temperament. *Child Development, 56,* 1314–1323.

Lewis, D. O., Shanok, S. S., Pincus, J. H., & Glaser, G. H. (1979). Violent juvenile delinquents: Psychiatric, neurological, psychological and abuse factors. *Journal of the American Academy of Child Psychiatry, 2,* 307–319.

Lezak, M. D. (1983). *Neuropsychological assessment.* New York: Oxford University Press.

Loeber, R. (1988). The natural histories of juvenile conduct problems, substance use, and delinquency: Evidence for developmental progressions. In B. B. Lahey & A. E. Kazdin (Eds.), *Advances in clinical child psychology,* vol. 11 (pp. 73–124). New York: Plenum.

Loehlin, J. C. (1989). Partitioning environmental and genetic contributions to behavioral development. *American Psychologist, 44,* 1285–1292.

Lou, H. C., Henriksen, L., & Bruhn, P. (1984). Focal cerebral hypoperfusion in children with dysphasia and/or attention deficit disorder. *Archives of Neurology, 41,* 825–829.

Luria, A. R. (1961). *The role of speech in the regulation of normal and abnormal behavior.* New York: Basic Books.

Luria, A. R., & Homskaya, E. D. (1964). Disturbance in the regulative role of speech with frontal lobe lesions. In J. M. Warren & K. Akert (Eds.), *The frontal granular cortex and behavior* (pp. 353–371). New York: McGraw Hill.

Lynam, D., Moffitt, T. E., & Stouthamer-Loeber, M. (1993). Explaining the relationship between IQ and delinquency: Class, race, test motivation, school failure or self-control? *Journal of Abnormal Psychology, 102,* 187–196.

Lytton, H. (1990). Child and parent effects in boys' conduct disorder: A reinterpretation. *Developmental Psychology, 26,* 683–697.

Maccoby, E. E., & Jacklin, C. N. (1983). The "person" characteristics of children and the family as environment. In D. Magnusson & V. L. Allen (Eds.), *Human development: An interactional perspective* (pp. 75–92). New York: Academic Press.

Maloney, M. P., & Ward, M. P. (1976). *Psychological assessment: A conceptual approach.* New York: Oxford University Press.

Martin, N. G., Jardine, R., & Eaves, L. J. (1984). Is there only one set of genes for different abilities? *Behavior Genetics, 14,* 355–370.

Meany, M. J., Aitken, D. H., van Berkel, C., Bhatnagar, S., & Sapolsky, R. M. (1988). Effect of neonatal handling on age-related impairments associated with the hippocampus. *Science, 239,* 766–768.

Milner, J. S., & McCanne, T. R. (1991). Neuropsychological correlates of physical child abuse. In J. S. Milner (Ed.), *The neuropsychology of aggression* (pp. 131–145). Boston: Kluwer Academic Publishers.

Milowe, I. D., & Lowrie, R. S. (1964). The child's role in the battered child syndrome. *Journal of Pediatrics, 65,* 1079–1081.

Moffitt, T. E. (1988). Neuropsychology and self-reported early delinquency in an unselected birth cohort: A preliminary report from New Zealand. In T. Moffitt, S. Mednick, & S. A. Stack (Eds.), *Biological contributions to crime causation* (pp. 93–120). New York: Martinus Nijhoff Press.

Moffitt, T. E. (1990a). Juvenile delinquency and attention-deficit disorder: Developmental trajectories from age 3 to 15. *Child Development, 61,* 893–910.

Moffitt, T. E. (1990b). The neuropsychology of delinquency: A critical review of theory and research. In N. Morris & M. Tonry (Eds.), *Crime and justice,* vol. 12 (pp. 99–169). Chicago: University of Chicago Press.

Moffitt, T. E., Gabrielli, W. F., & Mednick, S. A. (1981). Socioeconomic status, IQ, and delinquency. *Journal of Abnormal Psychology, 90,* 152–156.

Moffitt, T. E., & Heimer, K. (1988). Factoral analysis and construct validity of a research neuropsychological test battery. Unpublished manuscript, University of Wisconsin at Madison.

Moffitt, T. E., & Henry, B. (1989). Neuropsychological assessment of executive functions in self-reported delinquents. *Development and Psychopathology, 1,* 105–118.

Moffitt, T. E., & Henry, B. (1991). Neuropsychological studies of juvenile delinquency and violence: A review. In J. Milner (Ed.), *The neuropsychology of aggression* (pp. 67–91). Boston: Kluwer Academic Publishers.

Moffitt, T. E., & Silva, P. A. (1988a). IQ and delinquency: A direct test of the differential detection hypothesis. *Journal of Abnormal Psychology, 97,* 330–333.

Moffitt, T. E., & Silva, P. A. (1988b). Neuropsychological deficit and self-reported delinquency in an unselected birth cohort. *Journal of the American Academy of Child and Adolescent Psychiatry, 27,* 233–240.

Moffitt, T. E., & Silva, P. A. (1988c). Self-reported delinquency, neuropsychological deficit, and history of attention deficit disorder. *Journal of Abnormal Child Psychology, 16*, 553–569.

Needleman, H. L., & Beringer, D. C. (1981). The epidemiology of low-level lead exposure in childhood. *Journal of Child Psychiatry, 20*, 496–512.

Newman, J. P. (1987). Reaction to punishment in extroverts and psychopaths: Implications for the impulsive behavior of disinhibited individuals. *Journal of Research in Personality, 21*, 464–480.

Newman, J. P., & Howland, E. (1989). The effect of incentives on Wisconsin Card Sorting Task performance in psychopaths. Unpublished manuscript, University of Wisconsin at Madison.

Newman, J. P., & Kosson, D. S. (1986). Passive avoidance learning in psychopathic and nonpsychopathic offenders. *Journal of Abnormal Psychology, 95*, 257–263.

Patterson, G. R. (1982). *Coercive family process.* Eugene, Ore.: Castalia.

Patterson, G. R. (1986a). Performance models for antisocial boys. *American Psychologist, 41*, 432–444.

Patterson, G. R. (1986b). Maternal behavior: Determinant or product for deviant child behavior? In W. Hartup & Z. Rubin (Eds.), *Relationships and development* (pp. 73–94). Hillsdale, N.J.: Erlbaum.

Patterson, G. R., & Bank, L. (1990). Some amplifying mechanisms for pathologic processes in families. In M. R. Gunnar & E. Phelen (Eds.), *Systems and development: The Minnesota symposia on child psychology,* vol. 22 (pp. 167–209). Hillsdale, N.J.: Erlbaum.

Paulhus, D. L., & Martin, C. L. (1986). Predicting adult temperament from minor physical anomalies. *Journal of Personality and Social Psychology, 50*, 1235–1239.

Plomin, R. (1990). The role of inheritance in behavior. *Science, 248*, 183–188.

Plomin, R., Chipuer, H. M., & Loehlin, J. C. (1990). Behavioral genetics and personality. In L. A. Pervin (Ed.), *Handbook of personality theory and research* (pp. 225–243). New York: Guilford Press.

Plomin, R., Nitz, K., & Rowe, D. C. (1990). Behavioral genetics and aggressive behavior in childhood. In M. Lewis & S. M. Miller (Eds.), *Handbook of developmental psychopathology* (pp. 119–133). New York: Plenum.

Pontius, A. A. (1972). Neurological aspects in some type of delinquency, especially among juveniles: Toward a neurological model of ethical action. *Adolescence, 7*, 289–308.

Prentice, N. M., & Kelly, F. J. (1963). Intelligence and delinquency: A reconsideration. *Journal of Social Psychology, 60*, 327–337.

Raine, A. (1988). Evoked potentials and antisocial behavior. In T. Moffitt & S. Mednick, *Biological contributions to crime causation* (pp. 14–39). New York: Martinus Nijhoff Press.

Reiss, A. J., & Rhodes, A. L. (1961). The distribution of juvenile delinquency in the social class structure. *American Sociological Review, 26*, 720–732.

Robins, L. N. (1966). *Deviant children grown up.* Baltimore: Williams & Wilkins.

Robins, L. N. (1978). Sturdy childhood predictors of adult antisocial behaviour: Replications from longitudinal studies. *Psychological Medicine, 8*, 611–622.

Rodning, C., Beckwith, L., & Howard, J. (1989). Characteristics of attachment organization and play organization in prenatally drug-exposed toddlers. *Development and Psychopathology, 1*, 277–289.

Rothbart, M. K., & Derryberry, D. (1981). Development of individual differences in temperament. In M. E. Lamb & A. L. Brown (Eds.), *Advances in developmental psychology*, vol. 1 (pp. 37–66). Hillsdale, N.J.: Erlbaum.

Rourke, B. P. (1985). Statistical analysis of large neuropsychological data bases: Methodological and clinical considerations. *Journal of Clinical and Experimental Neuropsychology, 7*, 631.

Rourke, B. P., & Fiske, J. L. (1981). Socio-emotional disturbances of learning disabled children: The role of central processing deficits. *Bulletin of the Orton Society, 31*, 77–88.

Rutter, M. (1977). Brain damage syndromes in childhood: Concepts and findings. *Journal of Child Psychology and Psychiatry, 18*, 1–22.

Rutter, M. (Ed.). (1983). *Developmental neuropsychiatry*. New York: Guilford Press.

Rutter, M. (1983). Issues and prospects in developmental neuropsychiatry. In M. Rutter (Ed.), *Developmental neuropsychiatry* (pp. 577–598). New York: Guilford Press.

Sameroff, A., & Chandler, M. (1975). Reproductive risk and the continuum of caretaking casualty. In F. Horowitz, M. Hetherington, S. Scarr-Salapatek, & G. Siegel (Eds.), *Review of child development research*, vol. 4 (pp. 187–244). Chicago: University of Chicago Press.

Sandgrund, A. K., Gaines, R., & Green, A. (1974). Child abuse and mental retardation: A problem of cause and effect. *American Journal of Mental Deficiency, 79*, 327–330.

Savitsky, J. C., & Czyzewski, D. (1978). The reaction of adolescent offenders and nonoffenders to nonverbal emotional displays. *Journal of Abnormal Child Psychology, 6*, 89–96.

Scarr, S., & McCartney, K. (1983). How people make their own environments: A theory of genotype. *Child Development, 54*, 424–435.

Shapiro, S. K., Quay, H. C., Hogan, A. E., & Schwartz, K. P. (1988). Response perseveration and delayed responding in undersocialized aggressive conduct. *Journal of Abnormal Psychology, 97*, 371–373.

Short, J. F., & Strodtbeck, F. L. (1965). *Group process and gang delinquency*. Chicago: University of Chicago Press.

Shulman, H. M. (1929). *A study of problem boys and their brothers*. Albany, N.Y.: New York State Crime Commission.

Skoff, B. F., & Libon, J. (1987). Impaired executive functions in a sample of male juvenile delinquents. *Journal of Clinical and Experimental Neuropsychology, 9*, 60.

Snyder, J. J. (1977). Reinforcement analysis of interaction in problem and non-problem families. *Journal of Abnormal Psychology, 86*, 528–535.

Snyder, J., & Patterson, G. (1987). Family interaction and delinquent behavior. In H. Quay (Ed.), *Handbook of juvenile delinquency* (pp. 216–243). New York: Wiley.

Sobotowicz, W., Evans, J. R., & Laughlin, J. (1987). Neuropsychological function and social support in delinquency and learning disability. *The International Journal of Clinical Neuropsychology, 9*, 178–186.

Stamm, J. S., & Kreder, S. V. (1979). Minimal brain dysfunction: Psychological and neuropsychological disorders in hyperkinetic children. In M. Gazzaniga (Ed.), *Handbook of behavioral neurology: Vol. 2. Neuropsychology* (pp. 119–152). New York: Plenum.

Stewart, A. (1983). Severe perinatal hazards. In M. Rutter (Ed.), *Developmental neuropsychiatry* (pp. 15–31). New York: Guilford Press.

Stuss, D. T., & Benson, D. F. (1986). *The frontal lobes.* New York: Raven Press.

Szatmari, P., Reitsma-Street, M., & Offord, D. (1986). Pregnancy and birth complications in antisocial adolescents and their siblings. *Canadian Journal of Psychiatry, 31,* 513–516.

Tambs, K., Sundet, J. M., & Magnus, P. (1984). Heritability analysis of the TAIS subtests: A study of twins. *Intelligence, 8,* 283–293.

Tarter, R. E., Hegedus, A. M., Winsten, N. E., & Alterman, A. L. (1984). Neuropsychological, personality, and familial characteristics of physically abused delinquents. *Journal of the American Academy of Child Psychiatry, 23,* 668–674.

Tarter, R. E., Hegedus, A. M., Alterman, A. L., & Katz-Garris, L. (1983). Cognitive capacities of juvenile violent, nonviolent, and sexual offenders. *Journal of Nervous and Mental Disease, 171,* 564–567.

Thomas, A., & Chess, S. (1977). *Temperament and development.* New York: Brunner/Mazel.

Tinsley, B. R., & Parke, R. D. (1983). The person-environment relationship: Lessons from families with preterm infants. In D. Magnusson & V. L. Allen (Eds.), *Human development: An interactional perspective* (pp. 93–110). New York: Academic Press.

Vandenberg, S. G. (1969). A twin study of spatial ability. *Multivariate Behavioral Research, 4,* 273–294.

Walsh, A., Petee, T. A., & Beyer, J. A. (1987). Intellectual imbalance and delinquency: Comparing high verbal and high performance IQ delinquents. *Criminal Justice and Behavior, 14*(3), 370–379.

Waters, E., Vaughan, B., & Egeland, B. (1980). Individual differences in infant-mother attachment: Antecedents in neonatal behavior in an urban economically disadvantaged sample. *Child Development, 51,* 208–216.

Wechsler, D. (1944). *The measurement of adult intelligence* (3rd ed.). Baltimore: Williams & Wilkins.

Wender, P. H. (1971). *Minimal brain dysfunction in children.* New York: Wiley.

Werner, E., Simonian, K., Bierman, J., & French, F. (1967). Cumulative effect of perinatal complications and deprived environment on physical, intellectual, and social development of preschool children. *Pediatrics, 39,* 490–505.

West, D. J., & Farrington, D. P. (1973). *Who becomes delinquent?* London: Heinemann.

White, J., Moffitt, T. E., Caspi, A., Bartusch, D. J., Needles, D., & Stouthamer-Loeber, M. (1994). Measuring impulsivity and examining its relationship to delinquency. *Journal of Abnormal Psychology, 103,* 192–205.

White, J., Moffitt, T. E., Earls, F., Robins, L. N., & Silva, P. A. (1990). How early can we tell? Preschool predictors of boys' conduct disorder and delinquency. *Criminology, 28,* 507–533.

White, J., Moffitt, T. E., & Silva, P. A. (1989). A prospective replication of the protective effects of IQ in subjects at high risk for juvenile delinquency. *Journal of Clinical and Consulting Psychology, 57,* 719–724.

White, J., Moffitt, T. E., & Silva, P. A. (1992). Specific arithmetic disability: Neuropsychological and socio-emotional correlates. *Archives of Neuropsychology, 7,* 1–16.

Wilson, J. Q., & Herrnstein, R. J. (1985). *Crime and human nature.* New York: Simon and Schuster.

Wolff, P. H., Waber, D., Bauermeister, M., Cohen, C., & Ferber, R. (1982). The neuropsychological status of adolescent delinquent boys. *Journal of Child Psychology and Psychiatry, 23,* 267–279.

Wolfgang, M. E., Figlio, R. M., & Sellin T. (1972). *Delinquency in a birth cohort.* Chicago: The University of Chicago Press.

Yeudall, L. T. (1980). A neuropsychological perspective of persistent juvenile delinquency and criminal behavior. *Annals of the New York Academy of Science, 347,* 349–355.

8

The Development of Offending and Antisocial Behavior from Childhood to Adulthood

DAVID P. FARRINGTON

This chapter focuses on the Cambridge Study in Delinquent Development, which is a prospective longitudinal survey of crime, delinquency, and anti-social behavior. This is a follow-up study of 411 London boys, born mostly in 1953. The study began in 1961–62, and it was originally directed by Donald West. The present contributor has worked on it since 1969, taking over as director of the study in 1982.

Design of the Study

At the time they were first contacted, the boys were all living in a working-class area of London. The vast majority of the sample were chosen by taking all the boys who were then eight to nine years old and on the registers of six state primary schools within a one-mile radius of an established research office. Therefore, the boys were not really a carefully chosen sample but rather a complete population of boys of that age in that area at that time. The boys were almost all white and predominantly from working-class families.

The original aim of the study was to describe the development of delinquent and criminal behavior in inner-city males, to investigate how far it could be predicted in advance, and to explain why juvenile delinquency began, why it did or did not continue into adult crime, and why adult crime precipitously declined as men reached their twenties.

The boys were interviewed and tested in their schools when they were aged about eight, ten, and fourteen by male or female psychologists. They were interviewed in the research office at about sixteen, eighteen, and twenty-one and in their homes at about twenty-five and thirty-two by young male social science graduates. The tests in schools measured intelligence, attainment, personality, and psychomotor skills; the interviews collected information about living circumstances, employment histories, relationships with females, leisure activities such as drinking and fighting, and offending behavior.

In addition to interviews and tests of the boys, interviews with their parents were carried out by female social workers who visited their homes. These took place about once a year from when the boy was eight until when he was aged fourteen or fifteen and was in his last year of compulsory education. The primary informant was the mother, although many fathers were also seen. The parents provided details of such matters as their family income, family size, employment histories, child-rearing practices—including attitudes, discipline, and parental agreement—and degree of supervision of the boy, as well as information about his temporary or permanent separations from them.

The boys' teachers completed questionnaires when the boys were aged about eight, ten, twelve, and fourteen. These provided information about the boys' troublesome and aggressive school behavior, their school attainments, and their truancy. Ratings were also obtained from the boys' primary school peers on qualities such as their daring, dishonesty, troublesomeness, and popularity.

Searches were also carried out in the central Criminal Record Office in London to try to locate convictions of the boys, their parents, their brothers and sisters, and (in recent years) their wives or cohabitees. Since convictions were counted only if they were for offenses normally recorded in the Criminal Record Office, minor crimes such as common assault, traffic offenses, and drunkenness were excluded. The most common offenses were thefts, burglaries, and unauthorized takings of motor vehicles. Official records were supplemented with self-reports of offending from the boys themselves at every age from fourteen onwards.

The Cambridge Study in Delinquent Development has a unique combination of features:

♦ Eight personal interviews with the subjects have been completed over a period of twenty-four years (from age eight to age thirty-two).

♦ The main focus of interest is on crime and delinquency.

♦ The sample size of about four hundred is large enough for many statistical analyses but small enough to permit detailed case histories of the boys and their families.

♦ The attrition rate has been very low; 94 percent of the men still alive provided information at age thirty-two.

♦ Information has been obtained from multiple sources: the males, their parents, teachers, peers, and official records.

◆ Information has been obtained about a wide variety of theoretical constructs—including intelligence, personality, parental child-rearing methods, peer delinquency, school behavior, employment success, marital stability, etc.—thus facilitating investigation of the relative importance of these different factors as predictors and correlates of offending.

Criminal Careers

Following is a summary of some of the study's findings about criminal careers. Up to age thirty-two, over one-third of the study males (153, or 37 percent) were convicted of criminal offenses. While the peak age for the number of offenders and the number of offenses was seventeen, roughly equal numbers of offenses were committed by the study males as juveniles (age 10–16), as young adults (age 17–20), and as adults (age 21–32). There was considerable continuity in offending from the juvenile to the adult years. Nearly three-quarters of those convicted as juveniles were reconvicted between the ages of seventeen and twenty-four, and nearly half of the juvenile offenders were reconvicted between the ages of twenty-five and thirty-two.

The average age of onset of offending was seventeen, while the average age of desistance (that is, the age of the last offense) was twenty-three. An average of 4.5 offenses leading to convictions were committed in this six-year criminal career. Generally, the males first convicted at the earliest ages tended to become the most persistent offenders, committing large numbers of offenses at high rates over long periods.

The "chronic offenders" at age thirty-two were defined as the twenty-four men who had each committed at least nine officially recorded offenses. They had especially long criminal careers characterized by high rates of offending, and they accounted for nearly half of all the offenses committed by the sample. A study of offending by all family members (fathers, mothers, sons, and daughters) found that offending was even more concentrated in families. Just 4 percent of the four hundred families accounted for 50 percent of all the convictions of all family members. The worst offenders tended to be in large-sized, multiproblem families.

Most juvenile and young adult offenses were committed with others, but the incidence of co-offending declined with age. Burglary, robbery, and theft from vehicles were particularly likely to involve co-offenders. Co-offenders tended to be similar in age and sex to study males and lived close to their addresses and to the locations of the offenses. It was rare for study males to offend with their fathers, mothers, sisters, or wives, or with unrelated females. Co-offending with brothers was most likely when study males had brothers who were close to them in age.

Self-reported offending and official convictions showed that the most common crimes of burglary, shoplifting, theft of and from vehicles, and vandalism declined in prevalence from the teenage years to the twenties and thirties. However, theft from work increased with age. The cumulative prevalence of self-reported offending was very high; 96 percent of the males admitted committing at least one crime that might have led to a conviction. Hence, at least in this sample of urban working-class males, offending was not very deviant, although it was less common to commit relatively serious offenses such as burglary. Only 22 percent of the males admitted burglary, and only 14 percent were convicted of burglary. Generally, convictions and self-reports identified the same people as the worst offenders.

Predicting and Explaining Offending

At ages eight to ten, the most important predictors of later offending (whether measured by convictions or by self-reports) fell into six categories of theoretical constructs:

1. Antisocial child behavior, including troublesomeness in school, dishonesty, and aggressiveness
2. Hyperactivity-impulsivity-attention deficit, including poor concentration, restlessness, daring, and psychomotor impulsivity
3. Low intelligence and poor school attainment
4. Family criminality, including convicted parents and delinquent older siblings
5. Family poverty, including low family income, large family size, and poor housing
6. Poor parental child-rearing behavior, including harsh and authoritarian discipline, poor supervision, parental conflict, and separation from parents.

In prediction analyses, it was generally true that at least one factor from each of these categories predicted offending independently of all the other categories. The best predictors tended to be troublesomeness, daring, and convicted parents.

In order to explain the development of offending in males, the study proposed a four-stage theory, suggesting that offending depends on motivation, methods, internalized beliefs, and decision making. In the first stage, it is assumed that the main motives that ultimately lead to offending are desires for material goods, excitement, and status among intimate friends and relatives. These motives could reflect long-term differences between individuals or short-term fluctuations within individuals (e.g., when a state of boredom produces a desire for excitement). These desires may be greater among children from poorer families, perhaps because material goods, excitement, and status are more highly valued by poorer families.

In the second stage of the theory, these motives will produce antisocial tendencies if illegal methods of satisfying them are habitually chosen. It appears that some people (e.g., children from poorer families) are less able to satisfy their desires for material goods, excitement, and status by legal or socially approved methods and therefore tend to choose illegal or socially disapproved methods. The lower ability of poorer children to achieve goals by legitimate methods may be attributable to the fact that they tend to fail in school (possibly because of their relatively lower intelligence) and tend to have erratic, low-status job histories. School failure and low intelligence may be a consequence of the less stimulating intellectual environment in poorer homes and of the lesser emphasis on the future, planning, and abstract concepts in general (as opposed to more concrete issues of the present).

In the third stage, antisocial tendencies are inhibited or facilitated by internalized beliefs and attitudes about lawbreaking that have been accumulated in a learning process as a result of a history of rewards and punishments. The belief that offending is wrong, or a "strong conscience," tends to grow if parents are in favor of legal norms, if they exercise close supervision over their children, and if they consistently punish socially disapproved behavior using firm but kindly ("love-oriented") discipline. The belief that offending is legitimate, together with anti-establishment attitudes generally, tends to develop if children are exposed to attitudes and behavior favoring offending (e.g., in a modeling process), especially by their relatives and friends.

In the fourth stage, whether a person commits a crime in a given situation depends on opportunities and on the perceived probabilities, costs, and benefits of the different possible outcomes. The costs and benefits include immediate situational factors, such as the material goods that can be stolen and the likelihood and consequences of being caught by the police. They also include social factors, such as the likely disapproval of parents or spouses and the likely encouragement and approval of peers. In general, people tend to make hedonistic and rational decisions. However, more impulsive people are less likely to consider possible consequences, especially those that are long delayed, and tend to choose immediate gratification rather than long-term goals.

Applied explicitly to the Cambridge study, this theory shows that children from poorer families are more likely to offend because they are less able to achieve their goals legally and because they value some goals (e.g., excitement) especially highly. Children who are poor at manipulating abstract concepts tend to have low measured intelligence and to fail in school; since they cannot achieve their goals by legal methods, they therefore tend to offend. Impulsive children tend to offend because they do not give sufficient consideration to the possible consequences of offending, and because they prefer immediate gratification to long-term goals. Children who are exposed to poor parental child-rearing behavior, disharmony, or separation are likely to offend because they do not build up internal inhibitions against antisocial behavior. Finally, children from criminal families and those with delinquent friends tend to offend because they build up anti-establishment attitudes and the belief that offending is justifiable.

Offending tends to peak between ages fourteen and twenty because boys between these ages (especially those who were lower-class school failures) have high desires for excitement, material goods, and status; little chance of achieving these desires legally; and little to lose (since legal penalties are lenient and their close associates—male peers—approve of delinquency). In contrast, after age twenty, their desires become attenuated or more realistic, they have more possibility of achieving them legally, and the costs of delinquency are greater (since legal penalties are harsher and their intimates at these ages—wives or girlfriends—disapprove of delinquency). Hence, offending declines.

Antisocial Personality

Generally, offending is only one element of a much larger syndrome of antisocial behavior that tends to persist over time. For example, the study males who were convicted before age eighteen (most usually for offenses of dishonesty, such as burglary and theft) were significantly more socially deviant than the nonoffenders on almost every factor investigated at that age. The offenders drank more beer, got drunk more often, and were more likely to say that drink made them violent. They smoked more cigarettes, had started smoking at an earlier age, and were more likely to be heavy gamblers. They were more likely to have been convicted for minor driving offenses, to have driven after drinking at least 5 pints (3 liters) of beer, and to have been injured in road accidents. The offenders were more likely to have taken prohibited drugs such as marijuana or LSD, although few of them had convictions for drug offenses. Also, they were more likely to have had sexual intercourse, especially with a variety of different girls, and especially beginning at an early age, but they were less likely to have used contraceptives.

At age eighteen the convicted offenders tended to hold relatively well-paid but low-status jobs, and they were more likely to have erratic work histories including periods of unemployment. They were more likely to be living away from home, and they tended not to get on well with their parents. They were more likely to be tattooed, and they had significantly low pulse rates. The offenders were more likely to go out in the evenings, especially to spend time hanging about on the street. They tended to go around in groups of four or more and were more likely to be involved in group violence or vandalism. They were much more likely to have been involved in fights, to have started fights, to have carried weapons, and to have used weapons in fights. They were also more likely to have expressed aggressive and anti-establishment attitudes in a questionnaire.

Generally, the study males were less antisocial at age thirty-two than at age eighteen. Their offending and their aggressiveness declined with age, although their drinking and drug use tended to increase. At age thirty-two the convicted offenders were still relatively more deviant than the unconvicted males in a variety of respects, and this was especially true of those study males with convictions after age twenty-one. The offenders were more likely to rent their homes rather than own them, and they tended to move house more frequently. They were more likely to be separated or divorced from their wives, in conflict with and violent toward their wives or cohabitees, and separated from their children. They tended to have anti-establishment attitudes and a poor relationship with their parents. They were more likely to be unemployed and tended to have lower take-home pay. The convicted offenders went out more in the evenings, drank more, and got involved in more fights. Also, they were more likely to smoke heavily, drive when drunk, and take drugs, and more likely to commit different types of offenses according to their self-reports.

Generally, the study concluded that there was considerable continuity in an underlying antisocial personality that persisted from childhood to adulthood and had different behavioral manifestations at different ages.

Good Boys from Bad Backgrounds

The results described so far are probably not surprising to many people who work with offenders. Often, people are less interested in the continuity of an antisocial personality than in its discontinuity: Why do some boys from criminogenic backgrounds nevertheless become successful nonoffenders, and why do some boys from favorable backgrounds nevertheless become antisocial offenders? The study also explored good boys from bad backgrounds.

About one-sixth of the boys (63) were identified as vulnerable between the ages of eight and ten, because they possessed three out of five adverse background features (low family income, large family size, convicted parents, poor parental child-rearing behavior, and low nonverbal intelligence). Three-quarters of these vulnerable males were convicted of criminal offenses up to age thirty-two, and the vulnerable males were also likely to be juvenile delinquents, juvenile recidivists, and social failures at age thirty-two on a combined measure of living circumstances and behavior. The study investigated whether the unconvicted quarter of these boys were affected by any protective factors that might have helped them to achieve successful life outcomes.

The earlier research suggested that being nervous and withdrawn might act as a protective factor in insulating vulnerable boys against juvenile delinquency. Similar tendencies were apparent in the latest analyses up to age thirty-two, but the effects were relatively weak. The most important results of the study were that boys with few or no friends at age eight, and those without convicted parents or behavior problem siblings at age ten, tended to remain unconvicted; also, boys who were rated positively by their mothers at age ten tended to be leading relatively successful lives at age thirty-two. There was some evidence that shyness acted as a protective factor for nonaggressive boys and as an aggravating factor for aggressive boys.

One problem with these analyses is that at age thirty-two the unconvicted boys were not necessarily leading the most successful lives. The study examined the characteristics of unconvicted vulnerable men, convicted vulnerable men, unconvicted nonvulnerable men, and convicted nonvulnerable men at age thirty-two. Surprisingly, the unconvicted vulnerable men were often the most unsuccessful, for example in not being homeowners, in living in dirty home conditions, in having large debts, and in holding low-status, low-paid jobs. They were also the most likely never to have married, to have no wife or cohabitee, and to be living alone. In addition, they were the most likely to be in conflict with their parents, to have a real problem with a child, and to disagree with their wives or cohabitees about child rearing. However, they were generally well-behaved, for example in not taking drugs other than marijuana and in being least likely to commit offenses. Their good behavior may be connected with the fact that they were the most likely to stay in every night.

According to the research, the most protective factor against offending for boys from vulnerable backgrounds was the avoidance of contact with other boys in the neighborhood, with siblings, or with fathers, all of whom may have exerted undesirable influences. However, the unconvicted vulnerable males were not necessarily leading the most successful lives at age thirty-two. Their social isolation at age eight seemed to lead to social isolation as mature adults. For those vulnerable males who were the most successful at age thirty-two, the most protective factor seemed to be having a supportive mother to reinforce the boy's favorable self-concept.

Effects of Events on Development

An advantage of a longitudinal study is that it can investigate the effects of specific events on the course of development of offending by comparing "before" and "after" measures of offending and carrying out quasi-experimental analyses using each subject as his own control. For example, it is possible to study the effects on delinquent behavior of being found guilty in court. If convictions have a deterrent or reformative effect, a person's delinquent behavior should decline after he is convicted. On the other hand, if convictions have stigmatizing or contaminating effects, a person's delinquent behavior should increase after he is convicted.

These hypotheses were tested by studying self-reports of offending before and after a boy was first convicted. It was found that boys who were first convicted between the ages of fourteen and eighteen increased their self-reported offending afterwards, both in comparison with the level before and in comparison with the subsequent offending of a carefully matched group of unconvicted boys. The same result was obtained in relation to first convictions occurring between the ages of eighteen and twenty-one. There was some indication that the increase in self-reported offending was related to the penalties imposed in court, although the numbers were small. The most common consequences of a first conviction were fines and discharges. There was no increase in self-reported offending after a fine but a big increase after a discharge, suggesting that the increased offending may have been caused by a decrease in the boy's fear of a court appearance after he was discharged.

The effect on offending of going to different high schools was also investigated. At age eleven, most of the boys went to one of thirteen high schools. These schools differed dramatically in their official delinquency rates; one had 20 court appearances per 100 boys per year, whereas in another the corresponding figure was only 0.3. The key issue was whether the boys who went to high schools with a high delinquency rate became more likely to offend as a result, or whether the differing delinquency rates of the different high schools merely reflected differences in their intakes at age eleven.

The best predictor of delinquency in this survey was the rating of child troublesomeness at age eight to ten by teachers and peers. Generally, the continuity between troublesomeness and delinquency was not greatly affected by the kind of school to which a boy went. There was a marked tendency for the more troublesome boys to go to the high schools with high delinquency rates, and the delinquency rates of different high schools largely reflected their different intakes. The schools themselves had little effect on delinquency.

Another investigation of the effect of a specific event on offending was the study of the effect of unemployment. The complete job history of each boy between leaving school at an average age of fifteen and the interview at age eighteen was obtained, including all periods of unemployment. The key question was whether the boys committed more offenses (according to official records) during their periods of unemployment than during their periods of employment.

The results showed that the boys did indeed commit more offenses while unemployed than while employed. Furthermore, the difference was restricted to offenses involving financial gain, such as theft, burglary, robbery, and fraud. Unemployment had no effect on offenses such as violence, vandalism, and drug use, which suggests that the boys committed more offenses while they were unemployed because they were short of money at these times. Furthermore, the effect of unemployment was greatest for those with the highest prediction scores for crime, suggesting that unemployment had an especially criminogenic effect on those boys with the greatest prior potential for offending.

It is often believed that marriage to a good woman is one of the best treatments for male offending. When our males were asked in their twenties why they had stopped offending, they mentioned marriage and the influence of women, as well as the fact that they did not hang around so much with delinquent friends. The study assessed the effects of marriage by following both convictions and self-reported offending before and after marriage.

Marriage led to a decrease in offending, but only for offenders who married unconvicted women. Those who married convicted women continued to offend at the same rate after marriage as matched unmarried offenders. The same trends were evident for the men's fathers. Those who married convicted women incurred more convictions after marriage than those who married unconvicted women, independent of their conviction records before marriage.

Another event that was investigated was the effect of moving out of London. Most of those who left were upwardly mobile families who were moving to prosperous suburban areas in the surrounding counties, in many cases buying their own houses rather than renting in London. Both official and self-reported offending decreased after the men or their families moved out of London, possibly because of the effect of the move in breaking up delinquent groupings.

Recent Research

The most recent research has focused on bullying and on predictors of different groups of aggressive males. With bullying, there was a significant tendency for the males who reported that they were bullies at age fourteen also to report at age thirty-two that they were bullies and that their children were bullies. In other words, there seemed to be intragenerational and intergenerational continuity in bullying. In addition to being bullies themselves, the males who had child bullies tended to be poor readers, gamble heavily, and to have been unpopular in their teenage years; and they tended to have authoritarian parents.

The males were also asked at age thirty-two whether their children were being bullied. The males who had child victims tended to be those who had been unpopular and had few friends at age eight to ten, and those who were nervous and were regular smokers at age fourteen. Given that these factors are associated with being bullied, it is logical to conclude that there was intergenerational continuity in being bullied as well as in bullying.

The final set of analyses was designed to investigate the predictors of soccer violence at age eighteen and violence against spouses and cohabitees at age thirty-two. The best predictors of soccer violence were being relatively small, having a father who was not interested in his children, not attending church, not being nervous, leaving school early, and having authoritarian parents. Conceivably, relatively small boys whose fathers pay little attention to them might try to compensate for these handicaps by showing off and being aggressive in soccer crowds, especially if they are not inhibited by nervousness or religious beliefs.

The best predictors of spouse assault were having a convicted father, unpopularity, daring, separation from parents, and low intelligence. There seemed to be a link between experiencing parental disharmony and early separation from a parent in childhood, difficulties in relationships with peers and parents, and later difficulties in relationships with spouses and cohabitees. Teenage violence tended to develop into later spouse assault, particularly for those aggressive males who had long-standing difficulties in their relationships with other people.

Conclusions and Implications

The study's most important conclusion is that the types of acts that lead to convictions are only one aspect of a larger syndrome of antisocial behavior. It seems likely that individual differences between people in some underlying theoretical construct, which might be termed "antisocial personality," are relatively stable from childhood to adulthood. As already mentioned, the behavioral manifestations of this construct change with age. For example, adults cannot play truant from school, just as juveniles cannot hit their spouses. While the relative position of individuals on this underlying dimension is sufficiently stable to allow significant prediction from age eight to age thirty-two, the stability should not be exaggerated. Significant predictability does not mean that outcomes are inevitable or that people cannot and do not change.

The behavioral manifestations of antisocial personality probably vary with age according to social circumstances and social influence. Antisocial behavior is low at age eight to ten if a boy's parents exercise warm, consistent discipline, high in the teenage years if a boy hangs around with deviant peers, and then declines in the twenties if a man obtains a satisfactory job and settles down with a satisfactory woman. The worst offenders are those who are exposed to deviant social influences throughout their lives.

Social prevention experiments are clearly needed to prevent the development of crime and antisocial behavior. These could begin by targeting three important predictors of offending that may be both causal and modifiable: economic deprivation, school failure, and poor parental child-rearing behavior.

In this survey, as in many others, the worst offenders were drawn from the poorest families in the worst housing. Of all the factors measured at age eight to ten, low family income was the best predictor of general social failure at age thirty-two. These results suggest that more economic resources should be targeted selectively to the poorest families to try to improve their economic circumstances in comparison with other families.

Again, school failure has been shown in numerous surveys to be an important predictor and correlate of offending. There are indications from the United States that the preschool intellectual enrichment programs of the 1960s led to significant decreases in school failure and later offending. Therefore, it would be highly desirable to offer free, high-quality preschool intellectual enrichment programs to children at risk.

Poor parental child-rearing techniques (harsh or erratic discipline; cruel, passive, or neglecting attitudes; parental disharmony; and poor supervision) also predicted delinquency, especially at early ages. One possible implication of this is that offending might decrease if parents could be trained to use more appropriate child-rearing techniques. For example, parents could be educated to notice what children are doing, to state house rules clearly, to make rewards and punishments contingent upon behavior, and to negotiate disagreements so that conflicts do not escalate.

Because of the link between crime and numerous other social problems, any measure that succeeds in reducing crime will probably have benefits that go far beyond that achievement. Early social prevention that reduces crime will probably also reduce drinking, drunken driving, drug use, sexual promiscuity, and family violence; it may also reduce school failure, unemployment, and parental disharmony. Social problems are undoubtedly influenced by environmental as well as individual factors. However, to the extent that all of these problems reflect an underlying antisocial personality, they could all decrease together. It is clear from this research that problem children tend to grow up into problem adults and that problem adults tend to produce problem children. Sooner or later, serious efforts, firmly grounded on empirical research results, must be made to break this cycle.

References

Barnett, A., Blumstein, A., & Farrington, D. P. (1989). A prospective test of a criminal career model. *Criminology, 27,* 373–388.

Farrington, D. P., Gallagher, B., Morley, L., St. Ledger, R. J., & West, D. J. (1988). Are there any successful men from criminogenic backgrounds? *Psychiatry, 51,* 116–130.

Farrington, D. P., Gallagher, B., Morley, L., St. Ledger, R. J., & West, D. J. (1988). A 24-year follow-up of men from vulnerable backgrounds. In R. L. Jenkins & W. K. Brown (Eds.), *The abandonment of delinquent behavior: Promoting the turnaround* (pp. 155–173). New York: Praeger.

Farrington, D. P. (1989). Long-term prediction of offending and other life outcomes. In H. Wegener, F. Losel, & J. Haisch (Eds.), *Criminal behavior and the justice system: Psychological perspectives* (pp. 26–39). New York: Springer-Verlag.

Farrington, D. P., Gallagher, B., Morley, L., St. Ledger, R., & West, D. J. (1990). Minimizing attrition in longitudinal research: Methods of tracing and securing cooperation in a 24-year follow-up study. In D. Magnusson and L. Bergman (Eds.), *Data quality in longitudinal research* (pp. 122–147). Cambridge, England: Cambridge University Press.

Farrington, D. P. (1989). Later adult life outcomes of offenders and non-offenders. In M. Brambring, F. Losel, & H. Skowronek (Eds.), *Children at risk: Assessment, longitudinal research, and intervention* (pp. 220–244). Berlin: De Gruyter.

Farrington, D. P., & Hawkins, J. D. (1991). Predicting participation, early onset, and later persistence in officially recorded offending. *Criminal Behaviour and Mental Health, 1,* 1–33.

Farrington, D. P. (1989). Self-reported and official offending from adolescence to adulthood. In M. W. Klein (Ed.), *Cross-national research in self-reported crime and delinquency* (pp. 399–423). Dordrecht, Netherlands: Kluwer.

Farrington, D. P. (1991). Childhood aggression and adult violence: Early precursors and later life outcomes. In D. J. Pepler & K. H. Rubin (Eds.), *The development and treatment of childhood aggression* (pp. 5–29). Hillsdale, N.J.: Erlbaum.

Farrington, D. P. (1989). Early predictors of adolescent aggression and adult violence. *Violence and Victims, 4,* 79–100.

Farrington, D. P., & West, D. J. (1990). The Cambridge Study in Delinquent Development: A long-term follow-up of 411 London males. In H. J. Kerner & G. Kaiser (Eds.), *Kriminalität: Persönlichkeit, Lebensgeschichte und Verhalten* (Criminality: Personality, behavior and life history) (pp. 115–138). Berlin: Springer-Verlag.

Farrington, D. P. (1993). Childhood origins of teenage antisocial behaviour and adult social dysfunction. *Journal of the Royal Society of Medicine, 86,* 13–17.

Farrington, D. P. (1990). Implications of criminal career research for the prevention of offending. *Journal of Adolescence, 13,* 93–113.

Farrington, D. P. (1989). The origins of crime: The Cambridge Study in Delinquent Development. *Home Office Research Bulletin, 27,* 29–32.

Farrington, D. P. (1993). The stability and prediction of violence. To be published in German in F. Losel (Ed.), *Sozialisation von Gewalt* (Socialization of violence). Stuttgart, Germany: Enke-Verlag.

Farrington, D. P. (1990). Age, period, cohort, and offending. In D. M. Gottfredson & R. V. Clarke (Eds.), *Policy and theory in criminal justice: Contributions in honour of Leslie T. Wilkins* (pp. 51–75). Aldershot, England: Gower.

Farrington, D. P. (1991). Antisocial personality from childhood to adulthood. *The Psychologist, 4,* 389–394.

Farrington, D. P. (1992). Explaining the beginning, progress and ending of antisocial behaviour from birth to adulthood. In J. McCord (Ed.), *Facts, frameworks and forecasts: Advances in criminological theory,* vol. 3 (pp. 253–286). New Brunswick, N.J.: Transaction.

Farrington, D. P. (1992). Juvenile delinquency. In J. C. Coleman (Ed.), *The school years* (2nd ed.) (pp. 123–163). London: Routledge & Kegan Paul.

Farrington, D. P. (1994). Interactions between individual and contextual factors in the development of offending. In R. K. Silbereisen & E. Todt (Eds.), *Adolescence in context* (pp. 366–389). New York: Springer-Verlag.

Farrington, D. P. (1992). Criminal career research in the United Kingdom. *British Journal of Criminology, 32,* 521–536.

Farrington, D. P. (1993). Understanding and preventing bullying. In M. Tonry (Ed.), *Crime and justice,* vol. 17 (pp. 381–458). Chicago: University of Chicago Press.

Farrington, D. P. (1994). Childhood, adolescent and adult features of violent males. In L. R. Huesmann (Ed.), *Aggressive behaviour: Current perspectives* (pp. 215–240). New York: Plenum.

Farrington, D. P., & West, D. J. (1993). Criminal, penal, and life histories of chronic offenders: Risk and protective factors and early identification. *Criminal Behaviour and Mental Health, 3*, 492–523.

Farrington, D. P., & West, D. J. (1995). Effects of marriage, separation, and children on offending by adult males. In Z. S. Blau & J. Hagan (Eds.), *Current perspectives on aging and the life cycle*, vol. 4 (pp. 249–281). Greenwich, Conn.: JAI Press.

Nagin, D. S., & Farrington, D. P. (1992). The stability of criminal potential from childhood to adulthood. *Criminology, 30*, 235–260.

Nagin, D. S., & Farrington, D. P. (1992). The onset and persistence of offending. *Criminology, 30*, 501–523.

Reiss, A. J., & Farrington, D. P. (1991). Advancing knowledge about co-offending: Results from a prospective longitudinal survey of London males. *Journal of Criminal Law and Criminology, 82*, 360–395.

PART III
SOCIOLOGICAL THEORIES

Introduction

The central concern of the sociological theories of crime, dating back to Emile Durkheim's theory of the two laws of penal evolution (1964), is the "problem of order." Specifically, how may a given society establish and maintain social stability and cohesiveness? What Durkheim and the sociological theorists who followed him sought to provide was a third way of understanding social order that transcended the strictly contractual explanation of social order offered by the utilitarians and the strictly materialist conception of social order formulated by the economic determinists (Zeitlin, 1981). In his rebuttal of the utilitarians, Durkheim argued that contractual interests alone could not account for social order. According to Durkheim, all contractual relations that cumulatively produce social order contain noncontractual or sociomoral elements. While Durkheim agreed with the economic determinists that material inequality threatened social order, he rejected their conclusion that only through massive restructuring of the political economic system could such inequality be redressed, suggesting instead that the shift from primary institutions (family, church, and community) to secondary institutions (schools, courts, civic organizations, etc.) brought about by the increasing division of labor would both lessen the effects of economic inequality and create a more substantive system of justice, thereby establishing a new foundation for social order.

The sociological understanding of crime is drawn from Durkheim's conception of *anomie*. For Durkheim, the increasing division of labor brought with it a shift from mechanical to organic solidarity. In a mechanical society crime is conceived as normal. Crime invokes a sense of moral superiority among its noncriminal members that reinforces the society's collective conscience, which in turn increases social solidarity. In the Durkheimian analysis of anomie the increasing division of labor is seen as having gradually weakened the collective conscience upon which mechanical solidarity has rested and replaced it with a functional interdependence that serves as the foundation for organic solidarity. In the organic context, society regulates both the functional interactions of its various institutional components and the perceptions of its individual members. When the economic and social reality of individuals is not in line with their expectations, anomie will result. On a societal level, the incongruity between expectations and reality blurs the normative boundaries, leading to a crisis in the maintenance of order. The resulting "normlessness" manifests itself in elevated levels of deviance and crime.

Sociological theories of crime that have followed, beginning with Robert Merton's "Anomie and Social Structure," (1938) have defined anomie more as a permanent feature of society than as the transitory phenomenon described by Durkheim. The sociological theories have tended to locate the source of anomie in one of three societal levels: structural, institutional, or interactional. The chapters that follow include theories drawn from all three societal levels. The first two chapters, by Stark and Messner and Rosenfeld, use the more macro-level analysis of social structural theory. In his chapter, "Deviant Places: A Theory of the Ecology of Crime," Rodney Stark outlines an extensive set of facts about crime that expand the theoretical understanding of the social ecology of deviant behavior.

Using the classic works of the Chicago School (Park, Burgess, and McKenzie, 1925; Faris and Dunham, 1939; Shaw and McKay, 1931 and 1942), Stark begins by identifying the five major aspects of urban life that characterize areas of social disorganization: (1) density, (2) poverty, (3) mixed use, (4) transience, and (5) dilapidation. Stark extends the ecological analysis by examining the impact of these aspects of urban life on the moral order as people respond to them. In particular, Stark assesses the relationship of each of these five aspects of urban life to four potential responses to social disorganization: (1) moral cynicism, (2) increased opportunities for crime and deviance, (3) increased motivation to deviate, and (4) diminished social control. Stark extends the analysis further by demonstrating how these responses amplify the volume of deviance by attracting deviant and crime prone people and deviant and criminal activities to a neighborhood while at the same time driving out the least deviant residents, thereby further weakening both formal and informal mechanisms of social control. In summarizing his theoretical propositions, Stark broadly suggests that the five aspects of urban life long recognized as the major contributors to social disorganization work more indirectly in generating deviance and crime by encouraging a sense of moral cynicism and tolerance among residents that weakens both the *ability* of intermediate institutions (e.g., family, church, work) and the *will* of state institutions (e.g., police, schools) to exert effective social control.

Taking Robert Merton's structural understanding of anomie as their starting point, Messner and Rosenfeld use their institutional-anomie theory to identify the tension between cultural and social structures as the source of normlessness. In a point of departure with Merton, Messner and Rosenfeld suggest that the exceptionally high rate of crime in the United States (as compared with other industrialized Western societies) is the result of a fundamental imbalance in American institutional structure. According to Messner and Rosenfeld, an exaggerated emphasis on the goal of monetary success and a minimization of the importance of using institutional means have rendered impotent those elements of culture that in principle could counteract the anomic pressures because they lack firm institutional grounding. In America, they argue, the economy assumes dominance over other institutions that would otherwise (1) temper the goal of monetary success and (2) cultivate respect for the importance of normative restraint. As a result of this economic dominance, noneconomic factors tend to be devalued. For example, performance in noneconomic institutional realms (such as being a good parent) is assigned a low priority. Consequently, noneconomic roles must be accommodated to economic roles when conflicts emerge. Home schedules, for example, must be accommodated to work schedules. In addition, economic standards and norms penetrate into noneconomic realms. The language and logic of the economy govern the discourse and thinking about all other aspects of life. Family life, for example, is increasingly conceived of in terms of efficiency, effectiveness, and consumerism. Consequently, economic dominance undermines the basic function of social institutions (i.e., social control), thereby lessening control over individual members of society. Messner and Rosenfeld conclude their analysis by pointing out the paradox of capitalist social control, which implies that the greater the power of the economy over other institutions, the less control it is able to exert over the behavior of individual economic actors.

Analyzing crime causation on an institutional level, Robert Agnew reexamines strain theory in "Foundation for a General Strain Theory of Crime and Delinquency." Traditionally, strain theory has been conceived as a structural theory in which crime is a function of the conflict between the goals and desires individuals strive for and what they can realistically hope to achieve. Because of their social and economic disadvantage, lower-class individuals are unlikely to achieve success through conventional means. As a result, they feel frustration and resentment, which criminologists have defined in terms of social strain. Consequently, individuals experiencing such strain can either continue to use conventional means and scale back their expectations, or they can continue to pursue their original goal through unconventional means such as crime. Agnew's reexamination shifts the focus of strain theory from the structural to the institutional level. Agnew employs a social process analysis to counter both the persistent criticism of strain theory and its diminished influence as an explanation of crime causation. Agnew directs special attention to the actual social process by which strain is produced. Agnew constructs his theoretical analysis around the three major types of strain. He begins by identifying the failure to achieve positively valued goals resulting from the disjunction between individual expectations and achievements as a source of social strain. Agnew identifies the removal of positively valued stimuli from the individual (e.g., the death of a friend, divorce, change of schools) as a second source of strain. Agnew then describes the third source of strain as the presentation of negative stimuli (e.g., negative relations with parents, negative relations with peers, abuse, etc.). Agnew hypothesizes that the negative relations resulting from social strain have a cumulative impact. Employing an interactive model, similar to Howard Becker's sequential model of deviance formation, Agnew suggests that a person who has experienced one negative event may react with even more distress to a second negative event following soon after the first. Negative effects, according to Agnew, are better predictors of crime than predictions based on the relative weight of positive versus negative effects. Agnew concludes his theoretical overview by outlining the adaptations to strain, which he describes as coping strategies that can inhibit deviant and criminal impulses. These coping strategies are categorized by Agnew as either cognitive, behavioral, or emotional.

The final chapter that presents the social process perspective is Paternoster and Iovanni's "The Labeling Perspective and Delinquency: An Elaboration of the Theory and an Assessment of the Evidence." Paternoster and Iovanni begin their theoretical assessment by tracing the origins of labeling theory to both the conflict and symbolic interactionist perspectives. They use the conflict perspective to explain the political-economic backdrop of the labeling process. They suggest that labeling theory is predicated on a rejection of norm-based definitions of deviance. This macro-level component of labeling theory identifies conflict at three levels: (1) the rule-making level, where the definition of deviance is determined by the interest of the powerful; (2) the organizational-processing level, where middle-level social control agencies decide what powerless groups are to be singled out; and (3) the interpersonal level, where the consequences of rule enforcement for those who are singled out are felt. Once they have explained the process of who gets labeled, Paternoster and Iovanni turn their attention to what they consider the more important component of the labeling process—the generation of secondary deviance. They describe the concept of secondary deviance as the essence of labeling theory. Paternoster and Iovanni emphatically assert that the model of secondary deviance describes not an absolute position but rather the conditions under which an initial participation in deviance may produce subsequent problems of adjustment for the individual. Their analysis of the symbolic interactionist component of the labeling process begins with the negative reaction of society toward the criminal. Whether such a negative social reaction produces secondary deviance is dependent on the individual's relative access to three distinct audiences. According to Paternoster and Iovanni, secondary deviance is likely only when hostile audiences make access to normal associations and opportunities more difficult, and supportive nondeviant audiences, which may help to minimize the impact of the deviant label, are absent. In addition, deviant audiences that make the acceptance of the deviant label less isolating and provide additional deviant opportunities must be readily accessible to the individual. Paternoster and Iovanni further suggest that labeling is possible only when *intent* on the part of the actor is implied by others. Through this "essentializing" function, deviant motives become indicative of the actor's real or essential self. In Paternoster and Iovanni's analysis, special attention is directed to the reciprocal nature of the labeling process, which suggests that the exclusive social reactions from others may lead to an alteration of personal identity, which in turn may result in a closer affinity with deviant others. Paternoster and Iovanni, in reviewing the research on secondary deviance, conclude that because the labeling process itself has been poorly understood, a new research agenda must be pursued that would examine the three elements of the process—(1) the alteration of personal identity, (2) exclusion from conventional opportunities, and (3) probability of further deviance—sequentially rather than simultaneously.

References

Durkheim, E. (1964). *The division of labor in society.* New York: Free Press.

Merton, R. (1938). Social structure and anomie. *American Sociological Review, 3,* 672–682.

Zeitlin, I. (1981). *Ideology and the development of sociological theory.* Englewood Cliffs, N.J.: Prentice Hall.

9

Deviant Places: A Theory of the Ecology of Crime

RODNEY STARK

It is well known that high rates of crime and deviance can persist in specific neighborhoods despite repeated, complete turnovers in the composition of their populations. That this occurs suggests that more than "kinds of people" explanations are needed to account for the ecological concentration of deviance—that we also need to develop "kinds of places" explanations. This chapter attempts to codify more than a century of ecological research on crime and deviance into an integrated set of propositions and offers these as a first approximation of a theory of deviant places.

Norman Hayner, a stalwart of the old Chicago School of human ecology, noted that in the area of Seattle having by far the highest delinquency rate in 1934, "half the children are Italian." In vivid language, Hayner described the social and cultural shortcomings of these residents: "largely illiterate, unskilled workers of Sicilian origin. Fiestas, wine-drinking, raising of goats and gardens . . . are characteristic traits." He also noted that the businesses in this neighborhood were run down and on the wane and that "a number of dilapidated vacant business buildings and frame apartment houses dot the main street," while the area has "the smallest percentage of home-owners and the greatest aggregation of dilapidated dwellings and run-down tenements in the city" (Hayner, 1942:361–363). Today this district, which makes up the neighborhood surrounding Garfield High School, remains the prime delinquency area. But there are virtually no Italians living there. Instead, this neighborhood is the heart of the Seattle black community.

Thus we come to the point. How is it that neighborhoods can remain the site of high crime and deviance rates *despite a complete turnover in their populations?* If the Garfield district was tough *because* Italians lived there, why did it stay tough after they left? Indeed, why didn't the neighborhoods the Italians departed to become tough? Questions such as these force the perception that the composition of neighborhoods, in terms of characteristics of their populations, cannot provide an adequate explanation of variations in deviance rates. Instead, *there must be something about places as such* that sustains crime.[1]

This chapter attempts to fashion an integrated set of propositions to summarize and extend our understanding of ecological sources of deviant behavior. In so doing, the aim is to revive a *sociology* of deviance as an alternative to the social psychological approaches that have dominated for thirty years. That is, the focus is on traits of places and groups rather than on traits of individuals. Indeed, the chapter attempts to show that by adopting survey research as the *preferred* method of research, social scientists lost touch with significant aspects of crime and delinquency. Poor neighborhoods disappeared, to be replaced by individual kids with various levels of family income but no detectable environment at all. Moreover, the phenomena themselves become bloodless, sterile, and almost harmless; for questionnaire studies cannot tap homicide, rape, assault, armed robbery, or even significant burglary and fraud—too few people are involved in these activities to turn up in significant numbers in feasible samples, assuming that such people turn up in samples at all. So delinquency, for example, which once had meant offenses serious enough for court referrals, soon meant taking $2 out of mom's purse, having "banged up something that did not belong to you," and having a fist fight. This transformation soon led repeatedly to the "discovery" that poverty is unrelated to delinquency (Tittle, Villemez, and Smith, 1978).

Yet, through it all, social scientists somehow still knew better than to stroll the streets at night in certain parts of town or even to park there. And despite the fact that countless surveys showed that kids from upper- and lower-income families scored the same on delinquency batteries, even social scientists knew that the parts of town that scared them were not upper-income neighborhoods. In fact, when the literature was examined with sufficient finesse, it was clear that class *does* matter—that serious offenses are very disproportionately committed by a virtual underclass (Hindelang, Hirschi, and Weis, 1981).

So, against this backdrop, let us reconsider the human ecology approach to deviance. To begin, there are five aspects of urban neighborhoods that characterize high-deviance areas of cities. To my knowledge, no member of the Chicago School ever listed this particular set, but these concepts permeate their whole literature—starting with Park, Burgess, and McKenzie's classic, *The City* (1925). And they are especially prominent in the empirical work of the Chicago School (Faris and Dunham, 1939; Shaw and McKay, 1942). Indeed, most of these factors were prominent in the work of nineteenth-century moral statisticians such as the Englishmen Mayhew and Buchanan, who were doing ecological sociology decades before any member of the Chicago School was born. These essential factors are (1) density, (2) poverty, (3) mixed use, (4) transience, and (5) dilapidation.

Each of the five will be used in specific propositions. However, in addition to these characteristics of places, the theory also will incorporate some specific *impacts* of the five on the moral order as *people respond to them*. Four responses will be assessed: (1) moral cynicism among residents, (2) increased opportunities for crime and deviance, (3) increased motivation to deviate, and (4) diminished social control.

Finally, the theory will sketch how these responses further *amplify* the volume of deviance through the following consequences: (1) by attracting deviant and crime-prone people and deviant and criminal activities to a neighborhood, (2) by driving out the least deviant, and (3) by further reductions in social control.

The remainder of the chapter weaves these elements into a set of integrated propositions, clarifying and documenting each as it proceeds. Citations will not be limited to recent work, nor even to that of the old Chicago School, but will include samples of the massive nineteenth-century literature produced by the moral statisticians. The aim is to help contemporary students of crime and deviance rediscover the past and to note the power and realism of its methods, data, and analysis. In Mayhew's (1851) immense volumes, for example, he combines lengthy, first-person narratives of professional criminals with a blizzard of superb statistics on crime and deviance.

Before stating any propositions, one should note the relationship between this chapter and ongoing theoretical work, especially the deductive theory of religion presented by Stark and Bainbridge (1987). A major impediment to the growth of more formal and fully deductive theories in the social sciences is that usually one lacks the space necessary to work out the links between an initial set of axioms and definitions and the relevant set of propositions (statements deduced from the axioms and definitions). In consequence, it is not shown that the propositions outlined here follow logically from that axiomatic system, but they can be derived. Those interested in these matters can refer to the more complete formulation of control theory that was derived in *A Theory of Religion* (Stark and Bainbridge, 1987) to explain the conditions under which people are recruited by deviant religious movements. In any event, logical steps from one proposition to another will be clear in what follows, but the set as a whole must be left without obvious axiomatic ancestry.

Proposition 1: *The greater the density of a neighborhood, the more association between those most and least predisposed to deviance.*

At issue here is not simply the fact that there will be a higher proportion of deviance-prone persons in dense neighborhoods (although, as will be shown, that is true, too); rather, it is proposed that there is a higher average level of interpersonal interactions in such neighborhoods and that individual traits will have less influence on patterns of contact. Consider kids. In low-density neighborhoods—wealthy suburbs, for example—some active effort is required for one twelve-year-old to see another (a ride from a parent is often required). In these settings, kids and their parents can easily limit contact with bullies and those in disrepute. Not so in dense urban neighborhoods—the "bad" kids often live in the same building as the "good" ones, hang out close by, dominate the nearby playground, and are nearly unavoidable. Hence, peer groups in dense neighborhoods will tend to be inclusive, and all young people living there will face maximum peer pressure to deviate—as differential association theorists have stressed for so long.

Proposition 2: *The greater the density of a neighborhood, the higher the level of moral cynicism.*

Moral cynicism is the belief that people are much worse than they pretend to be. Indeed, Goffman's use of the dramaturgical model in his social psychology was rooted in the fact that we require ourselves and others to keep up appearances in public. We all, to varying degrees, have secrets, the public airing of which we would find undesirable. So long as our front-stage performances are credible and creditable, and we shield our backstage actions, we serve as good role models (Goffman, 1959, 1963). The trouble is that in dense neighborhoods it is much harder to keep up appearances—whatever morally discreditable information exists about us is likely to leak.

Survey data suggest that upper-income couples may be about as likely as lower-income couples to have physical fights (Stark and McEvoy, 1970). Whether that is true, it surely is the case that upper-income couples are much less likely to be *overheard* by the neighbors when they have such a fight. In dense neighborhoods, where people live in crowded, thin-walled apartments, the neighbors do hear. In these areas teenage peers, for example, will be much more likely to know embarrassing things about one another's parents. This will color their perceptions about what is normal, and their respect for conventional moral standards will be reduced. Put another way, people in dense neighborhoods will serve as inferior role models for one another—the same people would *appear* to be more respectable in less dense neighborhoods.

Proposition 3: *To the extent that neighborhoods are dense and poor, homes will be crowded.*

The proposition is obvious, but it serves as a necessary step to the next propositions on the effects of crowding, which draw heavily on the fine paper by Gove, Hughes, and Galle (1979).

Proposition 4: *Where homes are more crowded, there will be a greater tendency to congregate outside the home in places and circumstances that raise levels of temptation and opportunity to deviate.*

Gove and his associates reported that crowded homes caused family members, especially teenagers, to stay away. Since crowded homes will also tend to be located in mixed-use neighborhoods (see Proposition 9), when people stay away from home they will tend to congregate in places conducive to deviance (stores, pool halls, street corners, cafes, taverns, and the like).

Proposition 5: *Where homes are more crowded, there will be lower levels of supervision of children.*

This follows from the fact that children from crowded homes tend to stay out of the home and their parents are glad to let them. Moreover, Gove and his associates found strong empirical support for the link between crowding and less supervision of children.

Proposition 6: *Reduced levels of child supervision will result in poor school achievement, with a consequent reduction in stakes in conformity and an increase in deviant behavior.*

This is one of the most cited and strongly verified causal chains in the literature on delinquency (Thrasher, 1927; Toby and Toby, 1961; Hirschi, 1969; Gold, 1970; Hindelang, 1973). Indeed, Hirschi and Hindelang (1977:583) claim that the "school variables" are among the most powerful predictors of delinquency to be found in survey studies: "Their significance for delinquency is nowhere in dispute and is, in fact, one of the oldest and most consistent findings of delinquency research."

Here Toby's (1957) vital concept of "stakes in conformity" enters the propositions. Stakes in conformity are those things that people risk losing by being detected in deviant actions. These may be things we already possess as well as things we can reasonably count on gaining in the future. An important aspect of the school variables is their potential for future rewards, rewards that may be sacrificed by deviance, but only for those whose school performance is promising.

Proposition 7: *Where homes are more crowded, there will be higher levels of conflict within families, weakening attachments and thereby stakes in conformity.*

Gove and his associates found a strong link between crowding and family conflict, confirming Frazier's (1932:636) observations:

So far as children are concerned, the house becomes a veritable prison for them. There is no way of knowing how many conflicts in Negro families are set off by the irritations caused by overcrowding people, who come home after a day of frustration and fatigue to dingy and unhealthy living quarters.

Here we also recognize that stakes in conformity are not merely material. Indeed, given the effort humans will expend to protect them, our attachments to others are among the most potent stakes in conformity. We risk our closest and most intimate relationships by behavior that violates what others expect of us. People lacking such relationships, of course, do not risk their loss.

Proposition 8: *Where homes are crowded, members will be much less able to shield discreditable acts and information from one another, further increasing moral cynicism.*

As neighborhood density causes people to be less satisfactory role models for the neighbors, density in the home causes moral cynicism. Crowding makes privacy more difficult. Kids will observe or overhear parental fights, sexual relations, and the like. This is precisely what Buchanan noted about the dense and crowded London slums in 1846 (in Levin and Lindesmith, 1937:15):

> In the densely crowded lanes and alleys of these areas, wretched tenements are found containing in every cellar and on every floor, men and women, children both male and female, all huddled together, sometimes with strangers, and too frequently standing in very doubtful consanguinity to each other. In these abodes decency and shame have fled; depravity reigns in all its horrors.

Granted that conditions have changed since then and that dense, poor, crowded areas in the center cities of North America are not nearly so wretched. But the essential point linking "decency" and "shame" to lack of privacy retains its force.

Proposition 9: *Poor, dense neighborhoods tend to be mixed-use neighborhoods.*

Mixed use refers to urban areas where residential and commercial land use coexist, where homes, apartments, retail shops, and even light industry are mixed together. Since much of the residential property in such areas is rental, typically there is much less resistance to commercial use (landlords often welcome it because of the prospects of increased land values). Moreover, the poorest, most dense urban neighborhoods are often adjacent to the commercial sections of cities, forming what the Chicago School called the "zone of transition" to note the progressive encroachments of commercial uses into a previously residential area. Shaw and McKay (1942:20) describe the process as follows:

> As the city grows, the areas of commerce and light industry near the center encroach upon areas used for residential purposes. The dwellings in such areas, often already undesirable because of age, are allowed to deteriorate when such invasion threatens or actually occurs, as further investment in them is unprofitable. These residences are permitted to yield whatever return can be secured in their dilapidated condition, often in total disregard for the housing laws. . . .

Shaw and McKay were proponents of the outmoded concentric zonal model of cities, hence their assumption that encroachment radiates from the city center. No matter, the important point is that the process of encroachment occurs whatever the underlying shape of cities.

Proposition 10: *Mixed use increases familiarity with and easy access to places offering the opportunity for deviance.*

A colleague told me he first shoplifted at age eight, but that he had been "casing the joint for four years." This particular "joint" was the small grocery store at the corner of the block where he lived, so he didn't even have to cross a street to get there. In contrast, consider kids in many suburbs. If they wanted to take up shoplifting they would have to ask mom or dad for a ride. In purely residential neighborhoods there simply are far fewer conventional opportunities (such as shops) for deviant behavior.

Proposition 11: *Mixed-use neighborhoods offer increased opportunity for congregating outside the home in places conducive to deviance.*

It isn't just stores to steal from that the suburbs lack, they also don't abound in places of potential moral marginality where people can congregate. But in dense, poor, mixed-use neighborhoods, when people leave the house they have all sorts of places to go, including the street corner. A frequent activity in such neighborhoods is leaning. A bunch of guys will lean against the front of the corner store, the side of the pool hall, or up against the barber shop. In contrast, out in the suburbs young guys don't gather to lean against one another's houses, and since there is nowhere else for them to lean, whatever deviant leanings they might have go unexpressed. By the same token, in the suburbs, come winter, there is no close, *public* place to congregate indoors.

Thus, we can more easily appreciate some fixtures of the crime and delinquency research literature. When people, especially young males, congregate and have nothing special to do, the incidence of their deviance is increased greatly (Hirschi, 1969). Most delinquency, and a lot of crime, is a social rather than a solitary act (Erickson, 1971).

Proposition 12: *Poor, dense, mixed-use neighborhoods have high transience rates.*

This aspect of the urban scene has long attracted sociological attention. Thus, McKenzie wrote in 1926 (p. 145): "Slums are the most mobile . . . sections of a city. Their inhabitants come and go in continuous succession."

Proposition 13: *Transience weakens extrafamilial attachments.*

This is self-evident. The greater the amount of local population turnover, the more difficult it will be for individuals or families to form and retain attachments.

Proposition 14: *Transience weakens voluntary organizations, thereby directly reducing both informal and formal sources of social control* (see Proposition 25).

Recent studies of population turnover and church membership rates strongly sustain the conclusion that such membership is dependent upon attachments, and hence suffers where transience rates reduce attachments (Wuthnow and Christiano, 1979; Stark, Doyle, and Rushing, 1983; Welch, 1983; Stark and Bainbridge, 1985). In similar fashion, organizations such as PTAs or even fraternal organizations must suffer where transience is high. Where these organizations are weak, there will be reduced community resources to launch local, self-help efforts to confront problems such as truancy or burglary. Moreover, neighborhoods deficient in voluntary organizations will also be less able to influence how external forces such as police, zoning boards, and the like act vis-à-vis the community, a point often made by Park (1952) in his discussions of natural areas and by more recent urban sociologists (Suttles, 1972; Lee, Oropesa, Metch, and Guest, 1984; Guest, 1984).

In their important recent study, Simcha-Fagan and Schwartz (1986) found that the association between transience and delinquency disappeared under controls for organizational participation. This is not an example of spuriousness, but of what Lazarsfeld called "interpretation" (Lazarsfeld, Pasanella, and Rosenberg, 1972). Transience *causes* low levels of participation, which in turn *cause* an increased rate of delinquency. That is, participation is an *intervening variable* or *linking mechanism* between transience and delinquency. When an intervening variable is controlled, the association between X and Y is reduced or vanishes.

Proposition 15: *Transience reduces levels of community surveillance.*

In areas abounding in newcomers, it will be difficult to know when someone doesn't live in a building he or she is entering. In stable neighborhoods, on the other hand, strangers are easily noticed and remembered.

Proposition 16: *Dense, poor, mixed-use, transient neighborhoods will also tend to be dilapidated.*

This is evident to anyone who visits these parts of cities. Housing is old and not maintained. Often these neighborhoods are very dirty and littered as a result of density, the predominance of renters, inferior public services, and a demoralized population (see Proposition 22).

Proposition 17: *Dilapidation is a social stigma for residents.*

It hardly takes a real estate tour of a city to recognize that neighborhoods not only reflect the status of their residents but confer status upon them. In Chicago, for example, strangers draw favorable inferences about someone who claims to reside in Forest Glen, Beverly, or Norwood Park. But they will be leery of those who admit to living on the Near South Side. Granted, knowledge of other aspects of communities enters into these differential reactions, but simply driving through a neighborhood such as the South Bronx is vivid evidence that very few people would actually *want* to live there. During my days as a newspaper reporter, I discovered that to move just a block north, from West Oakland to Berkeley, greatly increased social assessments of individuals. This observation was underscored by the many times people told me they lived in Berkeley even though the phone book showed them with an Oakland address. As Goffman (1963) discussed at length, stigmatized people will try to pass when they can.

Proposition 18: *High rates of neighborhood deviance are a social stigma for residents.*

Beyond dilapidation, neighborhoods abounding in crime and deviance stigmatize the moral standing of all residents. To discover that you are interacting with a person through whose neighborhood you would not drive is apt to influence the subsequent interaction in noticeable ways. Here is a person who lives where homicide, rape, and assault are common; where drug dealers are easy to find; where prostitutes stroll the sidewalks waving to passing cars; where people sell TVs, VCRs, cameras, and other such items out of the trunks of their cars. In this sense, place of residence can be a dirty, discreditable secret.

Proposition 19: *Living in stigmatized neighborhoods causes a reduction in an individual's stake in conformity.*

This is simply to note that people living in slums will see themselves as having less to risk by being detected in acts of deviance. Moreover, as suggested below in Propositions 25–28, the risks of being detected also are lower in stigmatized neighborhoods.

Proposition 20: *The more successful and potentially best role models will flee stigmatized neighborhoods whenever possible.*

Goffman (1963) has noted that in the case of physical stigmas, people will exhaust efforts to correct or at least minimize them—from plastic surgery to years of therapy. Presumably it is easier for persons to correct a stigma attached to their neighborhood than one attached to their bodies. Since moving is widely perceived as easy, the stigma of living in particular neighborhoods is magnified. Indeed, as we see below, some people do live in such places because of their involvement in crime and deviance. But, even in the most disorderly neighborhoods, *most* residents observe the laws and norms. Usually they continue to live there simply because they can't afford better. Hence, as people become able to afford to escape, they do. The result is a process of selection whereby the worst role models predominate.

Proposition 21: *More successful and conventional people will resist moving into a stigmatized neighborhood.*

The same factors that *pull* the more successful and conventional out of stigmatized neighborhoods *push* against the probability that conventional people will move into these neighborhoods. This means that only less successful and less conventional people *will* move there.

Proposition 22: *Stigmatized neighborhoods will tend to be overpopulated by the most demoralized kinds of people.*

This does not mean the poor or even those engaged in crime or delinquency. The concern is with persons unable to function in reasonably adequate ways. For here will congregate the mentally ill (especially since the closure of mental hospitals), the chronic alcoholics, the retarded, and others with limited capacities to cope (Faris and Dunham, 1939; Jones, 1934).

Proposition 23: *The larger the relative number of demoralized residents, the greater the number of available "victims."*

As mixed use provides targets of opportunity by placing commercial firms within easy reach of neighborhood residents, the demoralized serve as human targets of opportunity. Many muggers begin simply by searching the pockets of drunks passed out in doorways and alleys near their residence.

Proposition 24: *The larger the relative number of demoralized residents, the lower will be residents' perception of chances for success, and hence they will have lower perceived stakes in conformity.*

Bag ladies on the corner, drunks sitting on the curbs, and schizophrenics muttering in the doorways are not advertisements for the American Dream. Rather, they testify that people in this part of town are losers, going nowhere in the system.

Proposition 25: *Stigmatized neighborhoods will suffer from more lenient law enforcement.*

This is one of those things that "everyone knows," but for which there is no firm evidence. However, evidence may not be needed, given the many obvious reasons for the police to let things pass in these neighborhoods that they would act on in better neighborhoods. First, the police tend to be reactive, to act upon complaints rather than seek out violations. People in stigmatized neighborhoods complain less often. Moreover, people in these neighborhoods frequently are much less willing to testify when the police do act—and the police soon lose interest in futile efforts to find evidence. In addition, it is primarily vice that the police tolerate in these neighborhoods, and the police tend to accept the premise that vice will exist *somewhere*. Therefore, they tend to condone vice in neighborhoods from which they do not receive effective pressures to act against it (see Proposition 14). They may even believe that by having vice limited to a specific area they are better able to regulate it. Finally, the police frequently come to share the outside community's view of stigmatized neighborhoods—as filled with morally disreputable people, who deserve what they get.

Proposition 26: *More lenient law enforcement increases moral cynicism.*

Where people see the laws being violated with apparent impunity, they will tend to lose their respect for conventional moral standards.

Proposition 27: *More lenient law enforcement increases the incidence of crime and deviance.*

This is a simple application of deterrence theory. Where the probabilities of being arrested and prosecuted for a crime are lower, the incidence of such crimes will be higher (Gibbs, 1975).

Proposition 28: *More lenient law enforcement draws people to a neighborhood on the basis of their involvement in crime and deviance.*

Reckless (1926:165) noted that areas of the city with "wholesome family and neighborhood life" will not tolerate "vice," but that "the decaying neighborhoods have very little resistance to the invasions of vice." Thus, stigmatized neighborhoods become the "soft spot" for drugs, prostitution, gambling, and the like. These are activities that require public awareness of where to find them, for they depend on customers rather than victims. Vice can function only where it is condoned, at least to some degree. In this manner, McKenzie (1926:146) wrote, the slum "becomes the hiding-place for many services that are forbidden by the mores but which cater to the wishes of residents scattered throughout the community."

Proposition 29: *When people are drawn to a neighborhood on the basis of their participation in crime and deviance, the visibility of such activities and the opportunity to engage in them increases.*

It has already been noted that vice must be relatively visible to outsiders in order to exist. Hence, to residents, it will be obvious. Even children not only will know *about* whores, pimps, drug dealers, and the like, they will *recognize* them. Back in 1840, Allison wrote of the plight of poor rural families migrating to rapidly growing English cities (p. 76):

> The extravagant price of lodgings compels them to take refuge in one of the crowded districts of the town, in the midst of thousands in similar necessitous circumstances with themselves. Under the same roof they probably find a nest of prostitutes, in the next door a den of thieves. In the room which they occupy they hear incessantly the revel of intoxication or are compelled to witness the riot of licentiousness.

In fact, Allison suggested that the higher social classes owed their "exemption from atrocious crime" primarily to the fact that they were not confronted by the temptations and seductions to vice that assail the poor. For it is the "impossibility of concealing the attractions of vice from the younger part of the poor in the great cities which exposes them to so many causes of demoralization."

Proposition 30: *The higher the visibility of crime and deviance, the more it will appear to others that these activities are safe and rewarding.*

There is nothing like having a bunch of pimps and bookies flashing big wads of money and driving expensive cars to convince people in a neighborhood that crime pays. If young girls ask the hookers on the corner why they are doing it, they will reply with tales of expensive clothes and jewelry. Hence, in some neighborhoods, deviants serve as role models that encourage residents to become "street wise." This is a form of "wisdom" about the relative costs and benefits of crime that increases the likelihood that a person will spend time in jail. The extensive recent literature on perceptions of risk and deterrence is pertinent here (Anderson, 1979; Jenson, Erickson, and Gibbs, 1978; Parker and Grasmick, 1979).

Conclusion

A common criticism of the ecological approach to deviance has been that although many people live in bad slums, most do not become delinquents, criminals, alcoholics, or addicts. Of course not. For one thing, as Gans (1962), Suttles (1968), and others have recognized, bonds among human beings can endure amazing levels of stress and thus continue to sustain commitment to the moral order even in the slums. Indeed, the larger culture seems able to instill high levels of aspiration in people even in the worst ecological settings. However, the fact that most slum residents aren't criminals is beside the point to claims by human ecologists that aspects of neighborhood structure can sustain high rates of crime and deviance. Such propositions do not imply that residence in such a neighborhood is either a necessary or a sufficient condition for deviant behavior. There is conformity in the slums and deviance in affluent suburbs. All the ecological propositions imply is a substantial correlation between variations in neighborhood character and variations in crime and deviance rates. What an ecological theory of crime is meant to achieve is an explanation of why crime and deviance are so heavily concentrated in certain areas, and to pose this explanation in terms that do not depend entirely (or even primarily) on *compositional* effects—that is, on answers in terms of "kinds of people."

To say that neighborhoods are high in crime because their residents are poor suggests that controls for poverty would expose the spuriousness of the ecological effects. In contrast, the ecological theory would predict that the deviant behavior of the poor would vary as their ecology varied. For example, the theory would predict less deviance in poor families in situations where their neighborhood is less dense and more heterogeneous in terms of income, where their homes are less crowded and dilapidated, where the neighborhood is more fully residential, where the police are not permissive of vice, and where there is no undue concentration of the demoralized.

As reaffirmed in the last paragraphs of this chapter, the aim here is not to dismiss "kinds of people" or compositional factors but to restore the theoretical power that was lost when the field abandoned human ecology. As a demonstration of what can be regained, let us examine briefly the most serious and painful issue confronting contemporary American criminology—black crime.

It is important to recognize that, for all the pseudobiological trappings of the Chicago School (especially in Park's work), their primary motivation was to refute "kinds of people" explanations of slum deviance based on Social Darwinism. They regarded it as their major achievement to have demonstrated that the real cause of slum deviance was social disorganization, not inferior genetic quality (Faris, 1967).

Today Social Darwinism has faded into insignificance, but the questions it addressed remain—especially with the decline of human ecology. For example, like the public at large, when American social scientists talk about poor central city neighborhoods, they mainly mean black neighborhoods. And, since they are not comfortable with racist explanations, social scientists have been almost unwilling to discuss the question of why black crime rates are so high. Nearly everybody knows that in and of itself, poverty offers only a modest part of the answer. So, what else can safely be said about blacks that can add to the explanation? Not much, *if* one's taste is for answers based on characteristics of persons. A lot, if one turns to ecology.

Briefly, my answer is that high black crime rates are, in large measure, the result of *where* they live.

For several years observations have been made about the strange fact that racial patterns in arrest and imprisonment seem far more equitable in the South than in the North and West. For example, the ratio of black prison inmates per 100,000 to white prison inmates per 100,000 reveals that South Carolina is the most equitable state (with a ratio of 3.2 blacks to 1 white), closely followed by Tennessee, Georgia, North Carolina, Mississippi, and Alabama; Minnesota (22 blacks to 1 white) is the least equitable, followed by Nebraska, Wisconsin, and Iowa. Black-white arrest ratios, calculated the same way, also show greater equity in the South; Minnesota, Utah, Missouri, Illinois, and Nebraska appear to be least equitable (Stark, 1986). It would be absurd to attribute these variations to racism. Although the South has changed immensely, it is not credible that police and courts in Minnesota are far more prejudiced than those in South Carolina.

But what *is* true about the circumstances of southern blacks is that they have a much more normal ecological distribution than do blacks outside the South. For example, only 9 percent of blacks in South Carolina and 14 percent in Mississippi live in the central core of cities larger than 100,000, but 80 percent of blacks in Minnesota live in large center cities and 85 percent of blacks in Nebraska live in the heart of Omaha. What this means is that large proportions of southern blacks live in suburbs, small towns, and rural areas, where they benefit from factors conducive to low crime rates. Conversely, blacks outside the South are heavily concentrated in precisely the kinds of places explored in this chapter—areas where the probabilities of *anyone* committing a crime are high. Indeed, a measure of black center-city concentration is correlated .49 with the black-white arrest ratio and accounts for much of the variation between the South and the rest of the nation (Stark, 1986).

"Kinds of people" explanations could not easily have led to this finding, although one might have conceived of "center-city resident" as an individual trait. Even so, it is hard to see how such an individual trait would lead to explanations of why place of residence mattered. Surely it is more efficient and pertinent to see dilapidation, for example, as a trait of a building rather than as a trait of those who live in the building.

Is there any reason for social scientists to cling to individual traits as the *only* variables that count? Do I hear the phrase "ecological fallacy"? What fallacy? It turns out that examples of this dreaded problem are very hard to find and usually turn out to be transparent examples of spuriousness—a problem to which *all* forms of nonexperimental research are vulnerable (Gove and Hughes, 1980; Stark, 1986; Lieberson, 1985).

Finally, it is not being suggested that we stop seeking and formulating "kinds of people" explanations. Age and sex, for example, have powerful effects on deviant behavior that are not rooted in ecology (Gove, 1985). What is suggested is that, although males will exceed females in terms of rates of crime and delinquency in all neighborhoods, males in certain neighborhoods will have much higher rates than will males in some other neighborhoods, and female behavior will fluctuate by neighborhood too. Or, to return to the insights on which sociology was founded, social structures are real and cannot be reduced to purely psychological phenomena. Thus, for example, we can be sure than an adult, human male will behave somewhat differently if he is in an all-male group than if he is the only male in a group—and no sex change surgery is required to produce this variation.

Note

1. This is *not* to claim that neighborhoods do not change in terms of their levels of crime and deviance. Of course they do, even in Chicago (Bursik and Webb, 1982). It also is clear that such changes in deviance levels often are accompanied by changes in the kinds of people who live there. The so-called gentrification of a former slum area would be expected to reduce crime and deviance there as the decline of a once nicer neighborhood into a slum would be expected to increase it. However, such changes involve much more than changes in the composition of the population. Great physical changes are involved too, and my argument is that these have effects of their own.

References

Allison, A. (1840). *The principles of population and the connection with human happiness.* Edinburgh: Blackwood.

Anderson, L. S. (1979). The deterrent effect of criminal sanctions: Reviewing the evidence. In P. J. Brantingham & J. M. Kress (Eds.), *Structure, law and power.* Beverly Hills, Calif.: Sage.

Erickson, M. L. (1971). The group context of delinquent behavior. *Social Problems, 19,* 114–129.

Faris, R. E. L. (1967). *Chicago sociology, 1920–1932.* San Francisco: Chandler.

Faris, R. E. L., & Dunham, W. (1939). *Mental disorder in urban areas.* Chicago: University of Chicago Press.

Frazier, E. F. (1932). *The Negro in the United States.* New York: Macmillan.

Gans, H. J. (1962). *The urban villagers.* New York: Free Press.

Gibbs, J. P. (1975). *Crime, punishment, and deterrence.* New York: Elsevier.

Goffman, E. (1959). *Presentation of self in everyday life.* New York: Doubleday.

Goffman, E. (1963). *Stigma.* Englewood Cliffs, N.J.: Prentice-Hall.

Gold, M. (1970). *Delinquent behavior in an American city.* Belmont, Calif.: Brooks/Cole.

Gove, W. R., Hughes, M. L., & Galle, O. R. (1979). Overcrowding in the home. *American Sociological Review, 44,* 59–80.

Guest, A. M. (1984). Robert Park and the natural area: A sentimental review. *Sociology and Social Research, 68,* 1–21.

Hindelang, M. J. (1973). Causes of delinquency: A partial replication and extension. *Social Problems, 20,* 471–478.

Hindelang, M. J., Hirschi, T., & Weis, J. G. (1981). *Measuring delinquency.* Beverly Hills, Calif.: Sage.

Hirschi, T. (1969). *Causes of delinquency.* Berkeley: University of California Press.

Hirschi, T., & Hindelang, M. J. (1977). Intelligence and delinquency: A revisionist view. *American Sociological Review, 42,* 571–587.

Jensen, G. F., Erickson, M. L., & Gibbs, J. (1978). Perceived risk of punishment and self-reported delinquency. *Social Forces, 57,* 57–58.

Jones, D. C. (1934). *The social survey of Merseyside*, Vol. III. Liverpool: University Press of Liverpool.

Lazarsfeld, P. F., Pasanella, A. K., & Rosenberg, M. (1972). *Continuities in the language of social research.* New York: Free Press.

Lee, B. A., Oropesa, R. S., Metch, B. J., & Guest, A. M. (1984). Testing the decline-of-community thesis: Neighborhood organizations in Seattle, 1929 and 1979. *American Journal of Sociology, 89,* 1161–1188.

Levin, Y., & Lindesmith, A. (1937). English ecology and criminology of the past century. *Journal of Criminal Law and Criminology, 27,* 801–816.

Mayhew, H. (1851). *London labor and the London poor.* London: Griffin.

McKenzie, R. (1926). The scope of human ecology. *Publications of the American Sociological Society, 20,* 141–154.

Park, R. E. (1952). *Human communities: The city and human ecology.* New York: Free Press.

Park, R. E., Burgess, E. W., & McKenzie, R. (1925). *The city.* Chicago: University of Chicago Press.

Parker, J., & Grasmick, H. G. (1979). Linking actual and perceived certainty of punishment: An exploratory study of an untested proposition in deterrence theory. *Criminology, 17,* 366–379.

Reckless, W. C. (1926). *Publications of the American Sociological Society, 20,* 164–176.

Shaw, C. R., & McKay, H. D. (1942). *Juvenile delinquency and urban areas.* Chicago: University of Chicago Press.

Simcha-Fagan, O., & Schwartz, J. E. (1986). Neighborhood and delinquency: An assessment of contextual effects. *Criminology, 24,* 667–699.

Stark, R., & Bainbridge, W. S. (1985). *The future of religion.* Berkeley: University of California Press.

Stark, R., & Bainbridge, W. S. (1987). *A theory of religion.* Bern & New York: Lang.

Stark, R., Doyle, D. P., & Rushing, J. L. (1983). Beyond Durkheim: Religion and suicide. *Journal for the Scientific Study of Religion, 22,* 120–131.

Stark, R., & McEvoy, J. (1970). Middle class violence. *Psychology Today, 4,* 52–54, 110–112.

Suttles, G. (1968). *The social order of the slum.* Chicago: University of Chicago Press.

Suttles, G. (1972). *The social construction of communities.* Chicago: University of Chicago Press.

Thrasher, F. M. (1927). *The gang.* Chicago: University of Chicago Press.

Tittle, C. R., Villemez, W. J., & Smith, D. A. (1978). The myth of social class and criminality: An empirical assessment of the empirical evidence. *American Sociological Review, 43,* 643–656.

Toby, J. (1957). Social disorganization and stake in conformity: Complementary factors in the predatory behavior of hoodlums. *Journal of Criminal Law, Criminology and Police Science, 48,* 12–17.

Toby, J., & Toby, M. L. (1961). *Law school status as a predisposing factor in subcultural delinquency.* New Brunswick, N.J.: Rutgers University Press.

Welch, K. (1983). Community development and metropolitan religious commitment: A test of two competing models. *Journal for the Scientific Study of Religion, 22,* 167–181.

Wuthnow, R., & Christiano, K. (1979). The effects of residential migration on church attendance. In R. Wuthnow (Ed.), *The religious dimension.* New York: Academic Press.

10

An Institutional-Anomie Theory of the Social Distribution of Crime

STEVEN F. MESSNER

RICHARD ROSENFELD

The Institutional-Anomie Theory of Crime

The point of departure for institutional-anomie theory is the premise that the nature and level of crime in a social system reflect the fundamental features of the social organization of that system, i.e., its culture and social structure. The theory is predicated on the assumption that, for a social system to function at all, cultural commitments and institutionalized patterns of behavior must be interrelated and integrated to a certain extent. However, concrete social systems are never perfectly integrated. Tensions or contradictions between the component elements of cultural and social structures are not only possible but highly likely (Merton, 1968:176). These normal contradictions of social organization are often the source of problems commonly viewed as abnormal, such as deviance and crime.[1] The exceptionally high rate of crime in the United States is due in large part to cultural contradictions that become particularly acute as a result of a fundamental imbalance in the institutional structure of American society.

To understand these criminogenic cultural contradictions, it is useful to begin with Merton's (1938) classic description of the prevailing success ethos, commonly referred to as the American Dream. Merton (1938) explained that the American Dream places an exaggerated emphasis on the goal of monetary success while at the same time minimizing the importance of using legitimate means to attain economic goals. This combination of strong pressures to succeed monetarily and weak restraints on the selection of means fosters a cultural climate that encourages people to pursue their goals by the technically most expedient means without regard to normative restraints. The American Dream, in other words, tends to promote goal attainment, in popular parlance, by any means necessary. Since the pioneering works of Durkheim ([1893] 1964; [1897] 1966), sociologists have referred to such deregulation as *anomie*.

What Merton and other proponents of the classical anomie perspective left unexplained is why the success ethos is able to assume such high priority in American culture. The American Dream obviously does not subsume all of culture. Other elements of culture run counter to the permissive success ethos and affirm socially approved forms of behavior. The cultural message associated with the American Dream to succeed "by any means necessary" is thus opposed to other cultural messages (including the formal legal norms) that explicitly place restraints on behavior.

Furthermore, the anomic tendencies to which Merton referred in his characterization of American culture can be viewed more generally as normal features of any capitalist society (see Gouldner, 1970:323–326; Orru, 1987:142; Passas, 1990). The logic of capitalism presupposes that social actors are highly responsive to monetary incentives and are willing to innovate in the competitive pursuit of monetary rewards. The capitalist mode of production, in other words, tends to encourage by its very nature a strong interest in monetary success and an orientation toward social norms and restraints that is at best highly calculative.

What is distinctive about American society, then, is not that anomic tendencies are built into its economic system but that they are allowed to develop to such an extraordinary degree. The reason for this, we propose, is that those elements of culture that could in principle counteract the anomic pressures of the American Dream are relatively impotent because they lack firm institutional grounding. This lack is due to the nature of the interrelationships among institutions, which may be termed the *institutional balance of power*. American culture promotes and sustains an institutional structure in which the economy assumes dominance over other institutions that might otherwise both temper the exaggerated emphasis on the goal of monetary success and cultivate respect for the importance of normative restraints.

Economic dominance in the institutional balance of power is manifested in at least three important ways. First, noneconomic functions and roles tend to be *devalued* in comparison with economic ones. Success is defined primarily in terms of achievements in one exclusive institutional domain: capital and labor markets. Accordingly, performances in other institutional realms, such as the family (being a good parent), the school (being a good student), or the polity (being a good citizen), are assigned lower priority and do not constitute appealing alternatives to the goal of monetary success.

Second, noneconomic roles typically must be *accommodated* to the requirements of economic roles when conflicts emerge. The schedules, routines, and demands of the workplace take priority over those of the home, the school, the community, and other aspects of social life. This subservience of noneconomic institutions to economic imperatives inevitably develops because the basic requirements for material subsistence and for the maintenance of noneconomic institutional arrangements must be satisfied through individual achievements in the marketplace.

Finally, economic standards and norms *penetrate* into noneconomic realms. The economy reproduces itself within other institutions. The language and logic of the economy tend to govern discourse and thinking about virtually all aspects of social life. To illustrate, spouses are "partners" who "manage" the "household division of labor." Courses and academic programs are evaluated on a "value-added" basis in the lower grades, where students are viewed as products, and in terms of quality standards applied to goods and services (e.g., cost-effectiveness, convenient delivery, attractive packaging) in the upper grades, where students are viewed as consumers. In the political realm, effective public officials are those who keep an eye on the bottom line and deliver the goods, for example, material benefits and low taxes.[2]

This imbalance of the American institutional structure ultimately contributes to high levels of crime in two ways. First, it enables the anomic tendencies inherent in capitalism to develop to a high degree, thereby weakening cultural restraints against crime. The cultural message that is propagated most forcefully tends to be that of the importance of realizing goals regardless of the means. Second, economic dominance undermines institutional control over the members of society. The basic function of institutions in any social system is to regulate behavior (see especially Parsons, 1990:331). Yet in the United States, where the institutional balance of power is skewed toward the economy, people become detached from noneconomic institutions. These institutions are then less capable of fulfilling their distinctive functions, including those of social control (Bellah et al., 1991:291).

The social forces conducive to crime, however, do not operate uniformly throughout the social structure. To the contrary, social positions are likely to vary with respect to their vulnerability to these forces. The key factor determining such vulnerability is the degree of embeddedness in noneconomic institutional spheres.

Institutional Embeddedness and the Social Distribution of Crime

The term "institutional embeddedness" has been widely used in research in organizational ecology to refer to "the interconnections between a population and its institutional environment" (Baum and Oliver, 1992:540). The term is used here in a similar way, although the present focus is on the embeddedness of social positions rather than organizations. In this analysis, institutional embeddedness refers to the level of engagement in the distinctive responsibilities and activities associated with a given institution. A social position in which the occupants participate actively and regularly in institutional tasks of a given type is thus strongly embedded in that institution. A position in which occupants perform such tasks rarely, or not at all, is relatively detached from that institution.

The tendency for monetary success to emerge as an all-encompassing cultural goal is less pronounced for occupants of social positions that are firmly embedded in noneconomic institutions. This is because persons who are actively involved in noneconomic roles are more likely to become committed to success measures other than the accumulation of wealth. These goals can then provide alternative measuring rods for assessing social standing and personal worth. The importance of success as defined purely in terms of economic roles is therefore reduced, and the pressure or encouragement to pursue such success by any means necessary is correspondingly weakened.[5]

In addition, by participating actively in institutional realms governed by noneconomic standards and criteria, occupants of embedded positions are more fully socialized into their distinctive logics and vocabularies of motive. They are less likely to view social life exclusively through the lens of a laissez-faire, deregulated marketplace and are more likely to be receptive to social restraints on self-interested behavior. In short, it can be hypothesized that social positions will be characterized by comparatively low levels of crime to the extent that they are embedded in noneconomic institutions that insulate occupants from anomic cultural pressures and the accompanying erosion of social control. In shorthand, this argument is referred to as the *embeddedness hypothesis.*

The Complex Association Between Class and Crime

The logic of this argument implies an association between social class and crime, although the expected relationship is not a simple one. Members of the upper classes have a greater capacity to cultivate the kind of noneconomic institutional embeddedness that restrains cultural pressures toward crime. From the vantage point of institutional-anomie theory, then, higher-class status is associated with a reduced likelihood of offending only insofar as it is translated into high levels of noneconomic institutional embeddedness. In fact, in the absence of such involvement in noneconomic institutions, the upper classes might be even more exposed than other social classes to the anomic tendencies of the dominant cultural ethos—the American Dream—and hence might be at particularly high risk of criminal involvement. In any event, economic opportunity is no guarantee against crime.

This argument requires some elaboration, because it runs against the grain of much contemporary thinking about the social sources of crime in American society. A dominant theme of liberal criminology links criminality to diminished economic opportunity for individuals and attributes high rates of serious offending to the economic marginality of entire social groups, such as the urban underclass (Currie, 1985:12–16). According to this line of reasoning, crime results when persons and groups are excluded from the full range of economic opportunities and rewards offered by the American Dream. Access to the benefits of the American Dream depends on continuing involvement in what is for most persons the core economic activity: employment. This view was succinctly put by *New York Times* columnist Bob Herbert (1993):

> In the U.S., employment is the cornerstone of everything else. It's the concrete reality that sustains the glorious myth of the American Dream. Take away the job and you take away the dream. Right now an awful lot of dreams are vanishing.

The liberal position is that criminogenic pressures are greatest for those *locked out* of the American Dream, whereas it has been argued here that crime increases for those who are, in effect, *locked in* the American Dream, subject to its anomic pressures. This argument shares with the liberal position the assumption that crime is related to access to economic resources. However, this relationship is mediated by institutional embeddedness. Crime results from economic deprivation only when resource deprivation lowers institutional embeddedness. Institutional-anomie theory also predicts that embeddedness is highly—if not perfectly—associated with access to economic resources.

As noted earlier, one of the distinctive manifestations of economic dominance in the institutional balance of power is "accommodation." Noneconomic roles are rendered subservient to, and therefore must be accommodated to, economic roles in instances of conflicting demands and requirements. Establishing and sustaining noneconomic involvements presupposes a sufficient level of economic resources. The difficulties of accommodating economic demands and sustaining meaningful involvement in noneconomic roles are appreciably lessened when resources are plentiful. It follows that access to economic resources facilitates noneconomic embeddedness and, in so doing, tempers the impact of anomic cultural pressures— pressures that are made all the more acute, ironically, in an institutional structure characterized by economic dominance.

Liberal criminology is deficient not, as conservative critics have charged, because it emphasizes the connection between resource deprivation and crime but because it neglects the institutional ramifications of resource deprivation (cf. Currie, 1985:144–179). Put differently, the conception of resources in liberal criminology focuses too narrowly on economic resources and should be broadened to encompass access to institutional resources—in a word, access to embeddedness. It is essential to complement the traditional liberal emphasis on the relationship between crime and deprivation with attention to the broader cultural and institutional contexts that condition and mediate this relationship in order to grasp some of the complexities in the distribution of crime in American society by gender, age, race, and class.

Notes

1. For a classic discussion of the ways in which the nature of deviance in a society reflects the distinctive features of that society, see Erikson (1966).
2. See Messner and Rosenfeld (1994) for an extended discussion of the penetration of economic standards into other institutional domains.

References

Baum, J. A. C., & Oliver, C. (1992). Institutional embeddedness and the dynamics of organizational populations. *American Sociological Review, 57*, 540–559.

Bellah, R. N., Madsen, R., Sullivan, W. M., Swidler, A., & Tipton, S. M. (1991). *The good society.* New York: Knopf.

Currie, E. (1985). *Confronting crime: An American challenge.* New York: Pantheon.

Durkheim, E. [1893] (1964). *The division of labor in society.* New York: Free Press.

Durkheim, E. [1897] (1966). *Suicide: A study in sociology.* New York: Free Press.

Gouldner, A. W. (1970). *The coming crisis of Western sociology.* New York: Basic Books.

Herbert, B. (1993, September 8). No job, no dream. *New York Times,* A19.

Merton, R. K. (1938). Social structure and anomie. *American Sociological Review, 3,* 672–682.

Merton, R. K. (1968). *Social theory and social structure.* New York: Free Press.

Messner, S. F. (1988). Merton's "social structure and anomie": The road not taken. *Deviant Behavior, 9,* 33–53.

Messner, S. F., & Rosenfeld, R. (1994). *Crime and the American dream.* Belmont, Calif.: Wadsworth.

Orru, M. (1987). *Anomie: History and meanings.* Boston: Allen & Unwin.

Parsons, T. (1951). *The social system.* New York: Free Press.

Passas, N. (1990). Anomie and corporate deviance. *Contemporary Crises, 14,* 157–178.

11

Foundation for a General Strain Theory of Crime and Delinquency

ROBERT AGNEW

The Major Types of Strain

Negative relationships with others are, quite simply, relationships in which others are not treating the individual as he or she would like to be treated. The classic strain theories of Merton (1938), A. Cohen (1955), and Cloward and Ohlin (1960) focus on only one type of negative relationship: relationships in which others prevent the individual from achieving positively valued goals. In particular, they focus on the goal blockage experienced by lower-class individuals trying to achieve monetary success or middle-class status. More recent versions of strain theory have argued that adolescents are concerned not only about the future goals of monetary success/middle-class status but also about the achievement of more immediate goals—such as good grades, popularity with the opposite sex, and doing well in athletics (Agnew, 1984; Elliott and Voss, 1974; Elliott et al., 1985; Empey, 1982; Greenberg, 1977; Quicker, 1974). The focus, however, is still on the achievement of positively valued goals. Most recently, Agnew (1985a) has argued that strain may result not only from the failure to achieve positively valued goals but also from the inability to escape legally from painful situations. If one draws on the above theories—as well as the stress, equity/justice, and aggression literatures—one can begin to develop a more complete classification of the types of strain.

Three major types of strain are described—each referring to a different type of negative relationship with others. Other individuals may (1) prevent

I would like to thank Helene Raskin White and Karen Hegtvedt for their comments.

one from achieving positively valued goals, (2) remove or threaten to remove positively valued stimuli that one possesses, or (3) present or threaten
to present one with noxious or negatively valued stimuli. These categories
of strain are presented as ideal types. There is no expectation, for example,
that a factor analysis of strainful events will reproduce these categories.
These categories, rather, are presented so as to ensure that the full range of
strainful events are considered in empirical research.

Strain as the Failure to Achieve Positively Valued Goals

At least three types of strain fall under this category. The first type encompasses most of the major strain theories in criminology, including the classic
strain theories of Merton, A. Cohen, and Cloward and Ohlin, as well as those
modern strain theories focusing on the achievement of immediate goals. The
other two types of strain in this category are derived from the justice/equity
literature and have not been examined in criminology.

STRAIN AS THE DISJUNCTION BETWEEN ASPIRATIONS
AND EXPECTATIONS/ACTUAL ACHIEVEMENTS

The classic strain theories of Merton, A. Cohen, and Cloward and Ohlin
argue that the cultural system encourages everyone to pursue the ideal goals
of monetary success and/or middle-class status. Lower-class individuals,
however, are often prevented from achieving such goals through legitimate
channels. In line with such theories, adolescent strain is typically measured
in terms of the disjunction between *aspirations* (or ideal goals) and *expectations* (or expected levels of goal achievement). These theories, however, have
been criticized for several reasons (see Agnew, 1986, 1991b; Clinard, 1964;
Hirschi, 1969; Kornhauser, 1978; Liska, 1987; also see Bernard, 1984; Farnworth and Leiber, 1989). Among other things, it has been charged that these
theories (1) are unable to explain the extensive nature of middle-class delinquency, (2) neglect goals other than monetary success/middle-class status,
(3) neglect barriers to goal achievement other than social class, and (4) do
not fully specify why only *some* strained individuals turn to delinquency.
The most damaging criticism, however, stems from the limited empirical
support provided by studies focusing on the disjunction between aspirations and expectations (see Kornhauser, 1978, as well as the arguments of
Bernard, 1984; Elliott et al., 1985; and Jensen, 1986).

As a consequence of these criticisms, several researchers have revised the
above theories. The most popular revision argues that there is a youth subculture that emphasizes a variety of immediate goals. The achievement of
these goals is further said to depend on a variety of factors besides social
class: factors such as intelligence, physical attractiveness, personality, and
athletic ability. As a result, many middle-class individuals find that they

lack the traits or skills necessary to achieve their goals through legitimate channels. This version of strain theory, however, continues to argue that strain stems from the inability to achieve certain ideal goals emphasized by the (sub)cultural system. As a consequence, strain continues to be measured in terms of the disjunction between *aspirations* and *actual achievements* (since we are dealing with immediate rather than future goals, actual achievements rather than expected achievements may be examined).

It should be noted that empirical support for this revised version of strain theory is also weak (see Agnew, 1991, for a summary). At a later point, several possible reasons for the weak empirical support of strain theories focusing on the disjunction between aspirations and expectations/achievements will be discussed. For now, the focus is on classifying the major types of strain.

Strain as the Disjunction between Expectations and Actual Achievements

As indicated above, strain theories in criminology focus on the inability to achieve *ideal* goals derived from the cultural system. This approach stands in contrast to certain of the research on justice in social psychology. Here the focus is on the disjunction between *expectations* and *actual achievements* (rewards), and it is commonly argued that such expectations are existentially based. In particular, it has been argued that such expectations derive from the individual's past experience and/or from comparisons with referential (or generalized) others who are similar to the individual (see Berger et al., 1972, 1983; Blau, 1964; Homans, 1961; Jasso and Rossi, 1977; Mickelson, 1990; Ross et al., 1971; Thibaut and Kelley, 1959). Much of the research in this area has focused on income expectations, although the above theories apply to expectations regarding all manner of positive stimuli. The justice literature argues that the failure to achieve such expectations may lead to such emotions as anger, resentment, rage, dissatisfaction, disappointment, and unhappiness—that is, all the emotions customarily associated with strain in criminology. Further, it is argued that individuals will be strongly motivated to reduce the gap between expectations and achievements—with deviance being commonly mentioned as one possible option. This literature has not devoted much empirical research to deviance, although limited data suggest that the expectations-achievement gap is related to anger/hostility (Ross et al., 1971).

This alternative conception of strain has been largely neglected in criminology. This is unfortunate, because the idea has the potential to overcome certain of the problems of current strain theories. First, one would expect the disjunction between expectations and actual achievements to be more emotionally distressing than that between aspirations and achievements. Aspirations, by definition, are *ideal* goals. They have something of the utopian in them, and for that reason the failure to achieve aspirations may not be taken seriously. The failure to achieve expected goals, however, *is* likely to be taken seriously, since such goals are rooted in reality—the individual has previously experienced such goals or has seen similar others experience such goals. Second, this alternative conception of strain assigns a central role to the social comparison process. As A. Cohen (1965) argued in a follow-up to his strain theory, the neglect of social comparison is a major shortcoming of strain theory. The above theories describe one way in which social comparison is important: Social comparison plays a central role in the formation of individual goals (expectations in this case; also see Suls, 1977). Third, the assumption that goals are culturally based has sometimes proved problematic for strain theory (see Kornhauser, 1978). Among other things, it makes it difficult to integrate strain theory with social control and cultural deviance theory (see Hirschi, 1979). These latter theories assume that the individual is weakly tied to the cultural system or tied to alternative/oppositional subcultures. The argument that goals are existentially based, however, paves the way for integrations involving strain theory.[1]

STRAIN AS THE DISJUNCTION BETWEEN JUST/FAIR OUTCOMES AND ACTUAL OUTCOMES

The above models of strain assume that individual goals focus on the achievement of specific outcomes. Individual goals, for example, focus on the achievement of a certain amount of money or a certain grade-point average. A third conception of strain, also derived from the justice/equity literature, makes a rather different argument. It claims that individuals do not necessarily enter interactions with specific outcomes in mind. Rather, they enter interactions expecting that certain distributive justice rules will be followed, rules specifying how resources should be allocated. The rule that has received the most attention in the literature is that of equity. An equitable relationship is one in which the outcome/input ratios of the actors involved in an exchange/allocation relationship are equivalent (see Adams, 1963, 1965; Cook and Hegtvedt, 1983; Walster et al., 1978). Outcomes encompass a broad range of positive and negative consequences, while inputs encompass the individual's positive and negative contributions to the exchange. Individuals in a relationship will compare the ratio of their outcomes and inputs to the ratio(s) of specific others in the relationship. If the ratios are equal to one another, they feel that the outcomes are fair or just. This is true, according to equity theorists, even if the outcomes are low. If outcome/input ratios are not equal, actors will feel that the outcomes are unjust and they will experience distress as a result. Such distress is especially likely when individuals feel they have been underrewarded rather than overrewarded (Hegtvedt, 1990).

The equity literature has described the possible reactions to this distress, some of which involve deviance (see Adams, 1963, 1965; Austin, 1977; Walster et al., 1973, 1978; see Stephenson and White, 1968, for an attempt to recast A. Cohen's strain theory in terms of equity theory). In particular, inequity may lead to delinquency for several reasons—all having to do with the restoration of equity. Individuals in inequitable relationships may engage in delinquency in order to (1) increase their outcomes (e.g., by theft); (2) lower their inputs (e.g., truancy from school); (3) lower the outcomes of others (e.g., vandalism, theft, assault); and/or (4) increase the inputs of others (e.g., by being incorrigible or disorderly). In highly inequitable situations, individuals may leave the field (e.g., run away from home) or force others to leave the field.[2] There has not been any empirical research on the relationship between equity and delinquency, although much data suggest that inequity leads to anger and frustration. A few studies also suggest that insulting and vengeful behaviors may result from inequity (see Cook and Hegtvedt, 1991; Donnerstein and Hatfield, 1982; Hegtvedt, 1990; Mikula, 1986; Sprecher, 1986; Walster et al., 1973, 1978).

It is not difficult to measure equity. Walster et al. (1978:234–242) provided the most complete guide to measurement.[3] Sprecher (1986) illustrated how equity may be measured in social surveys; respondents are asked who contributes more to a particular relationship and/or who "gets the best deal" out of a relationship. A still simpler strategy might be to ask respondents how fair or just their interactions with others, such as parents or teachers, are. One would then predict that those involved in unfair relations will be more likely to engage in current and future delinquency.

The literature on equity builds on the strain theory literature in criminology in several ways. First, all of the strain literature assumes that individuals are pursuing some specific outcome, such as a certain amount of money or prestige. The equity literature points out that individuals do not necessarily enter into interactions with specific outcomes in mind, but rather with the expectation that a particular distributive justice rule will be followed. Their goal is that the interaction conform to the justice principle. This perspective, then, points to a new source of strain not considered in the criminology literature. Second, the strain literature in criminology focuses largely on the individual's outcomes. Individuals are assumed to be pursuing a specific goal, and strain is judged in terms of the disjunction between the goal and the actual outcome. The equity literature suggests that this may be an oversimplified conception and that the individual's *inputs* may also have to be considered. In particular, an equity theorist would argue that inputs will condition the individual's evaluation of outcomes. That is, individuals who view their inputs as limited will be more likely to accept limited outcomes as fair. Third, the equity literature also highlights the importance of the social comparison process. In particular, the equity literature stresses that one's evaluation of outcomes is at least partly a function of the outcomes (and inputs) of those with whom one is involved in exchange/allocation relations. A given outcome, then, may be evaluated as fair or unfair depending on the outcomes (and inputs) of others in the exchange/allocation relation.

Strain as the Removal of Positively Valued Stimuli from the Individual

The psychological literature on aggression and the stress literature suggest that strain may involve more than the pursuit of positively valued goals. Certain of the aggression literature, in fact, has come to de-emphasize the pursuit of positively valued goals, pointing out that the blockage of goal-seeking behavior is a relatively weak predictor of aggression, particularly when the goal has never been experienced before (Bandura, 1973; Zillman, 1979). The stress literature has largely neglected the pursuit of positively valued goals as a source of stress. Rather, if one looks at the stressful life events examined in this literature, one finds a focus on (1) events involving the loss of positively valued stimuli and (2) events involving the presentation of noxious or negative stimuli (see Pearlin, 1983, for other typologies of stressful life events/conditions).[4] So, for example, one recent study of adolescent stress employs a life-events list that focuses on such items as the loss of a boyfriend/girlfriend, the death or serious illness of a friend, moving to a new school district, the divorce/separation of one's parents, suspension from school, and the presence of a variety of adverse conditions at work (see Williams and Uchiyama, 1989, for an overview of life-events scales for adolescents; see Compas, 1987, and Compas and Phares, 1991, for overviews of research on adolescent stress).[5]

Drawing on the stress literature, then, one may state that a second type of strain or negative relationship involves the actual or anticipated removal (loss) of positively valued stimuli from the individual. As indicated above, numerous examples of such loss can be found in the inventories of stressful life events. The actual or anticipated loss of positively valued stimuli may lead to delinquency as the individual tries to prevent the loss of the positive stimuli, retrieve the lost stimuli or obtain substitute stimuli, seek revenge against those responsible for the loss, or manage the negative affect caused by the loss by taking illicit drugs. While there are no data bearing directly on this type of strain, experimental data indicate that aggression often occurs when positive reinforcement previously administered to an individual is withheld or reduced (Bandura, 1973; Van Houten, 1983). And as discussed below, inventories of stressful life events, which include the loss of positive stimuli, are related to delinquency.

Strain as the Presentation of Negative Stimuli

The literature on stress and the recent psychological literature on aggression also focus on the actual or anticipated presentation of negative or noxious stimuli.[6] Except for the work of Agnew (1985a), however, this category of strain has been neglected in criminology. And even Agnew does not focus on the presentation of noxious stimuli per se but on the inability of adolescents to escape legally from noxious stimuli. Much data, however, suggest that the presentation of noxious stimuli may lead to aggression and other negative outcomes in certain conditions, even when legal escape from such stimuli is possible (Bandura, 1973; Zillman, 1979). Noxious stimuli may lead to delinquency as the adolescent tries to (1) escape from or avoid the negative stimuli; (2) terminate or alleviate the negative stimuli; (3) seek revenge against the source of the negative stimuli or related targets, although the evidence on displaced aggression is somewhat mixed (see Berkowitz, 1982; Bernard, 1990; Van Houten, 1983; Zillman, 1979); and/or (4) manage the resultant negative affect by taking illicit drugs.

A wide range of noxious stimuli have been examined in the literature; and experimental, survey, and participant observation studies have linked such stimuli to both general and specific measures of delinquency—with the experimental studies focusing on aggression. Delinquency/aggression, in particular, has been linked to such noxious stimuli as child abuse and neglect (Rivera and Widom, 1990), criminal victimization (Lauritsen et al., 1991), physical punishment (Straus, 1991), negative relations with parents (Healy and Bonner, 1969), negative relations with peers (Short and Strodtbeck, 1965), adverse or negative school experiences (Hawkins and Lishner, 1987), a wide range of stressful life events (Gersten et al., 1974; Kaplan et al., 1983; Linsky and Straus, 1986; Mawson, 1987; Novy and Donohue, 1985; Vaux and Ruggiero, 1983), verbal threats and insults, physical pain, unpleasant odors, disgusting scenes, noise, heat, air pollution, personal space violations, and high density (see Anderson and Anderson, 1984; Bandura, 1973, 1983; Berkowitz, 1982, 1986; Mueller, 1983). In one of the few studies in criminology to focus specifically on the presentation of negative stimuli, Agnew (1985a) found that delinquency was related to three scales measuring negative relations at home and school. The effect of the scales on delinquency was partially mediated through a measure of anger, and the effect held when measures of social control and deviant beliefs were controlled. And in a recent study employing longitudinal data, Agnew (1989) found evidence suggesting that the relationship between negative stimuli and delinquency was due to the *causal* effect of the negative stimuli on delinquency (rather than the effect of delinquency on the negative stimuli). Much evidence, then, suggests that the presentation of negative or noxious stimuli constitutes a third major source of strain.

Certain of the negative stimuli listed above, such as physical pain, heat, noise, and pollution, may be experienced as noxious largely for biological reasons (i.e., they may be unconditioned negative stimuli). Others may be conditioned negative stimuli, experienced as noxious largely because of their association with unconditioned negative stimuli (see Berkowitz, 1982). Whatever the case, it is assumed that such stimuli are experienced as noxious regardless of the goals that the individual is pursuing.

Each type of strain may create a *predisposition* to delinquency or function as a *situational event* that instigates a particular delinquent act. In the words of Hirschi and Gottfredson (1986), then, the strain theory presented in this chapter is a theory of both "criminality" and "crime" (or to use the words of Clarke and Cornish [1985], it is a theory of both "criminal involvement" and "criminal events"). Strain creates a predisposition to delinquency in those cases in which it is chronic or repetitive. Examples include a continuing gap between expectations and achievements and a continuing pattern of ridicule and insults from teachers. Adolescents subject to such strain are predisposed to delinquency because (1) nondelinquent strategies for coping with strain are likely to be taxed; (2) the threshold for adversity may be lowered by chronic strains (see Averill, 1982:289); (3) repeated or chronic strain may lead to a hostile attitude—a general dislike and suspicion of others and an associated tendency to respond in an aggressive manner (see Edmunds and Kendrick, 1980:21); and (4) chronic strains increase the likelihood that individuals will be high in negative affect/arousal at any given time (see Bandura, 1983; Bernard, 1990). A particular instance of strain may also function as the situational event that ignites a delinquent act, especially among adolescents predisposed to delinquency. Qualitative and survey data, in particular, suggest that particular instances of delinquency are often instigated by one of the three types of strain listed above (see Agnew, 1990; also see Averill, 1982, for data on the instigations to anger).

Examining the Cumulative Impact of Negative Relations

In most previous strain research in criminology, the impact of one type of negative relation on delinquency is examined with other negative relations ignored or held constant. So, for example, researchers will examine the impact of one type of goal blockage on delinquency, ignoring other types of goal blockage and other potential types of strain. This stands in sharp contrast to a central assumption in the stress literature, which is that stressful life events have a cumulative impact on the individual. Linsky and Straus (1986:17), for example, speak of the "accumulation theory," which asserts that "it is not so much the unique quality of any single event but the *cumulation* of several stressful events within a relatively short time span" that is consequential. As a result, it is standard practice in the stressful life-events literature to measure stress with a composite scale: a scale that typically sums the number of stressful life events experienced by the individual.

The precise nature of the cumulative effect, however, is unclear. As Thoits (1983:69) pointed out, stressful events may have an additive or interactive effect on outcome variables. The additive model assumes that each stressor has a fixed effect on delinquency, an effect independent of the level of the other stressors. Somewhat more plausible, perhaps, is the interactive model, which assumes that "a person who has experienced one event may react with even more distress to a second that follows soon after the first . . . two or more events . . . result in more distress than would be expected from the simple sum of their singular effects."

Whether the effect is additive or interactive, there is limited support for the idea that the level of stress/strain must pass a certain threshold before negative outcomes result (Linsky and Straus, 1986; Thoits, 1983). Below that level, stress/strain is unrelated to negative outcomes. Above that level, stress/strain has a positive effect on negative outcomes, perhaps an additive effect or perhaps an interactive effect.

Given these arguments, one should employ a composite index of strain in all analyses or examine the interactions between strain variables. Examining interactions can become very complex if there are more than a few indicators of strain, although it does allow one to examine the differential importance of various types of strain. If stressors have an interactive effect on delinquency, the interaction terms should be significant or the composite index should have a nonlinear effect on delinquency (see the discussion of interactions and nonlinear effects in Aiken and West, 1991). If the effect is additive, the interaction terms should be insignificant or the composite index should have a linear effect on delinquency (after the threshold level is reached). These issues have received only limited attention in the stress literature (see the review by Thoits, 1983), and they should certainly be explored when constructing measures of strain for the purpose of explaining delinquency. At a minimum, however, as comprehensive a list of negative events/conditions as possible should be examined.

There is also the issue of whether positive events/experiences should be examined. If prior stressors can aggravate the negative effect of subsequent stressors, perhaps positive events can mitigate the impact of stressors. Limited evidence from the stress literature suggests that lists of negative events predict better than lists examining the balance of negative and positive events (usually negative events minus positive events) (see Thoits, 1983: 58–59; Williams and Uchiyama, 1989:101; see Gersten et al., 1974, for a possible exception). This topic, however, is certainly in need of more research. In addition to looking at the *difference* between desirable and undesirable events, researchers may also want to look at the *ratio* of undesirable to desirable events.

It should be noted that tests of strain theory in criminology typically examine the disjunction between aspirations and expectations for one or two goals and ignore all of the many other types of strain. The tests also typically assume that strain has a linear effect on delinquency, and they never examine positive as well as negative events. These facts may constitute additional reasons for the weak empirical support given to strain theory in criminology.

Adaptations to Strain

What follows is a typology of the major cognitive, emotional, and behavioral adaptations to strain, including delinquency.

COGNITIVE COPING STRATEGIES

Several literatures suggest that individuals sometimes cognitively reinterpret objective stressors in ways that minimize their subjective adversity. Three general strategies of cognitive coping are described below; each strategy has several forms. These strategies for coping with adversity may be summarized in the following phrases: "It's not important," "It's not that bad," and "I deserve it." This typology represents a synthesis of the coping strategies described in the stress, equity, stratification, and victimization literatures (Adams, 1963, 1965; Agnew, 1985b; Agnew and Jones, 1988; Averill, 1982; Della Fave, 1980; Donnerstein and Hatfield, 1982; Pearlin and Schooler, 1978; Walster et al., 1973, 1978). The stress literature, in particular, was especially useful. Stress has been found to have a consistent, although weak-to-moderate, main effect on outcome variables. Researchers have tried to explain this weak-to-moderate effect by arguing that the impact of stressors is conditioned by a number of variables, and much of the attention has been focused on coping strategies (see Compas and Phares, 1991; Thoits, 1984).

Ignore/Minimize the Importance of Adversity. The subjective impact of objective strain depends on the extent to which the strain is related to the central goals, values, and/or identities of the individual. As Pearlin and Schooler (1978:7) state, individuals may avoid subjective strain "to the extent that they are able to keep the most strainful experiences within the least valued areas of their life." Individuals, therefore, may minimize the strain they experience by reducing the absolute and/or relative importance assigned to goals/values and identities (see Agnew, 1983; Thoits, 1991a).

In particular, individuals may claim that a particular goal/value or identity is unimportant in an absolute sense. They may, for example, state that money or work is unimportant to them. This strategy is similar to Merton's adaptations of ritualism and retreatism, and it was emphasized by Hyman (1953). Individuals may also claim that a particular goal/value or identity is unimportant in a relative sense—relative to other goals/values or identities. They may, for example, state that money is less important than status or that work is less important than family and leisure activities.

The strategy of minimizing strain by reducing the absolute and/or relative emphasis placed on goals/values and identities has not been extensively examined in the strain literature. Certain evidence, however, suggests that it is commonly employed and may play a central role in accounting for the limited empirical support for strain theory. In particular, research on goals suggests that people pursue a wide variety of different goals and that they tend to place the greatest absolute and relative emphasis on those goals they are best able to achieve (Agnew, 1983; McClelland, 1990; Rosenberg, 1979: 265–269; Wylie, 1979).

Maximize Positive Outcomes/Minimize Negative Outcomes. In the above adaptation, individuals acknowledge the existence of adversity but relegate such adversity to an unimportant area of their life. In a second adaptation, individuals attempt to deny the existence of adversity by maximizing their positive outcomes and/or minimizing their negative outcomes. This may be done in two ways: lowering the standards used to evaluate outcomes or distorting one's estimate of current and/or expected outcomes.

Lowering one's standards basically involves lowering one's goals or raising one's threshold for negative stimuli (see Suls, 1977). Such action, of course, makes one's current situation seem less adverse than it otherwise would be. Individuals may, for example, lower the amount of money they desire (which is distinct from lowering the importance attached to money). This strategy is also related to Merton's adaptations of ritualism and retreatism, and many of the critics of strain theory in criminology have focused on it. Hyman (1953) and others have argued that poor individuals in the United States are not strained because they have lowered their success goals— bringing their aspirations in line with reality. The data in this area are complex, but they suggest that this adaptation is employed by some—but not all—lower-class individuals (see Agnew, 1983, 1986; Agnew and Jones, 1988; see Cloward and Ohlin, 1960, and Empey, 1956, for data on "relative" aspirations).

In addition to lowering their standards, individuals may also cognitively distort their estimate of outcomes. As Agnew and Jones (1988) demonstrate, many individuals exaggerate their actual and expected levels of goal achievement. Individuals with poor grades, for example, often report that they are doing well in school. And individuals with little objective chance of attending college often report that they *expect* to attend college. (See Wylie, 1979, for additional data in this area.) In addition to exaggerating positive outcomes, individuals may also minimize negative outcomes—claiming that their losses are small and their noxious experiences are mild.

The self-concept literature discusses the many strategies individuals employ to accomplish such distortions (see Agnew and Jones, 1988; Rosenberg, 1979). Two common strategies, identified across several literatures, are worth noting. In "downward comparisons," individuals claim that their situation is less worse, or at least no worse than, that of similar others (e.g., Brickman and Bulman, 1977; Gruder, 1977; Pearlin and Schooler, 1978; Suls, 1977). This strategy is compatible with the equity literature, which suggests that one's evaluation of outcomes is conditioned by the outcomes of comparison others. Temporal comparisons may also be made, with individuals claiming that their situation is an improvement over the past. Recent research on the social comparison process suggests that individuals often deliberately make downward comparisons, especially when self-esteem is threatened (Gruder, 1977; Hegtvedt, 1991b; Suls, 1977). In a second strategy, "compensatory benefits," individuals cast "about for some positive attribute or circumstance within a troublesome situation . . . the person is aided in ignoring that which is noxious by anchoring his attention to what he considers the more worthwhile and rewarding aspects of experience" (Pearlin and Schooler, 1978:6–7). Crime victims, for example, often argue that their victimization benefited them in certain ways, such as causing them to grow as individuals (Agnew, 1985b).

Accept Responsibility for Adversity. Third, individuals may *minimize* the subjective adversity of objective strain by convincing themselves that they *deserve* the adversity they have experienced. There are several possible reasons why *deserved* strain is less adverse than undeserved strain. Undeserved strain may violate the equity principle, challenge one's "belief in a just world" (see Lerner, 1977), and—if attributed to the malicious behavior of another—lead one to fear that it will be repeated in the future. Such reasons may help explain why individuals who make internal attributions for adversity are less distressed than others (Kluegel and Smith, 1986; Mirowsky and Ross, 1990).

Drawing on equity theory, one may argue that there are two basic strategies for convincing oneself that strain is deserved. First, individuals may cognitively minimize their positive inputs or maximize their negative inputs to a relationship. Inputs are conceived as contributions to the relationship and/or status characteristics believed to be relevant to the relationship (see Cook and Yamagishi, 1983). Second, individuals may maximize the positive inputs or minimize the negative inputs of others. Della Fave (1980) uses both of these strategies to explain the legitimation of inequality in the United States. Those at the bottom of the stratification system are said to minimize their own traits and exaggerate the positive traits and contributions of those above them. They therefore come to accept their limited outcomes as just (also see Kluegel and Smith, 1986; Shepelak, 1987).

BEHAVIORAL COPING STRATEGIES

There are two major types of behavioral coping: those that seek to minimize or eliminate the source of strain and those that seek to satisfy the need for revenge.

Maximizing Positive Outcomes/Minimizing Negative Outcomes. Behavioral coping may assume several forms, paralleling each of the major types of strain. Individuals, then, may seek to achieve positively valued goals, protect or retrieve positively valued stimuli, or terminate or escape from negative stimuli. Their actions in these areas may involve conventional or delinquent behavior. Individuals seeking to escape from an adverse school environment, for example, may try to transfer to another school or may illegally skip school. This rather broad adaptation encompasses Merton's adaptations of innovation and rebellion, as well as those coping strategies described in the equity literature as "maximizing one's outcomes," "minimizing one's inputs," and "maximizing the other's inputs."

Vengeful Behavior. Data indicate that when adversity is blamed on others it creates a desire for revenge that is distinct from the desire to end the adversity. A second method of behavioral coping, then, involves the taking of revenge. Vengeful behavior may also assume conventional or delinquent forms, although the potential for delinquency is obviously high. Such behavior may involve efforts to minimize the positive outcomes, increase the negative outcomes, and/or increase the inputs of others (as when adolescents cause teachers and parents to work harder through their incorrigible behavior).

EMOTIONAL COPING STRATEGIES

Finally, individuals may cope by acting directly on the negative emotions that result from adversity. Rosenberg (1990), Thoits (1984, 1989, 1990, 1991b), and others list several strategies of emotional coping. They include the use of drugs such as stimulants and depressants, physical exercise and deep-breathing techniques, meditation, biofeedback and progressive relaxation, and the behavioral manipulation of expressive gestures through playacting or "expression work." In all of these examples, the focus is on alleviating negative emotions rather than cognitively reinterpreting or behaviorally altering the situation that produced those emotions. Many of the strategies are beyond the reach of most adolescents (Compas et al., 1988), and data indicate that adolescents often employ illicit drugs to cope with life's strains (Labouvie, 1986a, 1986b; Newcomb and Harlow, 1986). Emotional coping is especially likely when behavioral and cognitive coping are unavailable or unsuccessful.

It should be noted that individuals may employ more than one of the above coping strategies (see Folkman, 1991). Also, still other coping strategies, such as distraction, could have been listed. It is assumed, however, that the above strategies constitute the primary responses to strain.

FACTORS AFFECTING THE DISPOSITION TO DELINQUENCY

The selection of delinquent versus nondelinquent coping strategies is dependent not only on the constraints to coping but also on the adolescent's disposition to engage in delinquent versus nondelinquent coping. This disposition is a function of (1) certain temperamental variables (see Tonry et al., 1991); (2) the prior learning history of the adolescent, particularly the extent to which delinquency was reinforced in the past (Bandura, 1973; Berkowitz, 1982); (3) the adolescent's beliefs, particularly the rules defining the appropriate response to provocations (Bernard's, 1990, "regulative rules"); and (4) the adolescent's attributions regarding the causes of his or her adversity. Adolescents who attribute their adversity to others are much more likely to become angry, and as argued earlier, that anger creates a strong predisposition to delinquency. Data and theory from several areas, in fact, suggest that the experience of adversity is most likely to result in deviance when the adversity is blamed on another.[7] The attributions one makes are influenced by a variety of factors, as discussed in recent reviews by Averill (1982), Berwin (1988), R. Cohen (1982), Crittenden (1983, 1989), Kluegel and Smith (1986), and Utne and Kidd (1980). The possibility that there may be demographic and subgroup differences in the rules for assigning blame is of special interest (see Bernard, 1990; Crittenden, 1983, 1989).

A key variable affecting several of the above factors is association with delinquent peers. It has been argued that adolescents who associate with delinquent peers are more likely to be exposed to delinquent models and beliefs and to receive reinforcement for delinquency (see especially Akers, 1985). It may also be the case that delinquent peers increase the likelihood that adolescents will attribute their adversity to others.

The individual's disposition to delinquency, then, may condition the impact of adversity on delinquency. At the same time, it is important to note that continued experience of adversity may create a disposition toward delinquency. This argument has been made by Bernard (1990), Cloward and Ohlin (1960), A. Cohen (1955), Elliott et al. (1979), and others. In particular, it has been argued that under certain conditions the experience of adversity may lead to beliefs favorable to delinquency, lead adolescents to join or form delinquent peer groups, and lead adolescents to blame others for their misfortune.

Virtually all empirical research on strain theory in criminology has neglected the constraints to coping and the adolescent's disposition to delinquency. Researchers, in particular, have failed to examine whether the effect of adversity on delinquency is conditioned by factors such as self-efficacy and association with delinquent peers. This failure is likely a major reason for the weak empirical support for strain theory.

Notes

1. One need not assume that expectations are existentially based; they may derive from the cultural system as well. Likewise, one need not assume that aspirations derive from the cultural system. The focus in this chapter is on *types* of strain rather than *sources* of strain, although a consideration of sources is crucial when the macroimplications of the theory are developed. Additional information on the sources of positively valued goals—including aspirations and expectations—can be found in Alves and Rossi, 1978; Cook and Messick, 1983; Hochschild, 1981; Jasso and Rossi, 1977; Martin and Murray, 1983; Messick and Sentis, 1983; Mickelson, 1990; and Shepelak and Alwin, 1986.

2. Theorists have recently argued that efforts to restore equity need not involve the specific others in the inequitable relationship. If one cannot restore equity with such specific others, there may be an effort to restore "equity with the world" (Austin, 1977; Stephenson and White, 1968; Walster et al., 1978). That is, individuals who feel they have been inequitably treated may try to restore equity in the

context of a totally different relationship. The adolescent who is inequitably treated by parents, for example, may respond by inequitably treating peers. The concept of "equity with the world" has not been the subject of much empirical research, but it is intriguing because it provides a novel explanation for displayed aggression. It has also been argued that individuals may be distressed not only by their own inequitable treatment but also by the inequitable treatment of others (see Crosby and Gonzalez-Intal, 1984; Walster et al., 1978). We may have, then, a sort of vicarious strain, a type little investigated in the literature.

3. The equity literature has been criticized on a number of points, the most prominent being that there are a variety of distribution rules besides equity—such as equality and need (Deutsch, 1975; Folger, 1984; Mikula, 1980; Schwinger, 1980; Utne and Kidd, 1980). Much recent research has focused on the factors that determine the preference for one rule over another (Alves and Rossi, 1978; Cook and Hegtvedt, 1983; Deutsch, 1975; Hegtvedt, 1987, 1991a; Hochschild, 1981; Lerner, 1977; Leventhal, 1976; Leventhal et al., 1980; Schwinger, 1980; Walster et al., 1978). Also, the equity literature argues that individuals compare themselves with similar others with whom they are involved in exchange/allocation relations. However, it has been argued that individuals sometimes compare themselves with dissimilar others, make referential (generalized) rather than local (specific) comparisons, make internal rather than external comparisons, make group-to-group comparisons, or avoid social comparisons altogether (see Berger et al., 1972; Hegtvedt, 1991b; Martin and Murray, 1983; see Hegtvedt, 1991b, and Suls and Wills, 1991, for a discussion of the factors affecting the choice of comparison objects). Finally, even if one knows what distribution rule individuals prefer and the types of social comparisons they make, it is still difficult to predict whether they will evaluate their interactions as equitable. Except in unambiguous situations of the type created in experiments, it is hard to predict what inputs and outcomes individuals will define as relevant, how they will weight those inputs and outcomes, and how they will evaluate themselves and others on those inputs and outcomes (Austin, 1977; Hegtvedt, 1991a; Messick and Sentis, 1979, 1983; Walster et al., 1973, 1978). Fortunately, however, the above three problems do not prohibit strain theory from taking advantage of certain of the insights from equity theory. While it is difficult to predict whether individuals will define their relationships as equitable, it is relatively easy to measure equity after the fact.

4. The stress literature has also focused on positive events, based on the assumption that such events might lead to stress by overloading the individual. Accumulating evidence, however, suggests that it is only undesirable events that lead to negative outcomes such as depression (e.g., Gersten et al., 1974; Kaplan et al., 1983; Pearlin et al., 1981; Thoits, 1983).

5. Certain individuals have criticized the stress literature for neglecting the failure of individuals to achieve positively valued goals. In particular, it has been charged that the stress literature has neglected "nonevents," or events that are desired or anticipated but do not occur (Dohrenwend and Dohrenwend, 1974; Thoits, 1983). One major distinction between the strain literature in criminology and the stress literature in medical sociology, in fact, is that the former has focused on "nonevents" while the latter has focused on "events."

6. Some researchers have argued that it is often difficult to distinguish the presenta-

tion of negative stimuli from the removal of positive stimuli (Michael, 1973; Van Houten, 1983; Zillman, 1979). Suppose, for example, that an adolescent argues with parents. Does this represent the presentation of negative stimuli (the arguing) or the removal of positive stimuli (harmonious relations with one's parents)? The point is a valid one, yet the distinction between the two types of strain still seems useful since it helps ensure that all major types of strain are considered by researchers.

7. This is a major theme in the psychological research on aggression, in much of the recent research on equity, and in the emotions literature, and it is a central theme in Cloward and Ohlin's (1960) strain theory (e.g., Averill, 1982; Berkowitz, 1982; R. Cohen, 1982; Crosby and Gonzales-Intal, 1984; Garrett and Libby, 1973; Kemper, 1978; Leventhal, 1976; Mark and Folger, 1984; Martin and Murray, 1984; Weiner, 1982; Zillman, 1979).

References

Adams, J. S. (1963). Toward an understanding of inequity. *Journal of Abnormal and Social Psychology, 67*, 422–436.

Adams, J. S. (1965). Inequity in social exchange. In L. Berkowitz (Ed.), *Advances in experimental social psychology*. New York: Academic Press.

Agnew, R. (1983). Social class and success goals: An examination of relative and absolute aspirations. *Sociological Quarterly, 24*, 435–452.

Agnew, R. (1984). Goal achievement and delinquency. *Sociology and Social Research, 68*, 435–451.

Agnew, R. (1985a). A revised strain theory of delinquency. *Social Forces, 64*, 151–167.

Agnew, R. (1985b). Neutralizing the impact of crime. *Criminal Justice and Behavior, 12*, 221–239.

Agnew, R. (1986). Challenging strain theory: An examination of goals and goal-blockage. Paper presented at the annual meeting of the American Society of Criminology, Atlanta.

Agnew, R. (1989). A longitudinal test of the revised strain theory. *Journal of Quantitative Criminology, 5*, 373–387.

Agnew, R. (1990). The origins of delinquent events: An examination of offender accounts. *Journal of Research in Crime and Delinquency, 27*, 267–294.

Agnew, R. (1991). Strain and subcultural crime theory. In J. Sheley (Ed.), *Criminology: A contemporary handbook*. Belmont, Calif.: Wadsworth.

Agnew, R., & Jones, D. (1988). Adapting to deprivation: An examination of inflated educational expectations. *Sociological Quarterly, 29*, 315–337.

Aiken, L. S., & West, S. G. (1991). *Multiple regression: Testing and interpreting interactions*. Newbury Park, Calif.: Sage.

Akers, R. L. (1985). *Deviant behavior: A social learning approach*. Belmont, Calif.: Wadsworth.

Alves, W. M., & Rossi, P. H. (1978). Who should get what? Fairness judgments of the distribution of earnings. *American Journal of Sociology, 84*, 541–564.

Anderson, C. A., & Anderson, D. C. (1984). Ambient temperature and violent crime: Tests of the linear and curvilinear hypotheses. *Journal of Personality and Social Psychology, 46*, 91–97.

Austin, W. (1977). Equity theory and social comparison processes. In J. M. Suls & R. L. Miller (Eds.), *Social comparison processes*. New York: Hemisphere.

Averill, J. R. (1982). *Anger and aggression*. New York: Springer-Verlag.

Bandura, A. (1973). *Aggression: A social learning analysis*. Englewood Cliffs, N.J.: Prentice-Hall.

Bandura, A. (1983). Psychological mechanisms of aggression. In R. G. Geen and E. Donnerstein (Eds.), *Aggression: Theoretical and empirical reviews*. New York: Academic Press.

Berger, J., Zelditch, M., Jr., Anderson, B., & Cohen, B. (1972). Structural aspects of distributive justice: A status-value formulation. In J. Berger, M. Zelditch, Jr., & B. Anderson (Eds.), *Sociological theories in progress*. New York: Houghton Mifflin.

Berkowitz, L. (1978). Whatever happened to the frustration-aggression hypothesis? *American Behavioral Scientist, 21*, 691–708.

Berkowitz, L. (1982). Aversive conditions as stimuli to aggression. In L. Berkowitz (Ed.), *Advances in experimental social psychology*, vol. 15. New York: Academic Press.

Bernard, T. J. (1984). Control criticisms of strain theories: An assessment of theoretical and empirical adequacy. *Journal of Research in Crime and Delinquency, 21*, 353–372.

Bernard, T. J. (1990). Angry aggression among the "truly disadvantaged." *Criminology, 28*, 73–96.

Blau, P. (1964). *Exchange and power in social life*. New York: Wiley.

Brewin, C. R. (1988). Explanation and adaptation in adversity. In S. Fisher & J. Reason (Eds.), *Handbook of life stress, cognition and health*. Chichester, England: Wiley.

Brickman, P., & Bulman, R. J. (1977). Pleasure and pain in social comparison. In J. M. Suls & R. L. Miller (Eds.), *Social comparison processes*. New York: Hemisphere.

Clarke, R. V., & Cornish, D. B. (1985). Modeling offenders' decisions: A framework for research and policy. In M. Tonry & N. Morris (Eds.), *Crime and justice: An annual review of research*, vol. 6. Chicago: University of Chicago Press.

Clinard, M. B. (1964). *Anomie and deviant behavior*. New York: Free Press.

Cloward, R. A., & Ohlin, L. E. (1960). *Delinquency and opportunity*. New York: Free Press.

Cohen, A. K. (1955). *Delinquent boys*. New York: Free Press.

Cohen, A. K. (1965). The sociology of the deviant act: Anomie theory and beyond. *American Sociological Review, 30*, 5–14.

Cohen, R. L. (1982). Perceiving justice: An attributional perspective. In J. Greenberg & R. L. Cohen (Eds.), *Equity and justice in social behavior*. New York: Academic Press.

Compas, B. E. (1987). Coping with stress during childhood and adolescence. *Psychological Bulletin, 101*, 393–403.

Compas, B. E., Malcarne, V. L., & Fondacaro, K. M. (1988). Coping with stressful events in older children and young adolescents. *Journal of Consulting and Clinical Psychology, 56*, 405–411.

Compas, B. E., & Phares, V. (1991). Stress during childhood and adolescence: Sources of risk and vulnerability. In E. M. Cummings, A. L. Greene, & K. H. Karraker (Eds.), *Life-span developmental psychology: Perspectives on stress and coping*. Hillsdale, N.J.: Erlbaum.

Cook, K. S., & Hegtvedt, K. A. (1983). Distributive justice, equity, and equality. *Annual Review of Sociology, 9*, 217–241.

Cook, K. S., & Hegtvedt, K. A. (1991). Empirical evidence of the sense of justice. In

M. Gruter, R. D. Masters, & M. T. McGuire (Eds.), *The sense of justice: An inquiry into the biological foundations of law.* New York: Greenwood Press.

Cook, K. S., & Messick, D. (1983). Psychological and sociological perspectives on distributive justice: Convergent, divergent, and parallel lines. In D. M. Messick & K. S. Cook (Eds.), *Equity theory: Psychological and sociological perspectives.* New York: Praeger.

Cook, K. S., & Yamagishi, T. (1983). Social determinants of equity judgments: The problem of multidimensional input. In D. M. Messick & K. S. Cook (Eds.), *Equity theory: Psychological and sociological perspectives.* New York: Praeger.

Crittenden, K. S. (1983). Sociological aspects of attribution. *Annual Review of Sociology, 9,* 425–446.

Crittenden, K. S. (1989). Causal attribution in sociocultural context: Toward a self-presentational theory of attribution processes. *Sociological Quarterly, 30,* 1–14.

Crosby, F., & Gonzales-Intal, A. M. (1984). Relative deprivation and equity theories: Felt injustice and the undeserved benefits of others. In R. Folger (Ed.), *The sense of injustice: Social psychological perspectives.* New York: Plenum.

Della Fave, L. R. (1980). The meek shall not inherit the earth: Self-evaluations and the legitimacy of stratification. *American Sociological Review, 45,* 955–971.

Deutsch, M. (1975). Equity, equality, and need: What determines which value will be used as the basis of distributive justice. *Journal of Social Issues, 31,* 137–149.

Dohrenwend, B. S., & Dohrenwend, B. P. (1974). Overview and prospects for research on stressful life events. In B. S. Dohrenwend & B. P. Dohrenwend (Eds.), *Stressful life events: Their nature and effects.* New York: Wiley.

Donnerstein, E., & Hatfield, E. (1982). Aggression and equity. In J. Greenberg & R. L. Cohen (Eds.), *Equity and justice in social behavior.* New York: Academic Press.

Edmunds, G., & Kendrick, D. C. (1980). *The measurement of human aggressiveness.* New York: Wiley.

Elliott, D., & Voss, H. (1974). *Delinquency and dropout.* Lexington, Mass.: Lexington Books.

Elliott, D., Huizinga, D., & Ageton, S. (1985). *Explaining delinquency and drug use.* Beverly Hills, Calif.: Sage.

Empey, L. (1956). Social class and occupational aspiration: A comparison of absolute and relative measurement. *American Sociological Review, 21,* 703–709.

Empey, L. (1982). *American delinquency: Its meaning and construction.* Homewood, Ill.: Dorsey.

Farnworth, M., & Leiber, M. J. (1989). Strain theory revisited: Economic goals, educational means, and delinquency. *American Sociological Review, 54,* 263–274.

Folger, R. (1984). Emerging issues in the social psychology of justice. In R. Folger (Ed.), *The sense of injustice: Social psychological perspectives.* New York: Plenum.

Folkman, S. (1991). Coping across the life-span: Theoretical issues. In E. M. Cummings, A. L. Greene, & K. H. Karraker (Eds.), *Life-span developmental psychology: Perspectives on stress and coping.* Hillsdale, N.J.: Erlbaum.

Garrett, J., & Libby, W. L., Jr. (1973). Role of intentionality in mediating responses to inequity in the dyad. *Journal of Personality and Social Psychology, 28,* 21–27.

Gersten, J. C., Langer, T. S., Eisenberg, J. G., & Ozek, L. (1974). Child behavior and life events: Undesirable change or change per se. In B. S. Dohrenwend & B. P. Dohrenwend (Eds.), *Stressful life events: Their nature and effects.* New York: Wiley.

Greenberg, D. F. (1977). Delinquency and the age structure of society. *Contemporary Crises, 1,* 189–223.

Gruder, C. L. (1977). Choice of comparison persons in evaluating oneself. In J. M. Suls & R. L. Miller (Eds.), *Social comparison processes.* New York: Hemisphere.

Hawkins, J. D., & Lishner, D. M. (1987). Schooling and delinquency. In E. H. Johnson (Ed.), *Handbook on crime and delinquency prevention.* New York: Greenwood.

Healy, W., & Bonner, A. F. (1969). *New light on delinquency and its treatment.* New Haven, Conn.: Yale University Press.

Hegtvedt, K. A. (1987). When rewards are scarce: Equal or equitable distributions. *Social Forces, 66,* 183–207.

Hegtvedt, K. A. (1990). The effects of relationship structure on emotional responses to inequity. *Social Psychology Quarterly, 53,* 214–228.

Hegtvedt, K. A. (1991a). Justice processes. In M. Foschi & E. J. Lawler (Eds.), *Group processes: Sociological analyses.* Chicago: Nelson-Hall.

Hegtvedt, K. A. (1991b). Social comparison processes. In E. F. Borgotta & M. E. Borgotta (Eds.), *Encyclopedia of sociology.* New York: Macmillan.

Hirschi, T. (1969). *Causes of delinquency.* Berkeley: University of California Press.

Hirschi, T. (1979). Separate and unequal is better. *Journal of Research in Crime and Delinquency, 16,* 34–38.

Hirschi, T., & Gottfredson, M. (1986). The distinction between crime and criminality. In T. F. Hartnagel & R. A. Silverman (Eds.), *Critique and explanation.* New Brunswick, N.J.: Transaction Books.

Hochschild, J. L. (1981). *What's fair: American beliefs about distributive justice.* Cambridge, Mass.: Harvard University Press.

Homans, G. C. (1961). *Social behavior: Its elementary forms.* New York: Harcourt, Brace, & World.

Hyman, H. (1953). The value systems of the different classes: A social-psychological contribution to the analysis of stratification. In R. Bendix & S. M. Lipset (Eds.), *Class, status, and power.* New York: Free Press.

Jasso, G., & Rossi, P. H. (1977). Distributive justice and earned income. *American Sociological Review, 42,* 639–651.

Jensen, G. (1986). Dis-integrating integrated theory: A critical analysis of attempts to save strain theory. Paper presented at the annual meeting of the American Society of Criminology, Atlanta.

Kaplan, H. B., Robbins, C., & Martin, S. S. (1983). Toward the testing of a general theory of deviant behavior in longitudinal perspective: Patterns of psychopathology. In J. R. Greenley & R. G. Simmons (Eds.), *Research in community and mental health.* Greenwich, Conn.: Jai Press.

Kemper, T. D. (1978). *A social interactional theory of emotions.* New York: Wiley.

Kluegel, J. R., & Smith, E. R. (1986). *Beliefs about inequality.* New York: Aldine De Gruyter.

Kornhauser, R. R. (1978). *Social sources of delinquency.* Chicago: University of Chicago Press.

Labouvie, E. W. (1986a). Alcohol and marijuana use in relation to adolescent stress. *International Journal of the Addictions, 21,* 333–345.

Labouvie, E. W. (1986b). The coping function of adolescent alcohol and drug use. In R. K. Silbereisen, K. Eyfeth, & G. Rudinger (Eds.), *Development as action in context.* New York: Springer.

Lauritsen, J. R., Sampson, R. J., & Laub, J. (1991). The link between offending and victimization among adolescents. *Criminology, 29,* 265–292.

Lerner, M. J. (1977). The justice motive: Some hypotheses as to its origins and forms. *Journal of Personality, 45,* 1–52.

Leventhal, G. S. (1976). The distribution of rewards and resources in groups and organizations. In L. Berkowitz & E. Walster (Eds.), *Advances in experimental social psychology: Equity theory: Toward a general theory of social interaction.* New York: Academic Press.

Leventhal, G. S., Karuzajr, J., & Fry, W. R. (1980). Beyond fairness: A theory of allocation preferences. In G. Mikula (Ed.), *Justice and social interaction.* New York: Springer-Verlag.

Linsky, A. S., & Straus, M. A. (1986). *Social stress in the United States.* Dover, Mass.: Auburn House.

Liska, A. E. (1987). *Perspectives on deviance.* Englewood Cliffs, N.J.: Prentice-Hall.

McClelland, K. (1990). The social management of ambition. *Sociological Quarterly, 31,* 225–251.

Mark, M. M., & Folger, R. (1984). Responses to relative deprivation: A conceptual framework. In P. Shaver (Ed.), *Review of personality and social psychology,* vol. 5. Beverly Hills, Calif.: Sage.

Martin, J., & Murray, A. (1983). Distributive injustice and unfair exchange. In D. M. Messick & K. S. Cook (Eds.), *Equity theory: Psychological and social perspectives.* New York: Praeger.

Martin, J., & Murray, A. (1984). Catalysts for collective violence: The importance of a psychological approach. In R. Folger (Ed.), *The sense of injustice: Social psychological perspectives.* New York: Plenum.

Mawson, A. R. (1987). *Criminality: A model of stress-induced crime.* New York: Praeger.

Merton, R. (1938). Social structure and anomie. *American Sociological Review, 3,* 672–682.

Messick, D. M., & Sentis, K. (1979). Fairness and preference. *Journal of Experimental Social Psychology, 15,* 418–434.

Messick, D. M., & Sentis, K. (1983). Fairness, preference, and fairness biases. In D. M. Messick & K. S. Cook (Eds.), *Equity theory: Psychological and sociological perspectives.* New York: Praeger.

Michael, J. (1973). Positive and negative reinforcement, a distinction that is no longer necessary; or a better way to talk about bad things. In E. Ramp & G. Semb (Eds.), *Behavior analysis: Areas of research and application.* Englewood Cliffs, N.J.: Prentice-Hall.

Mickelson, R. A. (1990). The attitude-achievement paradox among black adolescents. *Sociology of Education, 63,* 44–61.

Mikula, G. (1980). *Justice and social interaction.* New York: Springer-Verlag.

Mikula, G. (1986). The experience of injustice: Toward a better understanding of its phenomenology. In H. W. Bierhoff, R. L. Cohen, & J. Greenberg (Eds.), *Justice in social relations.* New York: Plenum.

Mirowsky, J., & Ross, C. E. (1990). The consolation-prize theory of alienation. *American Journal of Sociology, 95,* 1505–1535.

Mueller, C. W. (1983). Environmental stressors and aggressive behavior. In R. G. Geen & E. I. Donnerstein (Eds.), *Aggression: Theoretical and empirical reviews,* vol. 2. New York: Academic Press.

Newcomb, M. D., & Harlow, L. L. (1986). Life events and substance use among adolescents: Mediating effects of perceived loss of control and meaninglessness in life. *Journal of Personality and Social Psychology, 51*, 564–577.

Novy, D. M., & Donohue, S. (1985). The relationship between adolescent life stress events and delinquent conduct including conduct indicating a need for supervision. *Adolescence, 78*, 313–321.

Pearlin, L. I. (1982). The social contexts of stress. In L. Goldberger & S. Berznitz (Eds.), *Handbook of stress*. New York: Free Press.

Pearlin, L. I. (1983). Role strains and personal stress. In H. Kaplan (Ed.), *Psychosocial stress: Trends in theory and research*. New York: Academic Press.

Pearlin, L. I., & Schooler, C. (1978). The structure of coping. *Journal of Health and Social Behavior, 19*, 2–21.

Quicker, J. (1974). The effect of goal discrepancy on delinquency. *Social Problems, 22*, 76–86.

Rosenberg, M. (1979). *Conceiving the self*. New York: Basic Books.

Rosenberg, M. (1990). Reflexivity and emotions. *Social Psychology Quarterly, 53*, 3–12.

Ross, M., Thibaut, J., & Evenback, S. (1971). Some determinants of the intensity of social protest. *Journal of Experimental Social Psychology, 7*, 401–418.

Schwinger, T. (1980). Just allocations of goods: Decisions among three principles. In G. Mikula (Ed.), *Justice and social interaction*. New York: Springer-Verlag.

Shepelak, N. J. (1987). The role of self-explanations and self-evaluations in legitimating inequality. *American Sociological Review, 52*, 495–503.

Shepelak, N. J., & Alwin, D. (1986). Beliefs about inequality and perceptions of distributive justice. *American Sociological Review, 51*, 30–46.

Short, J. F., & Strodtbeck, F. L. (1965). *Group process and gang delinquency*. Chicago: University of Chicago Press.

Sprecher, S. (1986). The relationship between inequity and emotions in close relationships. *Social Psychology Quarterly, 49*, 309–321.

Stephenson, G. M., & White, J. H. (1968). An experimental study of some effects of injustice on children's moral behavior. *Journal of Experimental Social Psychology, 4*, 460–469.

Straus, M. (1991). Discipline and deviance: Physical punishment of children and violence and other crimes in adulthood. *Social Problems, 38*, 133–154.

Suls, J. M. (1977). Social comparison theory and research: An overview from 1954. In J. M. Suls & R. L. Miller (Eds.), *Social comparison processes*. New York: Hemisphere.

Suls, J. M., & Wills, T. A. (1991). *Social comparison: Contemporary theory and research*. Hillsdale, N.J.: Erlbaum.

Thibaut, J. W., & Kelley, H. H. (1959). *The social psychology of groups*. New York: Wiley.

Thoits, P. (1983). Dimensions of life events that influence psychological distress: An evaluation and synthesis of the literature. In H. B. Kaplan (Ed.), *Psychosocial stress: Trends in theory and research*. New York: Academic Press.

Thoits, P. (1984). Coping, social support, and psychological outcomes: The central role of emotion. In P. Shaver (Ed.), *Review of personality and social psychology, 5*, Beverly Hills, Calif.: Sage.

Thoits, P. (1989). The sociology of emotions. In W. R. Scott & J. Blake (Eds.), *Annual review of sociology*, vol. 15. Palo Alto, Calif.: Annual Reviews.

Thoits, P. (1990). Emotional deviance research. In T. D. Kemper (Ed.), *Research agendas in the sociology of emotions*. Albany: State University of New York Press.

Thoits, P. (1991a). On merging identity theory and stress research. *Social Psychology Quarterly, 54,* 101–112.

Thoits, P. (1991b). Patterns of coping with controllable and uncontrollable events. In E. M. Cummings, A. L. Greene, & K. H. Karraker (Eds.), *Life-span developmental psychology: Perspectives on stress and coping.* Hillsdale, N.J.: Erlbaum.

Utne, M. K., & Kidd, R. (1980). Equity and attribution. In G. Mikula (Ed.), *Justice and social interaction.* New York: Springer-Verlag.

Van Houten, R. (1983). Punishment: From the animal laboratory to the applied setting. In S. Axelrod & J. Apsche (Eds.), *The effects of punishment on human behavior.* New York: Academic Press.

Vaux, A., & Ruggiero, M. (1983). Stressful life change and delinquent behavior. *American Journal of Community Psychology, 11,* 169–183.

Walster, E., Berscheid, E., & Walster, G. W. (1973). New directions in equity research. *Journal of Personality and Social Psychology, 25,* 151–176.

Walster, E., Walster, G. W., & Berscheid, E. (1978). *Equity: Theory and research.* Boston: Allyn & Bacon.

Weiner, B. (1982). The emotional consequences of causal attributions. In M. S. Clark & S. T. Fiske (Eds.), *Affect and cognition: The seventeenth annual Carnegie symposium on cognition.* Hillsdale, N.J.: Erlbaum.

Williams, C. L., & Uchiyama, C. (1989). Assessment of life events during adolescence: The use of self-report inventories. *Adolescence, 24,* 95–118.

Wylie, R. (1979). *The self-concept,* vol. 2. Lincoln: University of Nebraska Press.

Zillman, D. (1979). *Hostility and aggression.* Hillsdale, N.J.: Erlbaum.

12

The Labeling Perspective and Delinquency: An Elaboration of the Theory and an Assessment of the Evidence

RAYMOND PATERNOSTER

LEEANN IOVANNI

Edwin Lemert (1976:244) may have stated the case best when he noted over a decade ago that "labelling theory seems to be largely an invention of its critics." He also observed acutely that after critics of the theory enumerate assumptions and derive hypotheses that labeling theorists themselves would not necessarily accept, "they proceed to demonstrate the logical, methodological and empirical insufficiencies of the theory" (1974:244). Consequently, labeling proponents are put in a precarious position because they "must deny or refute that which they haven't said or defend ideas that they don't necessarily share, or accept only with qualifications" (Lemert, 1974:244; see also Kitsuse, 1980).[1] This description seems to be an accurate account of the labeling theory of deviance in the area of juvenile delinquency.

The criticisms directed against labeling theory have come from two somewhat different positions. Some critics attack its apparent theoretical imprecision: its failure to conceptualize key constructs, the fact that it has not been presented in axiomatic form and therefore is not testable, or that its intervening links have been poorly specified (Gibbs, 1966, 1972; Gove, 1980; Wellford,

We are most grateful to the three anonymous reviewers of this chapter and to the editorial efforts of Frank Cullen.

1975). Other critics, undaunted by the supposed theoretical inadequacies, have managed to derive at least two major labeling propositions. When tested, however, these critics claim that the data generally have failed to provide any support for labeling theory, leading them to the conclusion that it shows a disappointing "fit to the facts" (Hagan, 1974; Hirschi, 1975, 1980; Tittle, 1975a; Wellford, 1975).

In judging the adequacy of any theory one certainly is obligated to examine both its theoretical clarity and any lack of fit between the theory and the set of facts it is intended to explain. To permit an empirical test, it is incumbent on proponents of labeling theory to provide an unambiguous rendition of the theory and to accept the "bad news" of empirical falsification should the theory and a given set of facts about delinquency (or other forms of deviance) not converge (Gouldner, 1976). That is both acceptable theory construction and sound science.

Unfortunately, empirical tests of the labeling perspective have been conducted with rather inelegant formulations of a complex theory. Such research often is based on simplistic, unconditional hypotheses that even the staunchest proponent of the labeling doctrine would support only with substantial qualification. Although these crude hypothesis tests may be partially attributable to labeling theorists' own overstatements and ambiguities (see Kitsuse and Spector, 1975), critics often have failed to comprehend the theory's subtleties. For the most part, empirical tests of labeling propositions have been conducted with grossly misrepresented hypotheses that are more caricature than characteristic of the theory.

The concern in this chapter is the relevance of labeling theory to the study of juvenile delinquency. Specifically, it will examine three issues. First, the origins of labeling theory in both a conflict and a symbolic interactionist tradition will be discussed briefly. These two more general theoretical traditions were separately instrumental in the development of two major premises of labeling theory: (1) that political/economic power determines *what* is labeled and *who* is labeled—the conflict tradition—and (2) that the experience of being labeled is instrumental in the creation of both a more deviant character and a more deviant lifestyle—the symbolic interactionist tradition. Second, after the two major labeling theory hypotheses (and possible contingent conditions) have been specified, the form that empirical tests for its falsification should take will be suggested. Finally, the extant literature will be reviewed to determine to what extent critics are addressing these issues or instead are addressing others of their own construction.

Theoretical Origins of Labeling Theory

Conflict Theory

In an early formulation of the labeling perspective, Becker (1963:121) noted that a critical question for any theory of deviance is "when are rules made and enforced." In seeking an answer to this two-pronged question, early labeling theorists broke from the "norm-based definition of deviance" (Kitsuse, 1980:384) adopted by most criminologists by considering the role of political and economic conflict in the norm creation process (Becker, 1963; Erickson, 1962; Goode, 1970; Kitsuse, 1963; Lofland, 1969). Regarding rule creation, Lofland (1969:14) defined deviance explicitly as a power struggle between contending parties: "Deviance is the name of the conflict game in which individuals or loosely organized small groups with little power are strongly feared by a well-organized, sizeable minority or majority who have a large amount of power." As for the second dimension, rule enforcement, Becker observed that a central feature of deviance is that it involves power:

> To the extent that a group has to impose its rules on other groups in the society, we are presented with a second question: Who can, in fact, force others to accept these rules and what are the causes of their success? This is, of course, a question of political and economic power . . . (1963:17–18).

The conflict orientation in labeling theory is manifested at several levels of analysis. Schur (1971:148–51) noted that conflict occurs at the levels of (1) collective rule making, (2) organizational processing, and (3) interpersonal relations. Conflict at the level of collective rule making occurs when economically and politically powerful groups use their influence to define as unlawful those behaviors that they find offensive, and direct their rule making against identified groups involved in those activities. Examples of work conducted at this level of conflict include Becker's (1963) analysis of the Marijuana Tax Act, Gusfield's (1963) account of the temperance movement, and Platt's (1969) history of the child-saving movement.

Conflict at the organizational level concerns the process of labeling and label negotiation in middle-level social control agencies. Here, labeling theorists argue that the powerlessness of particular groups (blacks, members of the lower class, and perhaps females) makes it more likely that they will be singled out for more severe labels (being arrested rather than dismissed by the police, being incarcerated rather than fined or put on probation by the courts). There is an abundance of empirical studies at this level of analysis (for reviews see Hagan, 1974; Kleck, 1981; Tittle, 1980; Tittle and Curran, 1988).

Conflict at the level of interpersonal relations concerns the bargaining over labels in day-to-day encounters, such as between the sighted and the blind (Scott, 1969), between the deformed or the mentally ill and "normals" (Goffman, 1961, 1963), and between the delinquent and the court worker (Cicourel, 1968). At all three levels, a deviant outcome is taken to be the result of conflict between individuals or collectivities of actors with differential power.

Symbolic Interactionism

Symbolic interactionism is a second general theoretical source to which the labeling theory of deviance can be traced. In addition to focusing on the creation and enforcement of rules discussed above, labeling theorists also examine the consequences of rule enforcement for those at whom labels are directed. This concern has led labeling theorists to examine the creation and elaboration of deviant "careers." A key theme within this perspective is the idea that efforts at social control actually may have counterproductive results. Social reactions or attempts "to do something about deviance" may produce a heightened commitment to the very behavior that enforcement agents are attempting to eradicate. This idea is expressed most clearly by Lemert's (1967:63) now famous notion of secondary deviance.

Contrary to many interpretations and operationalizations of this theoretical construct, the idea of secondary deviance does not imply an absolute (deterministic) position: If labeling by social control agencies occurs, then in all instances more deviance will result. Rather, it describes the conditions under which an initial flirtation with deviance *may* produce subsequent problems of adjustment for the individual. These problems *may* facilitate additional deviant involvement. Although the symbolic interactionist heritage of labeling theory will be described in greater detail in a later section, it is instructive to point out here that labeling theorists characterize societal reaction and the labeling process as comprising (1) a hostile social audience making negative attributions of character, which may also restrict the actor's access to normal activities and opportunities; (2) a supportive nondeviant audience, which may make nondeviant imputations about the actor and may allow the actor to disavow the negative ascriptions and keep open normal routines; and (3) a supportive deviant audience, which may make the actor's acceptance of a deviant role less isolating while opening up deviant routines and opportunities.

The Secondary Deviance Hypothesis

Consequences of Labeling

It is the symbolic interactionist tradition within labeling theory that leads to the conceptualization of the "stigmatizing" and "segregating" effects of social control efforts. Labeling theorists believe that the reaction of social control agents, through the application of a "deviant" label, results in the actor's being typified or "cast" as a deviant (Garfinkel, 1956; Matza, 1969; Scheff, 1966). As a consequence of this typification process, the actor's identity is *simplified* to the extent that the deviant identity comes to be of primary importance and is considered to reflect the "essential" self. Simultaneously, other properties of the actor's character assume a secondary descriptive value; deviant ascription becomes a "master status" and "the deviant identi-fication becomes the controlling one" (Becker, 1963:33–34).

The process of typification or identity attribution has been outlined suc-cinctly by Hawkins and Tiedeman (1975:89–96) and needs only summariza-tion here. Briefly, when others perceive that the actor is aware of the consequences of his or her action and is willing to follow through on that action, *intent* on the part of the actor is implied by others (Jones and Davis, 1965). As suggested by Kelley (1967:208–9), this ascription of deviant mo-tives is facilitated and made particularly endurable as indicative of essential character whenever the actions of the individual at issue are atypical: "the fewer distinctive reasons a person might have for an action . . . the more informative that action is concerning the characteristics of that person." Thus, the deviant behavior becomes quintessential material for others in their ascription of motives to an actor. The ascription of deviant motives, however, is not limited to one facet of the actor's character. As Scott (1972:14) pointed out, this imputation process has an "essentializing" function in that motives become indicative of the actor's *essential* or *real self*. Through the motive ascription process, then, the actor becomes typified or labeled as an essential deviant. Once the actor is typed—labeled a deviant—the processes of stigmatization and segregation described by Lemert (1972) begin.

The central concern of labeling theorists in this tradition is, "What hap-pens to the individual after being labeled?" According to these theorists, being typified or labeled as a deviant has three main consequences: alter-ation of personal identity, exclusion from conventional opportunities, and an increase in the probability of further deviance. None is inevitable, how-ever, and they are not determined solely by those who impute the label. Figure 12.1 portrays the process leading to possible secondary deviance ef-fects. It shows, first of all, that the imposition of a label is unlikely to lead to secondary deviance if that fact is kept private. Not all instances of labeling are disclosed fully to others in the actors' social environment: Those appre-hended or arrested by the police may be released without further action; some hearings (juvenile) may be closed to the general public; and some of-fenders may be able to hide their label (drunken driver, shoplifter) from all but intimate others. Consequently, these instances of labeling would be unlikely to result in exclusion from the normal routines of life. If the actors' deviant status is generally broadcast, however (a successful "status degrada-tion ceremony," Garfinkel, 1957), it becomes *more likely* that they will face the exclusionary practices of others.

Although exclusion from the normal routines of life is a more likely out-come of a publicly known label than of a label kept private, it is not inevita-ble. Rather than accepting the deviant label as indicative of the actor's essential character, others instead may accept a different view (an under-standing of character known and accepted before the labeling) and may at-tempt to neutralize the consequences of negative character attribution by

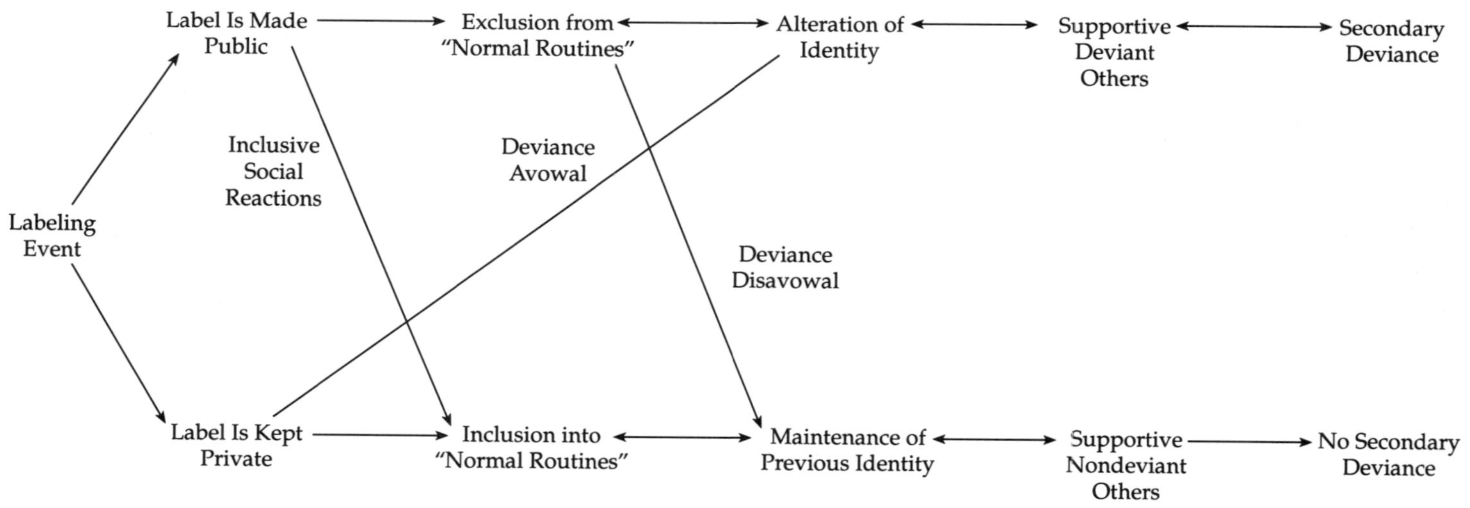

Figure 12.1 Processes Leading to Greater Probability of Secondary Deviance

what Orcutt (1973:260) calls "inclusive reactions." These inclusive social reactions are "attempts to control rule infractions by bringing the present or future behavior of the rule-breaker into conformity with the rules of the group without excluding him from it." It is possible, then, that others close to the labeled deviant can neutralize the consequences of the label by keeping the person within the group, thereby assisting in the maintenance of normal identity (see also Roman and Trice, 1971).

Figure 12.1 also suggests that even if the label is made public and one finds oneself excluded from many of the normal routines of life, the internalization of a deviant identity, though difficult to resist, is not an inevitable consequence. Though this phenomenon is ignored in much criminological writing from the social reaction perspective, it has been noted in the general deviance literature that labeled actors may resist or refuse to concur in others' judgment about their own deviant character. Davis (1961:120) refers to this process as *deviance disavowal* and defines it as a "refusal of those who are viewed as deviant to concur in the verdict"; if they do concur, "they usually place a very different interpretation on the fact or allegations than do their judges." Examples of these attempts at deviance disavowal include efforts by one's spouse to deny that the aberrant behavior of the other is indicative of mental illness (Sampson, Messinger, and Towne, 1962; Yarrow, Schwartz, Murphy, and Deasy, 1955) or of alcoholism (Jackson, 1954). Some of these attempts at deviance disavowal may be successful in that the actors may continue to be seen and to see themselves as "essentially normal" (or at least as not deviant in the way alleged), and may maintain their previous identity. If these deviance disavowal processes are activated and are successful, secondary deviance, as a solution to problems of adjustment, would be unlikely. Figure 12.1 also suggests that even in the case of exclusionary reactions from others and an alteration of identity toward one more consistent with the imputed label, secondary deviance is unlikely to occur unless the actor finds the company of others who both support and exemplify the deviant status.

The contingent nature of the labeling process can also be seen in the many routes to secondary deviance. At one level, Figure 12.1 suggests that secondary deviance is contingent on (1) the public nature of the label, (2) exclusionary reactions by others, (3) an alteration of personal identity, and (4) support from deviant others. Each one of these contingent conditions would have to be met in order to make further rule breaking a likely outcome of imposing a deviant label.

Figure 12.1 also shows that just as some persons may disavow the imposition of a deviant label, others may court such an identity. Turner (1972:308) used the term *deviance avowal* to refer to the process by which persons seek, accept, and identify with a deviant label. Finally, Figure 12.1 reveals clearly the reciprocal nature of the labeling process. Exclusive social reactions from others are likely to lead to an alteration of personal identity and to a closer affinity with deviant others. Such closer association with supportive deviants may lead in turn to additional exclusion (likely also as a result of intentional choice on the actor's part) and to a further recasting of self in line with the deviant label.

This process should make clear that escalation to secondary deviance rests heavily on the subjective effects of being labeled; that is, the labeling experience serves to recast individuals *in their own eyes* as well as in the eyes of others. From the standpoint of labeling theory, the individual faces the objective circumstance of the ascription of the deviant label and *may* begin to perceive himself as others have labeled him. This is not to say that the ascription of the deviant identity *determines* an individual's subjective reality. Rather, the identity construction process relies both on the objective information we receive from others and our subjective interpretation of that information.

Understanding this alteration of personal identity raises the question posed by Berger and Luckmann (1966:18; see also Berger, 1963): "How is it possible that subjective meanings become objective facticities?" or, for the present purpose, "How does the labeling experience become subjectively meaningful, resulting in the objective fact of the deviant career?" In pursuing this question, Blumer (1969) offered an illuminating discussion of George Herbert Mead on the self, the act, and social interaction. Blumer (1969:63) noted that Mead saw the self as a *reflexive* process, not merely as a psychological or personality structure:

> This reflexive process takes the form of the person making indications to himself, that is to say, noting things and determining their significance for his line of action. To indicate something is to stand over against it and to put oneself in the position of acting toward it instead of automatically responding to it . . . With the mechanism of self-interaction the human being ceases to be a responding organism where behavior is a product of what plays upon him from the outside, the inside or both.

Mead moved away from the deterministic view of traditional sociology and social psychology that prevailed during his time (represented most notably by Charles Horton Cooley), which saw human actors as a "mere medium for the operation of factors that produce behavior." Rather, Mead believed that human beings "act toward their world" on the basis of what they interpret and what is subjectively meaningful for them.

This definition of self as a process enables persons to maintain an active role in creating their own identities, deviant or conventional, in that it portrays human beings as self-determining agents who create their behavior with varying degrees of freedom and success. When actors are the recipient of a deviant label, they must assign meaning to that label in terms of their own understanding. Berger and Luckmann (1966:129) referred to this action as a process of internalization, "the immediate apprehension of an objective event as expressing meaning, that is, as a manifestation of another's subjective processes which thereby becomes subjectively meaningful to [the individual]."

Lemert (1972:65) explained this internalization process in terms of stigmatization, which he described as more than the formal action of "attaching visible signs of moral inferiority to persons." Individuals may or may not view their actions as inherently wrong, and may be capable of rationalizing them away (Davis's [1961] notion of deviance disavowal). Sometimes, however, rule infractions subject the individual to the opinions of the larger society. Confrontation with consistent opinions more numerous and more vocal than one's own may reduce the actor's confidence in an earlier understanding of self. This self-doubt may lead one in turn to entertain the reality of the newly ascribed identity. Of course, there is nothing inherently one-sided in this process; a recognition that identities are "socially bestowed" is not a tacit denial of the actors' capacities to resist such bestowal but only acknowledges the difficulties of such resistance.[2]

Schur (1971:69–70) refers to this individual-level process of identity transformation as *role engulfment*. Being typified by others as a deviant, then, may have two distinct consequences for the actor's self: One may view oneself as others do (as a deviant), and one may begin to perceive the self in a less favorable light, as less worthy. The "success" of this stigmatization or signification process as described by labeling theorists in the transformation of the individual's subjective reality is hastened and made easier by the objective effects of labeling. Berger and Luckmann (1966:157) noted that for successful alteration or resocialization "the most important social condition is the availability of an effective plausibility structure, that is a social base serving as a 'laboratory' of transformation." For labeling theory, the deviant identity is made even more plausible when the actor's access to conventional (normal) roles and opportunities becomes problematic (see Lofland's [1969] discussion of normal versus deviant hardware, places, and others).

Even in the absence of any physical and obvious forms of separation, such as those due to incarceration, once the actor is cast as generally deviant, he or she remains susceptible to exclusion from interactions with "normals." As Goffman (1963) observed, "normal" others, wishing to avoid "guilt by associating" with a known deviant, tend to structure situations so as to avoid encounters with these deviant others. Not only may the deviant actor be barred explicitly and implicitly from social interactions with normal others; such a person may also be barred from conventional opportunities, i.e., legitimate avenues of goal attainment. The essential character of the deviant label, then, may have the effect of curtailing the actor's interactions with normal others and his access to conventional opportunities. This exclusion in turn may fix the deviant identity more securely in the individual's (and others') mind.

The interaction process ultimately *may* result in the actor's involvement in secondary deviance; in that case, as Berger and Luckmann describe, subjective reality becomes objective fact for the individual and for the larger society. As Blumer notes with regard to behavior in general, however, secondary deviance is not determined in a one-sided fashion by the labeling experience. The actor, through interpretation and definition, is self-determining: "Action is built up in coping with the world instead of merely being released from a pre-existing psychological structure" (Blumer, 1969:64). For the actors secondary deviance becomes a direct response to problems created by the societal reaction to their deviance. When viewed as a problematic, contingent response to the application of a label, secondary deviance is both an attempt to cope meaningfully with the problems of a newly acquired identity and an expression of that identity. Though volition has limitations and restrictions, nowhere is the actor denied participation in the process of creating meaningful behavior (see Figure 12.1).

Review of Available Research: Secondary Deviance

As mentioned previously, the causal component of labeling theory entails three main consequences: alteration of personal identity, exclusion from conventional opportunities, and an increase in the probability of further deviance. Further, these consequences constitute a causal and contingent process with stigmatizing and exclusionary effects that act as intervening variables in the escalation to secondary deviance. The existing empirical literature, however, is limited to research that addresses these effects separately; in the case of the first two effects, tests have not necessarily been performed in a labeling context.

Some research has examined personal identity, in terms of both deviant identity (Ageton and Elliott, 1974; Eynon, Allen, and Reckless, 1971; Gibbs, 1974; Jensen, 1972; Thomas and Bishop, 1984) and self-worth (Gibbs, 1974; Harris, 1976; Jensen, 1972; Tittle, 1972). Taken as a whole, the results are inconsistent with labeling theory but not entirely contradictory. This is also true of research addressing the limitation on the actor's access to conventional others and opportunities. Studies have examined both the objective nature (Boshier and Johnson, 1974; Buikhuisen and Dijksterhuis, 1971; Fisher, 1972; Schwartz and Skolnick, 1962) and the subjective nature (Baum and Wheeler, 1968; Harris, 1975; Short, Rivera, and Tennyson, 1965; Snyder, 1971; Foster, Dinitz, and Reckless, 1972) of this effect.[3]

Of particular concern here are purported tests of the impact of labeling on secondary deviance (Farrington, 1977; Fisher and Erickson, 1973; Gold and Williams, 1969; Klein, 1974; McEachern, 1968; Meade, 1974; Thomas, 1977; Thomas and Bishop, 1984; Thornberry, 1971). Research of this nature generally examines the effect of varying sanction levels on behavior. Most of this research has contributed unjustifiably to the demise of labeling theory; by failing to consider the requisite intervening effects, the bulk of these studies do not constitute a valid test of labeling theory.

In addition, many of the tests that have been conducted are of questionable methodological rigor for several reasons. First of all, most tests of the labeling model use a relatively atypical sanction as the independent variable. In testing labeling theory, most studies examine recidivism within groups of youths subject to different types or degrees of sanction, such as juvenile court appearance, probation, or incarceration (Farrington, 1977; Gibbs, 1974; Harris, 1975, 1976; Thomas and Bishop, 1984; Tittle, 1972). What has been ignored until now is the labeling effect both of informal (unofficial) sanctions and of control agent activities experienced by a larger share of the population. With respect to the latter, the sievelike character of the juvenile justice system has been noted frequently (Empey, 1978; Nettler, 1978); when one takes for study a group that appears at the end of a long series of discretionary decisions, it is reasonable that the labeling process has run its course by that time. Having already experienced a repudiation of character and an exclusion from the normal routines of life, the "hard core" offenders may be immune to additional labeling effects. In addition, because only a small proportion of deviants undergo these experiences, it may be more germane from both a theoretical and a policy standpoint to examine the consequences of an experience common to a larger number of juveniles, such as encounters with the police. To date there has been little study of the possible effects of this more prevalent label (Ageton and Elliott, 1974; Jensen, 1972; Thomas and Bishop, 1984).

Second, much of the existing research has been concerned mainly with relative labeling effects rather than with absolute effects. In their discussion of deterrence, Zimring and Hawkins (1973) differentiated between these two conceptually distinct phenomena. Relative labeling effects concern the difference (in terms of secondary deviance) between two types of labels or degrees of labeling (probation versus incarceration, for example), while absolute labeling effects concern the difference between those who are labeled and those who are not. Labeling researchers traditionally have examined the behavioral effects of variations in labeling, assuming that the more severe the legal disposition, the greater the impact of labeling (Fisher and Erickson, 1973; Klein, 1974; McEachern, 1968; Meade, 1974; Thornberry, 1971; Tittle, 1975a), with generally inconclusive results. Although research along this line is worth considering, it should be noted that there have been few comparisons between an unlabeled group and a labeled group; those comparisons that have been conducted are generally more supportive of labeling theory predictions (Farrington, 1977; Gold, 1970; Thomas, 1977).

One recent example of the kind of research strategy that should be pursued further was published by Palamara, Cullen, and Gersten (1986). They examined the effect of police and mental health interventions on the postintervention delinquent and problem behavior of a sample of youths who had had no prior contact with the police at the time when the study began. Controlling for preintervention behavior, they found (1986:96) that in comparison with those youths not labeled, "acquiring a criminal record significantly affects subsequent levels of both delinquency and general psychological impairment."

The theoretical import of these findings is substantial. To say that one type of label has little additional effect on secondary deviance in relation to another is *not* to say that it has *no* deviance-generating effects at all. As already noted, it is doubtful that further increments in labeling will continue to produce further deviance; a "leveling off" point may be reached, where the process is at equilibrium. A failure to find evidence for incremental effects on secondary deviance is also to be expected theoretically. Personal identity may show continual decline, but once an actor is excluded from major conventional life situations it is not unreasonable to assume that further exclusion would have little additional meaning (Harris, 1976). This assumption would suggest that a clearly drawn conceptual distinction be maintained between absolute labeling effects (the effect of any label versus no label) and relative labeling effects (the effect of different types of labels).

A third limitation of past labeling models is that they were formulated simplistically—so simplistically that we would agree with Tittle's assessment (1975a:112) that they have "almost invited empirical negation." The traditional specification of the labeling process tends toward an unconditional "self-fulfilling prophecy model" (Becker, 1963) wherein the actor, once labeled a deviant, invariably internalizes the deviant label, perceives conventional avenues as closed to him, and becomes more deviant. Although labeling theorists themselves have contributed at times to this simplistic specification (Becker most notably), it is apparent from both early and more recent formulations that a more complex model of the labeling process is in order.

There are exceptions to this general trend, however; most notable is the recent research of Thomas and Bishop (1984). These authors cast their test of the secondary deviance hypothesis in terms of a causal sequence, with sanctions predicted as causing a change in delinquent behavior over time through an intervening process (alteration of self-conceptions). A proper test of the labeling model, specifying the intervening events in the causal process, would also entail an elucidation of the conditions under which social control has a labeling effect and the conditions under which no effect or a deterrent effect is observed (Tittle, 1975b; Tittle and Curran, 1988). The labeling literature contains evidence suggesting various class, race, and social psychological contingencies of the labeling process (Ageton and Elliott, 1974; Harris, 1976; Jensen, 1972), suggesting that just as the effects of status characteristics on juvenile justice decision making are not invariant, there is no uniform effect of public labeling.

The Revitalization of a Labeling Theory of Delinquency

What is the purpose of this extended discussion of the theoretical components of a labeling theory of delinquency and this review of the extant literature? What implications does it have for future work in this area? Hopefully, this chapter has shown that critics and those who work and write in the area of juvenile delinquency have understood the labeling perspective poorly and, as a result, have dismissed it prematurely. Ultimately we argue for a revitalization of labeling theory, a renaissance of the perspective. We hope this will take the form of a reworked version of traditional labeling theory arguments and an interest in putting the resulting theoretical framework to empirical test. This chapter has tried to suggest some of the components that such a neolabeling theory should have and to describe some of its unavoidable complexities, but this is certainly not the only formulation, or the most elegant. It is merely intended to be a starting point.

This effort need not be pursued completely in the dark. One successful revitalization effort, currently under way in the area of labeling theory and mental illness, can serve as a guide. Link and his colleagues (Link, 1987; Link, Cullen, Frank, and Wozniak, 1987; Link, Cullen, Struening, Shrout, and Dohrenwend, 1989) have developed and tested what they call a "modified" labeling theory. Briefly, this restatement of labeling theory follows closely the recommendations suggested in the present chapter. The modified labeling theory presented by Link et al. (1982, 1989) is highly critical of previous conceptualizations of the effects of a "mental patient" label. In two statements of this position, Link (1982:96, 1987) noted that previous statements overemphasized the "etiological aspects of labeling" to the neglect of specifying the intervening causal mechanisms through which ex-mental patients experience problems of adjustment because of their label.

In fact, labeling theory and research in this area, as well as critics' reactions to both, parallel the developments in juvenile delinquency. Commentators (Gove, 1970, 1980, 1982; Weinstein, 1983) have chosen to direct their critical work toward the more extreme positions of labeling theorists; they have taken the absence of any strong empirical support for such strong positions as reason enough to dismiss the salience of labels for persons adjusting to the problems of being an ex-mental patient. As was true for critics of labeling theory in delinquency, those working in mental health have concluded similarly that stigmatizing labels "[do] not appear to pose a severe problem" (Gove, 1982:280).

Link et al.'s presentation of a modified labeling theory, however, is a significant movement beyond simplistic assertions about labeling effects. Theirs is a complex causal model that links collectively held understandings about mental patients, a devalued role whose occupants experience discriminatory treatment, with a social psychological state of demoralization and with "real" problems of adjustment such as social isolation and employment difficulties. Link and his colleagues, then, specified more clearly the mechanisms intervening between the ascription of a mental illness label and subsequent problems of adjustment. In addition, they specified important contingent conditions of this process, such as the degree to which certain segments of the population perceive mental patients as dangerous persons (see Link et al., 1987). The utility of Link's and his colleagues' efforts for those working in juvenile delinquency is not only that they have presented an elaborate causal process of labeling effects; they have also begun an ambitious research effort to test various components of the overall model, with much success to date. They have demonstrated vividly that previous dismissals of labeling theory, which were based on stock caricatures of the societal reaction position, were premature, and that a complex version more faithful to the theory may have much more empirical support.

Notes

1. This is not a particularly original observation. In a 1978 article, Cullen and Cullen made a similar point concerning the critics of labeling theory rejecting theoretical positions that even the most ardent proponent would not assume without qualification: "The critiques of labeling theory are typically leveled against positions which have either never been held or held only by the most extreme and naive labeling theorist" (1978:28). In a perfectly apt phrase borrowed from Goode's (1973:64) discussion of functionalism's critics, they referred to this as "the empty castle phenomenon"; the structure is undefended because "there is no one inside against which [the] engines of war are mounted."

2. For years, labeling theory has had the undeserved reputation of being overdeterministic. This criticism has persisted even though the progeny of much labeling writing is symbolic interactionism, which emphasizes human will as a directing force in action. In part this reputation was created by labeling theorists themselves, for their sometimes one-sided portrayal of the role of the state and state agencies in creating deviant careers. To a large degree, however, the claim that labeling theorists denuded human activity of purpose and meaning was made by influential critics, such as Ronald Akers (1967:46) in his early critique of the new "societal reaction" school: "One sometimes gets the impression from reading this literature that people go about minding their business, and then—'wham'—bad society comes along and slaps them with a stigmatized label. Forced into the role of deviant the individual has little choice but to be deviant."

3. As will be suggested later in this chapter, delinquency researchers can learn from a recent reinterpretation of labeling theory by those in the mental health field. Research by Link and his colleagues (Link, 1982, 1987; Link et al., 1987, 1989) shows that the label "mental patient" carries stigmatization, as well as subsequent feelings of inferiority and of diminished objective and subjective opportunities.

References

Ageton, S., & Elliott, D. S. (1974). The effect of legal processing on delinquent orientation. *Social Problems, 22,* 87–100.

Akers, R. (1967). Problems in the sociology of deviance: Social definitions and behavior. *Social Forces, 46,* 455–65.

Baum, M., & Wheeler, S. (1968). Becoming an inmate. In S. Wheeler (Ed.), *Controlling delinquents* (pp. 153–85). New York: Wiley.

Becker, H. S. (1963). *Outsiders*. New York: Free Press.

Bell, D., Jr., & Lang, K. (1985). The intake dispositions of juvenile offenders. *Journal of Research in Crime and Delinquency, 22,* 309–28.

Berger, P. L. (1963). *Invitation to sociology: A humanistic perspective.* New York: Doubleday.

Berger, P. L., & Luckmann, T. (1966). *The social construction of reality.* New York: Doubleday.

Blumer, H. (1969). *Symbolic interactionism.* Englewood Cliffs, N.J.: Prentice-Hall.

Boshier, R., & Johnson, D. (1974). Does conviction affect employment opportunities? *British Journal of Criminology, 14,* 262.

Buikhuisen, W., & Dijksterhuis, P. H. (1971). Delinquency and stigmatization. *British Journal of Criminology, 11,* 185–87.

Cicourel, A. (1968). *The social organization of juvenile justice.* New York: Wiley.

Cullen, F. T., & Cullen, J. B. (1978). *Toward a paradigm of labeling theory.* Monograph No. 58. Lincoln: University of Nebraska Press.

Davis, F. (1961). Deviance disavowal: The management of strained interaction by the visibly handicapped. *Social Problems, 9,* 120–32.

Empey, L. T. (1978). *American delinquency.* Homewood, Ill.: Dorsey.

Erickson, K. T. (1962). Notes on the sociology of deviance. *Social Problems, 9,* 307–14.

Eynon, T., Allen, H. E., & Reckless, W. C. (1971). Measuring impact of a juvenile correctional institution by perceptions of inmates and staff. *Journal of Research in Crime and Delinquency, 8,* 93–107.

Farrington, D. P. (1977). The effects of public labelling. *British Journal of Criminology, 17,* 112–25.

Fisher, G. A., & Erickson, M. L. (1973). An assessment of the effects of official reactions to juvenile delinquency. *Journal of Research in Crime and Delinquency, 10,* 177–94.

Fisher, S. (1972). Stigma and deviant careers in school. *Social Problems, 20,* 78–83.

Foster, J. D., Dinitz, S., & Reckless, W. C. (1972). Perceptions of stigma following intervention for delinquent behavior. *Social Problems, 20,* 202–9.

Garfinkel, H. (1956). Conditions of successful degradation ceremonies. *American Journal of Sociology, 61,* 420–24.

Gibbs, J. P. (1966). Conceptions of deviant behavior: The old and the new. *Pacific Sociological Review, 9,* 9–14.

Gibbs, J. P. (1972). Issues in defining deviant behavior. In R. A. Scott & J. D. Douglas (Eds.), *Theoretical perspectives on deviance* (pp. 39–68). New York: Basic Books.

Gibbs, J. P. The effects of juvenile legal procedures on juvenile offenders' self-attitudes. *Journal of Research in Crime and Delinquency, 11,* 51–55.

Goffman, E. (1961). *Asylums.* New York: Doubleday.

Goffman, E. (1963). *Stigma.* Englewood Cliffs, N.J.: Prentice-Hall.

Gold, M. (1970). *Delinquent behavior in an American city.* Belmont, Calif.: Brooks/Cole.

Gold, M., & Williams, J. R. (1969). National study of the aftermath of apprehension. *Prospectus, 3,* 3–19.

Goode, E. (1970). *The marijuana smokers.* New York: Basic Books.

Goode, W. J. (1973). Functionalism: The empty castle. In *Explorations in social theory* (pp. 64–94). New York: Oxford University Press.

Gouldner, A. W. (1976). The dark side of the dialectic: Toward a new objectivity. *Sociological Inquiry, 46*, 3–15.

Gove, W. R. (1970). Societal reaction as an explanation of mental illness: An evaluation. *American Sociological Review, 35*, 873–84.

Gove, W. R. (1980). The labelling perspective: An overview. In W. R. Gove (Ed.), *The labelling of deviance* (2nd ed.) (pp. 9–33). Beverly Hills, Calif.: Sage.

Gove, W. R. (1982). The current status of the labelling theory of mental illness. In W. R. Gove (Ed.), *Deviance and mental illness* (pp. 273–300). Beverly Hills, Calif.: Sage.

Gusfield, J. R. (1963). *Symbolic crusade: Politics and the American temperance movement.* Urbana, Ill.: University of Illinois Press.

Hagan, J. (1974). Extra-legal attributes and criminal sentencing: An assessment of a sociological viewpoint. *Law and Society Review, 8*, 357–83.

Harris, A. R. (1975). Imprisonment and the expected value of criminal choice: A specification of the labeling perspective. *American Sociological Review, 40*, 71–87.

Harris, A. R. (1976). Race, commitment to deviance and spoiled identity. *American Sociological Review, 41*, 432–42.

Hawkins, R., & Tiedeman, G. (1975). *The creation of deviance.* Columbus, Ohio: Merrill.

Hirschi, T. (1975). Labeling theory and juvenile delinquency: An assessment of the evidence. In W. R. Gove (Ed.), *The labelling of deviance* (pp. 181–203). New York: Wiley.

Hirschi, T. (1980). Labelling theory and juvenile delinquency: An assessment of the evidence. In W. R. Gove (Ed.), *The labelling of deviance* (2nd ed.) (pp. 271–93). Beverly Hills, Calif.: Sage.

Jackson, J. K. (1954). The adjustment of the family to the crisis of alcoholism. *Quarterly Journal of Studies on Alcohol, 15*, 562–86.

Jensen, G. F. (1972). Delinquency and adolescent self-conceptions: A study of the personal relevance of infraction. *Social Problems, 20*, 84–103.

Jones, E. E., & Davis, K. E. (1965). From acts to dispositions: The attribution process in person perception. In L. Berkowitz (Ed.), *Advances in experimental social psychology,* vol. 2 (pp. 220–66). New York: Academic Press.

Kelley, H. H. (1967). Attribution theory in social psychology. In D. Levine (Ed.), *Nebraska symposium on motivation.* Lincoln: University of Nebraska Press.

Kitsuse, J. (1962). Societal reaction to deviant behavior: Problems of theory and method. *Social Problems, 9*, 247–56.

Kitsuse, J. (1980). The new conception of deviance and its critics. In W. R. Gove (Ed.), *The labelling of deviance* (2nd ed.) (pp. 381–91). Beverly Hills, Calif.: Sage.

Kleck, G. (1981). Racial discrimination in criminal sentencing: A critical evaluation of the evidence with additional evidence on the death penalty. *American Sociological Review, 46*, 783–805.

Klein, M. W. (1974). Labeling, deterrence and recidivism: A study of police dispositions of juvenile offenders. *Social Problems, 22*, 292–303.

Lemert, E. M. (1967). *Human deviance, social problems, and social control.* Englewood Cliffs, N.J.: Prentice-Hall.

Lemert, E. M. (1972). *Human deviance, social problems, and social control* (2nd ed.). Englewood Cliffs, N.J.: Prentice-Hall.

Lemert, E. M. (1974). Beyond Mead: The societal reaction to deviance. *Social Problems, 21*, 457–68.

Lemert, E. M. (1976). Response to critics, feedback and choice. In L. Coser & O. Larsen (Eds.), *The uses of controversy in sociology* (pp. 244–49). New York: Macmillan.

Link, B. (1982). Mental patient status, work and income: An examination of the effects of a psychiatric label. *American Sociological Review, 47,* 202–15.

Link, B. (1987). Understanding labeling effects in the area of mental disorders: An empirical assessment of the effects of expectations of rejection. *American Sociological Review, 52,* 96–112.

Link, B., Cullen, F. T., Frank, J., & Wozniak, J. F. (1987). The social rejection of former mental patients: Understanding why labels matter. *American Journal of Sociology, 92,* 1461–1500.

Link, B., Cullen, F. T., Struening, E., Shrout, P. E., & Dohrenwend, B. P. (1989). A modified labeling theory approach to mental disorders: An empirical assessment. *American Sociological Review, 54,* 400–23.

Lofland, J. (1969). *Deviance and identity.* Englewood Cliffs, N.J.: Prentice-Hall.

Matza, D. (1969). *Becoming deviant.* Englewood Cliffs, N.J.: Prentice-Hall.

McEachern, A. W. (1968). The juvenile probation system. *American Behavioral Scientist, 11,* 1.

Meade, A. C. (1974). The labeling approach to delinquency: State of the theory as a function of method. *Social Forces, 53,* 83–91.

Nettler, G. (1978). *Explaining crime.* New York: McGraw-Hill.

Orcutt, J. D. (1973). Societal reaction and the response to deviation in small groups. *Social Forces, 52,* 259–67.

Palamara, F., Cullen, F. T., & Gersten, J. C. (1986). The effect of police and mental health intervention on juvenile deviance: Specifying contingencies in the impact of formal reaction. *Journal of Health and Social Behavior, 27,* 90–105.

Platt, A. (1969). *The child savers.* Chicago: University of Chicago Press.

Roman, P. M., & Trice, H. M. (1971). Normalization: A neglected component to labeling theory. Paper presented at the annual meeting of the American Sociological Association, Denver.

Sampson, H., Messinger, S. L., & Towne, R. D. (1962). Family processes and becoming a mental patient. *American Journal of Sociology, 68,* 88–96.

Sampson, R. J. (1986). Effects of socioeconomic context on official reaction to juvenile delinquency. *American Sociological Review, 51,* 876–85.

Scheff, T. H. (1966). *Becoming mentally ill.* Chicago: Aldine.

Schur, E. M. (1971). *Labeling deviant behavior.* New York: Harper & Row.

Schwartz, R. D., & Skolnick, J. H. (1962). Two studies of legal stigma. *Social Problems, 10,* 133–42.

Scott, R. A. (1969). *The making of blind men.* New York: Russell Sage.

Scott, R. A. (1972). A proposed framework for analyzing deviance as a property of social order. In R. A. Scott & J. D. Douglas (Eds.), *Theoretical perspectives on deviance* (pp. 3–35). New York: Basic Books.

Short, J. F., Rivera, R., & Tennyson, R. (1965). Perceived opportunities, gang membership, and delinquency. *American Sociological Review, 30,* 56–67.

Snyder, E. (1971). The impact of the juvenile court hearing on the child. *Crime and Delinquency, 17,* 180–90.

Thomas, C. W. (1977). The effect of legal sanctions on juvenile delinquency. Unpublished monograph, Bowling Green State University, Bowling Green, Ohio.

Thomas, C. W., & Bishop, D. N. (1984). The effect of formal and informal sanctions on delinquency: A longitudinal comparison of labelling and deterrence theories. *Journal of Criminal Law and Criminology, 75,* 1222–45.

Thomas, C. W., & Cage, R. J. (1977). The effect of social characteristics on juvenile court dispositions. *Sociological Quarterly, 18,* 237–52.

Thornberry, T. P. (1971). Punishment and crime: The effect of legal dispositions on subsequent criminal behavior. Unpublished Ph.D. dissertation, University of Pennsylvania.

Tittle, C. R. (1972). Institutional living and self-esteem. *Social Problems, 20,* 65–77.

Tittle, C. R. (1975a). Labeling and crime: An empirical evaluation. In W. R. Gove (Ed.), *The labelling of deviance* (pp. 157–79). New York: Wiley.

Tittle, C. R. (1975b). Deterrent or labeling? *Social Forces, 53,* 399–410.

Tittle, C. R. (1980). Labelling and crime: An empirical evaluation. In W. R. Gove (Ed.), *The labelling of deviance* (2nd ed.) (pp. 241–63). Beverly Hills, Calif.: Sage.

Tittle, C. R., & Curran, D. (1988). Contingencies for dispositional disparities in juvenile justice. *Social Forces, 67,* 23–58.

Turner, R. H. (1972). Deviance avowal as neutralization of commitment. *Social Problems, 19,* 308–21.

Weinstein, R. (1883). Labeling theory and the attitudes of mental patients: A review. *Journal of Health and Social Behavior, 24,* 70–84.

Wellford, C. F. (1975). Labeling theory and criminology: An assessment. *Social Problems, 22,* 332–45.

Yarrow, M. R., Schwartz, C. G., Murphy, H. S., & Deasy, L. C. (1955). The psychological meaning of mental illness in the family. *Journal of Social Issues, 11,* 12–24.

Zimring, F. E., & Hawkins, G. J. (1973). *Deterrence.* Chicago: University of Chicago Press.

PART IV
INTEGRATED THEORIES

Introduction

In order to derive more powerful and robust explanations of crime, some criminologists are now integrating individual factors into complex, multifactor theories that attempt to blend seemingly independent concepts into coherent explanations of criminality.

There are a number of reasons for the recent popularity of integrated theory. One is practical: The development of large, computerized databases and software facilitating statistical analysis now makes theory integration practical. Criminologists of an earlier era simply did not have the tools to conduct the sophisticated computations necessary for theory integration.

A second reason for the development of integrated theories is substantive. Single-factor theories typically focus on the onset of crime; they tend to divide the population neatly into "criminals" and "noncriminals," those who maintain or are influenced by criminogenic conditions and those who have avoided these injurious influences. Consequently, they fail to distinguish between variations in criminal careers. They ignore differences between one-time, occasional, frequent, and chronic offenders. Scant effort is made to understand the frequency and variation in criminal acts. Why do some people escalate the frequency and seriousness of their criminal activity, and why do some terminate activity only to begin again? And although much attention is given to the factors that predict the onset of crime, little heed is paid to the reasons people desist from criminal behavior. We know, however, that most juvenile criminals do not become adult offenders. How can this "aging out" of crime be explained?

The view, then, that people can be classified as either "criminals" or "noncriminals" is now being challenged. Criminologists today are concerned not only with the onset of criminality but also with its termination. It has become important, too, to chart the natural history of a criminal career. Research has identified the existence of a relatively small group of chronic offenders who (1) commit a significant amount of all serious crimes and

(2) persist in criminal careers into adulthood. Single-factor theories, for example, those stressing the influence of environmental factors on behavior, have trouble explaining why only relatively few of the many individuals exposed to criminogenic influences in the environment actually become chronic offenders. Why do only a few adolescents in the most disorganized areas mature into chronic offenders? Why do so many underprivileged youths resist crime despite their exposure to social disorganization, poverty, and cultural deviance? There may be more than a single reason that one person engages in criminal behavior while another, living under similar circumstances, can avoid a criminal career.

By integrating a variety of ecological, socialization, psychological, biological, and economic factors into a coherent structure, criminologists are now attempting to answer these complex questions.

The first integrated theories attempted to show how a multitude of factors—including dysfunctional families, deteriorated neighborhoods, disrupted personalities, and destructive peers—exerted influence on criminal behavior. It was assumed that these factors were additive, and that a person exposed to the most damaging combination of them would also be the most likely to succumb to criminal behavior. Those who criticized this view argued that negative traits were highly correlated and that integrating factors together therefore did little to improve the predictive power of theory.

Today there are two separate and distinct visions of theory integration. The first, referred to here as latent trait theory, assumes a distribution across the population of a personal characteristic that controls the propensity to offend. This disposition, or latent trait, may be present at birth or established early in life; and it remains stable over time. Suspected latent traits include defective intelligence, impulsive personality, or genetic makeup.

Because latent traits are present in people who are antisocial during their adolescence, they are the ones most likely to be persistent criminals throughout their life span. Because latent traits are stable, fluctuations in offending rates reflect criminal opportunities and not the propensity to commit crime. According to this view, people age out of crime because the opportunity to commit crimes diminishes with age. Latent trait theory integrates concepts of biological and psychological determinism with rational choice and routine activity theories of crime.

A second theme that has emerged is the life-course view. According to this vision, a criminal career is a developmental process and the role of "criminal" is not always stable and unchanging. Some career criminals may desist from crime, only to resume their activities at a later date. Some commit offenses at a steady pace, whereas others escalate the rate of their criminal involvement. Offenders can begin to specialize in one type of crime or become "generalists" who commit a variety of illegal acts. Criminals may be influenced by family matters, financial needs, or changing lifestyles and interests. Although latent traits may be important, they alone do not influence the direction of criminal careers.

Life-course theories also recognize that as people mature, the factors that influence their behavior also undergo change. At first, family relations may be most influential; in later adolescence, school and peer relations predominate; in adulthood, marital relations may be the most critical influence. Some antisocial kids who are "in trouble" throughout their adolescence may later manage to find stable work and maintain intact marriages as adults; these life events help them desist from crime. In contrast, the less fortunate who develop arrest records and get involved with the "wrong crowd" later can only find menial jobs and are "at risk" for criminal careers. Social forces that are critical at one stage of life may have little meaning or influence at another.

This part includes two dominant latent trait views of crime: Gottfredson and Hirschi's general theory of crime and Wilson and Herrnstein's "crime as choice" theory. Both view criminal choice as being determined by one or more latent traits. The remaining chapters by Thornberry, Laub, Farrington, and Vila are important examples of the life-course perspective. Each shows that there are multiple influences on behavior, that the presence and intensity of these influences vary over the life course, and that persistence in and desistance from criminal activity can be explained by a multitude of factors.

13

The Nature of Criminality: Low Self-Control

MICHAEL R. GOTTFREDSON
TRAVIS HIRSCHI

Theories of crime lead naturally to interest in the propensities of individuals committing criminal acts. These propensities are often labeled "criminality." In pure classical theory, people committing criminal acts had no special propensities. They merely followed the universal tendency to enhance their own pleasure. If they differed from noncriminals, it was with respect to their location in or comprehension of relevant sanction systems. For example, the individual cut off from the community will suffer less than others from the ostracism that follows crime; the individual unaware of the natural or legal consequences of criminal behavior cannot be controlled by these consequences to the degree that people aware of them are controlled; the atheist will not be as concerned as the believer about penalties to be exacted in a life beyond death. Classical theories on the whole, then, are today called *control* theories, theories emphasizing the prevention of crime through consequences painful to the individual.

Although, for policy purposes, classical theorists emphasized legal consequences, the importance to them of moral sanctions is so obvious that their theories might well be called underdeveloped *social control* theories. In fact, Bentham's list of the major restraining motives—motives acting to prevent mischievous acts—begins with goodwill, love of reputation, and the desire for amity (1970:134–36). He goes on to say that fear of detection prevents crime in large part because of detection's consequences for "reputation, and the desire for amity" (p. 138). Put another way, in Bentham's view the restraining power of legal sanctions stems in large part from their connection to social sanctions.

If crime is evidence of the weakness of social motives, it follows that criminals are less social than noncriminals and that the extent of their asociality may be determined by the nature and number of their crimes. Calculation of the extent of an individual's mischievousness is a complex affair, but in general the more mischievous or depraved the offenses, and the greater their number, the more mischievous or depraved the offender (Bentham, 1970: 134–42). (Classical theorists thus had reason to be interested in the seriousness of the offense. The relevance of seriousness to current theories of crime is not so clear.)

Because classical or control theories assume that offenders are not restrained by social motives, it is common to think of them as emphasizing an asocial human nature. Actually, such theories make people only as asocial as their acts require. Pure or consistent control theories do not add criminality (i.e., personality concepts or attributes such as "aggressiveness" or "extraversion") to individuals beyond that found in their criminal acts. As a result, control theories are suspicious of images of an antisocial, psychopathic, or career offender, or of an offender whose motives to crime are somehow larger than those given in the crimes themselves. Indeed, control theories are compatible with the view that the balance of the total control structure favors conformity, even among offenders:

> For in every man, be his disposition ever so depraved, the social motives are those which . . . regulate and determine the general tenor of his life. . . . The general and standing bias of every man's nature is, therefore, towards that side to which the force of the social motives would determine him to adhere. This being the case, the force of the social motives tends continually to put an end to that of the dissocial ones; as, in natural bodies, the force of friction tends to put an end to that which is generated by impulse. Time, then, which wears away the force of the dissocial motives, adds to that of the social (Bentham 1970:141).

Positivism brought with it the idea that criminals differ from noncriminals in ways more radical than this, the idea that criminals carry within themselves properties peculiarly and positively conducive to crime. Being friendly to both the classical and positivist traditions, we expected to end up with a list of individual properties reliably identified by competent research as useful in the description of "criminality"—such properties as aggressiveness, body build, activity level, and intelligence. We further expected that we would be able to connect these individual-level correlates of criminality directly to the classical idea of crime. As the review progressed, however, it became clear that the success of positivism in establishing important differences between "criminals" and "noncriminals" beyond their tendency to commit criminal acts had been overestimated. Stable individual differences in the tendency to commit criminal acts were clearly evident, but many or even most of the other differences between offenders and nonoffenders were not as clear or pronounced as had been expected from reading the literature.[1]

If individual differences in the tendency to commit criminal acts (within an overall tendency for crime to decline with age) are at least potentially explicable within classical theory by reference to the social location of individuals and their comprehension of how the world works, the fact remains that classical theory cannot shed much light on the positivistic finding (denied by most positivistic theories) that these differences *remain reasonably stable with change in the social location of individuals and change in their knowledge of the operation of sanction systems.* This is the problem of self-control, the differential tendency of people to avoid criminal acts whatever the circumstances in which they find themselves. Since this difference among people has attracted a variety of names, this chapter begins by arguing the merits of the concept of self-control.

Self-Control and Alternative Concepts

The decision to ascribe stable individual differences in criminal behavior to self-control was made only after considering several alternatives, one of which (criminality) had been used before (Hirschi and Gottfredson, 1986). A major consideration was consistency between the classical conception of crime and this alternative conception of the criminal. It seemed unwise to try to integrate a choice theory of crime with a deterministic image of the offender, especially when such integration was unnecessary. In fact, the compatibility of the classical view of crime and the idea that people differ in self-control seems remarkable. Classical theory is a theory of social or external control, a theory based on the idea that the costs of crime depend on the individual's current location in or bond to society. What classical theory lacks is an explicit idea of self-control, the idea that people also differ in the extent to which they are vulnerable to the temptations of the moment. Combining the two ideas thus merely recognizes the simultaneous existence of social and individual restraints on behavior.

An obvious alternative is the concept of criminality. The disadvantages of that concept, however, are numerous. First, it connotes causation or determinism, a positive tendency to crime that is contrary to the classical model and, in this view, contrary to the facts. Whereas self-control suggests that people differ in the extent to which they are restrained from criminal acts, criminality suggests that people differ in the extent to which they are compelled to crime. The concept of self-control is thus consistent with the observation that criminals do not require or need crime, and the concept of criminality is inconsistent with this observation. By the same token, the idea of low self-control is compatible with the observation that criminal acts require no special capabilities, needs, or motivation; they are, in this sense, available to everyone. In contrast, the idea of criminality as a special tendency suggest that criminal acts require special people for their performance and enjoyment. Finally, lack of restraint or low self-control allows almost any deviant, criminal, exciting, or dangerous act; in contrast, the idea of criminality covers only a narrow portion of the apparently diverse acts engaged in by people at one end of the dimension now under discussion.

The concept of conscience comes closer than criminality to self-control and is harder to distinguish from it. Unfortunately, that concept has connotations of compulsion (to conformity) not, strictly speaking, consistent with a choice model (or with the operation of conscience). It does not seem to cover the behaviors analogous to crime that appear to be controlled by natural sanctions rather than social or moral sanctions, and in the end it typically refers to how people feel about their acts rather than to the likelihood that they will or will not commit them. Thus, accidents and employment instability are not usually seen as produced by failures of conscience, and writers in the conscience tradition do not typically make the connection between moral and prudent behavior. Finally, conscience is used primarily to summarize the results of learning via negative reinforcement, and even those favorably disposed to its use have little more to say about it (see, e.g., Eysenck, 1977; Wilson and Herrnstein, 1985).

It is now possible to describe the nature of self-control, the individual characteristic relevant to the commission of criminal acts. Assuming that the nature of this characteristic can be derived directly from the nature of criminal acts, it can thus be inferred from the nature of crime what people who refrain from criminal acts are like before they reach the age at which crime becomes a logical possibility. One can then work back further to the factors producing their restraint, back to the causes of self-control. In this view, lack of self-control does not require crime and can be counteracted by situational conditions or other properties of the individual. At the same time, it seems that high self-control effectively reduces the possibility of crime—that is, those possessing it will be substantially less likely at all periods of life to engage in criminal acts.

The Elements of Self-Control

Criminal acts provide *immediate* gratification of desires. A major characteristic of people with low self-control is therefore a tendency to respond to tangible stimuli in the immediate environment, to have a concrete "here and now" orientation. People with high self-control, in contrast, tend to defer gratification.

Criminal acts provide *easy or simple* gratification of desires. They provide money without work, sex without courtship, revenge without court delays. People lacking self-control also tend to lack diligence, tenacity, or persistence in a course of action.

Criminal acts are *exciting, risky, or thrilling.* They involve stealth, danger, speed, agility, deception, or power. People lacking self-control therefore tend to be adventuresome, active, and physical. Those with high levels of self-control tend to be cautious, cognitive, and verbal.

Crimes provide *few or meager long-term benefits.* They are not equivalent to a job or a career. On the contrary, crimes interfere with long-term commitments to jobs, marriages, family, or friends. People with low self-control thus tend to have unstable marriages, friendships, and job profiles. They tend to be little interested in and unprepared for long-term occupational pursuits.

Crimes require *little skill or planning.* The cognitive requirements for most crimes are minimal. It follows that people lacking self-control need not possess or value cognitive or academic skills. The manual skills required for most crimes are minimal. It follows that people lacking self-control need not possess manual skills that require training or apprenticeship.

Crimes often result in *pain or discomfort for the victim.* Property is lost, bodies are injured, privacy is violated, trust is broken. It follows that people with low self-control tend to be self-centered, indifferent, or insensitive to the suffering and needs of others. It does not follow, however, that people with low self-control are routinely unkind or antisocial. On the contrary, they may discover the immediate and easy rewards of charm and generosity.

Recall that crime involves the pursuit of immediate pleasure. It follows that people lacking self-control will also tend to pursue immediate pleasures that are *not* criminal: they will tend to smoke, drink, use drugs, gamble, have children out of wedlock, and engage in illicit sex.

Crimes require the interaction of an offender with people or their property. It does not follow that people lacking self-control will tend to be gregarious or social. However, it does follow that, other things being equal, gregarious or social people are more likely to be involved in criminal acts.

The major benefit of many crimes is not pleasure but relief from momentary irritation. The irritation caused by a crying child is often the stimulus for physical abuse. That caused by a taunting stranger in a bar is often the stimulus for aggravated assault. It follows that people with low self-control tend to have minimal tolerance for frustration and little ability to respond to conflict through verbal rather than physical means.

Crimes involve the risk of violence and physical injury, of pain and suffering on the part of the offender. It does not follow that people with low self-control will tend to be tolerant of physical pain or indifferent to physical discomfort. It does follow that people tolerant of physical pain or indifferent to physical discomfort will be more likely to engage in criminal acts whatever their level of self-control.

The risk of criminal penalty for any given criminal act is small, but this depends in part on the circumstances of the offense. Thus, for example, not all joyrides by teenagers are equally likely to result in arrest. A car stolen from a neighbor and returned unharmed before he notices its absence is less likely to result in official notice than is a car stolen from a shopping center parking lot and abandoned at the convenience of the offender. Teenagers who drink alcohol stolen from parents and consumed in the family garage are less likely to receive official notice than those who drink in the parking lot outside a concert hall. It follows that offenses differ in their validity as measures of self-control: Those offenses with large risk of public awareness are better measures than those with little risk.

In sum, people who lack self-control will tend to be impulsive, insensitive, physical (as opposed to mental), risk-taking, shortsighted, and nonverbal; and they will tend therefore to engage in criminal and analogous acts. Since these traits can be identified prior to the age of responsibility for crime, since there is considerable tendency for these traits to come together in the same people, and since the traits tend to persist through life, it seems reasonable to consider them as making up a stable construct useful in the explanation of crime.

The Many Manifestations of Low Self-Control

The image of the "offender" presented here suggests that crime is not an automatic or necessary consequence of low self-control. It suggests that many noncriminal acts analogous to crime (such as accidents, smoking, and alcohol use) are also manifestations of low self-control. This image therefore implies that no specific act, type of crime, or form of deviance is uniquely required by the absence of self-control.

Because both crime and analogous behaviors stem from low self-control (that is, both are manifestations of low self-control), they will all be engaged in at a relatively high rate by people with low self-control. Within the domain of crime, then, there will be much versatility among offenders in the criminal acts in which they engage.

Research on the versatility of deviant acts supports these predictions in the strongest possible way. The variety of manifestations of low self-control is immense. In spite of years of tireless research motivated by a belief in specialization, no credible evidence of specialization has been reported. In fact, the evidence of offender versatility is overwhelming (Hirschi, 1969; Hindelang 1971; Wolfgang, Figlio, and Sellin, 1972; Petersilia, 1980; Hindelang, Hirschi, and Weis, 1981; Rojek and Erickson, 1982; Klein, 1984).

The term versatility indicates that offenders commit a wide variety of criminal acts, with no strong inclination to pursue a specific criminal act or a pattern of criminal acts to the exclusion of others. Most theories suggest that offenders tend to specialize, whereby such terms as robber, burglar, drug dealer, rapist, and murderer have predictive or descriptive import. In fact, some theories create offender specialization as part of their explanation of crime. For example, Cloward and Ohlin (1960) created distinctive subcultures of delinquency around particular forms of criminal behavior, identifying subcultures specializing in theft, violence, or drugs. In a related way, books are written about white-collar crime as though it were a clearly distinct specialty requiring a unique explanation. Research projects are undertaken for the study of drug use, or vandalism, or teenage pregnancy (as though every study of delinquency were not a study of drug use and vandalism and teenage sexual behavior). Entire schools of criminology emerge to pursue patterning, sequencing, progression, escalation, onset, persistence, and desistance in the career of offenses or offenders. These efforts survive largely because their proponents fail to consider or acknowledge the clear evidence to the contrary. Other reasons for survival of such ideas may be found in the interest of politicians and members of the law enforcement community who see policy potential in criminal careers or "career criminals" (see, e.g., Blumstein et al., 1986).

Occasional reports of specialization seem to contradict this point, as do everyday observations of repetitive misbehavior by particular offenders. Some offenders rob the same store repeatedly over a period of years, or an offender commits several rapes over a (brief) period of time. Such offenders may be called "robbers" or "rapists." However, it should be noted that such labels are retrospective rather than predictive and that they typically ignore a large amount of delinquent or criminal behavior by the same offenders that is inconsistent with their alleged specialty. Thus, for example, the "rapist" will tend also to use drugs, to commit robberies and burglaries (often in concert with the rape), and to have a record for violent offenses other than rape. There is a perhaps natural tendency on the part of observers (and in official accounts) to focus on the most serious crimes in a series of events, but this tendency should not be confused with a tendency on the part of the offender to specialize in one kind of crime.

Recall that one of the defining features of crime is that it is simple and easy. Some apparent specialization will therefore occur because obvious opportunities for an easy score will tend to repeat themselves. An offender who lives next to a shopping area that is approached by pedestrians will have repeat opportunities for purse snatching, and this may show in his arrest record. But even here the specific "criminal career" will tend to run its course quickly and to be followed by offenses whose content and character are likewise determined by convenience and opportunity (which is why some form of theft is always the best bet about what a person is likely to do next).

The evidence that offenders are likely to engage in noncriminal acts psychologically or theoretically equivalent to crime is, because of the relatively high rates of these "noncriminal" acts, even easier to document. Thieves are likely to smoke, drink, and skip school at considerably higher rates than nonthieves. Offenders are considerably more likely than nonoffenders to be involved in most types of accidents, including household fires, auto crashes, and unwanted pregnancies. They are also considerably more likely to die at an early age (see, e.g., Robins, 1966; Eysenck, 1977; Gottfredson, 1984).

Good research on drug use and abuse routinely reveals that the correlates of delinquency and drug use are the same. As Akers (1984) has noted, "compared to the abstaining teenager, the drinking, smoking, and drug-taking teen is much more likely to be getting into fights, stealing, hurting other people, and committing other delinquencies." Akers goes on to say, "but the variation in the order in which they take up these things leaves little basis for proposing the causation of one by the other." In the view proposed here, the relation between drug use and delinquency is not a causal question. The correlates are the same, because drug use and delinquency are both manifestations of an underlying tendency to pursue short-term, immediate pleasure. This underlying tendency (i.e, lack of self-control) has many manifestations, as listed by Harrison Gough (1948):

> unconcern over the rights and privileges of others when recognizing them would interfere with personal satisfaction in any way; impulsive behavior, or apparent incongruity between the strength of the stimulus and the magnitude of the behavioral response; inability to form deep or persistent attachments to other persons or to identify in interpersonal relationships; poor judgment and planning in attaining defined goals; apparent lack of anxiety and distress over social maladjustment and unwillingness or inability to consider maladjustment qua maladjustment; a tendency to project blame onto others and to take no responsibility for failures; meaningless prevarication, often about trivial matters in situations where detection is inevitable; almost complete lack of dependability . . . and willingness to assume responsibility; and, finally, emotional poverty (p. 362).

This combination of characteristics has been revealed in the life histories of the subjects in the famous studies by Lee Robins. Robins is one of the few researchers to focus on the varieties of deviance and the way they tend to go together in the lives of those she designates as having "antisocial personalities." In her words: "We refer to someone who fails to maintain close personal relationships with anyone else, [who] performs poorly on the job, who is involved in illegal behaviors (whether or not apprehended), who fails to support himself and his dependents without outside aid, and who is given to sudden changes of plan and loss of temper in response to what appear to others as minor frustrations" (1978:255).

For thirty years Robins traced 524 children referred to a guidance clinic in St. Louis, Missouri, and she compared them to a control group matched on IQ, age, sex, and area of the city. She discovered that, in comparison to the control group, those people referred at an early age were more likely to be arrested as adults (for a wide variety of offenses), were less likely to get married, were more likely to be divorced, were more likely to marry a spouse with a behavior problem, were less likely to have children (but if they had children were likely to have more children), were more likely to have children with behavior problems, were more likely to be unemployed, had considerably more frequent job changes, were more likely to be on welfare, had fewer contacts with relatives, had fewer friends, were substantially less likely to attend church, were less likely to serve in the armed forces and more likely to be dishonorably discharged if they did serve, were more likely to exhibit physical evidence of excessive alcohol use, and were more likely to be hospitalized for psychiatric problems (1966:42–73).

Note that these outcomes are consistent with four general elements of our notion of low self-control: basic stability of individual differences over a long period of time; great variability in the kinds of criminal acts engaged in; conceptual or causal equivalence of criminal and noncriminal acts; and inability to predict the specific forms of deviance engaged in, whether criminal or noncriminal. The idea of an antisocial personality defined by certain behavioral consequences is too positivistic or deterministic, suggesting that the offender must do certain things given his antisocial personality. Thus, it should be said only that the subjects in question are *more likely* to commit criminal acts (as the data indicate they are). The commission of criminal acts is not part of the definition of the individual with low self-control.

Be this as it may, Robins's retrospective research showed that predictions derived from a concept of antisocial personality are highly consistent with the results of prospective longitudinal and cross-sectional research: Offenders do not specialize; they tend to be involved in accidents, illness, and death at higher rates than the general population; they tend to have difficulty persisting in a job regardless of the particular characteristics of the job (no job will turn out to be a good job); they have difficulty acquiring and retaining friends; and they have difficulty meeting the demands of long-term financial commitments (such as mortgages or car payments) and the demands of parenting.

Seen in this light, the "costs" of low self-control for the individual may far exceed the costs of his criminal acts. In fact, it appears that crime is often among the least serious consequences of a lack of self-control in terms of the quality of life of those lacking it.

The Causes of Self-Control

We know better what deficiencies in self-control lead to than where they come from. One thing is, however, clear: Low self-control is not produced by training, tutelage, or socialization. As a matter of fact, all of the characteristics associated with low self-control tend to show themselves in the absence of nurturance, discipline, or training. Given the classical appreciation of the causes of human behavior, the implications of this fact are straightforward: The causes of low self-control are negative rather than positive; self-control is unlikely in the absence of effort, intended or unintended, to create it. (This assumption separates the present theory from most modern theories of crime, where the offender is automatically seen as a product of positive forces, a creature of learning, particular pressures, or specific defect. This comparison will be reexamined once the present theory has been fully explicated.)

At this point it would be easy to construct a theory of crime causation, according to which characteristics of potential offenders lead them ineluctably to the commission of criminal acts. The simple task at this point would be to identify the likely sources of impulsiveness, intelligence, risk taking, and the like. But to do so would be to follow the path that has proven so unproductive in the past, the path according to which criminals commit crimes irrespective of the characteristics of the setting or situation.

This pitfall can be avoided by recalling the elements inherent in the decision to commit a criminal act. The object of the offense is clearly pleasurable, and universally so. Engaging in the act, however, entails some risk of social, legal, and/or natural sanctions. Whereas the pleasure attained by the act is direct, obvious, and immediate, the pains risked by it are not obvious, or direct, and are in any event at greater remove from it. It follows that though there will be little variability among people in their ability to see the pleasures of crime, there will be considerable variability in their ability to calculate potential pains. But the problem goes further than this: Whereas the pleasures of crime are distributed over the population reasonably equally, this is not true for the pains. Everyone appreciates money; not everyone dreads parental anger or disappointment upon learning that the money was stolen.

So, the dimensions of self-control can be seen as factors affecting calculation of the consequences of one's acts. The impulsive or shortsighted person fails to consider the negative or painful consequences of his acts; the insensitive person has fewer negative consequences to consider; the less intelligent person also has fewer negative consequences to consider (has less to lose).

No known social group, whether criminal or noncriminal, actively or purposefully attempts to reduce the self-control of its members. Social life is not enhanced by low self-control and its consequences. On the contrary, the exhibition of these tendencies undermines harmonious group relations and the ability to achieve collective ends. These facts explicitly deny that a tendency to crime is a product of socialization, culture, or positive learning of any sort.

The traits that low self-control comprises are also not conducive to the achievement of long-term individual goals. On the contrary, they impede educational and occupational achievement, destroy interpersonal relations, and undermine physical health and economic well-being. Such facts explicitly deny the notion that criminality is an alternative route to the goals otherwise obtainable through legitimate avenues. It follows that people who care about the interpersonal skill, educational and occupational achievement, and physical and economic well-being of those in their care will seek to rid them of these traits.

Two general sources of variation are immediately apparent in this scheme. The first is the variation among children in the degree to which they manifest such traits to begin with. The second is the variation among caretakers in the degree to which they recognize low self-control and its consequences and the degree to which they are willing and able to correct it. Obviously, therefore, even at this threshold level the sources of low self-control are complex.

There is good evidence that some of the traits predicting subsequent involvement in crime appear as early as they can be reliably measured; these include low intelligence, high activity level, physical strength, and adventuresomeness (Glueck and Glueck, 1950; West and Farrington, 1973). The evidence suggests that the connection between these traits and commission of criminal acts ranges from weak to moderate. Obviously, this does not mean to suggest that people are born criminals, inherit a gene for criminality, or anything of the sort. In fact, the theory presented here explicitly denies such notions. What it does suggest is that individual differences may have an impact on the prospects for effective socialization (or adequate control). Effective socialization is, however, always possible whatever the configuration of individual traits.

Other traits affecting crime appear later and seem to be largely products of ineffective or incomplete socialization. For example, differences in impulsivity and insensitivity become noticeable later in childhood when they are no longer common to all children. The ability and willingness to delay immediate gratification for some larger purpose may therefore be assumed to be a consequence of training. Much parental action is in fact geared toward suppression of impulsive behavior, toward making the child consider the long-range consequences of acts. Consistent sensitivity to the needs and feelings of others may also be assumed to be a consequence of training. Indeed, much parental behavior is directed toward teaching the child about the rights and feelings of others, and of how these rights and feelings ought to constrain the child's behavior. All of these points focus attention on child rearing.

Child Rearing and Self-Control: The Family

The major "cause" of low self-control thus appears to be ineffective child rearing. Put in positive terms, several conditions appear necessary to produce a socialized child. Perhaps the place to begin looking for these conditions is the research literature on the relationship between family conditions and delinquency. This research (e.g., Glueck and Glueck, 1950; McCord and McCord, 1959) has examined the connection between many family factors and delinquency. It reports that discipline, supervision, and affection tend to be missing in the homes of delinquents, that the behavior of the parents is often "poor" (e.g., excessive drinking and poor supervision [Glueck and Glueck, 1950:110–11]); and that the parents of delinquents are unusually likely to have criminal records themselves. Indeed, according to Michael Rutter and Henri Giller, "of the parental characteristics associated with delinquency, criminality is the most striking and most consistent" (1984:182).

Such information undermines the many explanations of crime that ignore the family, but in this form it does not represent much of an advance over the belief of the general public (and those who deal with offenders in the criminal justice system) that "defective upbringing" or "neglect" in the home is the primary cause of crime.

To put these standard research findings in perspective, it is necessary to define the conditions necessary for adequate child rearing to occur. The minimum conditions seem to be these: In order to teach the child self-control, someone must (1) monitor the child's behavior, (2) recognize deviant behavior when it occurs, and (3) punish such behavior. This seems simple and obvious enough. All that is required to activate the system is affection for *or* investment in the child. The person who cares for the child will watch his behavior, see him doing things he should not do, and correct him. The result may be a child more capable of delaying gratification, more sensitive to the interests and desires of others, more independent, more willing to accept restraints on his activity, and more unlikely to use force or violence to attain his ends.

In seeking the causes of low self-control, the question is where this system can go wrong. Obviously, parents do not prefer their children to be unsocialized in the terms described. We can therefore rule out in advance the possibility of positive socialization to unsocialized behavior (as cultural or subcultural deviance theories suggest). Still, the system can go wrong at any one of four places. First, the parents may not care for the child (in which case none of the other conditions would be met); second, the parents, even if they care, may not have the time or energy to monitor the child's behavior; third, the parents, even if they care *and* monitor, may not see anything wrong with the child's behavior; finally, even if everything else is in place, the parents may not have the inclination or the means to punish the child. So, what may appear at first glance to be unproblematic turns out to be problematic indeed. Many things can go wrong. According to much research in crime and delinquency, in the homes of problem children many things have gone wrong: "Parents of stealers do not track ([they] do not interpret stealing . . . as 'deviant'); they do not punish; and they do not care" (Patterson, 1980:88–89; see also Glueck and Glueck, 1950; McCord and McCord, 1959; West and Farrington, 1977).

Let us apply this scheme to some of the facts about the connection between child socialization and crime, beginning with the elements of the child-rearing model.

The Attachment of the Parent to the Child

Our model states that parental concern for the welfare or behavior of the child is a necessary condition for successful child rearing. Because it is too often assumed that all parents are alike in their love for their children, the evidence directly on this point is not as good or extensive as it could be. However, what exists is clearly consistent with the model. Glueck and Glueck (1950:125–28) reported that, compared to the fathers of delinquents, fathers of nondelinquents were twice as likely to be warmly disposed toward their sons and one-fifth as likely to be hostile toward them. In the same sample, 28 percent of the mothers of delinquents were characterized as "indifferent or hostile" toward the child as compared to 4 percent of the mothers of nondelinquents. The evidence suggests that stepparents are especially unlikely to have feelings of affection toward their stepchildren (Burgess, 1980), adding in contemporary society to the likelihood that children will be "reared" by people who do not especially care for them.

Parental Supervision

The connection between social control and self-control could not be more direct than in the case of parental supervision of the child. Such supervision presumably prevents criminal or analogous acts and at the same time trains the child to avoid them on his own. Consistent with this assumption, supervision tends to be a major predictor of delinquency, however supervision or delinquency is measured (Glueck and Glueck, 1950; Hirschi, 1969; West and Farrington, 1977; Riley and Shaw, 1985).

The general theory outlined here in principle provides a method of separating supervision as external control from supervision as internal control. For one thing, offenses differ in the degree to which they can be prevented through monitoring; children at one age are monitored much more closely than children at other ages; girls are supervised more closely than boys. In some situations, monitoring is universal or nearly constant; in other situations monitoring for some offenses is virtually absent. In the present context, however, the concern is with the connection between supervision and self-control, a connection established by the stronger tendency of those who were poorly supervised when young to commit crimes as adults (McCord, 1979).

Recognition of Deviant Behavior

In order for supervision to have an impact on self-control, the supervisor must perceive deviant behavior when it occurs. Remarkably, not all parents are adept at recognizing lack of self-control. Some parents allow their children to do pretty much as he or she pleases without interference. Extensive television viewing is one modern example, as is the failure to require completion of homework, to prohibit smoking, to curtail the use of physical force, or to see to it that the child actually attends school. (Truancy among second-graders presumably reflects on the adequacy of parental awareness of the child's misbehavior.) Again, the research is not as good as it should be, but evidence of "poor conduct standards" in the homes of delinquents is common.

Punishment of Deviant Acts

Control theories explicitly acknowledge the necessity of sanctions in preventing criminal behavior. They do not suggest that the major sanctions are legal or corporal. On the contrary, as has been shown, they suggest that disapproval by people one cares about is the most powerful of sanctions. Effective punishment by the parent or major caretaker therefore usually entails nothing more than explicit disapproval of unwanted behavior. The criticism of control theories that dwells on their alleged cruelty is therefore simply misguided or ill informed (see, e.g., Currie, 1985).

Not all caretakers punish effectively. In fact, some are too harsh and some are too lenient (Glueck and Glueck, 1950; McCord and McCord, 1959; West and Farrington, 1977; see generally Loeber and Stouthamer-Loeber, 1986). Given the alternative model, however, rewarding good behavior cannot compensate for failure to correct deviant behavior. (Recall the premise that deviant acts carry with them their own rewards.)

Given the consistency of the child-rearing model with this general theory and with the research literature, it should be possible to use it to explain other family correlates of criminal and otherwise deviant behavior.

Note

1. We do not mean to imply that stable individual differences between offenders and nonoffenders are nonexistent. The fact of the matter is, however, that substantial evidence documenting individual differences is not as clear to us as it appears to be to others. The evidence on intelligence is an exception. Here differences favoring nonoffenders have been abundantly documented (cf. Wilson and Herrnstein, 1985).

References

Akers, R. L. (1973). *Deviant behavior: A social learning approach.* Belmont, Calif.: Wadsworth.

Akers, R. L. (1984). Delinquent behavior, drugs, and alcohol: What is the relationship? *Today's Delinquent,* 3, 19–47.

Bentham, J. [1789] (1970). *An introduction to the principles of morals and legislation.* London: Athlone Press.

Blumstein, A., Cohen, J., Roth, J., & Visher, C. (1986). *Criminal careers and "career criminals."* Washington, D.C.: National Academy Press.

Cloward, R., & Ohlin, L. (1960). *Delinquency and opportunity.* New York: Free Press.

Eysenck, H. (1964). *Crime and personality.* London: Routledge & Kegan Paul.

Eysenck, H. (1977). *Crime and personality* (rev. ed.). London: Paladin.

Glueck, S., & Glueck, E. (1950). *Unraveling juvenile delinquency.* Cambridge, Mass.: Harvard University Press.

Gottfredson, M. R. (1984). *Victims of crime: The dimensions of risk.* London: Her Majesty's Stationery Office.

Gough, H. G. (1948). A sociological theory of psychopathy. *American Journal of Sociology, 53,* 359–66.

Hindelang, M. J. (1971). Age, sex, and the versatility of delinquent involvements. *Social Problems, 18,* 522–35.

Hindelang, M., Hirschi, T., & Weis, J. (1981). *Measuring delinquency.* Beverly Hills, Calif.: Sage.

Hirschi, T. (1969). *Causes of delinquency.* Berkeley: University of California Press.

Hirschi, T., & Gottfredson, M. R. (1986). The distinction between crime and criminality. In T. F. Hartnagel & R. Silveman (Eds.), *Critique and explanation: Essays in honor of Gwynne Nettler* (pp. 55–69). New Brunswick, N.J.: Transaction.

Klein, M. (1984). Offense specialization and versatility among juveniles. *British Journal of Criminology, 24,* 185–94.

McCord, W., & McCord, J. (1959). *Origins of crime: A new evaluation of the Cambridge-Somerville Study.* New York: Columbia University Press.

Patterson, G. R. (1980). Children who steal. In T. Hirschi & M. Gottfredson (Eds.), *Understanding crime* (pp. 73–90). Beverly Hills, Calif.: Sage.

Petersilia, J. (1980). Criminal career research: A review of recent evidence. In M. Tonry & N. Morris (Eds.), *Crime and justice: An annual review of research,* vol. 2 (pp. 321–79). Chicago: University of Chicago Press.

Robins, L. (1966). *Deviant children grown up.* Baltimore: Williams & Wilkins.

Robins, L. (1978). Aetiological implications in studies of childhood histories relating to antisocial personality. In R. Hare & D. Schalling (Eds.), *Psychopathic behavior* (pp. 255–71). New York: Wiley.

Rojek, D., & Erickson, M. (1982). Delinquent careers. *Criminology, 20,* 5–28.

Rutter, M., & Giller, H. (1984). *Juvenile delinquency: Trends and perspectives.* New York: Guilford Press.

West, D., & Farrington, D. P. (1973). *Who becomes delinquent?* London: Heinemann.

Wilson, J. Q., & Herrnstein, R. (1985). *Crime and human nature.* New York: Simon & Schuster.

Wolfgang, M., Figlio, R., & Sellin, T. (1972). *Delinquency in a birth cohort.* Chicago: University of Chicago Press.

14

Crime as Choice

JAMES Q. WILSON
RICHARD J. HERRNSTEIN

Theories of crime abound. The lay reader will wonder whether any theory can be an improvement on common sense, and the scholarly one will groan at the prospect of yet another theory. But what may be irrelevant to the former and redundant to the latter is, to us, important; for theories, whatever else they may do, direct our attention to some features of the situation and away from others. Much of the confusion about the sources of individual differences in criminality arises, we believe, from bad theories—that is, from views about how the world works that are incomplete and thus lead us to attend to some things but not to others.

For example, the theory that unemployment or economic want causes crime can lead us to look for increases in criminality during economic recessions but to overlook the possibility that crime may also be caused by prosperity (if it loosens the social bonds), by the distribution of income (if it causes social envy), or by some underlying factor that happens to cause both criminality and unemployment. More generally, theories that call attention to the social setting in which crime occurs (such as the attitudes of parents and peers, the perceived costs and benefits of crime, the influence of drugs and television) direct our attention away from preexisting individual traits that make people more or less susceptible to such social factors; by the same token, theories that emphasize the preferences of individuals tend to de-emphasize the situational factors that determine how, or even whether, those preferences affect behavior. The quarrels among lay persons and scholars about what causes crime are basically quarrels about the relative importance of those factors that occupy a central place in competing theories. These arguments are made more intense by the fact that sometimes people do not choose theories at random; very often, they choose them in part because the central factors in the theories—individual morality, social setting, economic circumstances, or the prospects of punishment—are ones that, for political or ideological reasons, the defenders of the theories *want* to believe are central.

We suggest that most of the common theories purporting to explain criminal behavior are but special cases of some more general theory. Specifying that larger theory is useful because, to the extent it is correct and comprehensive, it will keep before our eyes the full range of factors that cause individual differences in criminality. This, in turn, will restrain our tendency to give partial explanations of crime or to make partial interpretations of the empirical findings of criminologists. Ideally, of course, a theory should do much more than this. In principle, a theory is a testable statement of the relationships between or among two or more variables, so that, knowing the theory, we can say with some confidence that if we observe X, we will also observe Y. For instance: If we observe a left-handed, red-haired male, then we are 70 percent certain that we are observing a burglar. Unfortunately, theories about crime, even ours, often do not permit us to make such statements, but for the reasons already given, they are important nonetheless. If, given this state of affairs, "theory" sounds too grand a term for the systematic speculations we and others have produced, consider what we offer as an organized perspective on the causes of crime.

Our theory—or perspective—is a statement about the forces that control individual behavior. To most people, that is not a very interesting assertion, but to many scholars, it is a most controversial one. Some students of crime are suspicious of the view that explanations of criminality should be based on an analysis of individual psychology. Such a view, they argue, is "psychological reductionism" that neglects the setting in which crime occurs and the broad social forces that determine levels of crime. These suspicions, while understandable, are ill-founded. Whatever factors contribute to crime—the state of the economy, the competence of the police, the nurturance of the family, the availability of drugs, the quality of the schools—they must all affect the behavior of *individuals* if they are to affect crime. If people differ in their tendency to commit crime, we must express those differences in terms of how some array of factors affects their individual decisions. If crime rates differ among nations, it must be because individuals in those nations differ or are exposed to different arrays of factors. If crime rates rise or fall, it must be that changes have occurred in the variables governing individual behavior.

Our theory is eclectic, drawing from different, sometimes opposing, schools of thought. We incorporate both genetic predispositions and social learning and consider the influence of both delayed and immediate factors. An individual act is sometimes best understood as a reaction to immediate circumstances and at other times as an expression of enduring behavioral dispositions; both sorts of explanations have a place in our theory. Though eclectic, the theory is built upon modern behavioral psychology.[1]

Crime as Choice: The Theory in Brief

Our theory rests on the assumption that people, when faced with a choice, choose the preferred course of action. This assumption is quite weak; it says nothing more than that whatever people choose to do, they choose it because they prefer it. In fact, it is more than weak; without further clarification, it is a tautology. When we say people "choose," we do not necessarily mean that they consciously deliberate about what to do. All we mean is that their behavior is determined by its consequences. A person will do that thing the consequences of which are perceived by him or her to be preferable to the consequences of doing something else. What can save such a statement from being a tautology is how plausibly we describe the gains and losses associated with alternative courses of action and the standards by which a person evaluates those gains and losses.

These assumptions are commonplace in philosophy and social science. Philosophers speak of hedonism or utilitarianism, economists of value or utility, and psychologists of reinforcement or reward. We will use the language of psychology, but it should not be hard to translate our terminology into that of other disciplines. Though social scientists differ as to how much behavior can reasonably be described as the result of a choice, all agree that at least some behavior is guided, or even precisely controlled, by things variously termed pleasure, pain, happiness, sorrow, desirability, or the like. Our object is to show how this simple and widely used idea can be used to explain behavior.

At any given moment, a person can choose between committing a crime and not committing it (all these alternatives to crime we lump together as "noncrime"). The consequences of committing the crime consist of rewards (what psychologists call "reinforcers") and punishments; the consequences of not committing the crime (i.e., engaging in noncrime) also entail gains and losses. The larger the ratio of the net rewards of crime to the net rewards of noncrime, the greater the tendency to commit the crime. The net rewards of crime include, obviously, the likely material gains from the crime, but they also include intangible benefits, such as obtaining emotional or sexual gratification, receiving the approval of peers, satisfying an old score against an enemy, or enhancing one's sense of justice. One must deduct from these rewards of crime any losses that accrue immediately—that are, so to speak, contemporaneous with the crime. They include the pangs of conscience, the disapproval of onlookers, and the retaliation of the victim.

The value of noncrimes lies all in the future. It includes the benefits to the individual of avoiding the risk of being caught and punished and, in addition, the benefits of avoiding penalties not controlled by the criminal justice system, such as the loss of reputation or the sense of shame afflicting a person later discovered to have broken the law and the possibility that, being known as a criminal, one cannot get or keep a job.

The value of any reward or punishment associated with either crime or noncrime is, to some degree, uncertain. A would-be burglar can rarely know exactly how much loot he will take away or what its cash value will prove to be. The assaulter or rapist may exaggerate the satisfaction he thinks will follow the assault or the rape. Many people do not know how sharp the bite of conscience will be until they have done something that makes them feel the bite. The anticipated approval of one's buddies may or may not be forthcoming. Similarly, the benefits of noncrime are uncertain. One cannot know with confidence whether one will be caught, convicted, and punished, or whether one's friends will learn about the crime and as a result withhold valued esteem, or whether one will be able to find or hold a job.

Compounding these uncertainties is time. The opportunity to commit a crime may be ready at hand (an open, unattended cash register in a store) or well in the future (a bank that, with planning and preparation, can be robbed). And the rewards associated with noncrime are almost invariably more distant than those connected with crime, perhaps many weeks or months distant. The strength of reinforcers tends to decay over time at rates that differ among individuals. As a result, the extent to which people take into account distant possibilities—a crime that can be committed only tomorrow, or punishment that will be inflicted only in a year—will affect whether they choose crime or noncrime. All of these factors—the strength of rewards, the problems of uncertainty and delay, and the way in which our sense of justice affects how we value the rewards—will be examined in the remainder of this chapter.

Reinforcers

All human behavior is shaped by two kinds of reinforcers: primary and secondary. A primary reinforcer derives its strength from an innate drive, such as hunger or sexual appetite; a secondary reinforcer derives its strength from learning. The line dividing reinforcers that are innate from those that are learned is hard to draw; and people argue, often passionately, over where it ought to be drawn. When we disagree over whether people are innately altruistic, men are innately more aggressive than women, or mankind is innately warlike or competitive, we are disagreeing over whether behavior responds to primary or to secondary reinforcers.

In fact, most reinforcers combine primary and secondary elements. Part of the benefit that comes from eating either bread or spaghetti must derive from the fact that their common ingredient, wheat, satisfies an innate drive—hunger. In this sense, both are primary reinforcers. But bread and spaghetti differ in texture, flavor, and appearance; and the preferences we have for these qualities are in part learned. These qualities constitute secondary reinforcers. The diversity of the world's cuisines shows, to some extent, how extraordinarily varied are the secondary aspects of even a highly biological reinforcer such as food.

The distinction between primary and secondary reinforcers is important, in part because it draws attention to the link between innate drives and social conventions. For example, in every society men and women adorn themselves to enhance their sexual appeal. At the same time, styles in clothing and cosmetics vary greatly among societies and throughout history. As we are all immersed in the fashions of our place and time, we may suppose that fashion is purely arbitrary. But we are probably wrong, for these conventions of personal beauty are dependent on primary sexual reinforcers. But what constitutes acceptable adornment changes within broad limits. Once, for a woman to appear nude in a motion picture meant that she was wanton and the film was trash. Today, female nudity, though it is still offensive to some, is not construed by most viewers as an indication of the moral worth of the woman.

Not only do innate primary reinforcers become blended with learned secondary ones, the strength of even primary reinforcers (and of course of secondary reinforcers) will vary. Bread that we eat hungrily at seven o'clock in the morning may have no appeal to us at one o'clock in the afternoon, right after lunch. In fact, many forms of food may appeal to us before breakfast even though none may appeal after lunch. A class of reinforcers whose strengths vary together allows us to speak of a "drive"—in this case, the hunger drive.

Drives vary in strength. The various food drives can be depended on to assert themselves several times a day, but the sexual drive may be felt much less frequently, and then in ways powerfully affected by circumstances. The aggressive drive (to be discussed later in this chapter) may occur very rarely in some of us and frequently in others; and it may appear suddenly, in response to events, and blow over almost as quickly. We repeat these commonplace observations because we wish to emphasize that though much behavior, including criminal behavior, is affected by innate drives, this does not mean that crime is committed by "born criminals" with uncontrollable, antisocial drives. We can, in short, include innate drives (and thus genetic factors) in our theory without embracing a view of the criminal as an atavistic savage or any other sort of biological anomaly.

Secondary reinforcers change in strength along with the primary reinforcers with which they are associated. Those secondary reinforcers that change the least in strength are those associated with the largest variety of primary reinforcers. Money is an especially powerful reward, not because it is intrinsically valuable (paper currency has almost no intrinsic worth) but because it is associated with so many primary reinforcers that satisfy innate drives. Money can buy food, shelter, relief from pain, and even sexual gratification. (It can also buy status and power, but we will not discuss here the interesting question of whether the desire for these things is innate.) The reinforcing power of money is relatively steady because the many primary rewards with which it is connected make it somewhat impervious to fluctuations in the value of any one drive.

Because of the constant and universal reinforcing power of money, people are inclined to think of crimes for money gain as more natural, and thus more the product of voluntary choice and rational thought, than crimes involving "senseless" violence or sexual deviance. Stealing is an understandable, if not pardonable, crime; bestiality, "unprovoked" murder, and drug addiction seem much less understandable and therefore, perhaps, less voluntary or deliberate. People sometimes carry this line of thought even further: These "senseless" crimes are the result of overpowering compulsions or irrational beliefs. But this is a false distinction. Certain reinforcers may have a steadier, more predictable effect, but all behavior, even the bizarre, responds to reinforcement. It is sometimes useful to distinguish crimes that arise out of long-standing, hard-to-change reinforcers (such as money) from those that stem from short-acting, (possibly) changeable drives (such as sexual deviance), but we must always bear in mind that these are distinctions of degree, not of kind.

Conditioning

Thus far, we have spoken of the "association" between primary and secondary reinforcers. Now we must ask how that association arises. The answer is the process known as conditioning. The simplest form of conditioning is the well-known experiment involving Pavlov's dog. The dog repeatedly heard a buzzer a few moments before receiving some dried meat powder in its mouth. Soon, the dog salivated at the mere sound of the buzzer. Two different stimuli—meat and buzzers—were associated. The meat elicited an innate tendency to salivate; the buzzer came to elicit salivation through learning. Pavlov's successors extended his discovery to much more complex responses than salivation and to many other species, including man. These Pavlovian experiments involved what psychologists now call "classical conditioning," which typically involves the autonomic nervous system (that part of our neural structure controlling reflexive behavior—such as heartbeats, salivation, and perspiration—and internal emotional states—such as fear, anxiety, and relaxation) and in which the behavior of the subject (the dog or the man) does not affect the stimulus being administered.

Classical (or Pavlovian) conditioning can make an arbitrary stimulus reinforce behavior by associating the stimulus with either a primary (i.e., innate) reinforcer or some already learned secondary reinforcer. As we have seen, money is an arbitrary stimulus (a collection of scraps of paper and bits of metal) that has become one of the most universal and powerful secondary reinforcers. But there are many other examples. If a child is regularly praised for scrubbing his or her hands before dinner, then (provided that the praise is already felt to be rewarding) the child will in time scrub his hands without being told or praised. The satisfaction he feels in having scrubbed hands is now the internal feeling of reinforcement. In the same way, hand scrubbing can be taught by scolding a child who does not wash up. If the scolding is already felt by the child to be punishing, in time the child will feel uncomfortable whenever he has dirty hands.

Classical conditioning does not produce only secretions or muscle twitches. These external responses may be accompanied by a complex array of internalized dispositions. The child who learns to scrub his hands, because of either parental praise or parental disapproval, will have learned things on which his mind and his subsequent experience will come to work in elaborate ways. In time, the satisfaction he feels from having clean hands may merge with other similar satisfactions and become a general sense of cleanliness, which he may eventually believe is next to godliness. He imputes virtue to cleanliness and regards filth with great distaste, even when he finds it in the world at large rather than simply on his own hands. Of course, all this presupposes growing up in a society in which neighbors, friends, and even the government regularly praise cleanliness and condemn slovenliness.

Although it does not do justice to the subtlety and generality of the process or the way in which its outcome is linked to social settings, H. J. Eysenck's remark that "conscience is a conditioned reflex" is not far off the mark. And it calls attention to the intriguing possibility that individuals may differ in their susceptibility to classical conditioning. People are not alike in how readily they internalize rules, and thus they are not alike in the value they attach to the costs in conscience of a prospective crime. For some people, the benefits of a crime are not reduced as much by a "conscience decrement" as they are for persons who have been more successfully subjected to classical conditioning.

Many people have a conscience strong enough to prevent them from committing a crime some of the time but not all of the time. In ways that will become clearer later in the chapter, a reasonably strong conscience is probably sufficient to prevent a person from committing a crime that would have only a modest yield *and* that could not take place for, say, two days. This would be true even if the person was confident of not being caught. But now suppose the opportunity for committing the offense is immediately at hand—say, your poker-playing friends have left the room after the hand was dealt and you have a chance to peek at their cards, or the jewelry salesman has left the store with a tray of diamond rings open on the counter. Now, if the bite of conscience is not sufficient by itself to prevent the offense, the would-be offender will calculate, however roughly or inarticulately, the chances of being caught. He will know that if the friends suddenly return or the jewelry salesman is watching, he will lose things—in the first instance, reputation, and in the second, his freedom. People differ in how they calculate these risks. Some worry about any chance, however slight, of being caught and would be appalled at any loss of esteem, however small or fleeting; others will peek at the cards or grab a ring if they think they have any chance at all of getting away with it.

When present actions are governed by their consequences, "instrumental" (or operant) conditioning is at work. Unlike classically conditioned responses, instrumental conditioning involves behavior that affects the stimulus (e.g., not peeking at the cards or not taking the ring avoids the costs of the offense). Instrumental behavior affects the stimuli we receive, and this in turn affects subsequent behavior.

The distinction between classical and instrumental conditioning is by no means as clear as our simple definitions may make it appear. But if we bear in mind that behavior cannot be neatly explained by one or the other process, we can use the distinction to help us understand individual differences in criminality. Persons deficient in conscience may turn out to be persons who for various reasons resist classical conditioning—they do not internalize rules as easily as do others. Persons who, even with a strong conscience, commit crimes anyway may be persons who have difficulty imagining the future consequences of present action or who are so impulsive as to discount very heavily even those consequences they can foresee, and hence will resist the instrumental conditioning that might lead them to choose noncrime over crime.

The Context of Reinforcement

The effect of a reward or punishment is inversely proportional to the strength of all the reinforcements acting on a person at a given time. The more reinforcement a person is receiving, the less the value of any single reinforcement. The relativity of reinforcement has been demonstrated in the laboratory, but it can be illustrated by everyday experience. Ten dollars received just after payday is less reinforcing than ten dollars received just before payday, when money is running low. The gentle pleasures of the elderly or the infirm, for whom rewards have become fewer, may be as reinforcing to them as the more boisterous pleasures of the young and vigorous.

When the amount of reinforcement acting on a person increases, the strength of a small reward decreases relatively more than that of a large one. Since crime and noncrime usually have attached to them reinforcements of different magnitudes, changes in the context of reinforcement—that is, in the total amount of reinforcement operating—will affect the value of crime and noncrime differently. In Figure 14.1 the context of reinforcement is expanded. The increase in the context of reinforcement reduces the rewards attached to both crime and noncrime, but the rewards attached to crime

Figure 14.1 The Net Value of Crime and Noncrime

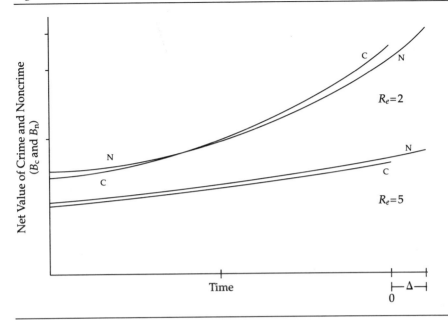

Note: The upper pair of curves represents the value of crime (C) and noncrime (N) in relation to the time interval between each behavior and its reward. Noncrime is assumed to have a larger reward than crime, but the reward for noncrime is Δ time units more delayed than the reward for crime. The criminal act takes *a* time units to execute. The crossing of the curves implies that crime will seem more rewarding when a criminal opportunity is at hand, but not when it is remote. The lower pair of curves shows the same choice between crime and noncrime after an increase in the general context of reward, R_e. When the context increases noncrime may rise above crime at all the delays of reward. A crime that would have occurred, given the opportunity, is forestalled by a general improvement in the context of reinforcement.

decrease more, with the result that now the person will not commit the crime. For example, a person who would commit a crime if the opportunity was sufficiently close in time and space (say, a boy who will grab a purse if he happens to come upon one being carried by a lone woman on the street) may not commit the crime if other reinforcers, having nothing to do with the value of crime or noncrime, start to operate (say, the boy has just fallen in love, is listening to some pleasant music on his portable stereo, and is enjoying a warm spring day).

There are other ways in which a changed context of reinforcement might affect the probability of the commission of a crime. Suppose not only that our boy has fallen in love, but that his girl has agreed to marry him. Suddenly he has more to lose from crime—that is, the value of noncrime has increased because now it includes retaining the affection of the girl and the respect of her parents. In this and other ways, the richer the supply of reinforcements operating on a person, the less chance he will commit a crime.

The Theory as a Whole

We began this chapter by asserting that the chief value of a comprehensive theory of crime is that it will bring to our attention all the factors that explain individual differences in criminality and thus prevent us from offering partial explanations or making incomplete interpretations of research findings.[2] The larger the ratio of the rewards (material and nonmaterial) of noncrime to the rewards (material and nonmaterial) of crime, the weaker the tendency to commit crimes. The bite of conscience, the approval of peers, and any sense of inequity will increase or decrease the total value of crime; the opinions of family, friends, and employers are important benefits of noncrime, as is the desire to avoid the penalties that can be imposed by the criminal justice system. The strength of any reward declines with time, but people differ in the rate at which they discount the future. The strength of a given reward is also affected by the total supply of reinforcers.

Some implications of the theory are obvious: Other things being equal, a reduction in the delay and uncertainty attached to the rewards of noncrime will reduce the probability of crime. But other implications are not so obvious. For instance, increasing the value of the rewards of noncrime (by increasing the severity of punishment) may not reduce a given individual's tendency to commit crime if he believes that these rewards are not commensurate with what he deserves. In this case, punishing him for preferring crime to noncrime may trigger hostility toward society in retaliation for the shortfall. The increased rewards for noncrime may be offset by an increased sense of inequity and hence an increased incentive for committing a crime. Or again: It may be easier to reduce crime by making penalties swifter or more certain, rather than more severe, if the persons committing crime are highly present-oriented (so that they discount even large rewards very sharply) or if they are likely to have their sense of inequity heightened by increases in the severity of punishment. Or yet again: An individual with an extroverted personality is more likely than one with an introverted one to externalize his feelings of inequity and act directly to correct them.

In laboratory settings involving both human and animal subjects, each element of the theory has received at least some confirmation, and the major elements have been confirmed extensively. Extrapolating these findings outside the laboratory into real-world settings is a matter on which opinions differ. Evidence from a variety of disciplines has a bearing on the connection between elements of the theory and the observed characteristics of crime and criminals.

The connection between crime and impulsiveness is clear, as is the link between (low) intelligence and crime. Those features of family life that produce stronger or weaker internalized inhibitions have a connection to the presence or absence of aggressiveness and criminality. Certain subcultures, such as street-corner gangs, appear to affect the value members attach to both crime and noncrime. The mass media, and in particular television, may affect both aggressiveness directly and a viewer's sense of inequity that can affect crime indirectly. Schooling may affect crime rates by bringing certain persons together into groups that reinforce either crime or noncrime and by determining the extent to which children believe that their skills will give them access to legitimate rewards. The condition of the economy will have a complex effect on crime depending on whether the (possibly) restraint-weakening impact of affluence dominates the restraint-strengthening influence of employment opportunities.

Though we will be using, for the most part, examples of rather common criminality to illustrate our argument, the theory is quite consistent with the more bizarre and unusual forms of crime. Psychopathic personalities lack to an unusual degree internalized inhibitions on crime. Persons possessed by some obsessive interest—for example, pyromania—attach an inordinately high value to the rewards of certain crimes. If everyone loved fire too much, society would try hard to teach the moral evil of fire, as well as its practical danger. As it is, what society does teach is sufficient to overcome whatever slight tendency toward pyromania every average person may have, but it is insufficient to inhibit the rare pyromaniac. One reason society punishes arsonists is not only to make it more costly for persons to use fire for material gain but also to provide extra moral education to the occasional person who loves fire for its own sake.

In addition to pathological drives, there are ordinary ones that can, under certain conditions, become so strong as to lead to crime. History and literature abound with normal men and women in the grip of a too powerful reinforcement. Many people have broken the law for love, honor, family, and country, as well as for money, sex, vengeance, or delusion. Such criminals may be psychologically unremarkable; they transgressed because as they perceived the situation, the reward for crime exceeded that for noncrime, and an opportunity presented itself. The legal system often tries to minimize the punishment inflicted on such people, which raises a number of separate issues.

Other Theories of Crime

Our approach to explaining individual differences in criminality is not meant to supplant but to encompass other theories. Following Travis Hirschi, we note that there are three main sociological perspectives on the causes of crime:

> According to *strain* or motivational theories, legitimate desires that conformity cannot satisfy force a person into deviance. According to *control* or bond theories, a person is free to commit delinquent acts because his ties to the conventional order have somehow been broken. According to *cultural deviance* theories,

the deviant conforms to a set of standards not accepted by the larger or more powerful society.

Strain theory assumes that people ordinarily obey society's rules but violate them when following those rules does not enable them to satisfy their legitimate aspirations. There is a strain between the goal they seek and the means at their disposal to reach that goal. Their opportunities are blocked; thus, strain theory is sometimes called the theory of differential opportunity. In some versions of strain theory, persons who are frustrated in their efforts to achieve middle-class goals abandon them and embrace antisocial values. In other versions, they persist in seeking wealth, property, and status but use criminal means to do so.

Advocates of strain theory are calling attention to the importance of certain reinforcers associated with noncrime, in particular the value of jobs and other sources of wealth and status, and suggesting that as these decline in strength (because they are not available or are of little value) the reinforcers associated with crime come to dominate the choices confronting the individual. This is a useful but partial observation. It properly reminds us of the importance to the individual of whatever alternatives to crime are available to him, but it neglects other components of the rewards of crime and noncrime and pays little attention to individual differences in impulsiveness and internalized inhibitions.

The reinforcers associated with noncrime include avoiding the penalties of the criminal justice system as well as obtaining the benefits of jobs; thus, the reinforcement supplied by noncrime can decline because *either* jobs become less available *or* sanctions decline in certainty or severity, or both. The theory also neglects the fact that the value of committing a crime is the sum not only of the money-supplying or status-conferring components of the crime but also of the costs (if any) of violating some internal inhibition and the benefits (if any) of rectifying a sense of inequity. Finally, strain theory ignores individual differences in time discounting (or impulsiveness).

Because of these limitations, strain theory cannot account for all of the observed facts about crime. It can offer no explanation, for example, of middle-class crime. If crime is disproportionately committed by lower-class persons because they find their lack of schooling and job opportunities a barrier to realizing their legitimate aspirations, then persons with adequate schooling and reasonable job prospects should not commit crimes, yet they do. If the people most likely to commit crimes are those in great need of legitimate rewards who find their access to those rewards blocked, then crime should be most common among men with families and heavy financial responsibilities, but in fact crime rates are highest among unattached males in the adolescent and young adult years.

Control theory directs our attention to the importance of learned inhibitions against crime. Unlike strain theory, which assumes that people naturally want to do the right thing but are prevented from doing it by circumstances, control theory suggests that it is first necessary to explain why anyone should want to do the right thing. This is an important suggestion because it reminds us of the intangible components of the reinforcements associated with both crime (the bite, if any, of conscience) and noncrime (the value, if any, of the good opinion of decent folk). Control theory asks how the social bond is formed and maintained. But important as this bonding may be, control theory does not explain all of the differences among individuals in criminality. In particular, it neglects differences in personality and orientation toward time: Some persons may commit crimes not because their attachment to legitimate norms is weak but because they are impulsive, unable to foresee the distant consequences of their actions, or confident that those consequences will not be costly. Moreover, control theory provides an incomplete account of the relationship between low intelligence and predatory criminality. The theory explains this connection largely by the claim that low-IQ individuals, frustrated by their inability to do well in their studies and jobs, fail to develop an attachment to school and work. This may well occur, but it is also possible that cognitive deficits affect criminality more directly because they are associated with having a short time horizon.

Cultural deviance theory also focuses on learning, but asserts that criminals have learned their values from deviant rather than law-abiding persons. Like control theory, this view directs our attention to the intangible reinforcers associated with crime and noncrime, suggesting that criminals are those who have learned that crime is worthwhile because it is reinforced by the good opinion of persons in whose company one commits the crime or who later learn of it. In some versions of this theory, deviant behavior is learned from other offenders by a process called "differential association"; in other versions, it is learned from a distinctive subculture composed of lower-class males who may not directly teach criminality but who value toughness, excitement, autonomy, and "street smarts" and have a fatalistic attitude toward the future. Useful as this perspective is, it cannot explain why some persons take their cues from street gangs while others take them from their families and other nondeviant individuals, nor is it consistent with the fact that high-rate delinquents seem to be boys who are *not* well integrated into gangs and who have few close or lasting friendships. In short, cultural deviance theory provides no explanation for individual differences and thus cannot account for the fact that in a given neighborhood or social class some boys adopt deviant values and others adopt conventional ones. And the theory has no place for those tangible reinforcements associated with crime and noncrime that may lead persons with conventional values to commit crimes (because they are so profitable) or dissuade persons with deviant values from committing them (because they are so unprofitable).

Notes

1. The specialist will recognize the debt we owe to, and the liberties we have taken with, the work of Edward L. Thorndike, Albert Bandura, B. F. Skinner, R. B. Cattell, H. J. Eysenck, I. P. Pavlov, and E. C. Tolman, among others.
2. There is an advantage to stating the theory mathematically. We thereby make it easier in principle to deal simultaneously with the interaction of several variables, and thus we resist the tendency in thinking about crime to keep only two or three things in mind at one time and to treat those few things as either-or propositions. But the essence of the theory can be grasped without the mathematical notation.

References

Bradshaw, C. M., Szabadi, E., & Lowe, C. F. (Eds.). (1981). *Quantification of steady-state operant behavior.* Amsterdam: Elsevier/North Holland Biomedical Press.

Catania, A. C. (1973). Self-inhibiting effects of reinforcement. *Journal of the Experimental Analysis of Behavior, 19,* 517–526.

Cloward, R. A., & Ohlin, L. E. (1960). *Delinquency and opportunity.* New York: Free Press.

Cohen, A. K. (1955). *Delinquent boys.* New York: Free Press.

Commons, M. L., Herrnstein, R. J., & Rachlin, H. (Eds.). (1982). *Quantitative analyses of behavior: Matching and maximizing accounts.* Cambridge, Mass.: Ballinger.

Donahoe, J. W. (1977). Some implications of a relational principle of reinforcement. *Journal of the Experimental Analysis of Behavior, 27,* 341–350.

Eysenck, H. J. (1977). *Crime and personality* (rev. ed.). London: Routledge & Kegan Paul.

Herrnstein, R. J. (1970). On the law of effect. *Journal of the Experimental Analysis of Behavior, 13,* 243–266.

Herrnstein, R. J. (1983). Some criminogenic traits of offenders. In J. Q. Wilson (Ed.), *Crime and public policy* (pp. 31–49). San Francisco: ICS Press.

Herrnstein, R. J., & Boring, E. G. (1965). *A sourcebook in the history of psychology.* Cambridge, Mass.: Harvard University Press.

Hirschi, T. (1969). *Causes of delinquency.* Berkeley: University of California Press.

Matza, D. (1964). *Delinquency and drift.* New York: Wiley.

Miller, W. B. (1958). Lower class culture as a generating milieu of gang delinquency. *Journal of Social Issues, 14,* 5–19.

Miller, W. B. (1961). Preference for delayed reinforcement and social responsibility. *Journal of Abnormal and Social Psychology, 62,* 1–7.

Premack, D. (1965). Reinforcement theory. In D. Levine (Ed.), *Nebraska Symposium on Motivation.* Lincoln, Neb.: University of Nebraska Press.

Premack, D. (1971). Catching up with common sense, or two sides of a generalization: Reinforcement and punishment. In D. Glaser (Ed.), *The nature of reinforcement.* New York: Academic Press.

Sutherland, E. H., & Cressey, D. R. (1966). *Principles of criminology* (7th ed.). Philadelphia: J. B. Lippincott.

15

Toward an Interactional Theory of Delinquency

TERENCE P. THORNBERRY

Contemporary theories of delinquency are seen as limited in three respects: They tend to rely on unidirectional causal structures that represent delinquency in a static rather than dynamic fashion, they do not examine developmental progressions, and they do not adequately link processual concepts to the person's position in the social structure. This chapter develops an interactional theory of delinquency that addresses each of these issues. It views delinquency as resulting from the freedom afforded by the weakening of the person's bonds to conventional society and from an interactional setting in which delinquent behavior is learned and reinforced. Moreover, the control, learning, and delinquency variables are seen as reciprocally interrelated, mutually affecting one another over the person's life. Thus, delinquency is viewed as part of a larger causal network, affected by social factors but also affecting the development of those social factors over time.

A variety of sociological theories have been developed to explain the onset and maintenance of delinquent behavior. Currently, three are of primary importance: social control theory (Hirschi, 1969), social learning theory (Akers, 1977), and integrated models that combine them into a broader body of explanatory principles (Elliott, Ageton, and Canter, 1979; Elliott, Huizinga, and Ageton, 1985).

Control theory argues that delinquency emerges whenever the social and cultural constraints over human conduct are substantially attenuated. As Hirschi stated in his classic presentation (1969), control theory assumes that

The present chapter was supported in part by the Office of Juvenile Justice and Delinquency Prevention, grant number 86-JN-CX-0007; the views expressed are mine and not necessarily those of the funding agency. I would like to thank Drs. Robert A. Silverman of the University of Alberta and Margaret Farnworth, Alan Lizotte, and Hans Toch of the University at Albany for providing helpful comments on earlier drafts of this article.

we would all be deviant if only we dared. Learning theory, on the other hand, posits that there is no natural impulse toward delinquency. Indeed, delinquent behavior must be learned through the same processes and mechanisms as conforming behavior. Because of these different starting points, control and learning models give causal priority to somewhat different concepts, and integrated models capitalize on these complementary approaches. Muting the assumptive differences, integrated theories meld together propositions from these (and sometimes other theories—for example, strain) to explain delinquent behavior.

Although these approaches have substantially informed our understanding of the causes of delinquency, they and other contemporary theories suffer from three fundamental limitations. First, they rely on unidirectional rather than reciprocal causal structures. By and large, current theories ignore reciprocal effects in which delinquent behavior is viewed as part of a more general social nexus, affected by, but also affecting, other social factors. Second, current theories tend to be nondevelopmental, specifying causal models for only a narrow age range, usually mid-adolescence. As a result, they fail to capitalize on developmental patterns to explain the initiation, maintenance, and desistance of delinquency. Finally, contemporary theories tend to assume uniform causal effects throughout the social structure. By ignoring the person's structural position, they fail to provide an understanding of the sources of initial variation in both delinquency and its presumed causes. In combination, these three limitations have led to theories that are narrowly conceived and provide incomplete and, at times, misleading models of the causes of delinquency.

Origins and Assumptions

The basic premise of the model proposed here is that human behavior occurs in social interaction and can therefore best be explained by models that focus on interactive processes. Rather than viewing adolescents as propelled along a unidirectional pathway to one or another outcome—that is, delinquency or conformity—it argues that adolescents interact with other people and institutions and that behavioral outcomes are formed by that interactive process. For example, the delinquent behavior of adolescents is formed in part by how they and their parents *interact* over time, not simply by their perceived, and presumably invariant, *level* of attachment to parents. Moreover, since it is an interactive system, the behaviors of others—for example, parents and school officials—are influenced both by each other and by the adolescents, including their delinquent behavior. If this view is correct, then interactional effects have to be modeled explicitly if we are to understand the social and psychological processes involved with initiation into delinquency, the maintenance of such behavior, and its eventual reduction.

Interactional theory develops from the same intellectual tradition as the theories mentioned above. It asserts that the fundamental cause of delinquency lies in the weakening of social constraints over the conduct of the individual. Unlike classical control theory, however, it does not assume that the attenuation of controls leads directly to delinquency. The weakening of controls simply allows for a much wider array of behavior, including continued conventional action, failure as indicated by school dropout and sporadic employment histories, alcoholism, mental illness, delinquent and criminal careers, or some combination of these outcomes. For the freedom resulting from weakened bonds to be channeled into delinquency, especially serious prolonged delinquency, an interactive setting is required in which delinquency is learned, performed, and reinforced.

Theoretical Concepts

Given these basic premises, an interactional model must respond to two overriding issues. First, how are traditional social constraints over behavior weakened, and second, once weakened, how is the resulting freedom channeled into delinquent patterns? To address these issues, this chapter presents an initial version of an interactional model, focusing on the interrelationships among six concepts: attachment to parents, commitment to school, belief in conventional values, associations with delinquent peers, adoption of delinquent values, and delinquent behavior. These concepts form the core of the theoretical model, since they are central to social psychological theories of delinquency and since they have been shown in numerous studies to be strongly related to subsequent delinquent behavior (see Elliott et al., 1985: chs. 1–3, for an excellent review of this literature).

The first three derive from Hirschi's version of control theory (1969) and represent the primary mechanisms by which adolescents are bonded to conventional middle-class society. When those elements of the bond are weakened, behavioral freedom increases considerably. For that freedom to lead to delinquent behavior, however, interactive settings that reinforce delinquency are required. In the model, those settings are represented by two concepts—associations with delinquent peers and the formation of delinquent values—that derive primarily from social learning theory.

For the purpose of explicating the overall theoretical perspective, each of these concepts is defined quite broadly. Attachment to parents includes the affective relationship between parent and child, communication patterns, parenting skills such as monitoring and discipline, parent-child conflict, and the like. Commitment to school refers to the stake in conformity the adolescent has developed and includes such factors as success in school, perceived importance of education, attachment to teachers, and involvement in school activities. Belief in conventional values represents the granting of legitimacy to such middle-class values as education, personal industry, financial success, deferral of gratification, and the like.

Three delinquency variables are included in the model. Association with delinquent peers includes the level of attachment to peers, the delinquent behavior and values of peers, and their reinforcing reactions to the adolescent's own delinquent or conforming behavior. It is a continuous measure that can vary from groups that are heavily delinquent to those that are almost entirely nondelinquent. Delinquent values refer to the granting of legitimacy to delinquent activities as acceptable modes of behavior as well as a general willingness to violate the law to achieve other ends.

Delinquent behavior, the primary outcome variable, refers to acts that place the youth at risk for adjudication; it ranges from status offenses to serious violent activities. Since the present model is an interactional one, interested in explaining not only delinquency but also the effects of delinquency on other variables, particular attention is paid to prolonged involvement in serious delinquency.

Model Specification

A causal model allowing for reciprocal relationships among the six concepts of interest—attachment to parents, commitment to school, belief in conventional values, association with delinquent peers, delinquent values, and delinquent behavior—is presented in Figure 15.1. This model refers to the period of early adolescence, from about ages eleven to thirteen, when delinquent careers are beginning, but prior to the period at which delinquency reaches its apex in terms of seriousness and frequency. In the following sections the model is extended to later ages.

The specification of causal effects begins by examining the three concepts that form the heart of social learning theories of delinquency—delinquent peers, delinquent values, and delinquent behavior. For now we focus on the reciprocal nature of the relationships, ignoring until later variations in the strength of the relationships.

Traditional social learning theory specifies a causal order among these variables in which delinquent associations affect delinquent values, and in turn both produce delinquent behavior (Akers, Krohn, Lanza-Kaduce, and Radosevich, 1979; Matsueda, 1982). Yet, for each of the dyadic relationships involving these variables, other theoretical perspectives and much empirical evidence suggest the appropriateness of reversing this causal order. For example, social learning theory proposes that associating with delinquents or, more precisely, people who hold and reinforce delinquent values increases the chances of delinquent behavior (Akers, 1977). Yet, as far back as the work of the Gluecks (1950) this specification has been challenged. Arguing that "birds of a feather flock together," the Gluecks proposed that youths who are delinquent seek out and associate with others who share those tendencies. From this perspective, rather than being a cause of delinquency, associ-

Figure 15.1 A Reciprocal Model of Delinquent Involvement at Early Adolescence*

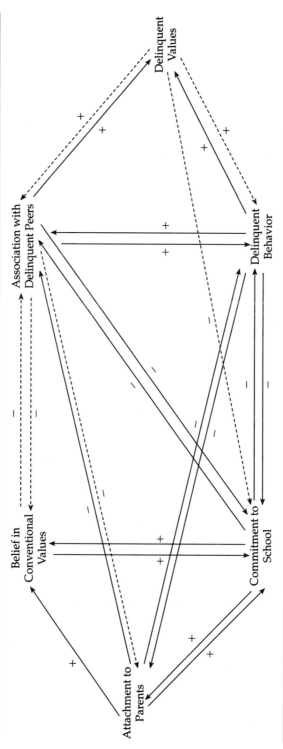

*Solid lines represent stronger effects; dashed lines represent weaker effects.

ations are the result of delinquents seeking out and associating with like-minded peers.

An attempt to resolve the somewhat tedious argument over the temporal priority of associations and behavior is less productive theoretically than capitalizing on the interactive nature of human behavior and treating the relationship as it probably is: a reciprocal one. People often take on the behavioral repertoire of their associates, but at the same time they often seek out associates who share their behavioral interests. Individuals clearly behave this way in conventional settings, and there is no reason to assume that deviant activities, such as delinquency, are substantially different in this regard.

Similar arguments can be made for the other two relationships among the delinquency variables. Most recent theories of delinquency, following the lead of social learning theory, posit that delinquent associations lead to the formation of delinquent values. Subcultural theories, however, especially those that derive from a cultural deviance perspective (Miller, 1958) suggest that values precede the formation of peer groups. Indeed, it is the socialization of adolescents into the "lower-class culture" and its particular value system that leads them to associate with delinquent peers in the first place. This specification can also be derived from a social control perspective as demonstrated in Weis and Sederstrom's social development model (1981) and Burkett and Warren's social selection model (1987).

Finally, the link between delinquent values and delinquent behavior restates, in many ways, the basic social psychological question of the relationship between attitudes and behavior. Do attitudes form behavior patterns, or does behavior lead to attitude formation? Social psychological research, especially in cognitive psychology and balance models (for example, Festinger, 1957; Brehm and Cohen, 1962), points to the reciprocal nature of this relationship. It suggests that people indeed behave in a manner consistent with their attitudes, but also that behavior is one of the most persuasive forces in the formation and maintenance of attitudes.

Such a view of the relationship between delinquent values and behavior is consistent with Hindelang's findings:

> This general pattern of results indicates that one can "predict" a respondent's self approval [of illegal behaviors] from knowledge of that respondent's involvement/non-involvement [in delinquency] with fewer errors than vice-versa (1974:382).

It is also consistent with recent deterrence research, which demonstrates that the "experiential effect," in which behavior affects attitudes, is much stronger than the deterrent effect, in which attitudes affect behavior (Paternoster, Saltzman, Waldo, and Chiricos, 1982; Paternoster, Saltzman, Chiricos, and Waldo, 1983).

Although each of these relationships appears to be reciprocal, the predicted strengths of the associations are not of equal strength during the early adolescent period (see Figure 15.1). Beliefs that delinquent conduct is acceptable and positively valued may be emerging, but such beliefs are not fully articulated for eleven- to thirteen-year-olds. Because of their emerging quality, they are viewed as more effect than cause, produced by delinquent behavior and associations with delinquent peers. As these values emerge, however, they have feedback effects, albeit relatively weak ones at these ages, on behavior and associations. That is, as the values become more fully articulated and delinquency becomes positively valued, it increases the likelihood of such behavior and further reinforces associations with like-minded peers.

Summary

When attention is focused on the interrelationships among associations with delinquent peers, delinquent values, and delinquent behavior, it appears that they are, in fact, reciprocally related. The world of human behavior is far more complex than a simple recursive one in which a temporal order can be imposed on interactional variables of this nature. Interactional theory sees these three concepts as embedded in a causal loop, each reinforcing the others over time. Regardless of where the individual enters the loop, the following obtains: Delinquency increases associations with delinquent peers and delinquent values; delinquent values increase delinquent behavior and associations with delinquent peers; and associations with delinquent peers increase delinquent behavior and delinquent values. The question now concerns the identification of factors that lead some youth, but not others, into this spiral of increasing delinquency.

Social Control Effects

As indicated at the outset of this chapter, the premise of interactional theory is that the fundamental cause of delinquency is the attenuation of social controls over the person's conduct. Whenever bonds to the conventional world are substantially weakened, the individual is freed from moral constraints and is at risk for a wide array of deviant activities, including delinquency. The primary mechanisms that bind adolescents to the conventional world are attachment to parents, commitment to school, and belief in conventional values; and the role of these mechanisms in the model can now be examined.

During the early adolescent years, the family is the most salient arena for social interaction and involvement, and because of this, attachment to parents has a stronger influence on other aspects of the youth's life at this stage than it does at later stages of development. With this in mind, attachment to parents* is predicted to affect four other variables. Since youths who are attached to their parents are sensitive to their wishes (Hirschi, 1969:16–19), and since parents are almost universally supportive of the conventional world, these children are likely to be strongly committed to school and to espouse conventional values. In addition, youths who are attached to their parents, again because of their sensitivity to parental wishes, are unlikely to associate with delinquent peers or to engage in delinquent behavior.

In brief, parental influence is seen as central to controlling the behavior of youths at these relatively early ages. Parents who have a strong affective bond with their children, who communicate with them, who exercise appropriate parenting skills, and so forth, are likely to lead their children toward conventional actions and beliefs and away from delinquent friends and actions.

On the other hand, attachment to parents is not seen as an immutable trait, impervious to the effects of other variables. Indeed, associating with delinquent peers, not being committed to school, and engaging in delinquent behavior are so contradictory to parental expectations that they tend to diminish the level of attachment between parent and child. Adolescents who fail at school, who associate with delinquent peers, and who engage in delinquent conduct are, as a consequence, likely to jeopardize their affective bond with their parents, precisely because these behaviors suggest that the "person does not care about the wishes and expectations of other people . . ." (Hirschi, 1969:18), in this instance, his or her parents.

Turning next to belief in conventional values, this concept is involved in two different causal loops. First, it strongly affects commitment to school and is in turn affected by commitment to school. In essence, this loop posits a behavioral and attitudinal consistency in the conventional realm. Second, a weaker loop is posited between belief in conventional values and associations with delinquent peers. Youths who do not grant legitimacy to conventional values are more apt to associate with delinquent friends who share those views, and those friendships are likely to attenuate further their beliefs in conventional values. This reciprocal specification is supported by Burkett and Warren's findings concerning religious beliefs and peer associations (1987). Finally, youths who believe in conventional values are seen as somewhat less likely to engage in delinquent behavior.

Although belief in conventional values plays some role in the genesis of delinquency, its impact is not particularly strong. For example, it is not affected by delinquent behavior, nor is it related to delinquent values. This is primarily because belief in conventional values appears to be quite invariant; regardless of class of origin or delinquency status, for example, most people strongly assert conventional values (Short and Strodtbeck, 1965:ch. 3). Nev-

---

*The term "attachment to parents" is used throughout the chapter, but it is clear that parent surrogates—for example foster parents or guardians—can also perform this function.

ertheless, these beliefs do exert some influence in the model, especially with respect to reinforcing commitment to school.

Finally, the impact of commitment to school is considered. This variable is involved in reciprocal loops with both of the other bonding variables. Youngsters who are attached to their parents are likely to be committed to and succeed in school, and that success is likely to reinforce the close ties to their parents. Similarly, youths who believe in conventional values are likely to be committed to school, the primary arena in which they can act in accordance with those values, and, in turn, success in that arena is likely to reinforce the beliefs.

In addition to its relationships with the other control variables, commitment to school also has direct effects on two of the delinquency variables. Students who are committed to succeeding in school are unlikely to associate with delinquents or to engage in substantial amounts of serious, repetitive delinquent behavior. These youths have built up a stake in conformity and should be unwilling to jeopardize that investment either by engaging in delinquent behavior or by associating with those who do.

Low commitment to school is not seen as leading directly to the formation of delinquent values, however. Its primary effect on delinquent values is indirect, via associations with delinquent peers and delinquent behavior (Conger, 1980:137). While school failure may lead to a reduced commitment to conventional values, it does not follow that it directly increases the acceptance of values that support delinquency.

Commitment to school, on the other hand, is affected by each of the delinquency variables in the model. Youths who accept values that are consistent with delinquent behavior, who associate with other delinquents, and who engage in delinquent behavior are simply unlikely candidates to maintain an active commitment to school and the conventional world that school symbolizes.

Summary

Attachment to parents, commitment to school, and belief in conventional values reduce delinquency by cementing the person to conventional institutions and people. When these elements of the bond to conventional society are strong, delinquency is unlikely, but when they are weak the individual is placed at much greater risk for delinquency. When viewed from an interactional perspective, two additional qualities of these concepts become increasingly evident.

First, attachment to parents, commitment to school, and belief in conventional values are not static attributes of the person, invariant over time. These concepts interact with one another during the developmental process. For some youths the levels of attachment, commitment, and belief increase as these elements reinforce one another, while for other youths the interlocking nature of these relationships suggests that a greater attenuation of the bond will develop over time.

Second, the bonding variables appear to be reciprocally linked to delinquency, exerting a causal impact on associations with delinquent peers and delinquent behavior; they are also causally affected by these variables. As the youth engages in more and more delinquent conduct and increasingly associates with delinquent peers, the level of his or her bond to the conventional world is further weakened. Thus, while the weakening of the bond to conventional society may be an initial cause of delinquency, delinquency eventually becomes its own indirect cause precisely because of its ability to weaken further the person's bonds to family, school, and conventional beliefs. The implications of this amplifying causal structure are examined below. First, however, the available support for reciprocal models is reviewed and the basic model is extended to later developmental stages.

Developmental Extensions

The previous section developed a strategy for addressing one of the three major limitations of delinquency theories mentioned in the introduction, namely, their unidirectional causal structure. A second limitation is the non-developmental posture of most theories, which tend to provide a cross-sectional picture of the factors associated with delinquency at one age but which do not provide a rationale for understanding how delinquent behavior develops over time. The present section offers a developmental extension of the basic model.

Middle Adolescence

First, a model for middle adolescence, when the youths are approximately fifteen or sixteen years of age, is presented (Figure 15.2). This period corresponds to the highest rates of involvement in delinquency and is the reference period, either implicitly or explicitly, for most theories of delinquent involvement. Since the models for the early and middle adolescent periods have essentially the same structure and causal relationships (Figures 15.1 and 15.2), discussion focuses on the differences between them and does not repeat the rationale for individual causal effects.

Perhaps the most important difference concerns attachment to parents, which is involved in relatively few strong relationships. By this point in the life cycle, the most salient variables involved in the production of delinquency are likely to be external to the home, associated with the youth's activities in school and peer networks. This specification is consistent with empirical results for subjects in this age range (Johnson, 1979:105; and Schoenberg, 1975, quoted in Johnson). Indeed, Johnson concluded that "an

Figure 15.2 A Reciprocal Model of Delinquent Involvement at Middle Adolescence*

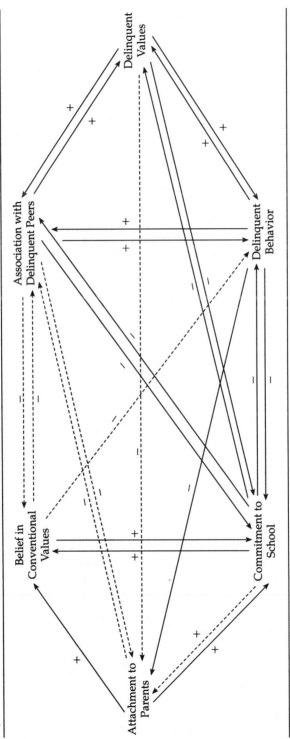

*Solid lines represent stronger effects; dashed lines represent weaker effects.

adolescent's public life has as much or more to do with his or her deviance or conformity than do 'under-the-roof' experiences" (1979:116).

This is not to say that attachment to parents is irrelevant; such attachments are involved in enhancing commitment to school and belief in conventional values, and in preventing associations with delinquent peers. It is just that the overall strength of parental effects is weaker than at earlier ages when the salience of the family as a locus of interaction and control was greater.

The second major change concerns the increased importance of delinquent values as a causal factor. It is still embedded in the causal loop with the other two delinquency variables, but now it is as much cause as effect. Recall that at the younger ages delinquent values were seen as emerging, produced by associations with delinquent peers and delinquent behavior. Given their emergent nature, they were not seen as primary causes of other variables. At mid-adolescence, however, when delinquency is at its apex, these values are more fully articulated and have stronger effects on other variables. First, delinquent values are seen as major reinforcers of both delinquent associations and delinquent behavior. In general, espousing values supportive of delinquency tends to increase the potency of this causal loop. Second, since delinquent values are antithetical to the conventional settings of school and family, youths who espouse them are less likely to be committed to school and attached to parents. Consistent with the reduced saliency of family at these ages, the feedback effect to school is seen as stronger than the feedback effect to parents.

By and large, the other concepts in the model play the same role at these ages as they do at the earlier ones. Thus, the major change from early to middle adolescence concerns the changing saliency of some of the theoretical concepts. The family declines in relative importance, while the adolescent's own world of school and peers takes on increasing significance. While these changes occur, the overall structure of the theory remains constant. These interactive variables are still seen as mutually reinforcing over time.

Later Adolescence

Finally, the causes of delinquency during the transition from adolescence to adulthood, about ages eighteen to twenty, can be examined (Figure 15.3). At these ages one should more properly speak of crime than delinquency, but for consistency we will continue to use the term delinquency in the causal diagrams and employ the terms delinquency and crime interchangeably in the text.

Two new variables are added to the model to reflect the changing life circumstances at this stage of development. The more important of these is commitment to conventional activities, which includes employment, attending college, and military service. Along with the transition to the world of work, there is a parallel transition from the family of origin to one's own

Figure 15.3   A Reciprocal Model of Delinquent Involvement at Later Adolescence*

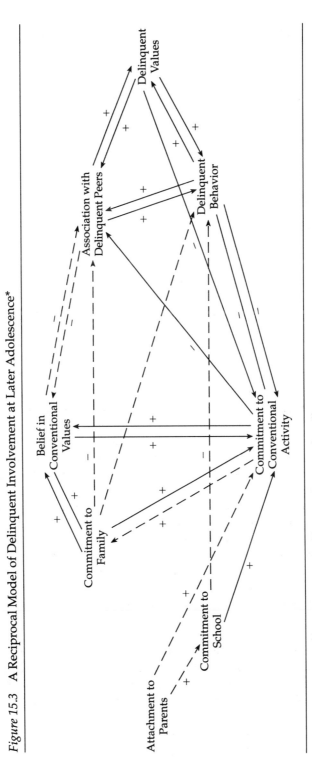

*Solid lines represent stronger effects; dashed lines represent weaker effects.

family. Although this transition does not peak until the early twenties, for many people its influence is beginning at this stage. Included in this concept are marriage, plans for marriage, and plans for child rearing. These new variables largely replace attachment to parents and commitment to school in the theoretical scheme; they represent the major sources of bonds to conventional society for young adults.

Both attachment to parents and commitment to school remain in the model but take on the cast of exogenous variables. Attachment to parents has only a minor effect on commitment to school, and commitment to school is proposed to affect only commitment to conventional activities and, more weakly, delinquent behavior.

The other three variables considered in the previous models—association with delinquent peers, delinquent values, and delinquent behavior—are still hypothesized to be embedded in an amplifying causal loop. As indicated above, this loop is most likely to occur among adolescents who, at earlier ages, were freed from the controlling influence of parents and school. Moreover, via the feedback paths delinquent peers, delinquent values, and delinquent behavior further alienate the youth from parents and diminish commitment to school. Once this spiral begins, the probability of sustained delinquency increases.

This situation, if it continued uninterrupted, would yield higher and higher rates of crime as the subjects matured. Such an outcome is inconsistent with the desistance that has been observed during this age period (Wolfgang, Thornberry, and Figlio, 1987). Rates of delinquency and crime begin to subside by the late teenage years, a phenomenon often attributed to "maturational reform." Such an explanation, however, is tautological, since it claims that crime stops when adolescents get older because they get older. It is also uninformative, since the concept of maturational reform is theoretically undefined.

A developmental approach, however, offers an explanation for desistance. As the developmental process unfolds, life circumstances change, developmental milestones are met (or, for some, missed), new social roles are created, and new networks of attachments and commitments emerge. The effects of these changes enter the processual model to explain new and often dramatically different behavioral patterns. In the present model, these changes are represented by commitment to conventional activity and commitment to family.

Commitment to conventional activity is influenced by a number of variables, including earlier attachment to parents, commitment to school, and belief in conventional values. And once the transition to the world of work is made, tremendous opportunities are afforded for new and different effects in the delinquency model. Becoming committed to conventional activities—work, college, military service, and so on—reduces the likelihood of delinquent behavior and associations with delinquent peers because it builds up a stake in conformity that is antithetical to delinquency.

Moreover, since the delinquency variables are still embedded in a causal loop, the effect of commitment to conventional activities tends to resonate throughout the system. But because of the increased saliency of a new variable—commitment to conventional activities—the reinforcing loop is now set in motion to *reduce* rather than increase delinquent and criminal involvement.

The variable of commitment to family has similar, albeit weaker effects, since the transition to the family is only beginning at these ages. Nevertheless, commitment to family is proposed to reduce both delinquent associations and delinquent values and to increase commitment to conventional activity. In general, as the individual takes on the responsibilities of family, the bond to conventional society increases, placing additional constraints on behavior and precluding further delinquency.

These changes do not occur in all cases, however; nor should they be expected to, since many delinquents continue on to careers in adult crime. In the Philadelphia cohort of 1945, 51 percent of the juvenile delinquents were also adult offenders, and the more serious and prolonged the delinquent careers were, the greater were the odds of an adult career (Wolfgang et al., 1987:ch. 4).

The continuation of criminal careers can also be explained by the nature of the reciprocal effects included in this model. In general, extensive involvement in delinquency at earlier ages feeds back upon and weakens attachment to parents and commitment to school (see Figures 15.1 and 15.2). These variables, as well as involvement in delinquency itself, weaken later commitment to family and to conventional activities (Figure 15.3). Thus, these new variables—commitment to conventional activities and to family—are affected by the person's situation at earlier stages and do not "automatically" alter the probability of continued criminal involvement. If the initial bonds are extremely weak, the chances of new bonding variables being established to break the cycle toward criminal careers are low, and it is likely that criminal behavior will continue.

Conclusion

The present chapter has developed an interactional theory of delinquent behavior. Unlike traditional theories of delinquency, interactional theory does not view delinquency merely as an outcome or consequence of a social process. On the contrary, it views delinquent behavior as an active part of the developmental process, interacting with other social factors over time to determine the person's ultimate behavioral repertoire.

The initial impetus toward delinquency comes from a weakening of the person's bond to conventional society, represented during adolescence by attachment to parents, commitment to school, and belief in conventional values. Whenever these three links to conformity are attenuated, there is a substantially increased potential for delinquent behavior.

For that potential to be converted to delinquency, however, especially prolonged serious delinquency, a social setting in which delinquency is learned and reinforced is required. This setting is represented by associations with delinquent peers and delinquent values. These two variables, along with delinquent behavior itself, form a mutually reinforcing causal loop that leads toward increasing delinquency involvement over time.

Moreover, this interactive process develops over the person's life cycle, and the saliency of the theoretical concepts varies as the person ages. During early adolescence, the family is the most influential factor in bonding the youth to conventional society and reducing delinquency. As the youth matures and moves through middle adolescence, the world of friends, school, and youth culture becomes the dominant influence over behavior. Finally, as the person enters adulthood, new variables, especially commitment to conventional activities and to family, offer a number of new avenues to reshape the person's bond to society and involvement with delinquency.

Finally, interactional theory posits that these process variables are systematically related to the person's position in the social structure. Class, minority-group status, and the social disorganization of the neighborhood of residence all affect the initial values of the interactive variables as well as the behavioral trajectories. Youths from the most socially disadvantaged backgrounds begin the process least bonded to conventional society and most exposed to the world of delinquency. Furthermore, the reciprocal nature of the process increases the chances that they will continue on to a career of serious criminal involvement. On the other hand, youths from middle-class families enter a trajectory that is strongly oriented toward conformity and away from delinquency.

But regardless of the initial starting points or the eventual outcome, the essential point of an interactional theory is that the causal process is a dynamic one that develops over the person's life. And delinquent behavior is a vital part of that process; it is clearly affected by, but it also affects, the bonding and learning variables that have always played a prominent role in sociological explanations of delinquency.

References

Akers, R. (1977). *Deviant behavior: A social learning perspective*. Belmont, Calif.: Wadsworth.

Akers, R. L., Krohn, M. D., Lanza-Kaduce, L., & Radosevich, M. (1979). Social learning theory and deviant behavior. *American Sociological Review, 44*, 635–655.

Brehm, J. W., & Cohen, A. R. (1962). *Explorations in cognitive dissonance*. New York: Wiley.

Burkett, S. R., & Warren, B. O. (1987). Religiosity, peer influence, and adolescent marijuana use: A panel study of underlying causal structures. *Criminology, 25,* 109–131.

Conger, R. D. (1980). Juvenile delinquency: Behavior restraint or behavior facilitation? In T. Hirschi & M. R. Gottfredson (Eds.), *Understanding crime.* Beverly Hills, Calif.: Sage.

Elliott, D. S., Ageton, S. S., & Canter, R. J. (1979). An integrated theoretical perspective on delinquent behavior. *Journal of Research on Crime and Delinquency, 16,* 3–27.

Elliott, D. S., Huizinga, D., & Ageton, S. S. (1985). *Explaining delinquency and drug use.* Beverly Hills, Calif.: Sage.

Festinger, L. (1957). *A theory of cognitive dissonance.* Stanford, Calif.: Stanford University Press.

Glueck, S., & Glueck, E. (1950). *Unraveling juvenile delinquency.* Cambridge, Mass.: Harvard University Press.

Hindelang, M. J. (1974). Moral evaluations of illegal behaviors. *Social Problems, 21,* 370–384.

Hirschi, T. (1969). *Causes of delinquency.* Berkeley: University of California Press.

Johnson, R. E. (1979). *Juvenile delinquency and its origins.* Cambridge, England: Cambridge University Press.

Matsueda, R. (1982). Testing social control theory and differential association. *American Sociological Review, 47,* 489–504.

Miller, W. B. (1958). Lower class culture as a generating milieu of gang delinquency. *Journal of Social Issues, 14,* 5–19.

Paternoster, R., Saltzman, L. E., Waldo, G. P., & Chiricos, T. G. (1982). Perceived risk and deterrence: Methodological artifacts in perceptual deterrence research. *Journal of Criminal Law and Criminology, 73,* 1238–1258.

Paternoster, R., Saltzman, L. E., Chiricos, T. G., & Waldo, G. P. (1983). Perceived risk and social control: Do sanctions really deter? *Law and Society Review, 17,* 457–479.

Schoenberg, R. J. (1975). A structural model of delinquency. Unpublished doctoral dissertation. Seattle: University of Washington.

Short, J. F., Jr., & Strodtbeck, F. L. (1965). *Group processes and gang delinquency.* Chicago: University of Chicago Press.

16

Crime in the Making: Pathways and Turning Points Through Life

JOHN H. LAUB

This chapter begins with two life histories. Both of the individuals concerned grew up in Boston during the Great Depression; both lived in disadvantaged neighborhoods; both had difficult family and school experiences; and, most important, both were juvenile delinquents and were incarcerated for their crimes in state reform schools. After presenting these life histories, the chapter recounts how these cases came to light and describes the larger study from which they are drawn. Next, it outlines an ongoing research project examining criminal and deviant behavior over the life course and discusses a theory of age-graded informal social control (see Sampson and Laub, 1993; Laub and Sampson, 1993). Finally, it explores the implications of this research for current thinking about crime and crime control.

Juvenile Delinquents Grown Up

Jimmy was born in Boston on August 8, 1926. He had an extensive record of criminal behavior as an adolescent and as an adult, totaling thirty-five arrests up to his death at age fifty-eight. Although his first arrest occurred at

This chapter was originally presented as the Thirtieth Annual Robert D. Klein University Lecture at Northeastern University in Boston on March 17, 1994. This research stems from an ongoing project using data from the Sheldon and Eleanor Glueck archives of the Harvard Law School Library, currently on long-term loan to the Henry A. Murray Research Center of Radcliffe College, and draws in large part from *Crime in the Making: Pathways and Turning Points Through Life,* co-authored with Robert J. Sampson (Harvard University Press, 1993). I thank Robert Sampson for comments on an earlier draft.

age twelve for burglary, Jimmy began stealing at age eight. He was eventually committed to the Lyman School for Boys a month before his fourteenth birthday. As an adolescent, Jimmy was committed to Lyman three times, serving a total of nineteen months. As a young man he was arrested for assault and battery, robbery, larceny, reckless driving—including leaving the scene of an accident—and public drunkenness.

Jimmy grew up in the West End and South End of Boston. He was one of eight children in his family. There was little parental control in the household, and Jimmy was not well supervised. At the age of six, Jimmy began staying out late at night. At the same time, he started to skip school on a regular basis. Although his IQ scores were relatively high, he refused to attend school, he had to repeat grades, and he eventually dropped out in the ninth grade. Throughout his childhood and early adolescence, Jimmy's best friends were juvenile delinquents like him.

At age twenty-four, Jimmy married. He lived with his wife and child in the Boston area. During the first year of his marriage, there were domestic difficulties. The couple separated on and off during the year. There were also indications of domestic violence. It appeared that on one occasion Jimmy grabbed his wife by the throat. In addition, he had repeatedly threatened her with violence. His wife stated that she was afraid of him, and Jimmy was later arrested for assault and battery on his wife as well as child neglect. The case was eventually dismissed in court because his wife was reluctant to move forward on the charges. The source of trouble was that Jimmy drank excessively, and this led to much arguing in the home. It was reported that Jimmy stayed out until 2 A.M. each night drinking to spite his wife.

Jimmy's problems with alcohol appeared prior to his marriage. While on parole, he enlisted in the navy at age seventeen. Although he served twenty-eight months, he eventually received a "bad conduct discharge"—the result of a general court martial for being AWOL. He also overstayed his leave several times while on liberty—"engaging in wild drinking bouts." Thus, a major source of difficulty in the military continued into his civilian life in the family setting.

Jimmy had similar problems when he began working at age sixteen as an "unskilled laborer." At age twenty-five, he was employed as a steel worker. He made no effort to improve his occupational status and appeared content just to drift from job to job. Jimmy's poor work habits appeared to be related to his drinking.

Jimmy did not change very much in later adulthood. At age thirty-two, Jimmy was being sought as a fugitive from justice. He had been living with his sister, her husband, and their two children. He was formally divorced, but he had lived with his wife after that, and they had a second child two years after the divorce. Jimmy's cruel and abusive treatment of his wife and children continued, as did his drinking. For instance, Jimmy was arrested for destroying property (a door) at his mother-in-law's house. He also threatened his wife on the street and at the secretarial school she attended, forcing her eventually to leave the school. Although employed as an iron worker, Jimmy frequently did not work, to avoid paying financial support to his wife and children.

Overall, Jimmy's antisocial behavior and related problems with family and work revealed remarkable stability over his life span, which included two arrests for driving under the influence of alcohol at the age of fifty and fifty-four.

Charlie was born in Boston on June 13, 1928. He had ten arrests as a juvenile, primarily for larcenies and burglaries. Charlie's first arrest occurred at the age of eight. Moreover, he was incarcerated three times (his first committal took place when he was eleven), and he spent a total of thirty months confined in reform schools. Despite this background of juvenile delinquency, Charlie had no record of criminal behavior as an adult.

In several ways, Charlie's early life was like Jimmy's. Charlie came from a large family—he was one of seven children. Charlie grew up in a poor neighborhood in East Boston and, like Jimmy, he was not well supervised by his parents. Although his IQ scores were much lower than Jimmy's, Charlie's school experiences were much the same—Charlie was frequently truant, he repeated grades, and he dropped out in the ninth grade. Charlie's best friends growing up were also involved in delinquent activities. His delinquent companions included his older brother and cousin.

At the age of eighteen, Charlie joined the U.S. Merchant Service. He remained with the same shipping line for two and a half years, working the eastern seaboard from Canada to Cuba. Once every three months, Charlie returned home. He gave virtually all of his earnings to his mother to bank for him.

During this same period (age eighteen to twenty), Charlie began a relationship with the woman who would eventually become his wife. Classmates together in high school, they began "an active courtship via letters" while he was in the merchant service.

Charlie was married in May 1949. He was almost twenty-one and his wife was nineteen at the time of the marriage. At age twenty-five, Charlie was living with his wife in East Boston. Charlie was devoted to his wife, and the couple appeared especially united in their mutual desire to advance economically. Their goal was to build their own home. During his early twenties, Charlie held a variety of factory jobs, and from all accounts he appeared to be a solid, industrious worker.

This portrait of Charlie did not change very much in later adulthood. At age thirty-two, he was living with his wife and two children in a suburb close to Boston. He appeared happy with his marriage and family. In his spare time, Charlie worked on home improvement. Charlie worked as a machine operator at a factory and was recently promoted to foreman. As of age sixty-five, Charlie had no record of criminal behavior in adulthood.

What accounts for these different life patterns? How is it that some juvenile delinquents are able to turn their lives around and change their criminal behavior so dramatically, whereas others display a pattern of continual antisocial behavior from childhood through adulthood? Can pathways to delinquency be explained? Once formed, can delinquent pathways be altered? In other words, are there "turning points" in life? These are some of the questions that the research program described below is trying to answer.

The Glueck Data

These two life histories are drawn from the case files from the Gluecks' classic study of juvenile delinquency and adult crime. For over forty years, Sheldon Glueck (1896–1980) and Eleanor Touroff Glueck (1898–1972) performed fundamental research in the field of criminology at the Harvard Law School (see Laub and De Lorenzo, 1992, for more details). Of their four pioneering studies, the Gluecks are best known for their work *Unraveling Juvenile Delinquency*, which was published in 1950. This study of the formation and development of criminal careers is considered to be one of the most influential studies in the history of criminological research.

The Gluecks' research sought to answer a basic, enduring, and ever popular question in the study of delinquency: What factors differentiate boys reared in poor neighborhoods who become serious and persistent delinquents from boys raised in the same neighborhoods who do *not* become delinquent or antisocial? Indeed, a classic film explored this question in 1938 as the Gluecks began planning their study. The film, *Angels with Dirty Faces*, starred James Cagney, Pat O'Brien, Humphrey Bogart, Ann Sheridan, and, of course, the Dead End Kids. James Cagney played the role of Rocky Sullivan, who was by contemporary definitions a high-rate, chronic offender—in other words, a "career criminal." Pat O'Brien played the role of Jerry Connelly, who became a priest in the local neighborhood parish. Both men were childhood friends, committed petty crime together, and were in fact products of the same slum environment. Yet both obviously had very different life experiences with respect to serious and persistent criminal activity.

About eight years ago, I uncovered the original case files for the delinquent subjects of the Gluecks' study in a dusty, dark subbasement of the Harvard Law School Library. These data, along with the Gluecks' eighteen-year follow-up of the 1,000 subjects from the *Unraveling* study, were given to the Harvard Law School Library by the Gluecks in 1972. The Gluecks also gave the library their personal papers, correspondence, books, photographs, and the like. The papers and other items were sorted and fully cataloged as part of the Glueck archive. The cartons of data were simply stored in the subbasement of the library. These data were of immense importance, yet the obstacles to analyzing them were formidable. For example, the data for the 500 delinquent subjects alone were contained in over fifty 12" by 15" cartons.

How could these data possibly be recoded and computerized? Moreover, as I began to sort through the case files, I soon discovered that these were not conventional data. And as I went on, I began to find out that the Gluecks themselves were not conventional researchers (see Laub and Sampson, 1991).

The boxes of data were moved eventually to the Murray Research Center archive; and since 1987 my colleague, Robert J. Sampson of the University of Chicago, and I have been recoding, computerizing, and reanalyzing the Gluecks' data—in short, reconstructing the Gluecks' data for an extensive long-term study of crime over the life course.

The Unraveling Juvenile Delinquency Design

The *Unraveling* study involved a comparison of 500 officially defined delinquents from two Massachusetts reform schools for boys and 500 nondelinquent boys as determined by official records and interviews with key informants (see Glueck and Glueck, 1950). Begun in 1940, the initial period of data collection took eight years.

A unique aspect of the *Unraveling* study was the matching design. Specifically, the 500 officially defined delinquents and 500 nondelinquents were matched *case by case* on age, race/ethnicity, measured intelligence, and neighborhood. The delinquents' ages averaged 14 years, 8 months and the nondelinquents' ages 14 years, 6 months when the study began. As to ethnicity, one-fourth of both groups were of English background; another fourth Italian; a fifth Irish; less than a tenth old American, Slavic, or French; and the remainder were Near Eastern, Spanish, Scandinavian, German, or Jewish. As measured by the Wechsler-Bellevue Test, the delinquents had an average IQ of 92 and nondelinquents 94. The two groups also grew up in similar high-risk environments of poverty and exposure to antisocial conduct. In brief, the 1,000 male subjects in the *Unraveling* study were matched on key criminological variables thought to influence both delinquent behavior and official reactions by the police and courts (Sampson, 1986). That 500 of the boys were persistent delinquents and 500 avoided delinquency in childhood thus cannot be attributed to age differences, ethnicity, IQ, or residence in urban slum areas.

The Unraveling Follow-ups

The original subjects in the *Unraveling* study were followed up at two different points in time—when they were twenty-five and again when they were thirty-two. This data collection effort took place from 1949 to 1963 (see Glueck and Glueck, 1968, for more details). As a result, extensive data are available for analysis relating to criminal career histories, criminal justice interventions, family life, school and employment history, and recreational activities for the matched subjects in childhood, adolescence, and young adulthood. Moreover, data are available for 438 of the original 500 delinquents (87 percent) and 442 of the original 500 nondelinquents (88 percent) at all three age periods. When adjusted for mortality, the follow-up success rate is approximately 92 percent—very high by current standards (see e.g., Wolfgang et al., 1987). The low attrition is testimony to the Gluecks' rigorous research strategy, and also to lower residential mobility and interstate migration rates in the 1940s and 1950s compared to today. It should be noted, though, that the follow-up of criminal histories and official records covered thirty-seven states—the most common involving California, New York, New Hampshire, Florida, and Illinois (Glueck and Glueck, 1968:xix).

An Age-Graded Theory of Informal Social Control

While we were organizing and reconstructing the Gluecks' data, two important books rocked the field of criminology—*Crime and Human Nature* by James Q. Wilson and Richard Herrnstein (1985), and *A General Theory of Crime* by Michael Gottfredson and Travis Hirschi (1990). Although certainly different, the thrust of these books was to redirect criminological attention to the importance of childhood factors in the explanation of crime. For example, Gottfredson and Hirschi (1990) argued that effective child rearing in the early formative years of a child's development produces high self-control, which in turn is a stable phenomenon that inhibits crime throughout the life course. The work of Wilson and Herrnstein (1985) pushed the explanation of crime back even earlier in life to constitutional differences (e.g., impulsiveness and temperament) in interaction with familial factors (see also Nagin and Paternoster, 1991; Grasmick et al., 1993).

Ironically, then, as we were resurrecting the Gluecks' data, new life was breathed into the primary thesis of the Gluecks—childhood temperament and family socialization matter most, and thus the "past is prologue" (Glueck and Glueck, 1968:167). Although attracted to this renewed emphasis on the importance of children and families to the explanation of delinquency, we were also troubled by the profound questions raised by the childhood stability argument. Are differences in child rearing and temperament all we need to know to understand patterns of adult crime? Are childhood differences in antisocial behavior invariably stable? Why does continuity in deviant behavior exist? Perhaps most important, what about individual change, salient life events, and turning points in adulthood?

Challenged by these and other questions, we set out to examine crime and deviance in childhood, adolescence, and adulthood in a way that recognized the significance of both continuity and change over the life course. To do so we synthesized and integrated the criminological literature on childhood antisocial behavior, adolescent delinquency, and adult crime with theory and research on the life course (Sampson and Laub, 1992). By also rethinking the findings produced by longitudinal research, this strategy eventually led us to develop an age-graded theory of informal social control to explain crime and deviance over the life span. We then tested this theory on the longitudinal data reconstructed from the Gluecks' study (see Sampson and Laub, 1993; Laub and Sampson, 1993).

The central idea of social control theory—that crime and deviance are more likely when an individual's bond to society is weak or broken—is an organizing principle in our theory of social bonding over the life course. Following Elder (1975, 1985), we differentiate the life course of individuals on the basis of age and argue that the important institutions of both formal and informal social control vary across the life span. However, we emphasize the role of age-graded *informal* social control as reflected in the structure of interpersonal bonds linking members of society to one another and to wider social institutions (e.g., work, family, school). Unlike formal sanctions, which originate in purposeful efforts to control crime, informal social controls "emerge as by-products of role relationships established for other purposes and are components of role reciprocities" (Kornhauser, 1978:24).

We also examine social relations between individuals (e.g., parent-child, teacher-student, and employer-employee) at each stage of the life course as a form of *social investment* or *social capital* (Coleman, 1988, 1990). Specifically, we posit that the social capital derived from strong social relations (or strong social bonds), whether it be as a child in a family, as an adolescent in school, or as an adult in a job, dictates the salience of these relations at the individual level. If these relations are characterized by interdependency (Braithwaite, 1989) they represent social and psychological resources that individuals can draw on as they move through life transitions that traverse larger trajectories. Thus, we see both social capital and informal social control as linked to social structure, and we distinguish both concepts as important in understanding changes in behavior over time.

By uniting a developmental, life-course perspective with research on antisocial and criminal behavior, we developed a new theory of crime and delinquency over the life course. This theory consists of three key ideas, which are presented below, along with highlights of the results of our study (see Sampson and Laub, 1993, for more details).

Structure and Process in Adolescent Delinquency

The first building block in our developmental theory is a focus on both structural and process variables. In explaining the onset of delinquency, criminologists have embraced either structural factors (e.g., poverty, broken homes) or process variables (e.g., attachment to parents or teachers). We believe such a separation is a mistake, and in our work we join structural and process variables along individual characteristics like temperament and early conduct disorder together into a single theoretical model.

To illustrate, we argue that informal social controls derived from the family (e.g., consistent use of discipline, monitoring, and attachment) mediate the effects of both individual and structural background variables. For instance, previous research on families and delinquency often failed to account for social structural disadvantage and how it influences family life. As Rutter and Giller (1983:185) argued, socioeconomic disadvantage has potentially adverse effects on parents, such that parental difficulties are more likely to develop and good parenting is impeded. If true, one would expect poverty and disadvantage to have their effects on delinquency transmitted through parenting. Our contention is that structural factors will strongly affect family and school social control mechanisms but that their influence will be largely indirect (though not unimportant) in the explanation of early delinquency. In a developmental model, proximate factors explain more variance than distal factors, but that does not mean that those distal factors are unimportant. Rather, it is the case that proximate factors mediate the effects of distal factors.

Overall, the results support our integrated version of social control theory, which recognizes the importance of both structure and process. When the bonds linking youth to society—whether via family or school—are weakened, the probability of delinquency is increased. Negative structural conditions (e.g., poverty, family disruption) also affect delinquency, but largely through family and school process variables (see Sampson and Laub, 1993: chs. 4 and 5).

The Importance of Continuity Between Childhood and Adulthood

There is considerable evidence that antisocial behavior is relatively stable across stages of the life course. As Caspi and Moffitt (1992:2) concluded, robust continuities in antisocial behavior have been revealed over the past fifty years in different nations (e.g., Canada, England, Finland, New Zealand, Sweden, and the United States) and with multiple methods of assessment (e.g., official records, teacher ratings, parent reports, and peer nominations of aggressive behavior). These replications across time and space yield an impressive generalization that is rare in the social sciences.

Criminologists still focus primarily on the teenage years in their studies of offending, apparently disregarding the connections between childhood delinquency and adult crime. Reversing this tide, the second building block of our theory incorporates the idea of continuity in childhood and adolescent antisocial behavior over the life course. We contend that childhood and adolescent antisocial behavior (e.g., juvenile delinquency, conduct disorder, violent temper tantrums) extends throughout adulthood across a variety of life's domains (e.g., crime, alcohol abuse, divorce, unemployment). In other words, antisocial behavior in childhood predicts a wide range of troublesome adult outcomes. Further, we argue that childhood delinquency is linked to dimensions of adult social bonding, including economic dependency, educational attainment, attachment to the labor force, and quality of marital experiences. Finally, we hold that these outcomes occur independent of traditional sociological and psychological variables such as social class, ethnicity, IQ, and even the family/school factors found to predict the onset of delinquency. As such, we propose that crime, deviance, and informal social control are intimately linked over the full life course.

Our analysis found that independent of age, IQ, neighborhood socioeconomic status, and ethnicity, the original delinquents and nondelinquents in the Gluecks' study displayed behavioral consistency well into adulthood. Indeed, delinquency and other forms of antisocial conduct in childhood were strongly related to troublesome adult behavior across a variety of life's domains (e.g., crime, military offenses, economic dependence, marital discord) (see Sampson and Laub, 1993:ch. 6).

The Significance of Change in the Life Course

Our third focus is changes in deviance and offending as individuals age. Having provided a role for continuity, we nonetheless believe that salient life events and social ties in adulthood can counteract, at least to some extent, the trajectories of early child development. Hence, a third thesis of our work is that social bonds in adulthood—especially *attachment to the labor force* and *cohesive marriage* (or cohabitation)—explain desistance from criminal behavior regardless of prior differences in criminal propensity. In other words, pathways to both crime and conformity are modified by key institutions of social control in the transition to adulthood (e.g., employment, military service, and marriage). For instance, late onset of criminal behavior can be accounted for by weak social bonds in adulthood, despite a background of nondelinquent behavior. Conversely, desistance from criminal behavior in adulthood can be explained by strong social bonds in adulthood, despite a background of delinquent behavior.

In contrast to many life-course models, we emphasize the quality or strength of social ties in these transitions more than the occurrence or timing of discrete life events (cf. Loeber and LeBlanc, 1990:430–432). For example, marriage *per se* may not increase social control, but close emotional ties and mutual investment increase the social bond between individuals and, all else equal, should lead to a reduction in criminal behavior (cf. Shover, 1985:94). Employment by itself also does not necessarily increase social control. It is employment coupled with job stability, commitment to work, and mutual ties binding workers and employers that should increase social control and, all else equal, lead to a reduction in criminal behavior.

In our analyses, we found that job stability and marital attachment in adulthood were significantly related to changes in adult crime—the stronger the adult ties to work and family, the less crime and deviance among both delinquents and controls. Despite differences in early childhood experiences, adult social bonds to work and family thus had similar consequences for the life trajectories of the 500 delinquents and 500 controls. Taken as a whole, then, our findings suggest that social ties embedded in adult transitions (e.g., marital attachment, job stability) explain variations in crime unaccounted for by childhood propensities (see Sampson and Laub, 1993, Chs. 7 and 8).

One additional finding deserves mention. We found that social bonds to employment were directly influenced by state sanctions. That is, incarceration as a juvenile and as an adult had negative effects on later job stability, and job stability was in turn negatively related to continued involvement in crime over the life course. Although we found little direct effect of incarceration on subsequent criminality, the indirect "criminogenic" effects appear substantively important (see Sampson and Laub, 1993:162–168). This point is discussed further below.

In sum, our theory attempts to unite continuity and change within the context of a sociological understanding of crime in the life course. Pathways and turning points are important concepts in the study of lives, and we have adapted this perspective to explore the lives of a disadvantaged sample of persistent adolescent delinquents. A major concept in our framework is the dynamic process whereby the interlocking nature of trajectories and transitions generate *turning points* or a change in life course (Elder, 1985:32). Turning points are closely linked to role transitions and, conceptually, turning points are helpful in understanding change in human behavior over the life course. Adaptation to life events is crucial, because the same event or transition followed by different adaptations can lead to different trajectories (Elder, 1985:35). That is, despite the connection between childhood events and experiences in adulthood, turning points can modify life trajectories— they can "redirect paths." Some positive turning points in the life courses we examined were cohesive marriage, meaningful work, and serving in the military. Clear negative turning points were prolonged incarceration, heavy drinking, and subsequent job instability during the transition to young adulthood. By refocusing attention on the significance of *both pathways and turning points in the life course,* our research agenda has the potential to unify divergent conceptions of stability and change in human development (see also Rutter et al., 1990).

Why This Study Is Important Today

The Need for a Long-Term Perspective

A staple of life-course research is examining how events in early life shape adult adjustment. As illustrated in the two life histories presented above, longitudinal studies are needed to provide a true understanding of pathways of delinquent and nondelinquent behavior from childhood through adulthood. Also, prospective longitudinal studies allow us to uncover turning points that may explain behavioral trajectories. Recently, George Vaillant pointed out, "Even a 15-year follow-up study is inadequate to capture the kind of changes that occur over the lifetime" (Becker, 1993:10).

Long-term studies of adult development and crime are especially rare, and to address this gap we are currently conducting a thirty-five-year follow-up of the original delinquents in the Glueck study. These men were born between 1924 and 1932; thus, in 1994 the oldest subject is seventy years of age and the youngest is sixty-two years of age. To date, we have collected criminal record histories at the state level, and these data provide information on criminal offenses committed in Massachusetts by the Glueck subjects since the age of thirty-two, the age at which they were last contacted by the Gluecks' research team. We have also gathered death records from the Massachusetts Registry of Vital Records and Statistics. Finally, we are launching a pilot study to trace and interview a small subset of subjects from the original study. These data will shed important light on the pattern of crime and human development over the full life course.

Scientific knowledge regarding crime and delinquency has been hampered by a lack of good longitudinal data. In this context, the Gluecks' data provide several key advantages. For example, the data cover a relatively long period of time; for most variables, information is available from birth to age thirty-two and, in some instances, up to age sixty-five. The Gluecks' data are also quite rich in the number and range of measures across a variety of important dimensions of juvenile and adult development such as educational attainment, occupational careers, and family relationships. To date, many longitudinal studies in criminology fail to measure background data and changes in life events over the life course. As many researchers have argued, to effectively distinguish the causal influences on crime one must first account for important background factors and the changing nature of salient life events such as leaving school, entering the military, and getting married—especially during the late adolescence to young adulthood transition.

Are the Glueck Data "Too Old" to Be Useful?

Despite these clear advantages, a researcher who takes on secondary data analysis is often confronted with the comment that the data are "old" and no longer useful for addressing important contemporary questions, especially those concerning policy. This attitude applies particularly to the Glueck project because the subjects (white males) grew up during the 1930s and early 1940s and reached adulthood in the late 1940s and early 1950s. In this social and historical context, drugs like "crack" cocaine were not even known, and the level of criminal violence, especially gun use, was below what we see today. The role of alcohol abuse, coupled with the virtual absence of other drug use (e.g., cocaine), thus suggests a strong period effect. Moreover, there is a sense that the responses of the juvenile justice and criminal justice systems to crime were very different then than they are now. So the question is raised: How can these data possibly be of any practical utility now? In other words, "Are these lives from a previous generation relevant to us today?" (Clausen, 1993:3).

We argue that precisely because these data are "old," they provide an unusual opportunity to assess whether the causes of juvenile delinquency and adult crime are specific to a historical period. Combined with the fact that the range of measures collected by the Gluecks will in all likelihood never be replicated in social science research again, the "age" of the Glueck data becomes a strength, not a weakness. Indeed, a focus on data collected between 1930 and 1960 leads to several interesting questions relevant to an understanding of current patterns of crime. For example, are the risk factors associated with crime similar across different structural contexts? Were characteristics of today's "underclass" (e.g., chronic joblessness, family disruption, poverty, criminal behavior) in fact found among earlier immigrant ethnic groups?

Our analyses suggest that crime in the Gluecks' era was not all that different from today in terms of its structural origins and underlying nature. Today we often hear discussions of crime that assume criminal behavior is inevitably linked to race and drugs. Yet crime in the historical context we are analyzing was primarily committed not by blacks but rather by white ethnic groups in structurally disadvantaged positions. And even though drugs were not pervasive, crime and alcohol abuse were quite rampant. The men in the Gluecks' delinquent sample were persistent, serious offenders, and many of them can be labeled "career criminals" in today's language. Therefore, the fact that in this study sample members were drawn from settings of social and economic disadvantage, yet were all white, provides an important comparative base to assess current concerns of race, crime, and the underclass. Furthermore, since use and sale of drugs like cocaine and heroin were not prevalent in this study, a unique opportunity is presented to learn about the relationship between drugs like alcohol and criminal behavior. In our view, criminological theory and policy are too often determined without a historical or longitudinal perspective, and our work shows why such a perspective is needed.

Our findings based on the Glueck data thus become a window from which to view contemporary research and begin a dialogue on crime and crime policy, especially in a nonrace-specific context. That is, the Glueck data allow us to discuss crime in a "deracialized" and, hopefully, depoliticized context. In this regard it appears that the causes of crime across the life course are rooted not in race and not simply in drugs, gangs, and guns—today's policy obsessions—but rather in structural disadvantage; weakened informal social bonds to family, school, and work; and the disruption of social relations between individuals and institutions that provide social capital. As John Clausen has noted, "The family, the school, and the peer group are still the primary agents that socialize the young and prepare them for adulthood. . . . the processes of development remain largely the same. Contexts change, but basic principles change far less" (1993:27).

Rethinking Current Crime Control Policy

The life-course perspective of our work also has implications for specific crime policies. Moreover, our analyses of the Glueck data can contribute to public discourse on crime and crime policy. The United States has embarked on a policy of unprecedented incarceration (see, for example, Steffensmeier and Harer, 1993). From all appearances, the major thrust of current crime control policy—whether aimed at drugs or violence—is to lock up offenders regardless of age. For those offenders with extensive prior records, even longer sentences of incarceration are being called for. And the most extreme formal sanction by the state—the death penalty—is being made available and increasingly used. Such policies assume that either individual deterrence or incapacitation will reduce further violence. Yet rates of violence have recently risen in many of our nation's cities despite unprecedented rates of imprisonment and executions (Hinds, 1990; James, 1991; Butterfield, 1992; Eckholm, 1993). How can this happen?

One clear possibility is that current policies are producing unintended "criminogenic" effects. From our perspective, imprisonment may have powerful negative effects on the prospects of future employment and job stability. In turn, low income, unemployment, and underemployment are themselves linked to heightened risks of family disruption (Wilson, 1987; Sampson, 1987). Through its negative effects on male employment, imprisonment may thus lead indirectly through family disruption to increases in future rates of crime and violence (Sampson, 1987). The extremely high incarceration rate of young black males (see Mauer, 1990) renders this scenario very real.

In our reanalysis of the Gluecks' data, we have also shown how long-term developmental effects of incarceration on crime and deviance may come about. Length of incarceration in both adolescence and adulthood has negative effects on job stability, which in turn lead to later crime and deviance. At the same time, our analysis revealed that intra-individual change is possible, and therefore it is critical that individuals have the opportunity to reconnect to institutions like family, school, and work *after* a period of incarceration (see also Cook, 1975; Braithwaite, 1989). Perhaps the most troubling aspect of our analysis was that the effects of long periods of incarceration appear quite severe when manifested in structural labeling—many of the Glueck men were simply cut off from the most promising avenues for desistance from crime.

Although the view is currently unpopular, we believe that it is time to take a renewed look at social policies that focus on *prevention* as opposed to after-the-fact approaches that ignore the structural context of crime and neglect the basic institutions of society—family, school, and work—that provide informal social control and social capital. This is not to suggest that imprisonment is unnecessary or undeserved, nor even that it has no deterrent effect on crime. Rather, our reservations about current crime policies reflect our fears that such policies do not reduce crime and may in fact be counterproductive. Nor are we convinced that "old ideas in new slogans" are the answer. Witness the popularity of the 'three strikes and you're out" bandwagon, which is totally inconsistent with a wide body of empirical research showing that violent offending is part of a larger syndrome of antisocial behavior. Focusing policies exclusively on violence and violent offenders seems contrary to what we know to be true, but empirical research is rarely the basis of crime control policies.

As an aside, Christopher Jencks (1991) has recently called for a constitutional amendment forbidding any reference to violent crime during a political campaign. It might also be good to have a constitutional amendment banning slogans masquerading as well-reasoned policies—take your pick of some recent offerings: "The War on Drugs," "Just Say No!", "One With a Gun Will Get You Two," and, my favorite, "If You Can't Do the Time, Don't Do the Crime."

Instead of cheap slogans, it is time for a broader crime policy that focuses on more than formal social control by the criminal justice system. Nongovernmental institutions like families, schools, work settings, and neighborhoods must be the centerpiece of any crime reduction policy. The government can and should take the lead in strengthening these basic social institutions. As such, a more complex and long-term perspective that recognizes the linkages among crime policies, employment, family cohesion, and the social organization of inner-city communities is needed. While these more complex crime policies are clearly not easily translated into specific programmatic initiatives, the costs of current crime policies are quite high, and their effects will be felt for the long term. As I speak, a generation of adolescent and adult offenders are being locked up and are at risk of being permanently severed from society. These offenders are being relegated to the structural role of the "dangerous, criminal class" (Brace, 1872; Hagan and Palloni, 1990), with the promise of a future life course that is very bleak indeed. Our work questions the wisdom and foundation of such a devastating and costly crime policy.

Reflecting this concern, this chapter has offered a theoretical and empirical framework from which to think in new ways about policies on crime. Public discourse about crime is dominated by television shows and radio call-in programs—forums that are inappropriate to discuss the causes of crime and the solutions to the crime problem. It is foolhardy to think that anyone can reduce the study of crime to a "30-second sound bite," as we have been asked to do in the past. Nonetheless, most citizens surely realize and appreciate the complexity of the crime problem, a complexity that is realized in our analyses. Using this knowledge we can reach those who are concerned about crime and who remain optimistic that social science research can inform dialogue on crime policy. We thus stubbornly cling to the belief that a well-reasoned and informed crime policy is possible and that our work can contribute to the development of that policy.

In closing, I wish to make a practical and self-interested argument for secondary analyses of longitudinal data over the life span. I began this research in 1987 when I was thirty-four years old. Imagine, if you will, that instead of pursuing a secondary analysis, I began a project like the Gluecks' study that involved original data collection. Following the lives of subjects who were on average fourteen years of age in 1987 until they were age sixty-five would take us well into the next century—2038, to be exact. This would mean that, assuming all else equal, I would be giving the Klein Lecture seven years later—at the ripe old age of ninety-two. That would have been very nice and, I am confident, quite interesting, but overall I am not sure how much I like the odds.

References

Becker, R. (1993). Study: Unhappy childhood need not limit adult success. *Harvard Gazette*, February 26, 3, 10.

Brace, C. L. (1872). *The dangerous classes of New York, and twenty years' work among them*. New York: Wynkoop.

Braithwaite, J. (1989). *Crime, shame, and reintegration*. Cambridge, England: Cambridge University Press.

Butterfield, F. (1992). Seeds of murder epidemic: Teen-age boys with guns. *The New York Times*, October 19, 8.

Caspi, A., & Moffitt, T. E. (1992). The continuity of maladaptive behavior: From description to understanding in the study of antisocial behavior. In D. Cicchetti & D. Cohen (Eds.), *Manual of developmental psychopathology*. New York: Wiley.

Clausen, J. A. (1993). *American lives: Looking back at the children of the Great Depression*. New York: Free Press.

Coleman, J. S. (1988). Social capital in the creation of human capital. *American Journal of Sociology, 94*, S95–120.

Coleman, J. S. (1990). *Foundations of social theory*. Cambridge, Mass.: Harvard University Press.

Cook, P. J. (1975). The correctional carrot: Better jobs for parolees. *Policy Analysis, 1*, 11–54.

Eckholm, E. (1993). Teen-age gangs are inflicting lethal violence on small cities. *The New York Times*, January 31, 1, 26.

Elder, G. H., Jr. (1975). Age differentiation and the life course. *Annual Review of Sociology, 1*, 165–190.

Elder, G. H., Jr. (1985). Perspectives on the life course. In G. H. Elder, Jr. (Ed.), *Life course dynamics*. Ithaca: Cornell University Press.

Glueck, S., & Glueck, E. (1950). *Unraveling juvenile delinquency*. New York: Commonwealth Fund.

Glueck, S., & Glueck, E. (1968). *Delinquents and nondelinquents in perspective*. Cambridge, Mass.: Harvard University Press.

Gottfredson, M. R., & Hirschi, T. (1990). *A general theory of crime*. Stanford, Calif.: Stanford University Press.

Grasmick, H., Tittle, C., Bursik, R. J., & Arneklev, B. (1993). Testing the core empirical implications of Gottfredson and Hirschi's general theory of crime. *Journal of Research in Crime and Delinquency, 30*, 5–29.

Hagan, J., & Palloni, A. (1990). The social reproduction of a criminal class in working-class London, circa 1950–1980. *American Journal of Sociology, 96*, 265–299.

Hinds, M. (1990). Number of killings soars in big cities across U.S. *The New York Times*, July 18, 1.

James, G. (1991). New York killings set record in 1990. *The New York Times*, April 23, A14.

Jencks, C. (1991). Is violent crime increasing? *The American Prospect, 4*, 98–109.

Kornhauser, R. (1978). *Social sources of delinquency*. Chicago: University of Chicago Press.

Laub, J. H., & Lorenzo, D. (1992). *Pioneers in criminology and criminal justice: Sheldon and Eleanor Touroff Glueck*. Cambridge, Mass.: President and Fellows of Harvard College.

Laub, J. H., & Sampson, R. J. (1991). The Sutherland-Glueck debate: On the sociology of criminological knowledge. *American Journal of Sociology, 96*, 1402–1440.

Laub, J. H., & Sampson, R. J. (1993). Turning points in the life course: Why change matters to the study of crime. *Criminology, 31*, 301–325.

Loeber, R., & LeBlanc, M. (1990). Toward a developmental criminology. In M. Tonry & N. Morris (Eds.), *Crime and justice*. Chicago: University of Chicago Press.

Mauer, M. (1990). *Young black men and the criminal justice system: A growing national problem*. Washington, D.C.: The Sentencing Project.

Nagin, D., & Paternoster, R. (1991). On the relationship of past and future participation in delinquency. *Criminology, 29*, 163–190.

Rutter, M., & Giller, H. (1983). *Juvenile delinquency: Trends and perspectives*. New York: Guilford Press.

Rutter, M., Quinton, D., & Hill, J. (1990). Adult outcomes of institution-reared children: Males and females compared. In L. Robins & M. Rutter (Eds.), *Straight and devious pathways from childhood to adulthood*. Cambridge, England: Cambridge University Press.

Sampson, R. J. (1986). Effects of socioeconomic context on official reaction to juvenile delinquency. *American Sociological Review, 51*, 876–885.

Sampson, R. J. (1987). Urban black violence: The effect of male joblessness and family disruption. *American Journal of Sociology, 93*, 348–382.

Sampson, R. J., & Laub, J. H. (1992). Crime and deviance in the life course. *Annual Review of Sociology, 18*, 63–84.

Sampson, R. J., & Laub, J. H. (1993). *Crime in the making: Pathways and turning points through life*. Cambridge, Mass.: Harvard University Press.

Shover, N. (1985). *Aging criminals*. Beverly Hills, Calif.: Sage.

Steffensmeier, D., & Harer, M. D. (1993). Bulging prisons, an aging U.S. population, and the nation's violent crime rate. *Federal Probation, 57*, 3–10.

Wilson, J. Q., & Herrnstein, R. (1985). *Crime and human nature*. New York: Simon & Schuster.

Wilson, W. J. (1987). *The truly disadvantaged: The inner city, the underclass and public policy*. Chicago: University of Chicago Press.

Wolfgang, M., Thornberry, T., & Figlio, R. (1987). *From boy to man: From delinquency to crime*. Chicago: University of Chicago Press.

17

The Explanation and Prevention of Youthful Offending

DAVID P. FARRINGTON

Explaining the Development of Offending

Summarizing the Major Risk Factors

The major risk factors for offending are socioeconomic deprivation, poverty, poor housing, and residence in public housing in inner-city, socially disorganized communities. They also include poor parental child-rearing techniques—such as poor supervision, harsh or erratic discipline, parental conflict, and separation from a biological parent. Additional factors are impulsivity (which may be linked to low physiological arousal) and low intelligence (which may reflect a poor ability to manipulate abstract concepts and deficits in the "executive functions" of the brain). It seems likely that communities influence parenting and that parenting influences the development of impulsivity and low intelligence, although both of these factors may have a large biological or genetic component.

Other risk factors are probably linked to poverty, poor parenting, and impulsivity and intelligence. For example, teenage mothers tend to live in poverty, tend to use poor child-rearing techniques, and tend to have impulsive children with low intelligence. Perinatal complications, in combination with other risk factors, may cause neurological dysfunction, which in turn causes impulsivity or low intelligence. Large family size may lead to poor parenting because of the problem of dividing attention among several children at once. Criminal parents may be poor supervisors of children and disproportionately separated, or alternatively there may be genetic transmission of a biological factor linked to offending. The links between delinquent peers and delinquent schools and offending are less clear. However, it is likely that the occurrence of offenses depends on situational factors such as costs, benefits, and opportunities.

In explaining the development of offending, a major problem is that most risk factors tend to coincide and tend to be interrelated. For example, adolescents living in physically deteriorated and socially disorganized neighborhoods tend also to come disproportionately from families with poor parental supervision and erratic parental discipline, as well as to have high impulsivity and low intelligence. The concentration and concurrence of these kinds of adversities make it difficult to establish their independent, interactive, and sequential influences on offending and antisocial behavior. Hence, any theory of the development of offending is inevitably speculative in the present state of knowledge.

It is important to establish which factors predict offending independently of other factors. In the Cambridge Study in Delinquent Development, it was generally true that each of six categories of variables (impulsivity, intelligence, parenting, antisocial family, socioeconomic deprivation, child antisocial behavior) predicted offending independent of any other category (Farrington, 1990b). For example, Farrington and Hawkins (1991) reported that the independent predictors of convictions between ages ten and twenty included high daring, low school attainment, poor parental child rearing, convicted parents, poor housing, and troublesomeness. Hence, it might be concluded that impulsivity, low intelligence, parenting, antisocial family, and socioeconomic deprivation, all contribute independently to the development of offending despite their interrelationship. In addition, of course, there is significant continuity in offending and antisocial behavior from childhood to adulthood, even though the prevalence of offending peaks in the teenage years. Any theory needs to give priority to explaining these results.

Building on Previous Theories

In proposing any new theory, it is important to build on previous theories that have not been disproved. As already mentioned, the classic delinquency theories of Cohen (1955) and Cloward and Ohlin (1960) aimed to explain why offenders disproportionately came from deprived, lower-class backgrounds. Cohen focused on the factors of poor parenting and impulsivity, whereas Cloward and Ohlin proposed that lower-class children adopted illegitimate means because they could not achieve their goals legitimately. Shaw and McKay (1969) aimed to explain why offenders disproportionately came from deprived inner-city areas, focusing on ineffective socialization processes and cultural transmission of antisocial values. Sutherland and Cressey (1974) also proposed that children learn to offend if they are surrounded by antisocial values, thus emphasizing the role of criminal families, delinquent peers, delinquent schools, and criminal areas.

In contrast to classic sociological theories, which aim to explain why people learn to offend, classic psychological theories aim to explain why people are inhibited from offending. As the latter may be less familiar to criminologists, they will be reviewed here in some detail. According to these theories, children learn to inhibit their antisocial tendencies and build up internal inhibitions against offending in a conditioning or social learning process as a result of the way their parents react to their transgressions. Conditioning theories focus on reinforcement and punishment, whereas social learning theories focus on modeling and thinking processes as well.

One of the most influential conditioning theories, propounded by Trasler (1962), suggests that when a child behaves in a socially disapproved way, the parent will punish the child. This punishment causes an anxiety reaction. After a number of pairings of the disapproved act and the punishment, the anxiety becomes classically conditioned to the act, and also to the sequence of events preceding the act. Consequently, when the child contemplates the disapproved act, the conditioned anxiety automatically arises and tends to block the tendency to commit the act, so the child becomes less likely to do it. Also, the anxiety generalizes to similar acts, so the child tends to feel anxious when contemplating similar acts. Hence, as Eysenck (1977) also argued, conscience is essentially a conditioned anxiety response.

However, whereas Eysenck emphasized individual, constitutional differences in conditionability, Trasler emphasized differences in parental child-rearing behavior as the major source of differences in criminal tendencies (conditioned anxiety). Children are unlikely to build up the link between disapproved behavior and anxiety unless their parents supervise them closely, use punishment consistently, and make punishment contingent on disapproved acts. Hence, poor supervision, erratic or inconsistent discipline, and conflict between parents are all conducive to offending by children. It is also important for parents to explain to children why they are being punished, so that they can discriminate precisely the behavior that is disapproved.

Trasler argued that middle-class parents are more likely to explain to children why they are being punished and to be concerned with long-term character building and the inculcation of general moral principles. This tendency is linked to the greater facility of middle-class parents with language and abstract concepts. In contrast, lower-class parents supervise their children less closely and are more inconsistent in their use of discipline. Generally, middle-class parents use love-oriented discipline, relying on withdrawal of love as the main sanction, whereas lower-class parents use much more physical punishment. Trasler contended that lower-class children commit more crimes because lower-class parents use less effective methods of socialization.

More recent learning theories tend to be cognitive social learning theories emphasizing the role of modeling, instruction, thought processes, and interpersonal problem-solving strategies (Bandura, 1977; Nietzel, 1979; Sarason, 1978). The individual is viewed as an information processor whose behavior depends on cognitive (thinking, problem-solving) processes as well as the history of rewards and punishments. Ross and Ross (1988) explicitly linked offending to cognitive deficits, arguing that offenders tended to be impulsive, egocentric, concrete rather than abstract in their thinking, and poor at interpersonal problem solving because they failed to understand how other people were thinking and feeling (Chandler, 1973). Many other scholars have argued that offenders are deficient in their thinking processes (e.g., Guerra, 1989). Whether they are also deficient in interpersonal social skills is less clear (Dishion et al., 1984; Hollin, 1990; Tisdelle and St. Lawrence, 1986).

Some modern criminological theories also aim to explain the development of internal inhibitions against offending. For example, Wilson and Herrnstein (1985) suggested that people differ in their underlying criminal tendency and that whether a person chooses to commit a crime in any situation depends on whether the expected benefits of offending outweigh the expected costs. The benefits of offending—including material gain, peer approval, and sexual gratification—tend to be contemporaneous with the crime. In contrast, many of the costs of offending, such as the risk of being caught and punished and the possible loss of reputation or employment, are uncertain and long delayed. Other costs—such as pangs of conscience (or guilt), disapproval by onlookers, and retaliation by the victim—are more immediate.

As in many psychological theories, Wilson and Herrnstein emphasized the importance of the conscience as an internal inhibitor of offending and suggested that it was built up in a process of classical conditioning according to parental reinforcement or punishment of childhood transgressions. Nevertheless, the key individual difference factor in Wilson and Herrnstein's theory is the extent to which people's behavior is influenced by immediate, as opposed to delayed, consequences. As in other theories, they suggested that individuals vary in their ability to think about or plan for the future, and that this variation is linked to intelligence. The major determinant of offending is a person's impulsivity. More impulsive people are less influenced by the likelihood of future consequences and hence are more likely to commit crimes.

Gottfredson and Hirschi (1990) castigated criminological theorists for ignoring the fact that people differ in underlying criminal propensities and that these differences appear early in life and remain stable over much of the life course. The key individual difference factor in their theory is low self-control, that is, the extent to which individuals are vulnerable to the temptations of the moment. People with low self-control are impulsive, take risks, have low cognitive and academic skills, are egocentric, have low empathy, and have short time horizons. Hence, they find it hard to defer gratification; and their decisions to offend are insufficiently influenced by the possible future painful consequences of offending.

Gottfredson and Hirschi argued that crimes were part of a larger category of deviant acts (including substance abuse, heavy smoking, heavy drinking, heavy gambling, sexual promiscuity, truanting, and road accidents), which were all behavioral manifestations of the key underlying theoretical construct of low self-control. They conceded that self-control, as an internal inhibitor, is similar to the conscience but preferred the term self-control because the idea of the conscience is less applicable to some of the wider category of acts that they were concerned with (e.g., accidents). Their theory easily explains the considerable versatility of antisocial behavior.

They argued that differences in self-control among individuals are present early in life (by ages six to eight), are remarkably stable over time, and are essentially caused by differences in parental child-rearing practices. Much parenting is concerned with suppressing impulsive behavior, with making children consider the long-range consequences of their acts, and with making them sensitive to the needs and feelings of others. Poor parental supervision contributes to low self-control, and poor parental supervision is more common in large families, among single parents, and among criminal parents. Ambitiously, Gottfredson and Hirschi aimed to present a theory that applies to all kinds of crimes in all kinds of cultures.

The Farrington Theory

The modern trend is to try to achieve increased explanatory power by integrating propositions derived from several earlier theories (e.g., Elliott et al., 1985; Hawkins and Weis, 1985; Pearson and Weiner, 1985). This writer's own theory of offending and antisocial behavior (Farrington, 1986b, 1992b, 1993c) is also integrative, and it distinguishes explicitly between the long-term development of antisocial tendency and the immediate occurrence of offenses and other antisocial acts. The level of antisocial tendency depends on energizing, directing, and inhibiting processes. The occurrence of offenses and other antisocial acts depends on the interaction between the individual (with a certain degree of antisocial tendency) and the social environment in a decision-making process.

The main energizing factors that ultimately lead to variations in antisocial tendency are desires for material goods, status among intimates, excitement, boredom, frustration, anger, and alcohol consumption. The desire for excitement may be greater among children from poorer families, perhaps because excitement is more highly valued by lower-class people than by middle-class ones, because poorer children think they lead more boring lives, or because poorer children are less able to postpone immediate gratification in favor of long-term goals (which could be linked to the emphasis in lower-class culture on the concrete and present as opposed to the abstract and future).

In the directing stage, these motivations lead to an increase in antisocial tendency if socially disapproved methods of satisfying them are habitually chosen. The methods chosen depend on maturation and behavioral skills; for example, a five-year-old would have difficulty stealing a car. Some people (e.g., children from poorer families) are less able to satisfy their desires for material goods, excitement, and social status by legal or socially approved methods and so tend to choose illegal or socially disapproved methods. The relative inability of poorer children to achieve goals by legitimate methods could be attributed to their tendency to fail in school and to have erratic, low-status employment histories. School failure in turn may often be a consequence of both the unstimulating intellectual environment that lower-class parents tend to provide for their children and their lack of emphasis on abstract concepts.

In the inhibiting stage, antisocial tendency can be reduced (or increased) by internalized beliefs and attitudes that have been built up in a social learning process as a result of a history of rewards and punishments. A strong conscience, that is, the belief that offending is wrong, tends to be built up if parents are in favor of legal norms, if they exercise close supervision over their children, and if they punish socially disapproved behavior using love-oriented discipline. Antisocial tendency can also be inhibited by empathy, which may develop as a result of parental warmth and loving relationships. There are individual differences in the development of these internal inhibitions. Because of associated neurological dysfunctions, children with high impulsivity and low intelligence are less able to build up internal inhibitions against offending, and therefore they tend to have a high level of antisocial tendency.

The level of antisocial tendency can also be increased in a social learning process if children are surrounded by antisocial models (criminal parents and siblings, delinquent peers in delinquent schools and criminal areas). The belief that offending is legitimate, and anti-establishment attitudes generally, tend to be built up if children have been exposed to attitudes and behavior favoring offending (e.g., in a modeling process), especially by members of their family, by their friends, and in their communities.

In the decision-making stage, which specifies the interaction between the individual and the environment, whether a person with a certain degree of antisocial tendency commits an antisocial act in a given situation depends on opportunities, costs, and benefits and on the subjective probabilities of the different outcomes. The costs and benefits include immediate situational factors, such as the material goods that can be stolen, and the likelihood and consequences of being caught by the police, as perceived by the individual. They also include social factors, such as likely disapproval by parents or spouses, and encouragement or reinforcement from peers. In general, people tend to make rational decisions. However, more impulsive people are less likely to consider the possible consequences of their actions, especially consequences that are likely to be long delayed.

The consequences of offending may, as a result of a learning process, lead to changes in antisocial tendency or in the cost-benefit calculation. Such changes are especially likely if the consequences are reinforcing (e.g., gaining material goods or peer approval) or punishing (e.g., legal sanctions or parental disapproval). Also, if the consequences involve labeling or stigmatizing the offenders, it may be more difficult for them to achieve their aims legally, hence they may increase their antisocial tendency. In other words, events that occur after offending may lead to changes in energizing, directing, inhibiting, or decision-making processes in a dynamic system.

When the theory is applied to explain some of the results reviewed here, it appears that children from poorer families may be likely to offend because they are less able to achieve their goals legally and because they value some goals (e.g., excitement) especially highly. Children with low intelligence may be more likely to offend because they tend to fail in school and hence cannot achieve their goals legally. Impulsive children, and those with a poor ability to manipulate abstract concepts, may be more likely to offend because they do not give sufficient consideration and weight to the possible consequences of offending. Also, children with low intelligence and high impulsivity are less able to build up internal inhibitions against offending.

Children who are exposed to poor child-rearing behavior, parental disharmony, or parental separation may be likely to offend because they do not build up internal inhibitions against socially disapproved behavior; children from criminal families and those with delinquent friends tend to build up anti-establishment attitudes and the belief that offending is justifiable. The whole process is self-perpetuating in that poverty, low intelligence, and early school failure lead to truancy and a lack of educational qualifications, which lead to low-status jobs and periods of unemployment, both of which in turn make it harder to achieve goals legitimately.

It is important to try to explain the onset, persistence, and desistance of offending. The onset of offending might be caused by increased motivation (an increasing need for material goods, status, and excitement), a growing likelihood of choosing socially disapproved methods (possibly linked to a change in dominant social influences from parents to peers), a growth in the facilitating influences of peers, greater opportunities (because of increasing freedom from parental control and more time spent with peers), or an increase in the expected utility of offending (because of the greater importance of peer approval and lesser importance of parental disapproval).

Persistence depends on the stability of the underlying antisocial tendency, which is built up in a long-term learning process. The relative ordering of people of antisocial tendency tends to stay relatively constant over time, because energizing, directing, and inhibiting factors are built up in childhood and thereafter change rather slowly. Desistance from offending could be linked to an increasing ability to satisfy desires by legal means (e.g., obtaining material goods through employment, achieving sexual gratification through marriage), a growth in the inhibiting influences of spouses and co-habitees, fewer opportunities (because of less time spent with peers), and a decrease in the expected utility of offending (because of the lesser impor-tance of peer approval and the greater importance of disapproval by spouses and cohabitees).

The prevalence of offending may increase to a peak between ages fourteen and twenty because boys (especially lower-class school failures) have high impulsivity; high desires for excitement, material goods, and social status between these ages; little chance of achieving their desires legally; and little to lose (since legal penalties are lenient and their intimates—male peers—often approve of offending). In contrast, after age twenty, desires become attenuated or more realistic, there is more possibility of achieving these more limited goals legally, and the costs of offending are greater (since legal penalties are harsher and their intimates—wives or girlfriends—disapprove of offending).

Prevention and Treatment

Risk Factors, Causes, and Prevention

Methods of preventing or treating antisocial behavior should be based on empirically validated theories about causes. In this section, implications about prevention and treatment are drawn from some of the risk factors and likely causes of antisocial behavior listed above. It will focus more on risk factors than on the theory being presented, although the theory aims to ex-plain the risk factors and is concordant with the prevention implications. The major emphasis is on the early prevention of offending. Gordon and Arbuthnot (1987), Kazdin (1985, 1987), and McCord and Tremblay (1992) have provided more extensive reviews of this topic. The focus here is on randomized experiments with reasonably large samples and with outcome measures of offending, since the effect of any intervention on offending can be demonstrated most convincingly in such experiments (Farrington, 1983; Farrington et al., 1986a). Many interesting experiments are either not ran-domized (Jones and Offord, 1989), do not have outcome measures of offend-ing (Kazdin et al., 1987, 1989), or are based on very small samples (Shore and Massimo, 1979).

It is difficult to know how and when it is best to intervene, because of the lack of knowledge about developmental sequences; ages at which causal factors are most salient; and influences on onset, persistence, and desistance. For example, if truancy leads to delinquency in a developmental sequence, intervening successfully to decrease truancy should lead to a decrease in delinquency. On the other hand, if truancy and delinquency are merely dif-ferent behavioral manifestations of the same underlying construct, tackling one symptom would not necessarily change the underlying construct. Experiments are useful in distinguishing between developmental sequences and different manifestations, and indeed Berg et al. (1979) found experimentally that decreases in truancy were followed by decreases in delinquency.

An important consequence of the continuity in antisocial behavior over time is that potential offenders can be identified at an early age with a reasonable degree of accuracy. In the Cambridge study, Farrington (1985) developed a prediction scale based on early antisocial behavior, convicted parents, socioeconomic deprivation, low intelligence, and poor parental child-rearing behavior—all measured at ages eight to ten. This scale was constructed in a randomly chosen half of the sample and validated in the other half, with very little shrinkage in predictive efficiency. The 55 boys with the highest prediction scores included the majority of chronic offenders with six or more convictions up to age twenty-five (15 out of 23), 22 other convicted males (out of 109 with between one and five convictions), and only 18 unconvicted males (out of 265).

The ideas of early intervention and preventive treatment raise numerous theoretical, practical, ethical, and legal issues. For example, should prevention techniques be targeted narrowly, on children identified as potential delinquents, or more widely, on all children living in a certain high-risk area (e.g., deprived public housing)? It would be most efficient to target the children who are most in need of the treatment. Also, some treatments may be ineffective if they are targeted widely, if they depend on raising the level of those at the bottom of the heap relative to everyone else. However, the most extreme group may also be the most resistant to treatment or difficult to engage, so there may be a greater payoff in targeting those who are not quite the most in need. Also, it might be argued that early identification could have undesirable labeling or stigmatizing effects, although the most extreme cases are likely to be stigmatized anyway, and there is no evidence that identification for preventive treatment in itself is damaging. The degree of stigmatization, if any, is likely to depend on the nature of the treatment. In order to gain political acceptance, it may be best to target areas rather than individuals.

The ethical issues raised by early intervention depend on the level of predictive accuracy and might perhaps be resolved by weighing the social costs against the social benefits. In the Cambridge study, Farrington et al. (1988a, 1988b) found that three-quarters of vulnerable boys identified at age ten were convicted. It might be argued that, if preventive treatment had been applied to these boys, the one-quarter who were "false positives" would have been treated unnecessarily. However, if the treatment consisted of extra welfare benefits to families and was effective in reducing the offending of the other three-quarters, the benefits might outweigh the costs, and early identification might be justifiable. Actually, the vulnerable boys who were not convicted had other types of social problems, among them having few or no friends at age eight and living alone in poor home conditions at age thirty-two. Therefore, even the unconvicted males in the survey might have needed and benefited from some kind of preventive treatment designed to alleviate their problems. Blumstein et al. (1985) developed an explicit method of taking social costs and benefits into account in prediction exercises.

Can Offending Be Prevented and Treated Successfully?

In the 1970s there was a widespread belief, stimulated by influential reviews by Martinson (1974) in the United States and Brody (1976) in England, that existing treatment techniques had no differential effects on the recidivism of detected offenders. This conclusion was substantially endorsed by a National Academy of Sciences panel in an impressive, methodologically sophisticated review (Sechrest et al., 1979). However, for a number of reasons, it should not be concluded that "nothing works," nor even that everything works equally well.

Martinson's (1974) conclusions were based on the Lipton et al. (1975) review of 231 studies of the effectiveness of correctional treatment between 1945 and 1967. However, Thornton (1987) found that only 38 of these studies met minimum methodological standards, contained matched or randomized comparison groups, and included an outcome measure of recidivism. For nearly all of these studies (34 out of 38), the treatment was "psychological" in nature, such as individual counseling, psychotherapy, or casework. Of these 34 psychological studies, 16 showed that the treatment was effective in reducing recidivism, 17 found no significant difference, and only one found that the treatment was harmful. These numbers were more compatible with the hypothesis that psychological treatment had beneficial effects than with the hypothesis that psychological treatment had no effect (since that would have predicted equal numbers of positive and negative results). Other commentators (e.g., Gendreau and Ross, 1979, 1987; Ross and Gendreau, 1980) also argued that there were many examples of effective correctional treatment. Also, Martinson (1979) later rejected his original conclusions about the ineffectiveness of treatment.

In the past decade, reviews of the effectiveness of correctional treatment have increasingly used the technique of meta-analysis (Hedges and Olkin, 1985) to summarize results from a number of studies. This technique requires the calculation of a comparable effect size (ES) in each study, usually defined as the difference between the average score of a treated group and the average score of a control group, expressed in standard deviation units. This ES measure is not very relevant to studies of correctional treatment, where the main interest is usually in the difference between the proportion of a treated group reconvicted and the proportion of a control group reconvicted. However, at least for effect sizes below 1, the difference in proportions is roughly half the ES. Thus, an ES of .2 corresponds to a 10 percent difference in recidivism rates (e.g., 40 percent versus 50 percent) between treated and control groups. An ES of .2 or greater has considerable practical significance.

The most important meta-analyses all focus on adjudicated juvenile delinquents. In an analysis of 111 institutional treatment studies, Garrett (1985) reported a mean ES of .37 for all outcomes of correctional treatment, but only .13 for recidivism specifically. Most of her outcome measures were of institutional or psychological adjustment or academic or vocational skills. Behavioral treatments were generally effective in reducing recidivism (mean ES = .18), but psychodynamic techniques were not (mean ES = −.01). In an analysis of ninety community-based treatment studies, Gottschalk et al. (1987) reported an identical mean ES of .37 for overall effectiveness in treatment-control comparisons but a higher ES for recidivism of .33. They considered that 56 percent of treatments had beneficial effects, 43 percent had no marked effect, and only 1 percent had harmful effects.

Whitehead and Lab (1989) drew more pessimistic conclusions from their meta-analysis of fifty studies of juvenile correctional treatment, largely because they set a very high criterion (a phi correlation of at least .2) for concluding that a treatment was effective. Only sixteen of their fifty studies met this criterion for recidivism. This value of the phi correlation approximates to a 20 percent difference in recidivism rates (Farrington and Loeber, 1989) and to an ES of .4. According to Lipsey (1992), their mean ES was .25, which has some practical significance. Andrews et al. (1990b) criticized Whitehead and Lab's review and reanalyzed their data, concluding that the mean phi correlation for "appropriate" treatments was .3, corresponding to a halving of recidivism rates in many cases. Overall, behavioral treatments had a high mean phi correlation of .29 (or a mean ES of about .6), whereas nonbehavioral treatments had a mean phi correlation of only .04 (Andrews et al., 1990a).

Roberts and Camasso (1991) reviewed 46 studies of juvenile correctional treatment published between 1980 and 1990 and reported a mean ES of .36 for recidivism. However, the largest meta-analysis, based on 443 studies, was completed by Lipsey (1992). Overall, he considered that the treatment reduced offending in 64 percent of studies, increased offending in 30 percent, and made no difference in 6 percent. The mean ES for delinquency outcomes in all studies was .17, and behavioral and skill-oriented programs were most effective, with mean ESs in the .2–.3 range after various adjustments.

It is reasonable to conclude from the meta-analyses that psychological, and especially behavioral, treatments generally succeed in reducing the recidivism rates of adjudicated juvenile offenders. The effect sizes are not large (of the order of .2–.3), but they correspond to reductions of 10 to 15 percent in the proportion reconvicted, which is a decrease of some practical significance. Personally, we prefer more traditional methods of reviewing and

268 DAVID P. FARRINGTON

summarizing the literature to meta-analysis. It seems more useful to identify the most adequate studies methodologically (e.g., randomized experiments with large samples, long follow-up periods, and outcome measures of offending) and to review the best studies in detail rather than to try to summarize a large number of projects with varying degrees of methodological adequacy and relevance.

Why do treatments not cause a greater reduction in recidivism? There are many possible reasons, including the fact that interventions may not be sufficiently powerful (e.g., averaging only one hour per week in the review by Gottschalk et al., 1987), especially in comparison to the overwhelming influence of environmental (e.g., family, peer, community) factors. Another problem is the persistence of offending and antisocial behavior over time. Kazdin (1987) suggested that serious antisocial behavior might be viewed as a chronic disease that requires continual monitoring and intervention over the life course. It might be desirable to distinguish chronic and less seriously delinquent juveniles and to apply different types of interventions to these two categories (LeBlanc and Frechette, 1989). If the chronics are the worst 5 percent, interventions applied to the next 10 percent may be more successful.

Conclusions

A great deal has been learned in the last twenty years, particularly from longitudinal surveys, about risk factors for offending and other types of antisocial behavior. Offenders differ significantly from nonoffenders in many respects, including impulsivity, intelligence, family background, peer influence, socioeconomic deprivation, and residence in deprived inner-city areas. These differences are present before, during, and after criminal careers. Since most is known about risk factors for prevalence and onset, more research is needed on risk factors for frequency, duration, escalation, and desistance. While the precise causal chains that link these factors with antisocial behavior—and the ways in which these factors have independent, interactive, or sequential effects—are not known, it is clear that individuals at risk can be identified with reasonable accuracy.

Offending is one element of a larger syndrome of antisocial behavior that arises in childhood and tends to persist into adulthood, with numerous different behavioral manifestations. However, while there is continuity over time in the relative ordering of people's antisocial behavior, changes are also occurring. It is commonly found that about half of a sample of antisocial children go on to become antisocial teenagers, and about half of antisocial teenagers go on to become antisocial adults. More research is needed on factors that vary within individuals and that predict these changes over time. Research is especially needed on changing behavioral manifestations and developmental sequences at different ages. More efforts should especially be made to identify factors that protect vulnerable children from developing into antisocial teenagers. More longitudinal surveys are needed.

The theory proposed here suggests that the key underlying construct is "antisocial tendency" and that offending depends on energizing, directing, inhibiting, decision-making, and social learning processes. It aims to explain how individuals interact with situations to produce offenses. In addition to explaining differences among individuals in the prevalence or frequency of offending, theories should explain changes within individuals: why people start offending, why they continue or escalate their offending, and why they stop offending. For example, onset may depend primarily on poor parental child-rearing behavior, persistence may depend on criminal parents and delinquent peers, and desistance may depend on settling down with spouses and cohabitees.

The stability of antisocial behavior from childhood to adulthood suggests that delinquency prevention efforts should be implemented as early in a child's life as possible. Teenage pregnancy, substance use in pregnancy, and perinatal complications (including low birth weight) are risk factors for a variety of undesirable outcomes, including low intelligence and attainment, hyperactivity and impulsivity, and child conduct problems of aggression and delinquency. Hence, it is important to mount delinquency prevention programs targeting these risk factors and to follow up the children into adolescence and adulthood to establish the long-term effects on delinquency and crime. Home-visiting programs that attempt to improve child-rearing methods and parental knowledge about child development seem to be quite effective. Cognitive-behavioral interpersonal skills training to improve self-control, preschool intellectual enrichment programs to develop cognitive skills, and parent management training also seem to be effective methods of preventing offending.

References

Andrews, D. A., Zinger, I., Hoge, R. D., Bonta, J., Gendreau, P., & Cullen, F. T. (1990a). A human science approach or more punishment and pessimism: A rejoinder to Lab and Whitehead. *Criminology, 28*, 419–429.

Andrews, D. A., Zinger, I., Hoge, R. D., Bonta, J., Gendreau, P., & Cullen, F. T. (1990b). Does correctional treatment work? A clinically relevant and psychologically informed meta-analysis. *Criminology, 28*, 369–404.

Bandura, A. (1977). *Social learning theory.* Englewood Cliffs, N.J.: Prentice-Hall.

Berg, I., Hullin, R., & McGuire, R. (1979). A randomly controlled trial of two court procedures in truancy. In D. P. Farrington, K. Hawkins, & S. Lloyd-Bostock (Eds.), *Psychology, law and legal processes* (pp. 143–151). London: Macmillan.

Blumstein, A., Farrington, D. P., & Moitra, S. (1985). Delinquency careers: Innocents, desisters and persisters. In M. Tonry & N. Morris (Eds.), *Crime and justice*, vol. 6 (pp. 187–219). Chicago: University of Chicago Press.

Brody, S. R. (1976). *The effectiveness of sentencing*. London: Her Majesty's Stationery Office.

Chandler, M. J. (1973). Egocentrism and antisocial behaviour: The assessment and training of social perspective-taking skills. *Developmental Psychology, 9*, 326–332.

Cloward, R. A., & Ohlin, L. E. (1960). *Delinquency and opportunity*. New York: Free Press.

Cohen, A. K. (1955). *Delinquent boys*. Glencoe, Ill.: Free Press.

Dishion, T. J., Loeber, R., Stouthamer-Loeber, M., & Patterson, G. R. (1984). Skill deficits and male adolescent delinquency. *Journal of Abnormal Child Psychology, 12*, 37–54.

Elliott, D. S., Huizinga, D., & Ageton, S. S. (1985). *Explaining delinquency and drug use*. Beverly Hills, Calif.: Sage.

Eysenck, H. J. (1977). *Crime and personality* (3rd ed.). London: Routledge & Kegan Paul.

Farrington, D. P. (1983). Randomized experiments on crime and justice. In M. Tonry & N. Morris (Eds.), *Crime and justice*, vol. 4 (pp. 257–308). Chicago: University of Chicago Press.

Farrington, D. P. (1985). Predicting self-reported and official delinquency. In D. P. Farrington & R. Tarling (Eds.), *Prediction in criminology* (pp. 150–173). Albany: State University of New York Press.

Farrington, D. P. (1986). Stepping stones to adult criminal careers. In D. Olweus, J. Block, & M. R. Yarrow (Eds.), *Development of antisocial and prosocial behaviour* (pp. 359–384). New York: Academic Press.

Farrington, D. P. (1990). Implications of criminal career research for the prevention of offending. *Journal of Adolescence, 13*, 93–113.

Farrington, D. P. (1992). Explaining the beginning, progress and ending of antisocial behaviour from birth to adulthood. In J. McCord (Ed.), *Facts, frameworks and forecasts: Advances in criminological theory*, vol. 3 (pp. 253–286). New Brunswick, N.J.: Transaction.

Farrington, D. P. (1993). Motivations for conduct disorder and delinquency. *Development and Psychopathology, 5*, 225–241.

Farrington, D. P., Gallagher, B., Morley, L., St. Ledger, R. J., & West, D. J. (1988a). A 24-year follow-up of men from vulnerable backgrounds. In R. L. Jenkins & W. K. Brown (Eds.), *The abandonment of delinquent behaviour* (pp. 155–173). New York: Praeger.

Farrington, D. P., Gallagher, B., Morley, L., St. Ledger, R. J., & West, D. J. (1988b). Are there any successful men from criminogenic backgrounds? *Psychiatry, 51*, 116–130.

Farrington, D. P., & Hawkins, J. D. (1991). Predicting participation, early onset, and later persistence in officially recorded offending. *Criminal Behaviour and Mental Health, 1*, 1–33.

Farrington, D. P., & Loeber, R. (1989). Relative improvement over chance (RIOC) and phi as measures of predictive efficiency and strength of association in 2×2 tables. *Journal of Quantitative Criminology, 5*, 201–213.

Farrington, D. P., Ohlin, L. E., & Wilson, J. Q. (1986). *Understanding and controlling crime*. New York: Springer-Verlag.

Garrett, C. J. (1985). Effects of residential treatment on adjudicated delinquents: A meta-analysis. *Journal of Research in Crime and Delinquency, 22*, 287–308.

Gendreau, P., & Ross, R. R. (1979). Effective correctional treatment: Bibliotherapy for cynics. *Crime and Delinquency, 25,* 463–489.

Gendreau, P., & Ross, R. R. (1987). Revivification of rehabilitation: Evidence from the 1980s. *Justice Quarterly, 4,* 349–407.

Gordon, D. A., & Arbuthnot, J. (1987). Individual, group and family interventions. In H. C. Quay (Ed.), *Handbook of juvenile delinquency* (pp. 290–324). New York: Wiley.

Gottfredson, M., & Hirschi, T. (1990). *A general theory of crime.* Stanford, Calif.: Stanford University Press.

Gottschalk, R., Davidson, W. S., Gensheimer, L. K., & Mayer, J. P. (1987). Community-based interventions. In H. C. Quay (Ed.), *Handbook of juvenile delinquency* (pp. 266–289). New York: Wiley.

Guerra, N. (1989). Consequential thinking and self-reported delinquency in high school youth. *Criminal Justice and Behaviour, 16,* 440–454.

Hawkins, J. D., Weis, J. G. (1985). The social development model: An integrated approach to delinquency prevention. *Journal of Primary Prevention, 6,* 73–97.

Hedges, L. V., & Olkin, I. (1985). *Statistical methods for meta-analysis.* Orlando, Fla.: Academic Press.

Hollin, C. R. (1990). Social skills training with delinquents: A look at the evidence and some recommendations for practice. *British Journal of Social Work, 20,* 483–493.

Jones, M. B., & Offord, D. R. (1989). Reduction of antisocial behaviour in poor children by non-school skill-development. *Journal of Child Psychology and Psychiatry, 30,* 737–750.

Kazdin, A. E. (1985). *Treatment of antisocial behaviour in children and adolescents.* Homewood, Ill.: Dorsey Press.

Kazdin, A. E. (1987). Treatment of antisocial behaviour in children: Current status and future directions. *Psychological Bulletin, 102,* 187–203.

Kazdin, A. E., Bass, D., Siegel, T., & Thomas, C. (1989). Cognitive-behavioural therapy and relationship therapy in the treatment of children referred for antisocial behaviour. *Journal of Consulting and Clinical Psychology, 57,* 522–535.

LeBlanc, M., & Frechette, M. (1989). *Male criminal activity from childhood through youth.* New York: Springer-Verlag.

Lipsey, M. W. (1992). Juvenile delinquency treatment: A meta-analytic inquiry into the variability of effects. In T. D. Cook, H. Cooper, D. S. Cordray, H. Hartmann, L. V. Hedges, R. J. Light, T. A. Louis, & F. Mosteller (Eds.), *Meta-analysis for explanation* (pp. 83–127). New York: Russell Sage.

Lipton, D., Martinson, R., & Wilks, J. (1975). *The effectiveness of correctional treatment.* New York: Praeger.

Martinson, R. M. (1974). What works? Questions and answers about prison reform. *The Public Interest, 35,* 22–54.

Martinson, R. M. (1979). New findings, new views: A note of caution regarding sentencing reform. *Hofstra Law Review, 7,* 243–258.

McCord, J., & Tremblay, R. (Eds.). (1992). *Preventing antisocial behaviour.* New York: Guilford Press.

Nietzel, M. T. (1979). *Crime and its modification.* New York: Pergamon.

Pearson, F. S., & Weiner, N. A. (1985). Toward an integration of criminological theories. *Journal of Criminal Law and Criminology, 76,* 116–150.

Roberts, A. R., & Camasso, M. J. (1991). The effect of juvenile offender treatment programmes on recidivism: A meta-analysis of 46 studies. *Notre Dame Journal of Law, Ethics and Public Policy, 5,* 421–441.

Ross, R. R., & Gendreau, P. (Eds.). (1980). *Effective correctional treatment.* Toronto: Butterworths.

Ross, R. R., & Ross, B. D. (1988). Delinquency prevention through cognitive training. *New Education, 10,* 70–75.

Sarason, I. G. (1978). A cognitive social learning approach to juvenile delinquency. In R. D. Hare & D. Schalling (Eds.), *Psychopathic behaviour* (pp. 299–317). Chichester: Wiley.

Sechrest, L., White, S. O., & Brown, E. D. (1979). *The rehabilitation of criminal offenders: Problems and prospects.* Washington, D.C.: National Academy of Sciences.

Shaw, C. R., & McKay, H. D. (1969). *Juvenile delinquency and urban areas* (rev. ed.). Chicago: University of Chicago Press.

Shore, M. F., & Massimo, J. L. (1979). Fifteen years after treatment: A follow-up study of comprehensive vocationally-oriented psychotherapy. *American Journal of Orthopsychiatry, 49,* 240–245.

Sutherland, E. H., & Cressey, D. R. (1974). *Criminology* (9th ed.). Philadelphia: J. B. Lippincott.

Thornton, D. M. (1987). Treatment effects on recidivism: A reappraisal of the "Nothing Works" doctrine. In B. J. McGurk, D. M. Thornton, & M. Williams (Eds.), *Applying psychology to imprisonment* (pp. 181–189). London: Her Majesty's Stationery Office.

Tisdelle, D. A., & St. Lawrence, J. S. (1986). Interpersonal problem-solving competency: Review and critique of the literature. *Clinical Psychology Review, 6,* 337–356.

Trasler, G. B. (1962). *The explanation of criminality.* London: Routledge & Kegan Paul.

Whitehead, J. T., & Lab, S. P. (1989). A meta-analysis of juvenile correctional treatment. *Journal of Research in Crime and Delinquency, 26,* 276–295.

Wilson, J. Q., & Herrnstein, R. J. (1985). *Crime and human nature.* New York: Simon & Schuster.

18

A General Paradigm of Criminality

BRYAN VILA

The Life Cycle

One must apply a *generational time scale* in order to gain a holistic understanding of the causes of individual criminal behavior. We begin in the same way an ecologist would approach the study of any organism—by examining the life cycle.

The Role of Early Life Experiences

Early life experiences appear likely to have an especially strong influence on the development of criminality, because individuals acquire traits sequentially. The traits people possess at any juncture are the result of the cumulative cognitive, affective, physical, and social effects of a sequence of events that began at conception. As a result of these events, individuals acquire a strategic style over the course of their lives. Some individuals develop *criminality*, a style that emphasizes the use of force, fraud, or stealth to obtain resources and is characterized by self-centeredness, indifference to the suffering and needs of others, and low self-control.

A complete review of factors affecting the development of criminality is beyond the scope of this chapter. Some of the more important factors, however, include parenting and family management practices associated both with how children are monitored, disciplined, and provided with positive reinforcement and with problem-solving styles and the level of parental involvement with children (e.g., Patterson et al., 1992:2). Also important are educational success, pre-, peri-, and postnatal stress (e.g., Wilson and Herrnstein, 1985), nutrition (e.g., Lozoff, 1989), and complex interactions between genes and environment (Fishbein, 1990; Plomin, 1989). Even the "goodness of fit" (Lerner and Lerner, 1983) between a child's temperamental style and parental demands and preferences can be important. Two especially important developmental factors are whether an environment helps or hinders a child's attempt to cope with his or her temperamental propensities and parents' ability to cope with or redirect the behaviors of a difficult child (e.g., Caspi et al., 1987; Olson et al., 1990).

Systematic relations between children and adult caregivers can have important effects on development. Because these relations are dynamic and can be self-reinforcing, interactions between a child's behavior and parental and family environmental factors can have cumulative effects on one another over time (Bell and Harper, 1977; Lytton, 1990). As Werner and Smith (1992) noted, children are placed at increasing risk of becoming involved in crime by factors such as economic hardship, residence in high-crime neighborhoods, serious caregiving deficits, and family disruption. These risks, however, appear to be buffered by factors such as an easy temperament, scholastic competence, educated mothers, and the presence of grandparents or older siblings who serve as alternative caregivers. The relative importance of risk and protective factors varies according to life stage, gender, and social environment (Featherman and Lerner, 1985:664).

Demographic stressors such as poverty, lack of education, and a high-crime environment, as well as family stressors such as unemployment, marital conflict, and divorce, all tend to influence development by disrupting family management practices (Sampson and Laub, 1993:83). Growing up in a disrupted or dysfunctional family is associated strongly with a child's antisocial behavior, of which crime is one type.

Generational time scales are needed for an understanding of criminal behavior because poor family management, antisocial behaviors, and susceptibility to stressors are often transmitted from grandparents to parents to children (Huesmann et al., 1984; Patterson et al., 1989). As will be discussed, the intergenerational transmission of risk factors may have important policy implications.

Figure 18.1 summarizes how people acquire traits that influence their behavior sequentially over the life course. Which traits are acquired depends on interactions between genes, social and individual learning, and environmental factors during development. Examples of important factors associated with development of criminality at each life stage are listed below the diagram.

An Example

As Figure 18.1 illustrates, parents may transmit genes that—in conjunction with pre-, peri-, and postnatal experiences—cause offspring to develop nervous and organ systems that make them much more difficult and irritable. This affects the probability that they will bond properly with a parent, especially if that parent is under extreme stress from economic, social, or per-

Figure 18.1   Acquisition of Behavior-Influencing Traits over the Human Life Cycle

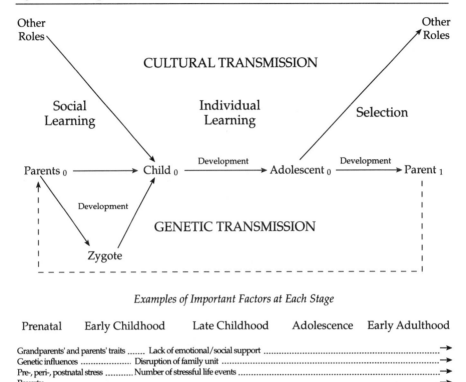

Examples of Important Factors at Each Stage

Prenatal	Early Childhood	Late Childhood	Adolescence	Early Adulthood

Grandparents' and parents' traits .... Lack of emotional/social support ....→
Genetic influences .... Disruption of family unit ....→
Pre-, peri-, postnatal stress .... Number of stressful life events ....→
Poverty..→
Nutrition .... Low scholastic competence .... Unemployment ....→
Environmental effects ....→

sonal factors. For example, children of poor parents beset by economic difficulties may be vulnerable to this dynamic, as may children of wealthy parents whose extreme focus on social and career concerns leads them to nurture their children irregularly (e.g., Binder et al., 1988:444–447). Moffitt (1993:682, 1994) described in detail the ways in which emergence of antisocial behaviors may be associated with interactions between problem children and problem parents in adverse rearing contexts. The parent-child bond affects how strongly a child values parental approval: Weakly bonded children tend to be much more impulsive and difficult to control. This situation can initiate a vicious cycle in which a child receives less affection and nurturance because of misbehavior and therefore seeks less and less to please. Over time, the child develops his or her strategic style in a setting where rewards are often unpredictable as parents struggle with alternating resentment and desire to nurture. Because the child perceives rewards as undependable, he or she learns to grasp opportunities for short-term gratification immediately rather than to defer them for future rewards. In this setting a child is also less likely to acquire conventional moral beliefs. In addition, the risk of physical and emotional child abuse—which further tend to fuel this vicious spiral toward criminality—may be greater (see Widom, 1989, 1992; Zingraff et al., 1992).

More impulsive children tend to do less well in school. Poor school performance strongly influences future life chances and thus affects how much stake the children develop in conventional society. It also increases the likelihood that they will associate with deviant peers and will learn criminal behavioral strategies from them. Both of these factors increase the likelihood of engaging in serious and frequent delinquency (Hirschi, 1969). Engaging in delinquency can further diminish conventional opportunities and weaken beliefs about the moral validity of specific laws, thus reinforcing criminality. This trajectory will tend to continue into adulthood until and unless it is altered. Sampson and Laub cited fundamental shifts in family relations and in work as the most important sources of potential change (1993:248; also see Caspi and Moffitt, 1993a). Unless the trajectory is deflected, this cycle of crime causation will tend to continue when people with high criminality become parents or role models (Figure 18.1). Thus, at the population level, this process can have an important effect on the evolution of the frequency, distribution, and character of crime.

Integrating Micro- with Macro-level Causes

A Paradigm of Crime Causation

An integrated paradigm of criminal behavior emerges when we consider how individual micro-level factors interact over time with ecological and macro-level factors to influence the evolution of criminal behaviors in a population. As Figure 18.2 illustrates, people acquire attributes such as knowledge, skills, attitudes, beliefs, and strategic styles over the life course via interactions among biological, sociocultural, and developmental factors. These attributes affect their "resource-holding potential" and "resource valuation" (Cohen and Machalek, 1988; Parker, 1974)—that is, their ability to obtain resources at a particular point in time and the way in which they value those resources. Thus, an individual's motivation to commit a crime is determined by these factors *plus the motivational effects of a tempting opportunity* (see Clarke and Felson, 1993). If motivation is sufficiently high and if an opportunity exists, a crime can occur. Resource-holding potential and resource valuation tend to vary substantially over the life course.

Moffitt's (1993) taxonomy of antisocial behavior provides an example of this dynamic. She proposed different causes for adolescence-limited and life-course-persistent antisocial behavior. According to her theory, adolescence-limited delinquency and antisocial behavior peak when resource-holding potential is lowest, and resource valuation tends to be most consistent with those types of behaviors. Compared with older people, adolescents

Figure 18.2   A General Model Integrating Individual and Societal Factors That
Cause Crime in an Ecological Context

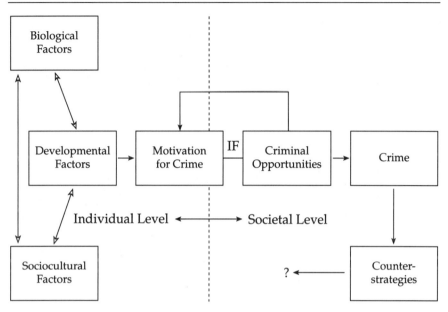

in contemporary industrial societies tend to be impoverished in the skills, status, and knowledge required to gain through conventional means the adult resources they value. At the same time, they tend to be less constrained by conventional attachments and to place greater value on thrills, prestige, and immediate gratification. Moffitt argued that this situation causes most normal adolescents to engage in at least some delinquent behavior. As relatively normal youths gain age, experience, and education, their resource-holding potential tends to increase; so do conventional opportunities and attachments. This process is consistent with their pattern of desistance from crime. In contrast, Moffitt contended that

> the life-course-persistent type [of antisocial behavior] has its origins in neuro-psychological problems that assume measurable influence when difficult children interact with criminogenic home environments. Beginning in childhood, discipline problems and academic failures accumulate increasing momentum, cutting off opportunities to practice prosocial behavior. As time passes, recovery is precluded by maladaptive individual dispositions and narrowing life options, and delinquents are channeled into antisocial adult lifestyles (1993:694–695).

Thus, life-course-persistent offenders tend not to desist from crime in early adulthood because their resource-holding potential deficit is *not* age-dependent, as is that of adolescence-limited delinquents.

The Evolution of Crime

When crimes occur, they tend to provoke counterstrategies (defensive responses). Over time, these ecological interactions cause individual and group responses to evolve. For example, higher crime rates often lead to more rigorous protective measures, which may cause crime rates to decline. In turn, barriers to crime may be relaxed as individuals and communities channel limited resources away from crime to deal with more pressing problems. Then, as crime rates decline, decreased vigilance and protective measures may make crime an easier and less risky behavioral strategy. Thus, as fewer individuals are attracted to crime, the potential rewards will tend to increase. Eventually, because of individual-level variation in resource-holding potential and resource valuation, *someone* in the population will find the rewards of a criminal strategy attractive enough to employ it. These dynamics—and the tendency of defensive counterstrategies to initiate a vicious cycle by provoking counter-counterstrategies from offenders—suggest that crime will probably always exist at some level in society (Cohen and Machalek, 1988, 1994; Vila and Cohen, 1993). Understanding the different ways in which counterstrategies address the causes of crime is the key to making criminological research relevant to public policy.

Counterstrategic Options

The Evolution of Counterstrategies

The paradigm offered here suggests that countervailing evolutionary forces affect the frequency and prevalence[1] of crime. On the one hand, the frequency of crime or of other expressions of criminality is fostered by co-evolutionary dynamics and by the tendency of frequency-dependent payoffs and risks to make rare criminal strategies more attractive. Some crime always will exist. The *amount* of crime, however, can be changed to some extent by counterstrategic forces that tend to make crime less attractive. Counterstrategies can be considered evolutionary forces in the sense that they may cause changes over time in the character, frequency, and distribution of criminal strategies and criminality. Counterstrategic considerations provide a natural link between research and policy.

The Problem of Crime

This paradigm and the general theory that it is hoped will one day flow from it are intended to guide both research and policy. For reasons discussed earlier, it is important to build stable links between research and policy. Traditional crime control strategies that emphasize use of the criminal justice system have largely failed to reduce serious crime. From 1971 to 1990, total constant dollar expenditures for federal, state, and local criminal justice system activities rose 88 percent, and imprisonment rates tripled (Maguire et al, 1993: Table 1.1, Fig. 6.4; U.S. Bureau of the Census, 1993: Table 755), becoming higher than in any other industrialized nation (Pease and Hukkila, 1990; UNAFEI, 1990). Yet rates of serious index crimes reported to the police increased by 40 percent, violent crimes by 85 percent, and more common property crimes by 35 percent (Maguire et al., 1993: Table 3.122).[2] Although the direct physical, material, mental, and emotional injuries sustained by victims of crime are obvious, the indirect damage to society is perhaps even more tragic. The responses of individuals and social control agents to crime often threaten personal freedoms, amplify mistrust and prejudice, and generally degrade social cohesion (Axelrod, 1984, 1986; Sampson and Groves, 1989; Shaw and McKay, 1969; Sugden, 1986; Vila and Cohen, 1993). Although a full discussion of policy implications is outside the scope of this chapter, some important links between research and policy are included in the following discussion to illustrate the utility of the paradigm.

Counterstrategies

In the past, most crime control proposals ignored the simple fact that criminality is influenced strongly by early life experiences because of the cumulative, sequential nature of development. As illustrated by the dashed arrows in Figure 18.3, we have usually employed counterstrategies that attempted to reduce opportunities for crime or deter it. *Protection or avoidance strategies* attempt to reduce criminal opportunities by changing people's routine activ-

Figure 18.3   Alternative Foci for Crime Control Strategies

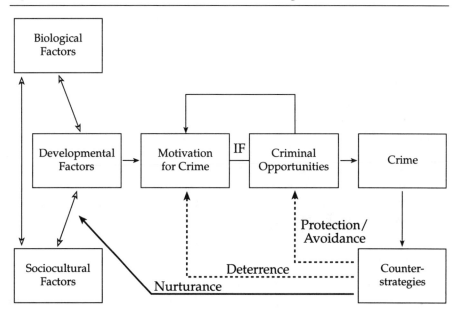

ities or by incapacitating convicted offenders via incarceration or electronic monitoring devices (Reiss and Roth, 1993:325). They may also increase guardianship by hardening targets, instituting neighborhood watch programs, and increasing the numbers or the effectiveness of police. *Deterrence strategies* attempt to diminish motivation for crime by increasing the perceived certainty, severity, or celerity of penalties. "Nonpunitive" deterrence approaches also advocate raising the costs of crime, but they emphasize increasing an individual's stake in conventional activities rather than punishing misbehavior (see Wilson and Herrnstein, 1985). *Nurturant strategies* (thick, solid arrow in Figure 18.3) have seldom been included on crime control agendas. They attempt to forestall development of criminality by improving early life experiences and channeling child and adolescent development.

Effectiveness of Protection and Avoidance

The long-term effectiveness of protection and avoidance strategies is limited. The evolutionary dynamics illustrated in Figure 18.3 indicate that protection strategies tend to stimulate "arms races" reminiscent of predator-prey co-evolution. Over time, for example, criminals adapt to better locks by learning to overcome them, to antitheft auto alarms by hijacking cars in traffic rather than while parked, to changes in people's routine activities by moving to areas with more potential targets (but see Barr and Pease, 1990). Protection strategies will obviously always be necessary in spite of their long-term limitations because of the opportunistic nature of much crime. This paradigm suggests that these strategies need to be able to evolve quickly in response to changes in criminal strategies because of the potentially rapid nature of cultural evolution. The effects of opportunity-reducing strategies such as incapacitation through incarceration are unclear, however, and may be confounded by the fact that younger offenders—who are least likely to be incarcerated—often commit the most crimes (see Reiss and Roth, 1993:292–294). Moreover, incarceration is expensive and perhaps often counterproductive. Sampson and Laub (1993:9) asserted that incarceration indirectly *causes* crime by disrupting families and ruining employment prospects (but see LeBlanc and Fréchette, 1989:191–193 for a discussion of the effectiveness of incarceration as an intervention for some chronic juvenile offenders). Newer alternatives such as incapacitation of convicted offenders by electronic monitoring in their homes are cheaper than incarceration and may have fewer undesirable side effects.

Effectiveness of Deterrence

Conventional deterrence strategies are also problematic. There is little evidence that, in a free society, they can be effective beyond some minimal threshold for controlling most crimes (Fisher and Nagin, 1978; Gibbs and Firebaugh, 1990; Reiss and Roth, 1993:292; Wilson and Herrnstein, 1985:397–399). One novel deterrence approach suggested recently by the National Research Council's Panel on the Understanding and Control of Violent Behavior might be more effective. It would attempt, through treatment and pharmacological intervention, to improve alcohol and psychoactive drug users' ability to calculate costs and benefits (Reiss and Roth, 1993:332–334).

Nonpunitive deterrence strategies that attempt to increase adolescents' and adults' stake in conventional life show promise for correcting life trajectories. Sampson and Laub's (1993) rigorous reanalysis of data from the Glueck Archive suggested that the best way to encourage most adult offenders to desist from crime is to increase their social capital by improving employment opportunities and family ties.[3] Evidence also exists to show that military service among young men may help to compensate for the criminogenic effects of earlier risk factors because it provides an opportunity to repair educational and vocational deficits (Elder, 1986; Werner and Smith, 1992).[4] The paradigm proposed here, however, suggests that nonpunitive deterrence strategies may still provide less potential crime control leverage than nurturant strategies do. Because criminality has its roots in the early life course, changing adults' strategic styles is generally more difficult than influencing children's development. To paraphrase Alexander Pope ([1734] 1961), it is easier to bend a twig than a mature oak.

EFFECTIVENESS OF NURTURANCE

This paradigm suggests that it should be possible to reduce the concentration of criminality in a population by improving early life experiences[5] and channeling child and adolescent development.[6] Nurturant strategies, however, such as educational, health care, and child care programs that address the roots of criminality early in the life course, have seldom been employed for crime control. Also, the results of educational and public health programs that attempted to improve early life-course factors have often been equivocal or disappointing (e.g., Haskins, 1989; Marris and Rein, 1973; Moynihan, 1969; Short, 1975). In fact, substantial increases in crime have accompanied what some observers would argue are enormous improvements during the past one hundred years in, for example, access to health care, public education about family management, and provision of counseling for abuse victims. How might this apparent inconsistency be explained?

Despite substantial improvements in these areas at the national level, their distribution undeniably has been uneven. Furthermore, increases in reported crime rates have been most dramatic during the last forty years. Much of the increase in crime during this period appears to have been associated with such factors as fluctuations in demographic and business cycles (e.g., Cohen and Land, 1987; Easterlin, 1987; Hirschi and Gottfredson, 1983) and changes in people's routine activities (Cohen and Felson, 1979). Increased urbanization, social disorganization, and concentration of those who are most deprived, as well as population growth, also appear to be very important (Land et al., 1991; W. J. Wilson, 1987; also see Sampson and Laub, 1993:64–98).

Time-lag effects may have confounded past attempts to *measure* the impact of nurturant strategies on crime rates. For example, previous empirical efforts to identify relationships between crime and social structural or economic variables (e.g., income inequality, poverty, and unemployment) by using aggregate data focused primarily on contemporaneous rather than lagged effects. The proposed importance of life-course thinking and intergenerational effects suggests that results of educational, health care, and child care programs implemented today should begin to be seen in about fifteen years—when today's newborns enter the fifteen- to twenty-nine-year-old age group, which is most at risk for criminal behavior. Even then, according to the paradigm, change would probably be gradual; the population-level concentration of criminality would continue to decline as each generation of more fully nurtured people became parents themselves. This means that change associated with nurturant strategies might require three or four generations.[7]

It is unclear whether the apparent failure of past nurturant programs (e.g., Cloward and Ohlin, 1960) reflects their lack of utility, faulty implementation, or a failure to pursue them *persistently* over generations. It is also possible that the effects of these programs have yet to be measured. Substantial payoffs could be realized if it were possible to implement programs such as these successfully over the long term. Strong evidence suggests that the 5 to 7 percent of male adolescents and young adults who are persistent chronic offenders are responsible for roughly 50 percent of all reported crimes.[8] Moffitt (1993) asserted that antisocial behavior in this group is most likely to be the result of early life-course factors.

Notes

1. The directional effect of frequency-dependent and co-evolutionary dynamics on *prevalence* is still unclear (Vila and Cohen, 1993:908).
2. Changes in victimization rates for often less serious crimes, calculated during a similar period by the National Crime Victimization Survey (NCVS), are less alarming; they show only a 3 percent decrease in crimes of violence but a 25 percent decrease in personal thefts and a 26 percent decrease in household crimes from 1973 to 1990 (U.S. Department of Justice, 1992: Table 1). Regardless of which measure is used, however, it seems clear that increases in criminal justice expenditures and incarceration rates are proportionately much greater than decreases (if any) in crime rates. The comparability of index crime data drawn from the Uniform Crime Reports and NCVS data is a complex issue (see Biderman and Lynch,

1991, and O'Brien, 1990, for overviews; for opposing positions see Blumstein et al., 1991, 1992; Menard, 1992).

3. Because improvement in employment opportunities appears to diminish the risk of offending, it is ironic that the United States, in comparison with most other industrialized nations, has largely ignored the occupational training needs of non-college graduates, who make up more than 80 percent of the U.S. adults over age twenty-five. The National Center on Education and the Economy notes that "America may have the worst school-to-work transition system of any advanced industrial country" (Havemann, 1993:A1).

4. In an apparent step in the right direction, the Clinton administration recently approved nonmilitary national service programs that might help smooth the school-to-work transition for young adults. (Also see Buckley, 1990.)

5. For example, nurturant strategies might attempt to (1) ensure that *all* women and children have access to high-quality prenatal, postnatal, and childhood health care; (2) educate as many people as possible about the basics of parenting and family management (e.g., Bank et al., 1987); (3) help people prevent unwanted pregnancies; (4) make help available for children who have been sexually, physically, and emotionally abused—and for their families; and (5) make available extended maternity leaves and high-quality child care for working parents.

6. Crime control strategies that *channel* tendencies such as impulsivity associated with increased risk of criminal behavior are necessary because biological, developmental, and environmental variation ensures that some people always will be more impulsive than others. Here the emphasis would be placed on improving the match between individuals and their environment. Channeling impulsivity might involve broad-based changes that improve the quality of education for all students (Committee for Economic Development, 1991; Linney and Seidman, 1989). For example, schools could place less emphasis on forcing children to sit all day and could allow them instead to participate in more active learning or to read in a preferred position. Similarly, self-regulation training, which improves self-control and diminishes impulsivity, would benefit all children. More impulsive students might also be encouraged to prepare for conventional occupations that reward people who prefer *doing* to sitting and talking and/or provide shorter-term gratification. This arrangement might help them to acquire a larger stake in conventional behavior and might diminish risks associated with school failure, thus making them less likely to develop or express criminality (Lemert, 1972; Sampson and Laub, 1993; Werner and Smith, 1992).

7. Attempts to measure past effects of nurturant strategies also might be confounded by immigration because, for example, national programs influencing early life-course factors would not have affected those whose childhoods were spent outside the country. *Legal* immigration as a percentage of total U.S. population growth has increased regularly from −0.1 percent during the Depression to 29.2 percent in 1980–1987 (U.S. Bureau of the Census, 1989; U.S. Immigration and Naturalization Service, 1986).

8. According to studies of large male cohorts, "chronic offenders" (those who had been arrested at least five times) accounted for 18 percent to 23 percent of all offenders (respectively, Wolfgang et al., 1972:88–94, and Tracy et al., 1990:82–92). See Farrington et al. (1986:50–52) for a review of these and similar studies.

References

Axelrod, R. (1984). *The evolution of cooperation.* New York: Basic Books.

Axelrod, R. (1986). An evolutionary approach to norms. *American Political Science Review, 80,* 1095–1111.

Bank, L., Patterson, G. R., & Reid, J. B. (1987). Delinquency prevention through training parents in family management. *The Behavior Analyst, 10,* 75–82.

Barr, R., & Pease, K. (1990). Crime placement, displacement, and deflection. In M. Tonry & N. Morris (Eds.), *Crime and justice: A review of research.* Chicago: University of Chicago Press.

Bell, R. Q., & Harper, L. V. (1977). *Child effects on adults.* Hillsdale, N.J.: Erlbaum.

Biderman, A. D., & Lynch, J. P. (1991). *Understanding crime incidence statistics: Why the UCR diverges from the NCS.* New York: Springer-Verlag.

Binder, A., Geis, G., & Bruce, D. (1988). *Juvenile delinquency: Historical, cultural, legal perspectives.* New York: Macmillan.

Blumstein, A. J., Cohen, J., & Rosenfeld, R. (1991). Trend and deviation in crime rates: A comparison of UCR and NCS data for burglary and robbery. *Criminology, 29,* 237–264.

Blumstein, A. J., Cohen, J., & Rosenfeld, R. (1992). The UCR-NCS relationship revisited: A reply to Menard. *Criminology, 30,* 115–124.

Buckley, W. F., Jr. (1990). *Gratitude: Reflections on what we owe our country.* New York: Random House.

Caspi, A., Elder, G. H., & Bem, D. J. (1987). Moving against the world: Life-course patterns of explosive children. *Developmental Psychology, 23,* 308–313.

Caspi, A., & Moffitt, T. E. (1993a). When do individual differences matter? A paradoxical theory of personality coherence. *Psychological Inquiry, 4,* 247–271.

Caspi, A., & Moffitt, T. E. (1993b). Paradox regained. *Psychological Inquiry, 4,* 313–321.

Clarke, R. V., & Felson, M. (Eds.) (1993). *Routine activity and rational choice.* New Brunswick, N.J.: Transaction.

Cloward, R., & Ohlin, L. (1960). *Delinquency and opportunity.* New York: Free Press.

Cohen, L. E., & Felson, M. (1979). Social change and crime rate trends: A routine activity approach. *American Sociological Review, 44,* 588–608.

Cohen, L. E., & Land, K. C. (1987). Age structure and crime: Symmetry versus asymmetry and the projection of crime rates through the 1990s. *American Sociological Review, 52,* 170–183.

Cohen, L. E., & Machalek, R. (1988). A general theory of expropriative crime. *American Journal of Sociology, 94,* 465–501.

Cohen, L. E., & Machalek, R. (1994). The normalcy of crime: From Durkheim to evolutionary ecology. *Rationality and Society, 6,* 286–308.

Committee for Economic Development (CED). (1991). *The unfinished agenda: A new vision for child development and education.* New York: CED.

Easterlin, R. A. (1987). *Birth and fortune.* Chicago: University of Chicago Press.

Elder, G. H. (1986). Military times and turning points in men's lives. *Developmental Psychology, 22,* 233–245.

Featherman, D. L., & Lerner, R. M. (1985). Ontogenesis and sociogenesis: Problematics for theory and research about development and socialization across the lifespan. *American Sociological Review, 50,* 659–676.

Fishbein, D. H. (1990). Biological perspectives in criminology. *Criminology, 28,* 27–72.

Fisher, F. M., & Nagin, D. (1978). On the feasibility of identifying the crime function in a simultaneous model of crime rates and sanction levels. In A. Blumstein (Ed.), *Deterrence and incapacitation: Estimating the effects of criminal sanctions on crime rates.* Washington, D.C.: National Academy of Sciences.

Gibbs, J. P., & Firebaugh, G. (1990). The artifact issue in deterrence. *Criminology, 28,* 347–365.

Haskins, R. (1989). Beyond metaphor: The efficacy of early childhood education. *American Psychologist, 44,* 274–282.

Havemann, J. (1993). The trade secrets of Denmark. *Los Angeles Times,* 3 July, A1.

Hirschi, T. (1969). *Causes of delinquency.* Berkeley: University of California Press.

Hirschi, T., & Gottfredson, M. R. (1983). Age and the explanation of crime. *American Journal of Sociology, 89,* 552–584.

Huesmann, L. R., Eron, L. D., Lefkowitz, M. M., & Walder, L. O. (1984). Stability of aggression over time and generations. *Developmental Psychology, 20,* 1120–1134.

Land, K. C., McCall, P. L., & Cohen, L. E. (1991). Characteristics of U.S. cities with extreme (high or low) crime rates: Results of discriminant analyses of 1960, 1970, and 1980 data. *Social Indicators Research, 24,* 209–231.

LeBlanc, M., & Fréchette, M. (1989). *Male criminal activity from childhood through youth: Multilevel and developmental perspectives.* New York: Springer-Verlag.

Lemert, E. M. (1972). *Human deviance, social problems, and social control.* Englewood Cliffs, N.J.: Prentice-Hall.

Lerner, J. V., & Lerner, R. M. (1983). Temperament and adaptation across life: Theoretical and empirical issues. In P. B. Baltes & O. G. Brim, Jr., (Eds.), *Life-span development and behavior,* vol. 5. New York: Academic Press.

Linney, J. A., & Seidman, E. (1989). The future of schooling. *American Psychologist, 44,* 336–340.

Lozoff, B. (1989). Nutrition and behavior. *American Psychologist, 44,* 231–236.

Lytton, H. (1990). Child and parent effects in boys' conduct disorder: A reinterpretation. *Developmental Psychology, 26,* 683–697.

Maguire, K., Pastore, A. L., & Flanagan, T. J. (1993). *Sourcebook of criminal justice statistics, 1992.* Washington, D.C.: U.S. Government Printing Office.

Marris, P., & Rein, M. (1973). *Dilemmas of social reform* (2nd ed.). Chicago: Aldine.

Menard, S. (1992). Residual gains, reliability, and the UCR-NCS relationship: A comment on Blumstein, Cohen, and Rosenfeld (1991). *Criminology, 30,* 105–114.

Moffitt, T. E. (1993). "Life-course-persistent" and "adolescence-limited" antisocial behavior: A developmental taxonomy. *Psychological Review, 100,* 674–701.

Moffitt, T. E. (1994). Natural histories of delinquency. In H.-J. Kerner & E. G. Weitekamp (Eds.), *Cross-national longitudinal research on human development and criminal behavior.* Dordrecht: Kluwer.

Moynihan, D. P. (1969). *Maximum feasible misunderstanding: Community action in the War on Poverty.* New York: Free Press.

O'Brien, R. M. (1990). Comparing detrended UCR and NCS crime rates over time: 1973–1986. *Journal of Criminal Justice, 118,* 229–238.

Olson, S. L., Bates, J. E., & Bayles, K. (1990). Early antecedents of childhood impulsivity: The role of parent-child interaction, cognitive competence, and temperament. *Journal of Abnormal Child Psychology, 18,* 317–334.

Parker, G. A. (1974). Assessment strategy and the evolution of fighting behaviour. *Journal of Theoretical Biology, 47,* 223–243.

Patterson, G. R., DeBaryshe, B. D., & Ramsey, E. (1989). A developmental perspective on antisocial behavior. *American Psychologist, 44*, 329–335.

Patterson, G. R., Reid, J. B., & Dishion, T. J. (1992). *Antisocial boys.* Eugene, Or.: Castalia.

Pease, K., & Hukkila, K. (Eds.). (1990). *Criminal justice systems in Europe and North America.* Helsinki: Helsinki Institute for Crime Prevention and Control.

Plomin, R. (1989). Environment and genes: Determinants of behavior. *American Psychologist, 44*, 105–111.

Pope, A. (1961). *Epistles to several persons* (1734), F. W. Bateson (Ed.) (2nd ed.). New Haven, Conn.: Yale University Press.

Reiss, A. J., Jr., & Roth, J. A. (1993). *Understanding and preventing violence.* Washington, D.C.: National Academy Press.

Sampson, R. J., & Groves, W. B. (1989). Community structure and crime: Testing social-disorganization theory. *American Journal of Sociology, 94*, 774–802.

Sampson, R. J., & Laub, J. H. (1993). *Crime in the making: Pathways and turning points through life.* Cambridge, Mass.: Harvard University Press.

Shaw, C. R., & McKay, H. (1969). *Juvenile delinquency in urban areas* (rev. ed.). Chicago: University of Chicago Press.

Short, J. F., Jr. (1975). The natural history of an applied theory: Differential opportunity and mobilization for youth. In N. J. Demerath, III, O. Larsen, & K. F. Schuessler (Eds.), *Social policy and sociology.* New York: Academic Press.

Sugden, R. (1986). *The economics of rights, co-operation and welfare.* Oxford: Basil Blackwell.

United Nations Asia and Far East Institute and Australian Institute of Criminology (UNAFEI). (1990). *Crime and justice in Asia and the Pacific.* Tokyo: UNAFEI.

U.S. Bureau of the Census. (1993). *Statistical abstract of the U.S., 1993.* Washington, D.C.: U.S. Government Printing Office.

U.S. Department of Justice, Bureau of Justice Statistics. (1992). *Criminal victimization in the United States: 1973–90 trends (NCJ-139564).* Washington, D.C.: U.S. Government Printing Office.

Vila, B. J., & Cohen, L. E. (1993). Crime as strategy: Testing an evolutionary ecological theory of expropriative crime. *American Journal of Sociology, 98*, 873–912.

Werner, E. E., & Smith, R. S. (1992). *Overcoming the odds: High risk children from birth to adulthood.* Ithaca: Cornell University Press.

Widom, C. S. (1989). The cycle of violence. *Science, 244*, 160–166.

Widom, C. S. (1992). *The cycle of violence.* National Institute of Justice Research in Brief, NCJ136607.

Wilson, J. Q., & Herrnstein, R. J. (1985). *Crime and human nature.* New York: Simon & Schuster.

Wilson, W. J. (1987). *The truly disadvantaged: The inner city, the underclass, and public policy.* Chicago: University of Chicago Press.

Wolfgang, M. E., Figlio, R. M., & Sellin, T. (1972). *Delinquency in a birth cohort.* Chicago: University of Chicago Press.

Zingraff, M. T., Leiter, J., Myers, K. A., & Johnsen, M. C. (1992). Child maltreatment and youthful problem behavior. *Criminology, 31*, 173–202.

PART V
CONFLICT THEORIES

Introduction

In explaining the presence of social order, criminologists have utilized two contrasting models of law and society. The consensus model asserts that society is based on a consensus of beliefs, values, and norms that reflect the general will of society's members. The state, in the form of criminal law, is viewed as the guarantor of this consensual social order (Vold and Bernard, 1986). When conflicts do arise, as the result of competing group interests, the state, in the form of civil and regulatory law, is viewed as a mediator between the conflicting groups, with the general societal will serving as the framework for conflict resolution. The contrasting model of social order begins with an assumption of conflict rather than consensus. The conflict model assumes that society is made up of groups with competing beliefs, values, and norms; and law is therefore viewed not as the embodiment of societal consensus but as an instrument of those groups with the power to determine the definition of crime and direct the mechanisms of social control (Turk, 1969).

Conflict theories can trace their origins to the political-economic theory of Karl Marx. Marx argued that in a capitalist state promulgation and implementation of law represent the average best interest of the dominant economic class, namely, those who own the means of production. Subsequent conflict theories have placed varying degrees of emphasis on either the legislative or enforcement component of Marx's original theory. Conflict theories have also been distinguished by their relative emphasis on the economic determinism first suggested by Marx. Willem Bonger's theory of criminality and economic conditions (1916) and, later, Richard Quinney's theory of the social reality of crime (1970) are examples of conflict theories that more closely reflect the economic determinism of Marx. Thorsten Sellin's culture conflict theory and George Vold's theory of group conflict trace the origin of group conflict to factors other than, or in addition to, the ownership of the means of production. Culture conflict theory identifies increasing societal complexity as the root of social conflict, whereas the theory of group conflict traces the sources of social conflict to the continuing struggle to maintain or improve one's place as a group in constant interaction with various ascendant, static, or descendant groups.

Contemporary conflict theories, beginning with Taylor, Walton, and Young's *The New Criminology* (1973), have tended to use Marx's economic analysis not as a singular explanation of conflict and crime but as one of a number of variables—including culture, race, gender, and ethnicity—that together explain how criminal definitions are determined and how criminal sanctions are applied, as well as the social conditions under which crime is likely to occur. The following selections represent the range of contemporary conflict theories. The first two chapters, by Lynch and DeKeseredy and Schwartz, are reformulations of original conflict theories that promote a more comprehensive critical analysis recognizing both the contextual importance of race, ethnicity, gender, and class and the legitimate fear of crime in poor and working-class communities. In "Assessing the State of Radical Criminology," Lynch begins by suggesting that there are strong connections between historically specific social structures and types of criminological theories generated during different political-economic eras. For Lynch radical criminology is a response to the construction of such ideologically biased explanations of crime. Through the use of radical history, Lynch traces the association between criminology's birth as a discipline and criminology's internalization of society's fear of the marginal groups as defined by race, ethnicity, class, and gender. Lynch argues that it is important to examine all crimes that carry punitive sanctions (including misdemeanors) as a form of control of the marginal groups in society. Using "radical linguistics," Lynch analyzes the language of criminology as a reflection of the connection between marginalization and the social construction of crime. Lynch concludes that radical criminology is essential because it offers an understanding of crime that is not shaped by culturally and historically specific (i.e., economic) forces.

In their discussion of left realism, DeKeseredy and Schwartz argue that any progressive analysis of the phenomenon of crime can no longer ignore the working-class communities' fear of street crime, as many conflict theories of the past have done. DeKeseredy and Schwartz identify left realism as an important phase in the evolution of critical criminology. Crime, according to the left realism perspective, is more than the function of moral panics by societal elites. Left realists caution that in critically analyzing crime in a capitalist system, it is important to note that working-class people are victimized from all directions. The left realist understanding of crime and social control focuses on the three variables that determine the criminological experience of the working class: victimization, fear of crime, and perception of the police. Taking into account these three variables, DeKeseredy and Schwartz offer a practical crime control strategy that includes the demarginalization of various disadvantaged groups, preemptive deterrence, democratic control of policing, and community participation in crime prevention initiatives. DeKeseredy and Schwartz also suggest a human ecology approach to crime that would shift the focus and resources of crime prevention away from the individual toward the political economy, the community, and the family.

The next two chapters, "Feminist Theory, Crime, and Justice" by Sally Simpson and "Feminism and Criminology" by Kathleen Daly and Meda Chesney-Lind, represent the recent development in conflict theory that focuses attention on how the dominant understanding of crime and its control affects specific marginalized groups, such as women. Simpson begins her analysis of gender and crime by differentiating among the major feminist theories. Although all theories take gender inequality as their starting point, they diverge on the question of structural causation. For liberal feminism, with its connection to the liberal bourgeois tradition, the system is not inherently unequal and discrimination is not systematic. Unequal treatment in the criminal justice system, as in any other social system, can be eliminated by simply increasing opportunity and freedom of choice for women. For radical feminism, gender oppression, which makes women much more likely to be victims of domestic violence and rape, is the result of men's control of women's sexuality through the system of patriarchy. In the radical critique, sexuality is the instrument of analysis and the personal experience of women constitutes the political dimension. The socialist feminist theory views the distinct victimization patterns of women and their patronizing treatment by the criminal justice system as an obvious feature of a capitalist economy that relegates women to a secondary economic position. Socialist feminism views the causes and control of crime as the result of the synthesis of two systems of domination: class *and* patriarchy. The theory of women of color argues for a heightened sensitivity to the complex interplay of gender, class, and race, ultimately leading to an alternative framework that would minimize the impact of these variables in the administration of justice. Simpson concludes her theoretical overview by outlining a feminist methodology that would transform traditional criminology from a social science based on masculine objectivity to a social action system based on a female subjectivity that is transdisciplinary, nonhierarchical, and empowering.

In their analysis of feminism and criminology, Daly and Chesney-Lind outline a two-stage theory that initially requires the achievement of full equality for women as a prerequisite for the development of a new vision of social order in which women's experiences and ways of knowing come to the fore. Daly and Chesney-Lind assert that it was feminist theory that originally challenged the separate spheres of men (the public) and women (the private), making men the final arbiters of morality and culture. The increasing equality of women, they argue, erodes the masculine monopoly of morality and culture. During the second stage of the transformation of criminological theory, Daly and Chesney-Lind call for a feminist conception of crime that denounces the domestic/private sphere as oppressive to women and replaces it with a unitary definition of crime that does not differentiate between acts committed in the public sphere and those committed in the private sphere. For a feminist vision of criminology to take hold, all gender-based laws and legal practices must be challenged. The authors conclude their theoretical analysis by demonstrating how a feminist vision of criminology, with its ability to connect clearly the conceptions of victimization and criminal offending, will inevitably lead to a reduction in violence toward women.

The final two selections, Herman Bianchi's "An Assensus Model of Justice" and Peter Cordella's "A Communitarian Theory of Social Order," propose alternative paradigms for dealing with crime. Both challenge the primary punitive response to crime that characterizes contemporary criminal justice and suggest as an alternative a criminological understanding predicated on peacemaking. Criminology as peacemaking redefines crime as conflict and replaces strictly punitive responses with a system of dispute settlement. Using historical and cross-cultural examples as support, each chapter outlines the conditions necessary for the successful establishment of a peacemaking system. Bianchi asserts that the definition of crime in a given society is determined by one of three models for interpreting norms and values: the consensus model, the dissensus model, and the assensus model. In the consensus model norms and values are seen as the embodiment of society's will, and any normative transgression is perceived to be a threat to the general will and is therefore defined as a crime requiring punitive action as a way of maintaining social solidarity. Conversely, the dissensus model suggests that values and norms reflect the interests of the powerful in society, and therefore any definition of crime must be viewed as a political action designed to maintain the existing power imbalance. For Bianchi the weaknesses of the consensus model are its inability to incorporate changing circumstances as a variable in determining criminality and is transference of participation in law from the people in general to a specialized bureaucracy. In the case of the dissensus model, Bianchi argues that even if crime is politically defined, the negative results of crime for the victim and the community are there and must be redressed. By contrast, the assensus model Bianchi proposes recognizes that interpretations of norms and values must be made in a neverending and open process of discussion. In Bianchi's assensus model, conflicts are transposed into dispute settlements between parties who are directly involved. In the case of crime, reconciliatory redress in the postcrime negotiations is a mandatory element of the discussion.

Cordella argues for an alternative paradigm for criminology in the form of a communitarian model of justice. Communitarian justice, according to Cordella, is based on a communicative and interactive system that combines the two functions of law, order maintenance and conflict resolution, into one unitary system. The added focus on conflict resolution requires the restorative system to reintegrate the actor while condemning the act. The legitimacy of communicative law is dependent upon its ability to engender remorse in the transgressor, provide reparations to the victim, and restore the community to its original state of harmony. Communicative law is conceived of as a cohesive discussion highlighting the mutual concerns and interests of the transgressor, the victim, and the community rather than as an edict separating the transgressor, the victim, and the community into competing constituencies. Communicative law is structured in such a way as to allow people to participate in the experience of its rules. Such rules are intentionally mutualist and life-supporting. They encourage people—law in hand—to discuss the main problems of their social life. Cordella traces the historical decline of restorative law in the West to the rise of bureaucracy. He asserts that as a result of the increasing bureaucratization of the legal process, people can no longer enjoy personal legal experience, which leads to the increasing disuse of normal abilities to deal with conflict. Cordella concludes his theory of restorative justice by suggesting that communicative and interactive systems of law are only possible within a larger mutualist or communitarian social context.

References

Taylor, I., Walton, P. & Young, J. (1973). *The new criminology.* New York: Harper and Row.

Turk, A. (1969). *Criminality and legal order.* Chicago: Rand McNally.

Vold, G., & Bernard, J. (1986). *Theoretical criminology.* New York: Oxford University Press.

19

Assessing the State of Radical Criminology

MICHAEL J. LYNCH

The situation of facts, events, behaviors, and eras within a political-economic frame of reference are the key ingredients of radically oriented history. There are several ways in which radically oriented histories of criminology could be constructed. Two paths are briefly outlined below.

One form a radical history of criminology could assume assesses the connections between historically specific social structures and the types of criminological ideas generated during specific political-economic eras (Lynch, 1988a). This type of radical history connects the history of criminological ideas to the history of a political, economic, and social structure. Bits and pieces of such a history exist, but there is no clear-cut or definitive work in this area.

A second radical history of criminology might emerge from an assessment of the association between the birth of criminology as a discipline and criminology's internalization of social fears of the marginal (dangerous) classes. This type of history would assess how criminology was (and is) employed to oppress or repress, generate fear of, and direct pain against marginalized segments of the population (Lynch, n.d.). The connection between the emergence of criminology; its theoretical rationale, justifications, and focus; and the growth of marginalized groups must necessarily be linked to economic conditions and processes if a "truly" radical history of criminology is to emerge from such an investigation.

Following the development of the two types of studies noted above, an attempt should be made to integrate all the various historical critiques and understandings generated by radical criminologists. This view would present a wide-ranging appraisal of criminology, in terms of both its theory and practice. Clearly, such a history has not been possible given the stage of development of radical criminology in particular and of criminology and the use of history in criminology in general. At this point, however, such histories can begin to be compiled; and in the next few years, as radical criminology matures further, these disparate histories can be further fleshed out and unified.

Constructing a radical history of criminology requires the fuller illumination of issues such as race, class, gender, and ethnicity; their connections to the construction of oppressive and biased theoretical explanations and justice practices; and their contextual importance in a historical sense. The next section examines the importance of incorporating race, ethnicity, and gender more fully into the radical tradition.

Class, Race, Ethnicity, and Gender

Traditionally, the radical model has been most fully understood and appreciated as a class model. And indeed, the origins of radical theory can be traced to Marx's class-linked analysis of capitalism. To be sure, a class-based model adds depth and insight to all forms of analysis, and it provides an indispensable mode of thinking about many issues that relate to inequality, particularly crime. For some issues, though, a staunch class model may be inappropriate, since it lacks the ability to deal with important dimensions of certain social, economic, and political issues (Messerschmidt, 1986, 1993)—specifically, forms of inequality that are unrelated to class (e.g., gender inequality, racial inequality, ethnic inequality). In other cases a pure economic focus may generate reductionistic explanations that exclude factors beyond class and economics (Lynch and Groves, 1989).

With these criticisms in mind, it is clear that at least three other important factors that generate inequality deserve further attention from radical criminologists—race, ethnicity, and gender. These three issues are simultaneously connected to and disconnected from the issue of class. This situation has not gone completely unnoticed by radical criminologists. There is currently much concern about race, ethnicity, and gender among a variety of radical criminologists (e.g., see Messerschmidt, 1993). These concepts have been redefined and incorporated into many recent radically oriented research projects (e.g., see special issue of Social Justice, vol. 19, no. 2, 1992). However, incorporation of these issues into radical criminology more generally has been tenuous to the extent that race, ethnicity, and gender issues have been almost completely separated from further development of the class-based model that informs radical criminology. In short, interest in issues other than class are certainly welcomed within radical models, and such interest has certainly done much to expand the focus of radical scholarship. However, in this process of expansion, radical theory itself has not been developed so that it may mature along with the interests of scholars who prefer this form of thinking. What is needed, in other words, is the construction of a radical theory that enables class, race, ethnicity, and gender to be connected as vital and viable components of our understanding of the operation of modern social systems.[1]

Class, gender, ethnicity, and race intersect in a number of distinct ways that cannot be explained by a unidimensional class-analytic model (Messerschmidt, 1993). As far as criminology is concerned, gender, ethnicity, race, and class affiliations all demarcate contextual boundaries. These boundaries need to be identified and addressed to answer more fully the question of how crime is constructed by criminal justice agents and the criminal (as subject and object) within a given political-economic setting.

In short, it is being argued here that radical feminist, radical class, radical race, and radical ethnicity models should no longer be seen as separate and competing concerns or interests. Rather, if radical criminology is to advance in its understanding of crime and justice, those adhering to this perspective will be required to think in ways that unite class, race, gender, and ethnicity and the various theoretical positions that support each as the key issue.

This does not mean to suggest that the issue of class should be marginalized in radically oriented research. Rather, the suggestion is that the class focus should make room for equally important, historically relevant forces that structure inequality. To radical criminologists, this means that their theories will always be in a state of flux, always emerging as a process of explanation (to the extent that the conditions these theories explain are constantly changing).

In the contemporary world, class continues to matter. Thus, this aspect of political economy should not be neglected. Yet, as the next section will discuss, the issue of class has already been marginalized to some extent within radical criminology, and this issue too needs to be addressed in the further development of radical criminology.

Marginalizing Research on Marginal Populations

One of the unique contributions radical criminology has to offer is its focus on marginalized populations and the relationship between marginalization and the social construction of crime. This focus has, however, been minimized in recent years by a number of new interests that fall within the realm of radical criminology (e.g., semiotics, deconstruction, postmodernism, peacemaking, left realism, etc.). Further, radical criminologists have limited the scope of inquiry in this area by focusing either on the association between marginalization and "serious" (felony street) crimes or on limited segments of the marginal population (e.g., unemployment; see Bohm, 1985, for a further critique).[2] In short, the critical theorists' focus on marginalization appears to have played itself out in many cases, but not because research into this issue has been exhaustive. Indeed, there are numerous ways in which this concern (marginalization) can be reincorporated into the core of radical theorizing.

For instance, the association among marginalization, social control, and misdemeanor offenses, while clear, needs much further analysis. Marginalization theory provides an excellent vehicle for understanding the distribution of misdemeanor crimes. This view begins with the observation that marginalized persons or bodies (Foucault, 1979) violate the spatial and temporal order of capitalism.[3] From the perspective of capital, marginalized bodies must be controlled, disciplined, punished, and forced back into the time-space dimension capitalism "allows" them to occupy. Consequently, marginalized persons are more likely to be controlled for infractions involving time-and-space disciplinary violations (e.g., vagrancy, loitering, public nuisance, no visible means of support, etc.; cf. Foucault, 1979) rather than other (violent-personal, property) crimes. Such infractions are only defined as criminal given the political economy of capitalism and the connection between inappropriate use of time and dislocation of the body from the strict space requirements (i.e., absence from work or from a working position) of capitalist economic arrangements. (This view has received some attention generally; see Foucault, 1979; Rusche and Kirchheimer, 1939; Melossi, 1976; Lynch, 1988b). Included in the array of minor time-space offenses that deserve greater attention are vagrancy, loitering, nonsupport statutes, public disturbance, and public drunkenness violations (some of which have been studied in the past; see Chambliss, 1964; Harring, 1983, 1982, 1981; Adler, 1991).

To some extent, the neglect of misdemeanor crimes and corresponding focus on the "most serious" forms of crime (i.e., street crime) is an interest radical criminologists have "inherited" from mainstream criminology. Clearly, certain felonious behavior is (life) threatening and therefore "serious." Statistically speaking, however, such crimes are rare events. The most likely form of crime in our society (as far as official statistics or victimization studies are concerned) is the misdemeanor or Part II Index Offense,[4] while the most widely used form of criminal justice control is the jail. The existence of misdemeanor crimes allows the criminal justice system to use the jail to control a large percentage of the marginal class. The average daily jail population in the United States, approximately 300,000, consists mainly of marginalized persons. On average, jail populations turn over about once every five days. Thus, in the space of a year the nation's jail population turns over about seventy-five times, resulting in jails controlling some 22.5 million marginal bodies during that time.[5]

Neglect of this large, class-specific, and state-controlled population is disconcerting for several reasons. Overlooking the obvious, let us turn to one reason internal to criminology and the battle between mainstream and critically oriented scholars: Misdemeanor offenses committed by marginalized persons are generally ignored entirely by mainstream criminologists. This means that an entire, rather large area of the crime problem is left untouched by any form of criminological explanation and is therefore ripe for capture by radically oriented explanation.

Statistical Models and Radical Subversion

Generally, radical criminologists have "shunned" statistical modeling of crime and responses to crime. The standard defense of this neglect is that statistical models are somehow "bourgeois" in nature—that the typical type of crime data available reflects and captures a capitalist-defined reality and nothing more. This argument is true in some ways (specifically, crime data contain class and race biases) but is quite misleading in others (e.g., in relation to empirical observation as a method of knowing and understanding). Extensive discussions of the nature of empirical observations have amassed enough evidence to demonstrate the fallaciousness of the general radical dismissal of empirical observation as a method (e.g., see Myrdal, 1969; Keats, 1979; Flakser, 1971; Irvine et al., 1979; Groves, 1985; Lynch, 1987; Greenberg, 1981). To review, Myrdal (1969) and Flakser (1971) among others (Lynch, 1987; Groves, 1985; Greenberg, 1981) argue that the biases contained in statistical methods are primarily the result of the need to contextualize or interpret empirical results, to place data within a frame of reference so that data acquire meaning. This suggestion is important for the following reason: When radicals avoid empirical models, there is little hope that interpretations of empirical data will emerge that favor radical expectations and theory. By avoiding data analyses, radicals have avoided their responsibility to lend radical meaning to the results of empirical tests within criminology. In sum, those radically oriented scholars who argue in favor of empirical analyses believe that "the total rejection of statistics is as one-sided [and one-dimensional] as an uncritical acceptance of statistical orthodoxy" (Irvine et al., 1979:2).

The real issue, however, is not the use or avoidance of data or empirical methods; it is the harm that has resulted from the debate over the use of empirical studies by radical criminologists. The division among radical criminologists between die-hard anti-empirical supporters and data-friendly radicals has distracted attention from the real issues and goals of data-based radical analyses and has created dissension where none should exist. Whether or not radicals accept the scientific model and its associated ideological truth claims (e.g., objectivity), radical criminologists must come to realize that empirical study is an important part of their challenge to mainstream criminology. This position is briefly explained below.

Traditional criminological positions, as we all know, are based upon a number of related assumptions about the nature of society, knowledge, and the means of acquiring knowledge. Internal or external challenges can be made to these assumptions (Lynch and Groves, forthcoming). Radical criminology, because it is based upon a different world view, typically attacks traditional criminology via the use of external criticism. Traditional criminology must reject such criticisms, which strike at the root beliefs of the traditional system and are incompatible with the logic of that system.

Conversely, radically oriented statistical models have the advantage of containing the type of evidence that offers an internally situated criticism of traditional criminology. Statistical tests cannot be rejected outright (in theory, at least) by the mainstream, because they contain the type of evidence valued by positivist social sciences. Consequently, where radical criminologists can (1) employ radically oriented variables in empirical tests and (2) pit these variables against variables representing traditional criminological perspectives, mainstream assumptions and findings can be challenged head on using a method of "acquiring knowledge" that mainstream circles recognize as legitimate.

In addition, the use of statistical methods to test radically oriented variables against traditional variables confers two other advantages on radical criminology and its adherents. First, this tactic constitutes an "offensive" attack against mainstream theory and evidence. This sets into motion a process whereby the mainstream must actively defend its position or accept the radical theory and explanation as superior. In short, it places mainstream rather than radical criminologists on the defensive.

Second, mainstream theorists must (in theory) accept the evidence radical criminologists offer in an empirical format. That is, they cannot challenge the form of presentation (i.e., the empirical or statistical format itself)[6] as inappropriate. In doing so, mainstream theorists would risk undermining the credibility of their own empirical models and assertions and the legitimacy of the positivistic frame of reference that is the backbone of mainstream criminological knowledge. This result, too, would be favorable to radical criminology.

In an ideal world, statistical studies could become a new way of communicating with the mainstream and altering the impact of radical theory on criminology and criminal justice practice more generally. That is, if criminologists actually reacted to empirical research in a nonideological manner, the radical empiricist might make greater headway in altering the mainstream view of crime. In the meantime, while radical criminologists attempt to build communication bridges with the mainstream, they also need to attend to the way in which they currently communicate with one another through language. The next section addresses this issue, taking a critical view of "radical linguistics."

Radical Linguistics: Who's Listening Anyway?

In recent years, radical or critical criminology has been increasingly influenced by a variety of related areas of concern. As the base of knowledge upon which radical criminology has been built expands, so too does the vocabulary of critical criminology. For example, ideas, phrases, and words from other languages that cannot be "properly translated" into English are increasingly introduced into critical theory. In the process of language or

term "importation," theorists often seem to fail to seek out the proper mean-
ing(s) or idea(s) these phrases and words represent in the culture into which
they are imported. In the process, radical criminologists have also failed to
learn to communicate with one another and the public.

These tendencies are particularly problematic and ironic from a radical,
critical, or Marxist perspective. In this view language is not universal but is
to a large extent shaped by culturally and historically specific (economic)
forces. Certain words and phrases, for example, have meaning in a language
because that language reflects the context in which that meaning makes
sense. Imported words often fail to make sense not simply because they are
in a foreign language but also because they are not relevant to the life context in which theorists attempt to apply them.

Support for this interpretation can be found in other (nonradical) views
on linguistics, in which language itself is viewed as a structure (e.g., Wittgenstein, 1960). In such a view, language and the thing(s) represented by
language, though connected, are in some manner severed; the link between
the two is mediated by other forces. Thus, in this view it also makes little
sense to examine words outside the context of their language structure. This
issue has been well examined by Wittgenstein (1960:5), who described the
problem as follows:

> If the meaning of the sign . . . is an image built up in our minds when we see or
> hear the sign, then first let us . . . replac[e] this mental image by some outward
> object seen, e.g., a painted or modelled image. Then why should the written
> sign plus the painted image be alive if the written sign alone was dead? In fact,
> as soon as you think of replacing the mental image by, say, a painted one, and
> as soon as the image thereby loses its occult character, it ceases to seem to
> impart any life to the sentence at all. (It was in fact just the occult character of
> the mental process which you needed for this purpose.)
>
> The mistake we are liable to make could be expressed thus: We are looking
> for the use of a sign, but we look for it as if it were an object coexisting with the
> sign. (One of the reasons for this mistake is again that we are looking for a
> "thing corresponding to a substantive.")
>
> The sign (the sentence) gets its significance from the system of signs, from
> the language to which it belongs. Roughly: understanding a sentence means
> understanding a language.

Building upon this logic and that contained within critically oriented theory, we can see that importing words across languages makes little sense.
The words themselves are unimportant. What may be important is the idea
or concept behind the words. Often, however, we are not led to take this
type of analytic step (i.e., assessing the concept or meaning behind a word
or phrase); rather, we accept the word at face value—as a word. The result:
Radical criminologists have tended to import cultural artifacts uncritically
without struggling to search for the meaning of this idea in our own cultural

circumstances. It may be, for example, that imported terms and phrases have no significance for the political, economic, and/or cultural conditions in which we produce criminological and criminal justice theory in the United States; the imported phraseology arises from particular contradictions or reproductive conditions alien to our own experience as a society or people. This possibility must be exposed and searched—analyzed—so that the language we use expresses the context of life as we live it in our society and culture—not life as it is lived in another society in connection with another language and another social structure.

In addition, by importing language and theoretically dense structures that may have little meaning to our circumstances or to nonacademicians, we have participated in building an impassable wall around critical theory that denies access to all but a chosen few. These tendencies (which could be described as elitist) are detrimental to the critical position's health and vitality.

Linguistically, critical theory has become increasingly dense in recent years as it adopts the guise of a science (remember, one of the distinguishing features of a science as defined in philosophy of science literature is the development of its own unique language). Looking, or at least sounding, like a science may be professionally appealing; however, sounding like a science distances critical theory from the working class and, often, from working-class issues and concerns. If forms of oppression, their consequences, and remedies cannot be clearly communicated to a broad audience with clear and concise language, then there is little hope that critical criminology will enjoy broad appeal and support.

Certainly, it is easy for us as academics to create a language that only we understand. It is much more difficult to think about what the terms we employ mean and to use the ideas contained in those terms in a way that makes our work accessible (see Mills, 1959, for further discussion). By masking what we say with an apparently "scientific" language full of difficult, imported, and convoluted terms and writings, we shield ourselves from certain types of criticism. No one knows exactly what we are talking about, and therefore they cannot assess what our position says. It is surely better to be clear and risk criticism that takes the theorist to task for his or her views than to be ignored as an obtuse egghead by an audience that has little time to waste attempting to decipher criminological hieroglyphics.

In any event, the "language game" (Wittgenstein, 1960) that we have played within and with radical criminology is a major obstacle to the further development of this area of research. We are currently in grave danger of falling into the trap of "Grand Theorists" such as Parsons, a trap C. Wright Mills so carefully dissected over thirty years ago. This trap entails developing a discipline or specialty caught up in itself. A discipline caught up in itself expands exponentially without developing the capability of (1) addressing real problems encountered by real individuals as they live out their lives each and every day and (2) addressing problems in a language and manner that makes the problem visible to those who experience it.

Notes

1. Historically, race, ethnicity, and gender may not have been as important in all societies. In the future, these issues may also become less important. Currently these forces clearly play a large role in determining power relations in the United States as well as around the world, a world in the midst of several ethnic cleansing battles. In short, a historically contingent qualifier is attached to this call for greater attention to issues of race, ethnicity, and gender.

2. Admittedly, I am guilty of some of these same tendencies in my research (Lynch, 1988b; Lynch et al., 1994). Where I am guilty of this, I have purposely chosen to focus upon felony street crimes to address the criticisms leveled against radical criminology by mainstream criminologists. I fully realize that the radical approach has broader import. In addition to explaining misdemeanor offenses, this view can be used to explore the issue of corporate crime (Frank and Lynch, 1992; Simon and Eitzen, 1992; Reiman, 1990; Michalowski, 1985).

3. Of course the contradiction is, as all radicals know, that the organization of capitalism creates marginalized groups that cannot fit within the "normal" (i.e., laboring or time-space) segment of a capitalist economy or class structure.

4. This position excludes the striking observation made by numerous radical criminologists (e.g., Reiman, 1990; Michalowski, 1985; Quinney, 1980; Messerschmidt, 1986; Simon and Eitzen, 1992; Box, 1983; Frank and Lynch, 1992) who have pointed out that the most serious and widespread form of crime in our society is corporate, white-collar, and political crime. White-collar and corporate crimes are, however, omitted from consideration here for two reasons: (1) Much radical research has focused on white-collar and corporate crimes, and these can hardly be considered neglected areas; and (2) the assumption that there are more white-collar and corporate crimes than any other form of illegal activity may be true, but it remains unprovable owing to the lack of a valid and comprehensive source of data on such crimes.

5. This figure is calculated simply by taking the average daily population rate and multiplying that figure by the number of times the population turns over in one year. The figure is misleading to the extent that many persons are jailed several times in any given year. However, the numbers demonstrate the amount of control that the jail can exert.

6. In theory, mainstream theorists are bound to specific assumptions concerning the use and meaning of data. When empirically oriented radical scholarship is at issue, however, many of these assumptions seem to be dismissed. Where they are not, there is an attempt to dismiss the analysis using a variety of methodological and statistical caveats—and few analyses could meet those standards. Yet when the data support a radical interpretation, the empirical standards, in my experience at least, appear to be much stricter than at other times and when testing other theories.

References

Adler, J. (1989). A historical analysis of the law of vagrancy. *Criminology, 27, 2,* 209–229.

Bohm, R. (1985). Beyond unemployment: Toward a radical solution to the crime problem. *Crime and Social Justice, 21–22,* 213–222.

Box, S. (1983). *Power, crime and mystification.* London: Tavistock.

Chambliss, W. (1964). A sociological analysis of the law of vagrancy. *Social Problems, 12,* 67–77.

Flasker, D. (1971). *Marxism, ideology and myth.* New York: Philosophical Library.

Frank, N., & Lynch, M. J. (1992). *Corporate crime, corporate violence.* New York: Harrow & Heston.

Foucault, M. (1979). *Discipline and punish: The birth of the prison.* New York: Vintage.

Garza, C. (1992). Postmodern paradigms and Chicana feminist thought: Creating a "space and language." *Critical Criminologist, 4, 3–4,* 1–2, 11–13.

Greenberg, D. (1981). *Crime and capitalism.* Palo Alto, Calif.: Mayfield.

Groves, W. B. (1985). Marxism and positivism. *Crime and Social Justice, 23,* 129–150.

Groves, W. B., & Frank, N. (1986). Punishment and structured choice. In W. B. Groves & G. R. Newman (Eds.), *Punishment and privilege.* New York: Harrow & Heston.

Groves, W. B., & Lynch, M. J. (1990). Structuralism and subjectivity. *Journal of Research in Crime and Delinquency, 27, 4,* 348–375.

Groves, W. B., & Sampson, R. J. (1986). Critical theory and criminology. *Social problems, 33, 6,* 58–80.

Harring, S. (1983). *Policing in a class society.* New Brunswick, N.J.: Rutgers University Press.

Harring, S. (1982). The police institution as a class question: Milwaukee socialists and police, 1900–1915. *Science and Society, 46, 2,* 197–221.

Harring, S. (1981). Policing a class society: The expansion of the urban police in the late nineteenth and early twentieth centuries. In D. Greenberg (Ed.), *Crime and capitalism.* Palo Alto, Calif.: Mayfield.

Henry, S., & Milovanovic, D. (1993). Back to basics: A postmodern redefinition of crime. *The Critical Criminologist, 5, 2–3,* 1–2, 6, 12.

Henry, S., & Milovanovic, D. (1991). Constitutive criminology: The maturation of critical criminology. *Criminology, 29,* 293–315.

Irvine, J., Miles, I., & Evans, J. (1979). The critique of official statistics. In J. Irvine, I. Miles, & J. Evans (Eds.), *Demystifying social statistics.* London: Pluto Press.

Keats, R. (1979). Positivism and statistics in social science. In J. Irvine, I. Miles, & J. Evans (Eds.), *Demystifying social statistics.* London: Pluto Press.

Lynch, M. J. (n.d.). Evil heart: The underside of criminology and criminal justice. Unpublished manuscript.

Lynch, M. J. (1988a). The poverty of historical analysis in criminology. *Social Justice, 15, 1,* 329–344.

Lynch, M. J. (1988b). Surplus value, crime, and punishment: A preliminary examination. *Contemporary Crises, 12,* 329–344.

Lynch, M. J., (1987). Quantitative analysis and Marxist criminology: Some solutions to a dilemma in Marxist criminology. *Crime and Social Justice, 29,* 110–127.

Lynch, M. J., Groves, W. B., & Lizotte, A. (1994). The rate of surplus value and crime: A theoretical and empirical examination of Marxian economics and crime. *Crime, Law and Social Change, 21, 1,* 15–48.

Melossi, D. (1976). The penal question in capital. *Crime and Social Justice, 5,* 26–33.

Messerschmidt, J. (1993). *Masculinities and crime.* Totowa, N.J.: Rowman, Littlefield.

Messerschmidt, J. (1986). *Capitalism, patriarchy and crime.* Totowa, N.J.: Rowman, Littlefield.

Michalowski, R. (1985). *Order, law and crime.* New York: Random House.

Mills, C. W. (1959). *The sociological imagination.* New York: Oxford.

Milovanovic, D. (1992). *Post modern law and disorder: Psychoanalytic semiotics, chaos and juridic exegesis.* Merseyside, U.K.: Deborah Charles Publications.

Milovanovic, D. (1993). Lacan, chaos and practical discourse in law. In R. Kevelson (Ed.), *Flux, complexity and illusion in law.* New York: Peter Lang.

Milovanovic, D., & Henry, S. (1991). Constitutive penology. *Social Justice, 18,* 204–224.

Quinney, R. (1980). *Class, state, and crime.* New York: Longman.

Reiman, J. (1990). *The rich get richer and the poor get prison.* New York: Wiley.

Rusche, G., & Kirchheimer, O. (1939) [1968]. *Punishment and social structure.* New York: Columbia University Press.

Simon, D. R., & Eitzen, D. S. (1992). *Elite deviance.* Boston: Simon & Schuster.

Wittgenstein, L. (1960). *The blue and brown books.* New York: Harper Torchbooks.

20

British and U.S. Left Realism: A Critical Comparison

WALTER S. DEKESEREDY

MARTIN D. SCHWARTZ

The most important movement in radical criminology in the 1980s was the response by U.S. and British scholars to their respective governments' "law and order" programs with progressive analyses that accepted as legitimate the working-class communities' fear of street crime (e.g., Currie, 1985, 1989; Gross, 1982; Jones et al., 1986; Lea and Young, 1984; Matthews and Young, 1986; Michalowski, 1983). In doing so, they answered Taylor's (1981:xxi) famed call for the "reconstruction of socialist criminal politics" by proposing practical crime control strategies. These methods were meant as important alternatives not only to the programs of liberals and conservatives but also to those programs implicit in the analyses of the "left idealists" who have had a tendency to idealize oppressed groups and to overlook antisocial behavior within them (Young, 1988).

Despite their common ground, however, there are important differences between U.S. and British radical realists, rooted in very distinct political agendas. Thus, the principal objective of this chapter is to articulate the differences and the similarities between the American and British left realist positions.* Perhaps ironically, although coming from a country noted in Europe for being practical to a fault, the U.S. theorists have tended to discuss

We would like to thank several people for their helpful comments and suggestions on earlier and related articles. They include Alan Hunt, Ray Michalowski, Tony Platt, Brian MacLean, Hal Pepinsky, and Joe Sim.

*Although not essential to a comparison between U.S. and U.K. left realism, it is important to note the contributions made by Canadian (e.g., Alvi, 1986; DeKeseredy, 1988; Lowman, 1987, 1989; MacLean, 1988, 1989a, 1988b; McMullan, 1986, 1987) and Australian scholars (e.g., Boehringer, Brown, Edgeworth, Hogg, and Ramsey, 1983; C.C.J., 1988; Hogg, 1988; Hogg and Brown, 1988) when attempting an overall picture of the debates.

the wider and perhaps more abstract aspects of government, the economy, and crime, whereas the British have tended to dominate the more specific discussions of concrete policy suggestions. Certainly this is not the tendency of American criminology as a whole, which has been highly concrete to the point of being almost nontheoretical for at least two decades.

Another major difference is that there has been a more receptive audience, at least at the local level, for socialist suggestions in Great Britain. The marginalization of U.S. socialist academics, when combined with a limited discussion of concrete recommendations for change on the local level, has meant that they have had less impact on social policy than the British left realists.

Left Realism in Britain

Although there are different scenarios of the origin of British left realism, there is no question that it is a response to the law and order policies of the Thatcher government. Some locate the history in a reaction by some leftists to the violent British inner-city riots of 1980 and 1981 (e.g., Taylor, 1988), while others see it as a natural evolution of dissatisfaction with the direction of radical criminology in Britain (e.g., Young, 1988). In either case, left realism can only be adequately understood in the context of both British academic criminology and also the complex interests of the Labour Party. Although American academic criminology will be covered in more detail later in this chapter, it is important to note that socialists in the U.S. are outsiders in the best of circumstances; the language of socialist reform is not in the American vocabulary. In Britain, however, socialists have often seen in the Labour Party the real possibility of victory in the class struggle through the establishment of a proletarian state. Within the Labour Party, left-wing criminology has had a much more receptive audience. In the 1980s, faced with a central state and a rabidly right-wing popular press intent on exploiting racist and classist crime fears, British left realists struggled to develop crime control strategies that could be placed immediately into action with the help of Labour Party allies. Their struggle may have intensified as the Thatcher government's crushing defeats of the Labour Party on the national level made it seem more essential to work on specific and detailed projects with local Labour borough councils.

Proponents of British left realism are, by and large, affiliated with the Middlesex Polytechnic and the University of Edinburgh. Since the basic principles of their school of thought have been well documented elsewhere (Kinsey, Lea, and Young, 1986; Lea and Young, 1984; Matthews and Young, 1986; Young, 1986), only a brief summary will be provided here.

First, predatory street crime is seen as a serious problem for the working class. British left realists maintain that crime is more than a function of moral panics and that working-class people are victimized from all directions in capitalist societies. Specifically, the left realists reject the popular notion that crime rates are an epiphenomenon of social control. This point is a central notion of British left realists and occupies a great deal of space in most of their writings. Although they never identify by name whom they are attacking, it is essential that they see themselves in opposition to the "left idealists," who are the criminologists who minimize the effect of crime on working-class communities and may even idealize the proletarian criminal (Schwartz and DeKeseredy, 1991).

Second, British realism provides a theory of crime and its control that includes four major variables: the victim, the offender, the state, and the community (Jones, MacLean, and Young, 1986). Their explanation attempts to relate macro- and micro-levels of analysis. Although Marxist thought plays a significant role in realist discourse, this discourse is also influenced by other criminological approaches; it has been particularly affected by American academic thought such as subcultural theory, victimology, strain theory, and select ecological theories (Matthews, 1987).

Third, left realists defend the value of quantitative methods while rejecting abstract empiricism. They have conducted surveys on victimization, fear of crime, and perceptions of the police (e.g., Jones et al., 1986; Kinsey, Lea, and Young, 1986) and advocate research designs that consist of both quantitative and qualitative methods (Phipps, 1986).

Fourth, they try to provide practical crime control strategies that both challenge the right-wing law and order campaign and address working-class communities' legitimate fear of street crime. Examples of these "middle range policy alternatives which do not compromise any overall design for radical social change" (Cohen, 1979:49) are (1) demarginalization, (2) preemptive deterrence, (3) democratic control of policing, and (4) community participation in crime prevention and policy development (Lea and Young, 1984).

Except for research on violence against children, women, and ethnic groups (e.g., Breines and Gordon, 1983; Dobash and Dobash, 1979; Pearson, 1976; Russell, 1984, 1990; Schechter, 1982), left-wing scholars generally have not paid significant attention to the causes and control of intraworking-class crime. British radical realism makes a salient contribution to critical criminology by providing a "radical victimology" (Phipps, 1986) that includes an explanation of street crime and transitional, socialist policies to reduce it.

As one might expect, British left realism has not escaped attacks from opponents. For example, left realists have been criticized for ignoring feminist concerns (DeKeseredy and Schwartz, 1991; Edwards, 1989; Taylor, 1988). Others are critical of their failure to address the power of police subcultures (Gilroy and Sim, 1987), their discussions on race and crime (Bridges and Gilroy, 1982; Gilroy, 1982; Sim, Scraton, and Gordon, 1987), and their very use of the concept "crime" (Hulsman, 1986; Steinert, 1985). Their strongest critics have accused the realists of accommodating the repressive crime control policies of the Thatcher government (Gilroy and Sim, 1982), and come from those with other left-wing proposals (Taylor, 1988).

While these problems warrant further attention, especially the realists' responses to the above criticisms, it is beyond the scope of this chapter to reproduce these concerns. Rather, our concern is to compare British left realism with its U.S. counterpart, an objective that has not been adequately achieved in earlier critique.

British and U.S. Left Realism: Similarities and Differences

Compared to the much-discussed and influential British left realist project, U.S. left realist criminology has received little attention. The main reason for its relatively faint presence is that there is no clearly identifiable left realist perspective in American critical criminology (Taylor, 1988), just as it is impossible to identify a clear-cut left realist movement in Australia or Canada (Hogg and Brown, 1988; Schwartz, 1989). U.S. progressives have tended to provide individual commentaries, while the British left realists have produced a series of books and papers with a united perspective on street crime and its control. To the extent that there is a U.S. movement, it consists heavily of articles first published in the journal *Crime and Social Justice* (e.g., Boostrom and Henderson, 1983; Gross, 1982; Michalowski, 1983).

One major reason for the divergence of the two groups of scholars is their dissimilar academic histories. Although in the late 1960s and early 1970s academic sociologists were radicalized into the New Left in both Britain and the United States, the next steps were very different. In the United States, radicals rarely gained control over an entire department and where they did, for example at the University of California at Berkeley, the result was more likely to be the disbanding of the department than the establishment of a beachhead of progressive theory. Although isolated radicals have often been tolerated if they could not cause much trouble, radical criminologists and critical legal studies scholars have been heavily victimized by "academic McCarthyism" (Friedrichs, 1989). Further, fueled by extraordinary funding from the Law Enforcement Assistance Administration of the U.S. Department of Justice for tuition scholarships for law enforcement personnel, the main drive in U.S. academic life was to found departments of criminal justice. With the majority of the students in these departments often either in-service or preservice law enforcement, the major subject matter taught was commonly administrative criminology and technological law enforcement. To staff hundreds of departments starting almost simultaneously, many schools hired line personnel from police and corrections agencies with limited training in academic criminology. These faculty members in later years duplicated themselves by requiring line experience in law enforcement for new faculty. Although, to be sure, many radicals still taught courses in criminology or the sociology of deviant behavior, these courses were often mar-

ginalized to the edges of the discipline or taught only in sociology departments as electives for sociology majors. At the same time, enormous sums
of money were available to criminologists doing research in administrative
criminology, particularly for studies designed to improve efficiency in criminal justice system operations.

The situation was quite different in Britain, where deviance courses were
taught by sociology departments and often by instructors affiliated with the
National Deviancy Conference. Radicals established "power bases" in various polytechnics (e.g., Middlesex, "home" of the left realists), universities,
and colleges of education (Young, 1988). Since scholars such as those belonging to the left realist cohort were able to work in close proximity to one
another, it is not surprising that united schools of thought were able to develop in Britain. One of these schools of thought, of course, is left realism.

Another major difference is in the effect that scholars have had outside the
ivory towers of the academy. As with socialists generally, American radical
criminologists have been marginalized on every level. Not only was there no
national radical conference founded, but it was not until 1988 that radical
criminologists felt strong enough to begin to work toward institutionalizing
themselves as a division within the American Society of Criminology. Academic isolation and marginalization have precluded the development of a
united left realist perspective on predatory street crime.

In Britain, critical criminological discourse has influenced Labour Party
politics; especially at the local level in the early 1980s when Young (1988:
170) wrote

> . . . a new wave of young Labour politicians, many of them schooled in the New
> Left Orthodoxy of the sixties, were brought into power in the inner-city Labour
> strongholds. They—and in particular the police committee support units which
> they brought into being—became important political focuses for the ideas and
> concerns of radical criminology.

This connection between politicians and academics provided opportunities
that were rarely available in the United States. Although, just as in the
United States, the Home Office provided research grants only to administrative criminologists, the opportunity existed for radical criminologists to
work through Labour-controlled local government offices. Further, there is
no political group in the United States similar to the British Labour Party or
the Canadian New Democratic Party, where socialists are drawn to participate in mainstream political activities. To a small extent the Democratic
Party adheres to some socialist principles, but that remains a slight variation
within a dominant order committed to perpetuating and legitimating capitalist social relations (Miliband, 1969). Democratic Party meetings do not
bring U.S. radicals together to formulate agendas such as left realism, because their voices are likely to be ignored. Certainly the Democratic Party

has not provided research opportunities for radical criminologists, even at the most local levels.

In sum, political and academic forces have indirectly contributed to the development of a united left realist perspective in Britain. Operating within more repressive political and academic contexts, U.S. realists have been forced to "go it alone." Their individual contributions, however, are important and warrant attention here.

U.S. realists, like their British counterparts, take working-class crime seriously. However, some of their anticrime proposals move beyond the limited realm of both the street and the criminal justice system. For the purpose of this article, U.S. left realist strategies can be categorized under the following headings: economic policies, social services, and community crime prevention.

Economic Policies

Lea and Young (1984) stated that Taylor's (1981) *Law and Order: Arguments for Socialism* helped contribute to the development of British left realism. However, they have not addressed Taylor's (1981:184) warning that

> a socialist policy toward reform must be predicated primarily on its transformative economic policies; socialist policies of reform, for example in the area of law or welfare, must properly be formulated in terms of this initial premise. This is to say that policies towards the reform of law or towards policing cannot be substitutes for the initial, fundamental economic and social reconstruction. Demands for the democratization of policing, therefore, are not in themselves a part of an integrated program of socialist transformation, and they are not, and cannot be, substitutes for any such program.

Undoubtedly the British left realists would concur with Taylor's argument. Since their principal goals are to fill the vacuum in New Left thinking about street crime and to provide a criminology that offers progressive alternatives to the right-wing law and order agenda, it may not be fair to criticize them for excluding strategies to curb economic inequality. However, a discourse on this subject is clearly necessary, because a silent response to the relationship between wider political economic forces and crime perpetuates a dominant tendency "to compartmentalize social problems along bureaucratic lines" (Currie, 1985:18).

For example, it is an important argument of North Americans that those who assume that the criminal justice system is solely responsible for dealing with crime and that other state agencies should manage the social, economic, or family problems that cause it do not consider how decisions on economic issues (e.g., factory closures, reductions in welfare benefits, goods and services taxes) may significantly influence the rate of predatory street crime. Consequently, according to Currie (1985:19),

The failure to make these necessary connections between causes and consequences stifles the development of intelligent policies to prevent criminal violence, and burdens the criminal justice system with the impossible job of picking up the pieces after broader social policies have done their damage.

The policy proposals provided by several U.S. realists are sensitive to these concerns. Their contributions clearly address the relationship between inequality and crime. Michalowski, for example, provided economic policies to reduce street crime that are designed to be a financial burden for capitalists instead of the welfare state. Examples of his strategies include (1983: 14–18):

♦ Tax surcharges on industries attempting to close plants or permanently reduce a community's work force

♦ Government laws demanding retraining and job placement for all workers displaced by new technology

♦ A minimum wage level that is approximately 150 percent of the poverty level

In contrast to Michalowski's proposed structural changes, Currie's (1985, 1989) agenda requires both increased public and private support. His "social environmental" or "human ecological" approach calls for the following economic measures:

♦ Increased wages for women

♦ A wage policy based on Scandinavia's "solidaristic" (Rhen, 1985) scheme

♦ Publicly supported, community-oriented job creation

♦ Upgrading the quality of work available to disenfranchised people

♦ Intensive job training and supported work designed to help prepare the young and disabled for stable careers

♦ Paid work leaves

♦ Job creation in local communities

Such economic strategies certainly move beyond the limited realm of criminal justice reform (Gross, 1982). They attempt to address the wider structural forces that are seen by the realists to be the major sources of interpersonal crime, and to respond to the limitations of compartmentalizing social problems along bureaucratic lines.

Although some of these suggestions have been successfully implemented in other nations (Currie, 1985), and many U.S. theorists agree that they would reduce the rates of predatory street crime in America, whether politicians and voters are ready to hear the news remains questionable. Barak (1986:201) has contended that crime policies based on such principles will not be formulated and implemented by governing bodies until "politicians, policy analysts, and the public are exorcised of current crime causation myths, and not until many people are ready to challenge some of our most inbred cultural and political assumptions." The "exorcism" that Barak is calling for will not be an easy task when essential parts of the proposals include eliminating the gains the powerful in America have made under the current capitalist social order.

Platt (1984) has pointed out that the Right is also likely to respond to the Left's struggle by intensifying its "ideological combat" against progressive viewpoints. Thus, he argued, it is essential that progressives develop strategies to mobilize a broad base of activism. As he suggested, whereas British realists have begun to work with politicians to implement their ideas, progressives in the United States who ignore these concerns will develop strategies that will remain only blueprints for action.

Social Services

As U.S. conservative criminologists such as Wilson (1985) have taken great delight in pointing out, state-sponsored social services provided in the 1960s failed to reduce crime. Moreover, the failure of state-funded social programs has been successfully exploited by the Right for the purpose of gaining popular support for both reducing social funding and for its draconian law and order campaign in the 1970s and 1980s. The conservative approach has failed just as badly in both the United States and Britain, however, and is beginning to experience a major crisis of credibility (Currie, 1989) in both countries.

The British realists' anticrime agenda does not include a specific discourse on social programs, although there are occasional suggestions that they would be amenable to developing one. A particular burden they must carry is that the heritage of the New Left in England has been a heavy criticism of the interventions of the welfare state (Hood, 1987; Young, 1988). The cuts imposed by the Thatcher government were so heavy, however, Young (1988) argued, that many radicals quickly converted to become supporters of welfare state programs.

The major U.S. platform on social services comes from Currie (1985, 1989), who suggested that a limitation of earlier social service programs was that they were not sensitive to the powerful influences of the political economy, community, and family. Ironically, while liberal theories stated that social and economic inequality foster crime, only rarely did liberal U.S. crime control strategies deal with these factors. Instead, they attempted to increase individuals' "human capital" so that they could make better use of the limited opportunities that were given to them. Few attempts were made to deal with the structural disintegration of troubled individuals' familial and neighborhood environments.

Currie's progressive agenda for the future called for a variety of social services to the family to help them cope with both problems and abuse, recognizing the importance of the family's role in shaping prosocial behavior. Although both conservatives and liberals can agree with this basic point, Currie provided a sharp contrast with social environmental reforms that clearly recognize family dynamics as shaped by wider political economic forces. For example, as he contended (1989:10):

> A preschool on every ghetto corner won't overcome the structural disintegration of the surrounding communities—a disintegration whose sources lie well beyond the disadvantaged child and family, beyond the local community, and beyond the reach of the school, and which may well intensify in the coming decades.

Community Crime Prevention

Practically every variant of critical criminology calls for local, community-based strategies to curb crime. The rationale for proposing popular initiatives is based on the fact that some community efforts can reduce crime (Cohen, 1986; Michalowski, 1983). Hence, it is no surprise that both U.K. and U.S. left realists propose community initiatives. Some of their strategies are, however, plainly distinct from each other.

For example, British radical realists' community crime control measures focus primarily on street crime rather than suite crime. They don't actually assert that the fight against the former should precede the struggle against the latter. In fact, Lea and Young (1984) have contended that the working class is victimized from all directions and that a "double thrust" against both types of crime is required. This said, they simply do not provide further discussion or strategies based on this argument.

Instead, their local strategies are designed to foster democratic accountability of police to local communities and local police authorities. This is an important ambition, because the British police are experiencing a significant crisis, generally perceived as an inability to solve two major problems: the rising rate of crime among the disenfranchised and decreasing clear-up rates. Kinsey, Lea, and Young (1986) have argued that the British police's inability to curb crime is the result of a breakdown in police-community relations caused by the transition from "consensus" to "military" policing. For example, "hard" tactics (e.g., stop and search) have been used more extensively in recent years to reduce growing rates of street crime. These measures, however, alienate communities and influence many people to withhold support and information. Consequently, the police respond with more military tactics, which in turn lead to more community alienation from the police.

Kinsey, Lea, and Young have referred to this process as a "vicious circle," and have offered a community-based policy aimed at destroying it. Their left realist alternative is rooted in a theory of "minimal policing" and is distinct from community approaches advocated by liberals and conservatives. They have written (1986:192) "Minimal policing entails a strict limit on police powers working from the premise that it is for the police to cooperate with and respond to the demands of the public, rather than vice versa." The principles of minimal policing are maximum public initiation of police action, minimum necessary coercion by the police, minimal police intervention, and maximum public access to the police. The achievement of these goals would be a major change in British policing, but given the powerful law and order campaign in the United Kingdom, it is unlikely that we will see these four developments in the near future.

The U.K. left realist arguments about minimal policing have been greeted with great interest, if not complete acceptance. Nevertheless, if British left realists are correct in their own arguments that the working class is victimized from all directions, then any crime control strategy that seeks to be truly critical would attempt to work simultaneously in all directions. Unfortunately, American realist community-based strategies are quite similar in addressing street crime at the expense of white-collar, corporate, and state crime (e.g., Browning, 1982; Boostrom and Henderson, 1983; Currie, 1985, 1989; Gross, 1982). The attack on these positions, simply put, is that they all have the potential of becoming "simply a mechanism to get the working class to police itself" (Michalowski, 1983:19).

One American who provides a sharp contrast to one-sided community crime initiatives is Michalowski, who has suggested a popular crime control strategy that deals with crime from all directions. He proposed that citizen patrols based on democratic principles, and representative of all members of the community, should be organized to prevent both street and suite crime. With regard to the latter, Michalowski contended that citizen patrols could be used to gather information and to study complaints of business crimes. Local citizen groups could use their data to pressure businesses to stop harming the general public, or to initiate legal action against offenders.

Michalowski recognized that the small-scale initiatives of community patrols will not significantly alter the "deep structure" of corporate crime. Nevertheless, they may offset the dominant belief that only working-class people commit crimes. In addition, these strategies may sensitize people to the fact that they can start to control the private-sector economy.

Although there has been great interest in community crime strategies, those proposed by leftists on both sides of the Atlantic have been the subject of extensive critiques. Depending on who ultimately gains control over the mechanisms, such strategies have the potential to be extensions of state control over the powerless (Baskin, 1988; Cohen, 1985; Santos, 1980; Selva and Bohm, 1987). In many cases, they tend to advance what Platt (1984) referred to as a "vague populism" devoid of class analysis. The fear that local communities will enforce and reinforce racism, sexism, and class inequality through community crime strategies has further made some critics wary (Iadicola, 1986).

The Influence of Feminist Theory

A similarity in U.S. and U.K. left realism, and a major problem with both, is that it essentially ignores the problems of both a patriarchal society and the victimization of women. Both groups give extensive lip service to the problems raised by feminist authors, but both fail to integrate these concerns into their analyses or solutions in any meaningful way (DeKeseredy and Schwartz, 1991; Gelsthorpe and Morris, 1988; Kelly and Radford, 1987). A major feminist criminological concern is the effect of patriarchal structures on relations between men (Daly and Chesney-Lind, 1988). For example, Messerschmidt (1988) argued that it is impossible to understand violent street crime by the powerless without taking into account the power accorded males in this society, and that an attack on the sexual division of labor is essential to ending street crime. However, such an analysis is rare, particularly in criminology literature that is not explicitly feminist.

Similarly, although many feminist writers have discussed the nature of violence against women, few critical criminologists have integrated such concerns into their analyses. A very few Americans, such as Currie (1985) and Messerschmidt (1986), have made serious attempts to do so, but the response of the U.K. left realists has been no stronger than noting that the problem exists (Schwartz and DeKeseredy, 1991).

Summary and Conclusion

U.S. and British left realists have enlivened debates on anticrime strategies by providing significant challenges to conservative, liberal, and left idealist approaches. Although realist scholars from both sides of the Atlantic are dedicated to reducing predatory street crime, the British perspective has clearly been more influential theoretically and politically (Hogg and Brown, 1988). The reason for British realism's greater success is that it is the project of a clearly defined, united school of thought. British realists were able to join forces because, unlike their American counterparts, they have considerable influence in both the academy and the broader political realm (Young, 1988).

A critical examination of both types of left realist criminology reveals two important differences. First, American radicals have given more attention to reconstructing social and economic policies as well as criminal justice reform. British critical realists' proposals have been, by and large, restricted to the limited realm of the criminal justice system. Thus, they may be open to the criticism that they tend to reproduce what Currie (1985:18) called "the tendency to compartmentalize social problems along bureaucratic lines."

The second difference between American and British realism is that some U.S. strategies address crime from all directions (e.g., Michalowski, 1983; Schwartz and Ellison, 1982) while British proposals are concerned primarily with street crime. Of course the British cohort's primary interest is in filling the vacuum in radical thinking about street crime.

Given both the many criticisms and concerns raised in this chapter, two brief comments about the future of left realism are in order. First, since realists from both sides of the Atlantic have similar political concerns yet different agendas, it can only be fruitful for each to establish stronger relations with the other. Increased communication between British and U.S. radicals may contribute to each school of thought's struggle against law and order policies. One of the greater difficulties for Americans and Canadians in dealing with British left realist proposals for police reform is that so much of it is tied directly to the British experience and thus is only partially relevant to American police practice (Schwartz and DeKeseredy, 1991). Cooperation may make it possible to synthesize what is relevant and useful from the British experience for the North American audience.

Second, if left realism is to emerge as significant discourse in the United States, it requires a greater interchange of ideas within the criminological community. Currie (1989:5) pointed out: "We are poised uneasily at the end of one criminological era and the beginning of a new one, and it will be up to us to define just what the new one will look like." Given the geographic problems of distance in North America, this may mean careful attention to the possibilities of united schools of thought. Realist panels have been among the best attended at recent American Society of Criminology meetings, and a new Division on Critical Criminology has been organized within the ASC; hence, it seems that many North Americans are interested in such developments.

References

Barak, G. (1986). Is America really ready for the Currie challenge? *Crime and Social Justice, 25,* 200–203.

Boostrom, R., & Henderson, J. (1983). Community action and crime prevention: Some unresolved issues. *Crime and Social Justice, 19,* 24–30.

Breines, W., & Gordon, L. (1983). The new scholarship on family violence. *Signs: Journal of Women in Culture and Society, 8,* 491–553.

Bridges, L., & Gilroy, P. (1982). Striking back. *Marxism Today, 26,* 34–35.

Browning, F. (1982). Nobody's soft on crime anymore. *Mother Jones,* August, 24–31.

Cohen, S. (1979). Guilt, justice and tolerance: Some old concepts for a new criminology. In D. Downes & P. Rock (Eds.), *Deviance and social control.* London: Martin Robertson.

Cohen, S. (1986). Community control. In H. Bianchi & R. van Swanningen (Eds.), *Abolitionism* (pp. 127–132). Amsterdam: Free University Press.

Currie, E. (1985). *Confronting crime: An American challenge.* New York: Pantheon.

Currie, E. (1989). Confronting crime: Looking toward the twenty-first century. *Justice Quarterly, 6,* 5–26.

Daly, K., & Chesney-Lind, M. (1988). Feminism and criminology. *Justice Quarterly, 5,* 497–535.

DeKeseredy, W., & Schwartz, M. (1991). Left realism and woman abuse. In H. Pepinsky & R. Quinney (Eds.), *Criminology as peacemaking.* Bloomington: Indiana University Press.

Dobash, R., & Dobash, R. (1979). *Violence against wives.* New York: Free Press.

Edwards, S. (1989). *Policing "domestic" violence.* London: Sage.

Friedrichs, D. (1989). Critical criminology and critical legal studies. *Critical Criminologist, 1, 7.*

Gelsthorpe, L., & Morris, A. (1988). Feminism and criminology in Britain. *British Journal of Criminology, 28*(2), 93–110.

Gilroy, P. (1982). The myth of black criminality. In R. Miliband & J. Saville (Eds.), *Socialist register 1982.* London: Merlin Press.

Gilroy, P., & Sim, J. (1987). Law, order and the state of the left. In P. Scraton (Ed.), *Law, order and the authoritarian state* (pp. 1–70). Philadelphia: Open University Press.

Gross, B. (1982). Some anticrime proposals for progressives. *Crime and Social Justice, 17,* 51–54.

Hogg, R., & Brown, D. (1988). Law and order politics, left realism and criminology: An overview. Paper presented at the annual meeting of the American Society of Criminology, Chicago.

Hood, R. (1987). Some reflections on the role of criminology in public policy. *Criminal Law Review,* 527–538.

Hulsman, L. (1986). Critical criminology and the concept of crime. *Contemporary Crises, 10,* 63–80.

Jones, T., MacLean, J., & Young, J. (1986). *The Islington crime survey.* Aldershot, England: Gower.

Kelly, L., & Radford, J. (1987). The problem of men: Feminist perspectives on sexual violence. In P. Scraton (Ed.), *Law, order and the authoritarian state* (pp. 237–253). Philadelphia: Open University Press.

Kinsey, R., Lea, J., & Young, J. (1986). *Losing the fight against crime.* London: Basil Blackwell.

Lea, J., & Young, J. (1984). *What is to be done about law and order?* New York: Penguin.

Matthews, R. (1987). Taking realist criminology seriously. *Contemporary Crises, 11,* 371–401.

Matthews, R., & Young, J. (Eds.). (1986). *Confronting crime.* London: Sage.

Messerschmidt, J. (1986). *Capitalism, patriarchy, and crime: Toward a socialist feminist criminology.* Totowa, N.J.: Rowman & Littlefield.

Michalowski, R. (1983). Crime control in the 1980s: A progressive agenda. *Crime and Social Justice, 19,* 13–23.

Pearson, G. (1976). Paki-bashing in a north-east Lancashire cotton town. In G. Mungham & G. Pearson (Eds.), *Working class youth culture* (pp. 138–158). London: Routledge & Kegan Paul.

Phipps, A. (1986). Radical criminology and criminal victimization. In R. Matthews & J. Young (Eds.), *Confronting crime* (pp. 97–117). London: Sage.

Platt, T. (1984). Criminology in the 1980s: Progressive alternatives to law and order. *Crime and Social Justice, 21/22,* 191–199.

Rhen, G. (1985). Swedish active labour market policy: Retrospect and prospect. *Industrial Relations, 24* (Winter).

Russell, D. (1990). *Rape in marriage* (rev. ed.). Bloomington: Indiana University Press.

Russell, D. (1984). *Sexual exploitation: Rape, child sexual abuse, and workplace harassment.* Beverly Hills, Calif.: Sage.

Santos, B. (1980). Law and the community: The changing nature of state power in late capitalism. *International Journal of Sociology of Law, 8,* 379–397.

Schechter, S. (1982). *Women and male violence.* Boston: South End.

Schwartz, M., & Ellison, C. (1982). Criminal sanctions for corporate misbehavior: A call for capitalist punishment. *Humanity and Society, 6*(3), 267–293.

Schwartz, M., & DeKeseredy, W. (1991). Left realist criminology: Strengths, weaknesses and the feminist critique. *Law, Crime and Social Change: An International Journal, 15*(1), 51–72.

Schwartz, M. (1989). The undercutting edge of criminology. *Critical Criminologist, 1,* 1, 2, 5.

Selva, L., & Bohm, R. (1987). A critical examination of the informalism experiment in the administration of justice. *Crime and Social Justice, 29,* 43–57.

Sim, J., Scraton, P., & Gordon, P. (1987). Introduction: Crime, the state and critical analysis. In P. Scraton (Ed.), *Law, order and the authoritarian state* (pp. 1–70). Philadelphia: Open University Press.

Steinert, H. (1985). The amazing new left and order campaign: Some thoughts on antiutopianism and possible futures. *Contemporary Crises, 9,* 327–334.

Taylor, I. (1981). *Law and order: Arguments for socialism.* London: Macmillan.

Taylor, I. (1988). Left realism, the free market economy and the problem of social order. Paper presented at the annual meeting of the American Society of Criminology, Chicago.

Wilson, J. Q. (1985). *Thinking about crime* (rev. ed.). New York: Vintage.

Young, J. (1986). The failure of criminology. In R. Matthews & J. Young (Eds.), *Confronting crime* (pp. 4–30). London: Sage.

Young, J. (1988). Radical criminology in Britain: The emergence of a competing paradigm. *British Journal of Criminology, 28,* 289–313.

21

Feminist Theory, Crime, and Justice

SALLY S. SIMPSON

Feminist research has expanded beyond its origins in women's studies to influence the more traditionally bounded academic disciplines. Criminology has not been immune to these excursions. This chapter presents an overview of feminist theory and methods and their applications within select areas of crime and justice studies. Points of intratheoretical divergence as well as directions for future feminist contributions are noted.

"Why Can't a Woman Be More like a Man?"

One is tempted to respond to Henry Higgins's familiar lament with a cynical observation: Criminological theory assumes a woman *is* like a man. As many feminist criminologists have noted (early critics include Heidensohn, 1968; Klein, 1973; and Smart, 1976), most middle-range and macro theories of crime generously assume that what is true for the gander is true for the goose (see also Harris, 1977). As tempting as this simple assertion might be, however, a closer inspection reveals a more complicated picture.

Some feminist critics (Daly and Chesney-Lind, 1988) have suggested that criminology, like other social sciences, is androcentric, that is, study of crime and the justice process is shaped by male experiences and understandings of the social world. Such studies form the core of "general" theories of crime and deviance without taking female experience, as crime participant or victim, into account:

My thanks to Kathleen Daly, Nicole Hahn Rafter, and N. Craig Smith for their insightful comments on a draft of this chapter. I was assisted in my revisions by the criticisms of three anonymous reviewers. All of the above are to be commended for their assistance, but none is responsible for the ideas and arguments contained herein.

[Men] create the world from their own point of view, which then becomes the truth to be described . . . Power to create the world from one's point of view is power in its male form (MacKinnon, 1982:23).

Not all criminological research has ignored women, but all too often, pre-1970s research on female offenders and victims of crime fell prey to unreflecting sexism and, in its more extreme form, misogyny. Females who deviated from expected roles were viewed as morally corrupt, hysterical, diseased, manipulative, and devious (Glueck and Glueck, 1934). Law-violating and -conforming behaviors were believed to stem from the same etiological source—the female nature (Edwards, 1985; Klein, 1973).[1] A woman, it seemed—whether good or bad—could never be like a man.

These observations are not new, but they reflect a different voice, a feminist voice, that has been added to the criminological discourse. The purpose of this review essay is to introduce feminist criminology and its intellectual parent, feminism, to the uninitiated reader. It would be presumptuous to suggest that all relevant studies and arguments about gender and crime are included here. Such an extensive review is more appropriate for a book, and depending on the topic, it has likely already been done and done well (e.g., Eaton, 1986; Freedman, 1981; Heidensohn, 1985; Mann, 1984; Naffine, 1988; Smart, 1976). Instead, illustrative examples of different types of feminist thinking are presented to show how feminism has reframed our points of reference, underlying assumptions, and understandings about crime, victimization, and the justice process.

To achieve these aims, the chapter is organized into three sections. First, the perspectives and methods that constitute feminist analysis are sorted and differentiated. Second, three areas of criminological study (the female offender, female victim, and criminal justice processing) are discussed because they are key areas in which feminist approaches have been incorporated. Third, directions for further integration are suggested.

Feminism: Perspectives and Methods

Feminism is best understood as both a world view and a social movement that encompasses assumptions and beliefs about the origins and consequences of gendered social organization as well as strategic directions and actions for social change. As such, feminism is both analytical and empirical. In its incipient form, feminist research almost exclusively focused on women—as a way of placing women at the center of inquiry and building a base of knowledge. As it has matured, feminism has become more encompassing, taking into account the gendered understanding of all aspects of human culture and relationships (Stacey and Thorne, 1985:305).

It would be a mistake, however, to think of feminism as a single theory. Feminism has expanded into a diverse set of perspectives and agendas, each based on different definitions of the "problem," competing conceptions of the origins and mechanisms of gender inequality and oppression, and divergent strategies for its eradication. Collectively, these perspectives share a concern with identifying and representing women's interests, interests judged to be insufficiently represented and accommodated within the mainstream (Oakley, 1981:335).

Liberal Feminism

Liberal feminism was conceived within a liberal bourgeois tradition that called for women's equality of opportunity and freedom of choice (Eisenstein, 1981). For the most part, liberal feminists see gender inequality[2] emerging from the creation of separate and distinct spheres of influence and traditional attitudes about the appropriate role of men and women in society (Pateman, 1987). Such attitudes are reinforced by discrimination against women in education, the workplace, politics, and other public arenas.

Liberals do not believe the system to be inherently unequal; discrimination is not systemic. Rather, men and women can work together to "androgynize" gender roles (i.e., blend male and female traits and characteristics; Bem, 1974) and eliminate outdated policies and practices that discriminate against women. Affirmative action, the equal rights amendment, and other equal opportunity laws and policies are advocated as redistributive measures until a meritocratic gender restructuring of society occurs.

Socialist Feminism

For socialists, gender oppression is an obvious feature of capitalist societies. Depending on whether one is a socialist woman (Marxist feminist) or a socialist feminist, however, the weight that one gives to capitalism as a necessary and/or sufficient cause of that oppression will vary (Eisenstein, 1979). If one is the former, gender (and race) oppression is seen as secondary to and reflective of class oppression.

Socialist feminists attempt a synthesis between two systems of domination, class and patriarchy (male supremacy). Both relations of production and reproduction are structured by capitalist patriarchy (Beauvoir, 1960; Hartmann, 1979; Mitchell, 1971). Gender difference, as a defining characteristic of power and privilege in a capitalist society can be attacked only by constructing a completely different society, one that is free of gender and class stratification (Oakley, 1981).

Radical Feminism

The origins of patriarchy, and the subordination of women therein, are seen by radical feminists to rest in male aggression and control of women's sexuality. Men are inherently more aggressive than women, who, because of their relative size disadvantages and dependency on men during childbearing years, are easy to dominate and control. The arguments of radical feminists (e.g., Atkinson, 1974; Barry, 1979; Firestone, 1970; Rich, 1980) bring sexuality to the analytical fore. The "personal" is "political" (Millett, 1971). Sex, not gender, is the crucial analytical category; male domination, not class, is the fundamental origin of female subordination. Radical feminists' political and social agendas encompass lesbian separatism (Atkinson, 1984) and technological control of reproduction (Firestone, 1970).

Women of Color

In her eloquent "Ain't I a Woman" speech, Sojourner Truth (1851) informed white suffragists of their myopia about race by highlighting how as a black woman her experience was different from theirs. Joseph and Lewis (1981) reminded us that Truth's commentary is no less relevant today. Many women of color see the women's liberation movement as hopelessly white and middle class, immune to their concerns. As Hooks (1987:62) observed,

> Most people in the United States think of feminism . . . as a movement that aims to make women the social equals of men. . . . Since men are not equals in white supremacist, capitalist, patriarchal class structure, which men do women want to be equal to?

The alternative frameworks developed by women of color heighten feminism's sensitivity to the complex interplay of gender, class, and race oppression. Patriarchy permeates the lives of minority women, but it does not take the same form that it does for whites (Brittan and Maynard, 1984). Though these contributions may not have coalesced yet into a coherent theoretical framework (at least according to Jagger and Rothenberg, 1984), radical (Lorde, 1988), socialist (Mullins, 1986), and Marxist (Davis, 1981) women of color have provided possible points of integration with theories of race oppression (e.g., Joseph, 1981a, 1981b; Wellman, 1977).

In sum, feminist theory is not one perspective; it is a cacophony of comment and criticism "concerned with demystifying masculine knowledge as objective knowledge" (Brittan and Maynard, 1984:210) and offering insights from a woman's perspective.

Feminist Methods

> The male epistemological stance, which corresponds to the world it creates, is objectivity; the ostensibly uninvolved stance, the view from a distance and from no particular perspective, apparently transparent to its reality. It does not comprehend its own perspectivity, does not recognize what it sees as subject like itself, or that the way it apprehends its world is a form of its subjection and presupposes it (MacKinnon, 1982:23–24).

Concern over the nonobjective consequences of so-called objective normal science (Kuhn, 1970) has led some feminists to challenge the scientific enterprise. Keller (1982) has arranged these challenges on a political spectrum from slightly left of center (liberal feminists) to the more radical left. The liberal critique takes an equal employment opportunity approach by observing the relative absence of women from the scientific community. This view "in no way conflicts either with traditional conceptions of science or with current liberal, egalitarian politics" (p. 114).

From this point, however, the criticisms become increasingly fundamental to the way knowledge is produced; they range from charges of bias in selecting research topics and interpreting results to rejecting rationality and objectivity as purely male products. More radical feminists have adopted a methodological strategy that is in direct opposition to the scientific method. In order to "see" women's existence (which has been invisible to objective scientific methods) "feminist women must deliberately and courageously integrate . . . their own experiences of oppression and discrimination . . . into the research process" (Miles, 1983:121). *Feminist methods* are necessarily subjectivist, transdisciplinary, nonhierarchical, and empowering.

Where one falls along Keller's feminist-political spectrum will determine one's choice of methods (i.e., quantitative versus qualitative) and whether one sees methods and theory as interrelated as opposed to separate and distinct. Thus, methods used by feminists are more diverse than typically credited (for examples, see Jayarate, 1983; Reinhartz, 1983; Stacey and Thorne, 1985).

Together, the above theoretical and methodological points form a feminist perspective. All have been incorporated into criminology, but some have had a greater impact than others. The goal in the next section is to identify the ways in which these approaches and methods have changed the way criminologists address the problems of crime and justice.

Incorporating the Frameworks

The Female Offender

The stirrings of feminist criminology are nearly two decades old. Heidensohn (1968:171), in a "prefeminist" paper, bemoaned the state of knowledge about female deviance and called for a "crash programme of research which telescopes decades of comparable studies of males." Later, Klein (1973) and Smart (1976) were to bring explicitly feminist perspectives to their critiques of extant theoretical and empirical work on the female offender. Klein, a Marxist feminist, noted the absence of economic and other social explanations for female crime. Smart, working within more of a radical feminist perspective, stressed the linkages among sexist theory, patriarchy, and sexism in practice—specifically identifying the relationship between stereotypical assumptions about the causes of female crime and how female offenders are controlled and treated.

Both Klein and Smart set an agenda for a new feminist criminology, but their more radical approaches were derailed by the publication of Simon's *Women and Crime* and F. Adler's *Sisters in Crime* (1975). Claiming that a "new" female offender was emerging (white collar and/or male like), Simon and Adler generated tremendous interest in female crime (a clear aim of incipient feminism). But tying the female offender's emergence to women's liberation brought about a "moral panic" (Smart, 1976), which was viewed by some as a backlash to the women's movement.[3] In Chesney-Lind's (1980:29) words, it represented "another in a century long series of symbolic attempts to keep women subordinate to men by threatening those who aspire for equality with the images of the witch, the bitch, and the whore."[4]

As with many social problems of our day, female crime became interesting only when it transcended the expected boundaries of class, race, and gender. As a "quasi-theory," the liberation-crime relationship had great appeal for nonfeminist criminologists.[5] But tests of the thesis were less than supportive. In fact most discredited it (Austin, 1982; Giordano et al., 1981), and others found evidence of a link between female crime and economic marginalization (Datesman and Scarpitti, 1980; Gora, 1982; Mukherjee and Fitzgerald, 1981; Steffensmeier, 1978, 1981; Steffensmeier and Cobb, 1981). The new female offender identified by Simon and Adler was more myth than reality (Steffensmeier, 1978). These conclusions did not differ substantially from Klein's (1973), yet they came years after her original critique—a fact that dramatically illustrates the marginality of feminist criminology at the time. Yet subsequent research on the causes of female crime has clearly buttressed the economic/class perspectives of Marxist/socialist feminists as well as the "opportunity" perspectives of the liberal feminists (Ageton, 1983; Box, 1983; Box and Hale, 1984; Elliott and Ageton, 1980; Giordano et al., 1981).

In retrospect, feminist criminology both gained and lost from the narrow focus on liberation and crime. On the plus side, it gained a better insight into the historical (Mukherjee and Fitzgerald, 1981) and cross-cultural (F. Adler, 1981; Plenska, 1980) patterns of female crime. But because the liberation thesis was so limited, it diverted attention from the material and structural forces that shape women's lives and experiences. It is in these areas that women of color and socialist and radical feminist criminologists are more apt to focus etiological attention (Hagan et al., 1985, 1987; Lewis, 1981; Miller, 1985; Rafter and Natalizia, 1981; Wilson, 1985).

Women Victims: The Radical Feminist Critique

Liberal feminism has dominated studies of the female offender, but the same is not true of victimology (Daly and Chesney-Lind, 1988). Shifting away from analyses that blame the victim for her victimization (Amir, 1967),[6] radical feminists have constructed alternative interpretations of offender-victim relationships and victim experiences of criminal justice (Chapman and Gates, 1978; Klein, 1981; Wood, 1981).

Brownmiller's (1975) historical and cross-cultural study of rape brought a radical feminist perspective to the center of public consciousness. Building on the argument that rape is not a crime of sex but rather an act of power and dominance (Greer, 1970), Brownmiller concluded that rape is a tool in the arsenal of all men to control all women.

Radical feminists have reframed the ways in which rape is commonly understood in our society. Rather than a crime of sex, it is more apt to be viewed as one of male power, control, and domination. Brownmiller's work, coupled with that of other radical feminists (e.g., Griffin, 1979; Riger and Gordon, 1981), opened a floodgate of inquiry into rape and other types of victimizations that are "uniquely feminine" (Wilson, 1985:4), such as pornography (Dworkin, 1981), battering (Dobash and Dobash, 1979; Martin, 1976; Straus et al., 1980), incest (Finkelhor, 1979; Moyer, 1985; Stanko, 1985), and sexual harassment (MacKinnon, 1979; Stanko, 1985).

Guiding much of this research is the radical feminist critique of official conceptions and definitions of violence, which are viewed as male-centered and incapable of incorporating the full range of female experiences of violence (i.e., from intimidation and coercion to physical violence and death). A woman-centered definition of violence is one that portrays violence as a form of social domination rather than a random and/or noninstrumental form of expression (Hanmer, 1981:32).

Radical feminists have dominated but not monopolized feminist perspectives in this area. Socialist feminists, liberals, and women of color have also participated in the dialogue. Gordon's (1988) research of family violence was implicitly critical of some radical feminists' overly deterministic conception of patriarchy. Such an image, she argued, denies agency to women and cannot incorporate "the chronic conflict, unpredictability, and ambivalent emotions that have characterized relations between the sexes" (pp. xi–xii).

In another historical study, Tomes (1978) linked variations in spousal abuse to changes in the economic position of the working class generally and the male's position within the family specifically. As the working class improved its economic position and males cemented greater power within their families, the official incidence of working-class battering decreased.

Based on her findings, Tomes argued that feminists may need to reconceptualize the relationship among male power, female economic dependency, and battering. Dependency is not necessarily tied to greater abuse; in fact, the opposite may be true. A wife's economic independence may exert a greater challenge to male authority within the family, thus creating a climate in which husbands resort to battering as a means to reestablish their control.

Studies that find great variety in the cross-cultural prevalence and incidence of rape and battering (e.g., Pagelow, 1981; Sanday, 1981) have forced feminists to examine patriarchal relations across different societal and situational arrangements (e.g., Wilson, 1985). If female victimization is a function of changing the needs of a capitalist and patriarchal system, then male domination and its relationship to female victimization need not be viewed as inevitable or immutable.

Around the themes of rape and control of sexuality, patriarchy and racism marry and divorce in intricate ways (Davis, 1981). In the United States, white racism and fear gave rise to mythological constructions of black sexuality. Black males are perceived as sexual threats and have been hunted and hanged for their "rape potential." For black victims of rape, the justice process is not simply gendered—it is racially gendered. Data indicate that black-on-black rapes are not taken as seriously by authorities as those that involve white victims (Kleck, 1981; LaFree, 1980). Such findings have led one prominent black scholar (Joseph, 1981b:27) to comment, "It must be considered an impossibility for white men to rape Black women in the eyes of justice and in the minds of many. Black women apparently are considered as something other than 'women.' "

Gender and Justice Processing

A final area to be discussed in this literature review is gendered justice. Comedian Richard Pryor once called attention to discrimination in the U.S. criminal justice system by defining justice as "just us." His concern with differential sentencing practices is one shared by feminists who primarily study the conditions under which criminal justice is gendered and with what consequences. Although liberal approaches typically dominate the gender-and-justice research, other feminist perspectives are gaining ground—especially in research on courts and corrections.

There are many stages in the criminal justice system at which gender may have an impact on decision making. The findings of some of the better-known studies of several strategic points in the decision-making process are summarized below.

POLICE

Arguments about whether and how justice is gendered must begin with police behavior. That police decisions to arrest can be influenced by extralegal factors such as the demeanor of the offender (Black, 1980) has been established. It is less clear how gender, either alone or in conjunction with other characteristics, may consciously or inadvertently influence police behavior.

In the liberal "equal treatment" tradition, Moyer and White (1981) tested police bias in response decisions under "probable" responses to hypothetical situations. Neither gender nor race had an effect on police behavior once crime type, especially as it interacts with the demeanor of the offender, was controlled. On the other hand, Freyerhern's (1981) comparison of juvenile male and female probabilities of transition from self-report incident to police contact and arrest found males to be more likely to incur police contact and arrest than females. Both of these studies are methodologically problematic, however. Moyer and White could not generalize their findings to real police encounters, and Freyerhern (1981:90) does not calculate transition probabilities across individual offense categories, nor does he include status offenses. Avoiding some of these methodological traps but still working within a liberal tradition, Visher (1983) found the interaction between race and gender to be a key factor influencing arrest decision. Visher found police chivalry only toward white females once "legal" factors were controlled. She hypothesized that black females are treated more harshly than their white counterparts because they are less apt to display expected (i.e., traditional) gender behaviors and characteristics when they encounter a mostly white and male police force.

Race and gender are also found to interact through victim characteristics (Smith et al., 1984). An analysis of 272 police-citizen encounters, in which both a suspected offender and victim were present, revealed that white female victims received more preferential treatment from police than black female victims. Thus, although chivalry may be alive and well for white women, it appears to be dead (if it ever existed) for blacks.

COURTS

Police contact is not the only point in justice processing at which discrimination can occur. Women have been found to receive more lenient treatment in the early stages of court processing (i.e., bail, release on own recognizance, and/or cash alternatives to bail; I. Nagel, 1983) and further into the process, e.g., conviction and sentencing (Bernstein et al., 1977; S. Nagel and Weitzman, 1972; Simon, 1975). Other studies found no gender bias when controlling for crime seriousness and prior record (Farrington and Morris, 1983) or little effect from extralegal factors when legal factors and bench bias were controlled (I. Nagel, 1983). Variation in sentencing may be related to so-called countertype offenses, that is, women are treated more harshly when processed for nontraditional female crimes, like assault (Bernstein et al., 1977; S. Nagel and Weitzman, 1972), or when they violate female sexual norms (Chesney-Lind, 1973; Schlossman and Wallach, 1978). Given variable-specification problems, however, some of these findings are potentially spurious.

Once again, race may confound these effects. Spohn et al. (1982) addressed the issue of paternalism in sentencing, especially for black women. Controlling for prior record and attorney type, they found that black women are incarcerated significantly less often than black men, but about as often as white men. They concluded that the apparently lenient treatment of black women is not due to paternalism in their favor but rather to the racial discrimination against black vis-à-vis white men.

Studies of court processing are not entirely dominated by liberal perspectives. More critical perspectives emphasize social power and patriarchal control as the primary mechanisms through which justice is gendered (Kruttschnitt, 1982, 1984). Eaton (1986:35) argued that magistrate courts in Great Britain (the lower courts) reinforce the dominant imagery of justice (i.e., courts are ostensibly fair and just) while they maintain the status quo: "It is in these courts that the formal rules of society—the laws—are endorsed; it is here, too, that the informal, unwritten rules regulating social relations [e.g., gender, class, and race] are re-enacted."

When are females apt to be subjected to formal mechanisms of control? When other, more informal, constraints are lacking or disrupted. Kruttschnitt (1982, 1984) suggested that sentencing outcomes are affected by a woman's social status and/or her respectability. Differential sentencing among women is tied to the degree to which women are subjected to formal versus informal social control in their everyday lives.

Daly (1987a, 1989b) and Eaton (1986, 1987) offered convincing evidence that the most important factor determining sentence outcome, once prior record and offense seriousness are controlled, is marital and/or familial status.[7] Marital status has been found to matter for women (married receive more lenient sentences) but not for men (Farrington and Morris, 1983; I. Nagel, 1981) or to be as important for both (Daly, 1987a, 1987b).

Pretrial release and sentencing are seen to be both "familied" and "gendered." They are familied in that court decisions regarding the removal of men and women from families "elicit different concerns from the court" (Daly, 1987a:154). They are gendered in that women's care of others and male economic support for families represent "different types of dependencies in family life" (p. 154). Men and women without family responsibilities are treated similarly, but more harshly than familied men and women. Women with families, however, are treated with the greatest degree of leniency due to "the differing social costs arising from separating them from their families" (Daly, 1987b:287). The economic role played by familied men can, more easily, be covered by state entitlement programs, but it is putatively more difficult to replace the functional role of familied women. Judges rationalize such sentencing disparities as necessary for keeping families together (Daly, 1989b).

As these latter studies suggest, much of the observed gender bias in processing may not be a case of overt discrimination for or against women relative to men. Instead, judicial decisions may be influenced by broader societal concerns about protecting nuclear families (Daly, 1989b) and the differing roles and responsibilities contained therein (Eaton, 1986). It is not clear that such forms of justice are overtly paternalistic, nor are they necessarily racist.

Rather, in a society that stratifies other rights and privileges by gender, race, and class, "equality" in sentencing may not be just (Daly, 1989a).

Eaton (1986:10–11) took a somewhat different view of familied justice. In her opinion, the courts reflect the needs and interests of patriarchy and capitalism, in which attendant inequities are reproduced. "Family-based" justice is a visible manifestation of the patriarchal and capitalist need to maintain and protect the nuclear family—within which gender and productive/reproductive relations first emerge.

CORRECTIONS

As it became clear that, compared with males, female prisoners were treated differently (in some cases more leniently and in others more harshly), liberal feminist perspectives came to dominate research questions and policy considerations (see Haft, 1980; Heide, 1974; Simon, 1975).

The linkages between female incarceration and male control of female sexuality have been developed by radical feminists (Chesney-Lind, 1973; Smart, 1976). Rasche (1974), for example, described how prostitutes with venereal disease were prosecuted and institutionalized, with the "cure" as a condition of release. Nondiseased prostitutes were less likely to go to jail or prison. Certain prison practices, such as checking for evidence of a hymen during forced physical examinations and vaginal contraband searches, have been used as techniques to control the sexuality of youthful offenders and to humiliate and degrade female inmates (Burkhart, 1973; Chesney-Lind, 1986).

Socialist feminists emphasize how prison tenure and treatment vary by class and race (Freedman, 1981; French, 1977, 1978; Lewis, 1981; Rafter, 1985). In her historical accounting of the development of women's prisons, Rafter (1985:155) observed how race determined whether and where a woman was sent to prison.

> Comparison of incarceration rates and in-prison treatment of black women and white women demonstrates that partiality was extended mainly to whites. Chivalry filtered them out of the prison system, helping to create the even greater racial imbalances among female than male prisoner populations. And partiality toward whites contributed to the development of a bifurcated system, one track custodial and predominantly black, the other reformatory and reserved mainly for whites.

The bifurcated system of women's corrections emerges in part from two competing images of female nature. In one view, women are seen as fragile and immature creatures, more childlike than adult. Consequently, the female offender is perceived as a "fallen woman," in need of guidance but not a true danger to society (Rasche, 1974). The reformatory is perfectly suited to such an offender. Primarily staffed by reform-minded, middle-class women, reformatory training programs emphasized skills that would turn the white, working-class misdemeanants into proper (and class-appropriate) women, that is, good servants or wives (Rafter, 1985:82).

In custodial prisons, however, a different archetype dominated. Women's "dark side," their inherent evil and immorality (Smart, 1976) shaped prison philosophy. Here, the predominantly black felons (who were perceived as more masculine, more self-centered, volatile, and dangerous) were treated like men—only, given the conditions of their incarceration (i.e., fewness of numbers and at the mercy of violent male offenders), their equality was tantamount to brutal treatment and often death (Rafter, 1985:181).

The degree to which prisons function as something other than just places of punishment and/or treatment is a popular theme in neo-Marxist literature. Extending this interpretation to women, Marxist feminists (e.g., Wilson, 1985; Hartz-Karp, 1981) argued that prisons, like other institutions of social control (e.g., mental health facilities), retool deviant women for gender-appropriate roles in capitalist patriarchal societies:

> If deviant women are more frequently assigned to the mental health system for social control than to the criminal justice system, it is perhaps because of the superior ability of the mental health system to "re-tool" worn-out or rebellious domestic workers (Wilson, 1985:18).

Societal control of female deviance serves the needs of capital. When those needs change, so too will the mechanisms and directions of social control.[8]

In this vein, Carlen (1983) demonstrates how "down, out and disordered" women in Scotland are disciplined through medical and judicial apparatuses. Most of the imprisoned are poor women; many have histories of alcohol and drug abuse, and a large number come from violent homes. These life experiences combine, setting into motion a cycle of deviance, imprisonment, and patriarchal and class discipline that is tenacious and defeating:

> Being seen as neither wholly mad nor wholly bad, [women] are treated to a disciplinary regime where they are actually infantilised at the same time as attempts are made to make them feel guilty about their double, triple, quadruple, or even quintuple refusal of family, work, gender, health, and reason (Carlen, 1983:209).

Where to Go from Here?

In 1976, Carol Smart suggested a number of topics for feminist research.[9] A decade later, feminist criminology has amassed a considerable body of knowledge in most of these areas—so much so, in fact, that feminists now are more self-critical—especially in the areas of policy and legislative changes (see Daly and Chesney-Lind, 1988). This is a positive step. It suggests that a feminist voice is not only being heard but that it is loud enough to produce disagreement and intellectual exchange. Nonetheless, certain areas in criminology have either been underexposed or are resistant to feminist concerns. Thus, some new directions for feminist criminology are discussed below.[10]

Race and Crime

Poorly conceived offender self-report surveys provided criminologists with the empirical justification to ignore the race-crime relationship, and the prevailing political climate reinforced our myopia. There is enormous risk in ignoring that relationship, however. First, based on more sophisticated crime measures (e.g., National Youth Survey, National Crime Survey, cohort studies), it is clear that the race-crime relationship is an essential one. Second, and not unlike the gender-crime relationship, such reticence leaves the interpretive door open to less critical perspectives.

Feminist criminologists have great potential in this area, but the data are sparse and problematic and the analytic contributions few. Too often we rely on quantitative studies that dichotomize race into white and black, or the nonwhite category is broadened to include groups other than blacks (see, e.g., Tracey et al., in press). In the former instance, other ethnic/racial groups are ignored; in the latter, such inclusive categorizations assume etiological and historical/cultural invariance between groups.

Clearly, one of the first places for feminists to start is to target women of color for greater research. Available data indicate that there are significant differences between black and white female crime rates (Ageton, 1983; Chilton and Datesman, 1987; Hindelang, 1981; Laub and McDermott, 1985; Mann, 1987; Young, 1980). Simpson (1988), Miller (1985), and Lewis (1981) have argued that the unique structural and cultural positioning of black women produces complex cultural typescripts that exert push-pull pressures for crime, pressures that may not exist for white women.

Miller's (1985:177–178) ethnography of lower-class deviant networks described how certain types of male and female criminality (e.g., hustling, pimping, and other instrumental crimes) are interdependent in minority communities. Female crime also appears to have a group-directed and -enacted dimension (see Young, 1980). The collective nature of such minority offending may stem from the fact that it emerges, in part, from the integrated and extended domestic networks of underclass blacks (Miller, 1985) and from joint participation in gang activities (Campbell, 1984).

These observations do not imply, however, that patriarchy is absent from these communities. Male dominance and control are reproduced within interpersonal relationships (not necessarily familial) and embodied in informal organizations, like gangs (Campbell, 1984) and state social service agencies. Some female offending can be interpreted as challenging patriarchal control and asserting independence (Campbell, 1984:135); much can be attributed to both economic necessity and the pull and excitement of street life (Campbell, 1984; Miller, 1985). Female participation in violent crime may stem from abusive relationships between men and women (Browne, 1987; Mann, 1987) and/or the frustration, alienation, and anger that are associated with racial and class oppression (Simpson, 1988).

Research by Hill and Suval (1988) suggested that the causes of crime may differ for black and white women, which raises questions about whether current theories of female crime, including feminist perspectives, are white-female-centered. Given the paucity of data on how gender structures relationships within minority communities and families, it is impossible to say. More quantitative research is needed on minority groups other than blacks (e.g., Chicanos and other Hispanics, Asians, Native Americans) to establish a better knowledge base, but qualitative studies that probe culture and subjective differences between women of color and whites are also essential (Mullins, 1986). Feminist criminologists are guilty of the "add race and stir" shortsightedness that pervades feminist thinking. We would do well to heed Spelman's (1988:166) reminder of how to understand and approach differences among women:

> If we assume there are differences among women, but at the same time they are all the same as women, and if we assume the woman part is what we know from looking at the case of white middle-class women, then we appear to be talking only about white middle-class women. This is how white middle-class privilege is maintained even as we purport to recognize the importance of women's differences.

Notes

1. This is not to suggest that biological reductionism is absent in studies/theories of male criminality. Such explanations of male crime abound (e.g., Wilson and Herrnstein, 1985). However, with the demise of phrenology, social factors replaced biology as key etiological forces. These explanations have not been seriously challenged. Conversely, until the feminist critique of the 1970s, biogenic/psychogenic models of female crime went, for the most part, unchallenged.
2. Phillips (1987) argues that the choice of terms describing gender relations imply particular views of what the problem is. So, inequality (a term favored by liberals and some women of color) suggests that women deserve what men and/or whites are granted. Oppression (socialists and women of color) implies a complex combination of forces (ideological, political, and economic) that keep woman in her place. Subordination is a term favored by radical feminists and some women of color who identify the holder of power as the culprit (men and whites respectively).
3. The links between women's liberation and changing patterns of female criminality were made before. Bishop (1931) complained that women's liberation during the 1920s had three negative results: (1) More women were turning criminal; (2) a

"better" class of women were becoming criminal more often; and (3) women were becoming sexually criminal at a younger age (cited in Rasche, 1974).

4. To be fair, both Simon and Adler had more to offer than mere speculation about the "dark side" of women's liberation. Simon's research documents the basic inequities between male and female correctional facilities and treatments. By attributing these differences to male chivalry toward women, she takes a liberal feminist approach to the problem of gender and justice, an approach that heavily influenced later works in this area. Adler's work, while more impressionistic than Simon's, attempted to explain differences in crime rates between white and black females. Although her interpretations gave rise to more systematic examinations of intragender race differences in crime that are highly critical of her interpretations and methods, the issues she raised are of primary importance to most feminist criminologists today.

5. A research focus on gender alone does not qualify one as a feminist, just as a focus on class does not make one a Marxist. Rather, as part of their endeavor, feminist criminologists must seriously consider the nature of gender relations and the peculiar brand of oppression that patriarchal relations bring (Leonard, 1982).

6. Precipitous behavior has ranged from dressing provocatively, saying no to sex while "meaning" yes, "nagging" a spouse, Lolita-like seductiveness on the part of the victim, and so on.

7. These effects appear to be strongest for black defendants (Daly, 1989a).

8. Cloward and Piven (1979) and Box (1983) asserted that female deviance is handled by the medical community, in part, because women are more likely to direct their deviance inward (i.e., they privatize it into self-destructive behaviors, like depression and suicide). Such behavior is conceptualized as sickness (like "hysteria" earlier) and is thus subject to the formal control of the psychiatric community.

9. The relevant topics are the female offender and the attitudes of criminal justice personnel toward her; criminal justice processing; gender and corrections; and the structure and purpose of law.

10. To suggest that feminists need to identify areas "appropriate" for feminist critique implies that knowledge, as currently constructed, is selectively androcentric. I would argue that criminology as a whole, like other academic disciplines, needs a feminist "overhaul."

References

Adler, F. (1981). *The incidence of female criminality in the contemporary world*. New York: New York University Press.

Adler, P. (1985). *Wheeling and dealing: An ethnography of an upper-level drug dealing and smuggling community*. New York: Columbia University Press.

Ageton, S. S. (1983). The dynamics of female delinquency, 1976–1980. *Criminology, 21*, 555–584.

Amir, M. (1967). Victim precipitated forcible rape. *Journal of Criminal Law, Criminology, and Police Science, 58*, 493–502.

Atkinson, T. G. (1974). Radical feminism and love. In *Amazon odyssey*. New York: Links Books.

Austin, R. L. (1982). Women's liberation and increases in minor, major, and occupational offenses. *Criminology, 20,* 407–430.

Barry, K. (1979). *Female sexual slavery.* New York: Avon Books.

Beauvoir, S. de (1960). *The second sex.* London: Four Square Books.

Bem, S. (1974). The measurement of psychological androgyny. *Journal of Consulting and Clinical Psychology, 42,* 155–162.

Bernstein, I. N., Kick, E., Leung, J., & Schulz, B. (1977). Charge reduction: An intermediary stage in the process of labelling criminal defendants. *Social Forces, 56,* 362–384.

Bishop, C. (1931). *Women and crime.* London: Chatto & Windus Press.

Black, D. (1980). *On the manners and customs of the police.* New York: Academic Press.

Block, A. (1977). Aw! Your mother's in the mafia: Women criminals in progressive New York. *Contemporary Crises, 1,* 5–22.

Box, S. (1983). *Power, crime, and mystification.* London: Tavistock.

Box, S., & Hale, C. (1984). Liberation/emancipation, economic marginalization, or less chivalry: The relevance of three theoretical arguments to female crime patterns in England and Wales, 1951–1980. *Criminology, 22,* 473–497.

Brittan, A., & Maynard, M. (1984). *Sexism, racism and oppression.* Oxford: Basil Blackwell.

Brownmiller, S. (1975). *Against our will: Men, women, and rape.* New York: Simon & Schuster.

Burkhart, K. W. (1973). *Women in prison.* Garden City, N.Y.: Doubleday.

Bureau of Justice Statistics. (1987). *Special report: White-collar crime.* Washington, D.C.: U.S. Department of Justice.

Campbell, A. (1984). *The girls in the gang: A report from New York City.* Oxford: Basil Blackwell.

Chapman, J. R., & Gates, M. (Eds.). (1978). *The victimization of women.* Beverly Hills, Calif.: Sage.

Chesney-Lind, M. (1973). Judicial enforcement of the female sex role. *Issues in Criminology, 8,* 51–69.

Chesney-Lind, M. (1980). Rediscovering Lilith: Misogyny and the "new" female criminal. In C. T. Griffiths & M. Nance (Eds.), *The female offender.* Criminology Research Centre. Burnaby, B.C.: Simon Fraser University.

Chilton, R., & Datesman, S. K. (1987). Gender, race, and crime: An analysis of urban arrest trends, 1960–1980. *Gender and Society, 1,* 152–171.

Daly, K. (1987a). Discrimination in the criminal courts: Family, gender and the problem of equal treatment. *Social Forces, 66,* 152–175.

Daly, K. (1987b). Structure and practice of familial-based justice in a criminal court. *Law and Society Review, 21,* 267–290.

Daly, K. (1988). Gender and varieties of white-collar crime. Revised version of a paper presented at the annual meeting of the American Society of Criminology, Atlanta.

Daly, K. (1989a). Neither conflict nor labeling nor paternalism will suffice: Intersections of race, ethnicity, gender, and family in criminal court decisions. *Crime and Delinquency, 35,* 136–168.

Daly, K. (1989b). Rethinking judicial paternalism: Gender, work-family relations, and sentencing. *Gender and Society, 3,* 9–36.

Daly, K., & Chesney-Lind, M. (1988). Feminism and criminology. *Justice Quarterly, 5,* 497–538.

Datesman, S. K., & Scarpitti, F. R. (Eds.). (1980). *Women, crime, and justice.* New York: Oxford University Press.

Davis, A. (1981). *Women, race, and class.* New York: Random House.

Dobash, R. E., & Dobash, R. (1979). *Violence against wives: A case against the patriarchy.* New York: Free Press.

Dworkin, A. (1981). *Pornography: Men possessing women.* New York: Perigee Books.

Eaton, M. (1986). *Justice for women? Family, court, and social control.* Philadelphia: Open University Press.

Eaton, M. (1987). The question of bail: Magistrates' responses to applications for bail on behalf of men and women defendants. In P. Carlen & A. Worrall (Eds.), *Gender, crime and justice.* Philadelphia: Open University Press.

Edwards, S. M. (1985). *Women on trial: A study of the female suspect, defendant, and offender in the criminal law and criminal justice system.* Manchester, N.H.: Manchester University Press.

Eisenstein, Z. (1979). *Capitalist patriarchy and the case for socialist feminism.* New York: Monthly Review Press.

Eisenstein, Z. (1981). *The radical future of liberal feminism.* New York: Monthly Review Press.

Elliott, D., & Ageton, S. S. (1980). Reconciling race and class differences in self-reported and official estimates of delinquency. *American Sociological Review, 45,* 95–110.

Farrington, D., & Morris, A. (1983). Sex, sentencing and reconviction. *British Journal of Criminology, 23,* 229–248.

Finkelhor, D. (1979). *Sexually victimized children.* New York: Free Press.

Finley, N. J., & Grasmick, H. G. (1985). Gender roles and social control. *Sociological Spectrum, 5,* 317–330.

Firestone, S. (1970). *The dialectic of sex: The case for feminist revolution.* New York: Bantam.

Freedman, E. (1981). *Their sisters' keepers: Women's prison reform in America, 1830–1930.* Ann Arbor: University of Michigan Press.

French, L. (1977). An assessment of the black female prisoner in the South. *Signs, 3,* 483–488.

French, L. (1978). The incarcerated black female: The case of social double jeopardy. *Journal of Black Studies, 8,* 321–335.

Freyerhern, W. (1981). Gender differences in delinquency quantity and quality. In L. H. Bowker (Ed.), *Women and crime in America.* New York: Macmillan.

Gilligan, C. (1982). *In a different voice: Psychological theory and women's development.* Cambridge, Mass.: Harvard University Press.

Giordano, P., Kerbel, S., & Dudley, S. (1981). The economics of female criminality: An analysis of police blotters 1890–1975. In L. H. Bowker (Ed.), *Women and crime in America.* New York: Macmillan.

Glueck, S., & Glueck, E. (1934). *Five hundred delinquent women.* New York: Knopf.

Gora, J. G. (1982). *The new female criminal: Empirical reality or social myth?* New York: Praeger.

Gordon, L. (1988). *Heroes of their own lives: The politics and history of family violence.* New York: Penguin.

Greer, G. (1970). *The female eunuch*. New York: McGraw-Hill.

Griffin, S. (1979). *Rape: The power of consciousness*. San Francisco: Harper & Row.

Haft, M. G. (1980). Women in prison: Discriminatory practices and some legal solutions. In S. Datesman & F. R. Scarpitti (Eds.), *Women, crime, and justice*. New York: Oxford University Press.

Hagan, J., Gillis, A. R., & Simpson, J. (1985). The class structure of gender and delinquency: Toward a power control theory of common delinquent behavior. *American Journal of Sociology, 90*, 1151–1178.

Hagan, J., Simpson, J., & Gillis, A. R. (1979). The sexual stratification of social control: A gender-based perspective on crime and delinquency. *British Journal of Sociology, 30*, 25–38.

Hagan, J., Simpson, J., & Gillis, A. R. (1987). Class in the household: A power-control theory of gender and delinquency. *American Journal of Sociology, 92*, 788–816.

Hanmer, J. (1981). Violence and the social control of women. *Feminist Issues, 1*, 29–46.

Harris, A. R. (1977). Sex and theories of deviance: Toward a functional theory of deviant typescripts. *American Sociological Review, 42*, 3–16.

Hartman, H. (1979). The unhappy marriage of Marxism and feminism: Toward a more progressive union. *Capital and Class* (Summer), 1–13.

Hartz-Karp, J. (1981). Women in constraints. In S. K. Mukherjee & J. A. Scutt (Eds.), *Women and crime*. Sydney: Australian Institute of Criminology with Allen & Unwin.

Heide, W. S. (1974). Feminism and the "fallen woman." *Criminal Justice and Behavior, 1*, 369–373.

Heidensohn, F. (1968). The deviance of women: A critique and an enquiry. *British Journal of Sociology, 19*, 160–175.

Heidensohn, F. (1985). *Women and crime*. London: Macmillan.

Hill, G. D., & Suval, E. M. (1988). Women, race, and crime. A revised version of a paper presented at the annual meeting of the American Society of Criminology, Chicago.

Hindelang, M. (1981). Variations in sex-race-age-specific incidence rates of offending. *American Sociological Review, 46*, 461–474.

Hooks, B. (1987). Feminism: A movement to end sexist oppression. In A. Phillips (Ed.), *Feminism and equality*. Oxford: Basil Blackwell.

Jayarate, T. E. (1983). The value of quantitative methodology for feminist research. In G. Bowles & R. D. Klein (Eds.), *Theories of women's studies*. Boston: Routledge & Kegan Paul.

Joseph, G. I. (1981a). The incompatible ménage à trois: Marxism, feminism, and racism. In L. Sargent (Ed.), *Women and revolution*. Boston: South End Press.

Joseph, G. I. (1981b). White promotion, black survival. In G. I. Joseph & J. Lewis (Eds.), *Common differences: Conflicts in black and white feminist perspectives*. Boston: South End Press.

Joseph, G. I., & Lewis, J. (Eds.). (1981). *Common differences: Conflicts in black and white feminist perspectives*. Boston: South End Press.

Keller, E. F. (1982). Feminism and science. In N. O. Keohane, M. Z. Rosaldo, & B. C. Gelpi (Eds.), *Feminist theory*. Chicago: University of Chicago Press.

Klein, D. (1973). The etiology of female crime: A review of the literature. *Issues in Criminology, 8*, 3–29.

Klein, D. (1981). Violence against women: Some considerations regarding its causes and its elimination. *Crime and Delinquency, 27,* 64–80.

Kohlberg, L. (1981). *The philosophy of moral development.* San Francisco: Harper & Row.

Kruttschnitt, C. (1982). Respectable women and the law. *The Sociological Quarterly, 23,* 221–234.

Kruttschnitt, C. (1984). Sex and criminal court dispositions: The unresolved controversy. *Journal of Research in Crime and Delinquency, 21,* 213–232.

Kuhn, T. (1970). *The structure of scientific revolutions* (2nd ed.). Chicago: University of Chicago Press.

Laub, J., & McDermott, M. J. (1985). An analysis of serious crime by young black women. *Criminology, 23,* 81–98.

Lewis, D. (1981). Black women offenders and criminal justice: Some theoretical considerations. In M. Warren (Ed.), *Comparing female and male offenders.* Beverly Hills, Calif.: Sage.

MacKinnon, C. A. (1979). *The sexual harassment of working women.* New Haven, Conn.: Yale University Press.

MacKinnon, C. A. (1982). Feminism, Marxism, method, and the state: An agenda for theory. In N. O. Keohane, M. Z. Rosaldo, & B. C. Gelpi (Eds.), *Feminist theory.* Chicago: University of Chicago Press.

Mann, C. R. (1984). *Female crime and delinquency.* Tuscaloosa: University of Alabama Press.

Mann, C. R. (1987). Black female homicide in the United States. Paper presented at the Conference on Black Homicide and Public Health, Baltimore.

Martin, D. (1976). *Battered wives.* New York: Pocket Books/Simon & Schuster.

Miles, M. (1983). Toward a methodology for feminist research. In G. Bowles & R. D. Klein (Eds.), *Theories of women's studies.* Boston: Routledge & Kegan Paul.

Miller, E. M. (1985). *Street woman.* Philadelphia: Temple University Press.

Millett, K. (1971). *Sexual politics.* London: Rupert Hart-Davis.

Mitchell, J. (1971). *Woman's estate.* New York: Random House.

Moyer, I. L. (1985). *The changing roles of women in the criminal justice system: Offenders, victims, and professionals.* Prospect Heights, Ill.: Waveland Press.

Moyer, I. L., & White, G. F. (1981). Police processing of female offenders. In L. H. Bowker (Ed.), *Women and crime in America.* New York: Macmillan.

Mukherjee, S. K., & Fitzgerald, R. W. (1981). The myth of rising female crime. In S. K. Mukherjee & J. A. Scutt (Eds.), *Women and crime.* Sydney: Australian Institute of Criminology with Allen & Unwin.

Naffine, N. (1988). *Female crime: The construction of women in criminology.* Boston: Allen & Unwin.

Nagel, I. H. (1981). Sex differences in the processing of criminal defendants. In A. Morris & L. Gelsthorpe (Eds.), *Women and crime.* Cambridge, England: Cambridge Institute of Criminology.

Nagel, I. H. (1983). The legal/extra-legal controversy: Judicial decisions in pretrial release. *Law and Society Review, 17,* 481–515.

Nagel, S., & Weitzman, L. J. (1972). Double standard of American justice. *Society, 9,* 18–25, 62–63.

Oakley, A. (1981). *Subject women.* New York: Pantheon.

Pagelow, M. (1981). Sex roles, power, and woman battering. In L. H. Bowker (Ed.), *Women and crime in America.* New York: Macmillan.

Pateman, C. (1987). Feminist critiques of the public/private dichotomy. In A. Phillips (Ed.), *Feminism and equality*. Oxford: Basil Blackwell.

Phillips, A. (Ed.). (1987). *Feminism and equality*. Oxford: Basil Blackwell.

Plenska, D. (1980). Women's criminality in Poland. In C. T. Griffiths & M. Nance (Eds.), *The female offender*. Criminology Research Centre. Burnaby, B.C.: Simon Fraser University.

Rafter, N. H. (1985). *Partial justice: Women in state prisons, 1800–1935*. Boston: Northeastern University Press.

Rafter, N. H., & Natalizaia, E. (1981). Marxist feminist: Implications for criminal justice. *Crime and Delinquency, 27*, 81–98.

Rasche, C. (1974). The female offender as an object of criminological research. *Criminal Justice and Behavior, 1*, 301–320.

Reinhartz, S. (1983). Experimental analysis: A contribution to feminist research. In G. Bowles & R. D. Klein (Eds.), *Theories of women's studies*. Boston: Routledge & Kegan Paul.

Reiss, A. J., Jr., & Biderman, A. P. (1980). *Data sources on white-collar law-breaking*. National Institute of Justice. Washington, D.C.: U.S. Department of Justice.

Rich, A. (1980). Compulsory heterosexual and lesbian existence. *Signs, 5*, 631–660.

Richards, P., & Tittle, C. R. (1981). Gender and perceived chances of arrest. *Social Forces, 59*, 1182–1199.

Riger, S., & Gordon, M. T. (1981). The fear of rape: A study in social control. *Journal of Social Issues, 37*, 71–92.

Schlossman, S., & Wallach, S. (1978). The crime of precocious sexuality: Female juvenile delinquency in the progressive era. *Harvard Educational Review, 48*, 65–94.

Simpson, S. S. (1987). Women in elite deviance: A grounded theory. Paper presented at the annual meeting of the American Society of Criminology, Montreal.

Simpson, S. S. (1988). Caste, class, and crime: Violence and the disenfranchised black female. Revised version of a paper presented at the annual meeting of the American Society of Criminology, Chicago.

Simon, R. (1975). *Women and crime*. Lexington, Mass.: D. C. Heath.

Smart, C. (1976). *Women, crime and criminology: A feminist critique*. London: Routledge & Kegan Paul.

Smith, D., Visher, C., & Davidson, L. (1984). Equity and discretionary justice: The influence of race on police arrest decisions. *Journal of Criminal Law and Criminology, 75*, 234–249.

Spelman, E. V. (1988). *Inessential woman: Problems of exclusion in feminist thought*. Boston: Beacon.

Spohn, C., Gruhl, J., & Welch, S. (1982). The effect of race on sentencing: A re-examination of an unsettled question. *Law and Society Review, 16*, 71–88.

Stacey, J., & Thorne, B. (1985). The missing feminist revolution in sociology. *Social Problems, 32*, 301–316.

Stanko, E. A. (1985). *Intimate intrusions: Women's experience of male violence*. London: Routledge & Kegan Paul.

Steffensmeier, D. J. (1978). Crime and the contemporary woman: An analysis of changing levels of female property crime, 1960–75. *Social Forces, 57*, 566–584.

Steffensmeier, D. J. (1981). Patterns of female property crime, 1960–1975: A postscript. In L. H. Bowker (Ed.), *Women and crime in America*. New York: Macmillan.

Steffensmeier, D. J. (1983). Organization properties and sex-segregation in the underworld: Building a sociological theory of sex differences in crime. *Social Forces, 61*, 1010–1043.

Steffensmeier, D. J., & Cobb, M. J. (1981). Sex differences in urban arrest patterns, 1934–79. *Social Problems, 29*, 37–50.

Straus, M. A., Gelles, R. J., & Steinmetz, S. K. (1980). *Behind closed doors: Violence in the American family.* Garden City, N.Y.: Anchor/Doubleday.

Tomes, N. (1978). A "torrent of abuse": Crimes of violence between working-class men and women in London, 1840–1875. *Journal of Social History, 11*, 328–345.

Tracy, P. E., Wolfgang, M. E., & Figlio, R. M. (In press). *Delinquent careers in two birth cohorts.* New York: Plenum.

Tronto, J. C. (n.d.). "Women's morality": Beyond gender difference to a theory of care. Unpublished paper, Hunter College of the City University of New York.

Truth, S. (1851). Cited in G. I. Joseph & J. Lewis (Eds.), *Common differences: Conflicts in black and white feminist perspectives.* Boston: South End Press.

Visher, C. (1983). Gender, police arrest decisions, and notions of chivalry. *Criminology, 21*, 5–28.

Wellman, D. (1977). *Portraits of white racism.* New York: Cambridge University Press.

Wilson, J. Q., & Herrnstein, R. J. (1985). *Crime and human nature.* New York: Simon & Schuster.

Wilson, N. K. (1985). Witches, hookers, and others: Societal response to women criminals and victims. Paper presented at the annual meeting of the American Society of Criminology, San Diego.

Wood, P. (1981). The victim in a forcible rape case: A feminist view. In L. H. Bowker (Ed.), *Women and crime in America.* New York: Macmillan.

Young, V. D. (1980). Women, race, and crime. *Criminology, 18*, 26–34.

Zietz, D. (1981). *Women who embezzle or defraud: A study of convicted felons.* New York: Praeger.

22

Feminism and Criminology

KATHLEEN DALY
MEDA CHESNEY-LIND

This chapter sketches core elements of feminist thought and demonstrates their relevance for criminology. After reviewing the early feminist critiques of the discipline and the empirical emphases of the 1970s and early 1980s, it appraises current issues and debates in three areas: building theories of gender and crime, controlling men's violence toward women, and gender equality in the criminal justice system. The reader is invited to reflect on the androcentrism of the discipline and to appreciate the promise of feminist inquiry for rethinking problems of crime and justice.

The last decade has seen an outpouring of feminist scholarship in the academy. Theories, research methods, and pedagogies have been challenged across the disciplines (e.g., Abel and Abel, 1983; Bowles and Klein, 1983; Culley and Portuges, 1985; DuBois, Kelly, Kennedy, Korsmeyer, and Robinson, 1985; Griffin and Hoffman, 1986; Harding and Hintikka, 1983; Klein, 1987; Sherman and Beck, 1979; Spender, 1981; Stanley and Wise, 1983). Feminist thought has deepened and broadened. Whereas in the early years of second-wave feminism[1] there was a collective sense of a "we" to feminist theorizing, today postmodern thought and "fractured identities" have decentered feminism (Alcoff, 1988; Flax, 1987; Harding, 1986). Previously the emphasis was on women gaining equality with men within existing social institutions, but today feminist thought emphasizes a new vision of the social order in which women's experiences and ways of knowing are brought to the fore, not suppressed (Gross, 1986). Theories and concepts rooted in men's experience formerly monopolized intellectual inquiry, but today dis-

Our thanks to Rebecca Bordt and Joanne Belknap for comments on an earlier draft.

ciplinary debates in some fields reflect the impact of feminist thought, albeit uneven, across the disciplines (Stacey and Thorne, 1985).

How has criminology been affected by these developments? With the exception of feminist treatments of rape and intimate violence, the field remains essentially untouched. The time has come for criminologists to step into the world of feminist thought and for feminist scholars to move more boldly into all areas of criminology. This task will not be easy; we write as feminists interested in problems of crime and justice, and find that we lead a double life. As feminists,[2] we grapple with the many strands of feminist thought and activism, educate ourselves and others about the impact of gender relations on social life, and ponder our role as academics in a social movement. As criminologists, we grapple with the field's many theoretical and policy strands, educate ourselves and others on the conditions and social processes that make crime normal and deviant, and ponder the state's role in creating and reducing crime. All the while we wonder if it is possible to reconcile these double lives.

Defining Feminism

What Is Feminism?

In their introduction to *What Is Feminism?* Mitchell and Oakley (1986:3) suggested that it is "easier to define feminism in its absence rather than its presence." Delmar (1986) offered a "baseline definition" on which feminists and nonfeminists might agree: A feminist holds that women suffer discrimination because of their sex, that they have needs that are negated and unsatisfied, and that the satisfaction of these needs requires a radical change. "But beyond that," Delmar said, "things immediately become more complicated" (1986:8).

This complication arises because feminism is a set of theories about women's oppression *and* a set of strategies for social change. Cott (1987) identified the paradoxes of first-wave feminism (the "woman movement" in the nineteenth and early twentieth centuries), which reflected the merging of these theoretical and political impulses. These paradoxes include acknowledging diversity among women but claiming women's unity, requiring gender consciousness but calling for an eradication of gender-based distinctions and divisions, and aiming for individual freedom and autonomy by mobilizing a mass-based movement. The same paradoxical elements are seen in second-wave feminism (the contemporary women's movement beginning in the 1960s). Unfriendly interpretations of these contrary tendencies include, "These women don't know what they want" or "They want it both ways." Yet as Harding (1986:244) suggested, "The problem is that we [feminists] do not know and should not know just what we want to say about a number of conceptual choices with which we are presented—except that the choices themselves create no-win dilemmas for our feminisms." The task of describing *and* changing a spectrum of women's experiences, which have been formed by particular and often competing allegiances to class, race, and other social groups, is not straightforward but a blurred and contingent enterprise.

Distinguishing Feminist from Nonfeminist Analyses

It is not easy to know when a work or action is feminist. Delmar asked, for example, "Are all actions and campaigns prompted or led by women, feminist?" (1986:11). "Can an action be 'feminist' even if those who perform it are not?" (1986:12). She contrasted several views of feminism. It may be diffuse activity, any action motivated out of concern for women's interests, whether or not actors or groups acknowledge them as feminist. This view empties feminism of any meaning because all actions or analyses having women as their object fall into the same category. Delmar opted instead for another approach, to "separate feminism and feminists from the multiplicity of those concerned with women's issues." Feminism can be defined as a field—even though diverse—but feminists can "make no claim to an exclusive interest in or copyright over problems affecting women" (1986:13).

Neither a scholar's gender nor the focus of scholarship—whether women, gender difference, or anything else—can be used to distinguish feminist, nonfeminist, or even antifeminist works. Scholars' theoretical and methodological points of view are defined by the way in which they frame questions and interpret results, not by the social phenomenon alone. Thus, to Morris's (1987:15) question, "Does feminist criminology include criminologists who are feminist, female criminologists, or criminologists who study women?" we reply that research on women or on gender difference, whether conducted by a male or a female criminologist, does not in itself qualify it as feminist. Conversely, feminist inquiry is not limited to topics on or about women; it focuses on men as well. For criminology, because most offenders and criminal justice officials are men, this point is especially relevant; allied social institutions such as the military have not escaped feminist scrutiny (Enloe, 1983, 1987). When feminist, nonfeminist, or not-really-feminist distinctions are drawn, the main source of variation is how inclusively scholars (or activists) define a continuum of feminist thought.

Pateman (1986), for example, has compared theories addressing "women's issues" with those that are "distinctly feminist." She has termed the former "domesticated feminism" and sees it in liberal and socialist thought when scholars try to fit women or gender relations into existing theories, making "feminism . . . safe for academic theory" (1986:4). Such efforts deny that "sexual domination is at issue, or that feminism raises a problem [patriarchy], which is repressed in other theories" (1986:5). A more distinctive feminist approach assumes that individuals are gendered, and that "individuality is not a unitary abstraction but an embodied and sexually differentiated expression of the unity of humankind" (1986:9).

The implications of a distinctive feminist approach are profound—in Pateman's and others' words, "subversive"—for social, political, criminological, and other theories. It is one thing to say that women have been excluded from general theories of social phenomena. It is another matter to wonder how theories would appear if they were fashioned from women's experiences and if women had a central place in them. In addition, it is equally important to query the gender-specific character of existing theories fashioned from men's experiences.

Although some scholars (typically, liberal and Marxist feminists who do not accord primacy to gender or to patriarchal relations) assume that previous theory can be corrected by including women, others reject this view, arguing that a reconceptualization of analytic categories is necessary. Working toward a reinvention of theory is a major task for feminists today. Although tutored in "male-stream" theory and methods,[3] they work within and against these structures of knowledge to ask new questions, to put old problems in a fresh light, and to challenge the cherished wisdom of their disciplines. Such rethinking comes in many varieties, but these five elements of feminist thought distinguish it from other types of social and political thought:

♦ Gender is not a natural fact but a complex social, historical, and cultural product; it is related to, but not simply derived from, biological sex difference and reproductive capacities.

♦ Gender and gender relations order social life and social institutions in fundamental ways.

♦ Gender relations and constructs of masculinity and femininity are not symmetrical but are based on an organizing principle of men's superiority and social and political-economic dominance over women.

♦ Systems of knowledge reflect men's views of the natural and social world; the production of knowledge is gendered.

♦ Women should be at the center of intellectual inquiry, not peripheral, invisible, or appendages to men.

These elements take different spins, depending on how a scholar conceptualizes gender, the causes of gender inequality, and the means of social change. Generally, however, a feminist analysis draws from feminist theories or research, problematizes gender, and considers the implications of findings for empowering women or for change in gender relations. Finally, we note that scholars may think of themselves as feminists in their personal lives, but they may not draw on feminist theory or regard themselves as feminist scholars. For personal or professional reasons (or both), they may shy away from being marked as a particular kind of scholar.

Tracing Developments: The Awakening to the 1980s

The Awakening

In the late 1960s, Bertrand (1969) and Heidensohn (1968), respectively a Canadian and a British female criminologist, drew attention to the omission of women from general theories of crime. Although they were not the first to do so, their work signaled an awakening of criminology from its androcentric slumber. Several years earlier Walter Reckless had made the following observation in the third edition of *The Crime Problem* (1961:78):

> If the criminologist, before propounding or accepting any theory of crime or delinquency, would pause to ask whether that theory applied to women, he would probably discard it because of its inapplicability to women.

Then, as today, the problem identified by Bertrand, Heidensohn, and Reckless had two dimensions. First, it is uncertain whether general theories of crime can be applied to women's (or girls') wrongdoing. Second, the class-, race-, and age-based structure of crime forms the core of criminological theory, but the gender-based structure is ignored. Although related, these dimensions pose different questions for criminology. The first is whether theories generated to describe men's (or boys') offending can apply to women or girls (the *generalizability problem*). The second is why females commit less crime than males (the *gender ratio problem*). Both questions now occupy a central role in research on gender and crime, which will be addressed below. The early feminist critiques of criminology, however, centered on a third and more obvious problem: intellectual sexism in theories of female crime and institutional sexism in the juvenile and criminal justice systems.

Early Feminist Critiques

In the now classic reviews of the literature on female crime, Klein (1973) and Smart (1976) analyzed how such crime had been described and explained. Millman (1975) offered a related analysis for the literature on women's deviance. These reviews and recent summaries in Carlen and Worrall (1987: 1–14), Heidensohn (1985:110–62), and Morris (1987:1–18, 41–78) identified the following problems: Women's and girls' crime and deviance were explained more often by biological factors than by social or economic forces; representations of their motives or of the circumstances leading to crime were wrong or distorted; and sexual deviance (which could range from broken hymens to "immorality" or prostitution) was merged with criminal deviance. These critiques focused on the sexist assumptions of predominantly, but not exclusively, male criminologists who aimed to describe women's or girls' crime but who seemingly had little understanding of their social worlds.

At about the same time, several papers appeared that examined the assumptions and practices then operating in the juvenile and criminal justice systems in response to delinquency and crime. Chesney-Lind (1973) pointed out that girls' wrongdoing was "sexualized" and that noncriminal status offenses such as running away or curfew violations formed a larger portion of girls' than of boys' delinquency subject to juvenile justice control and intervention. Temin (1973) analyzed current gender-based differences in sentencing statutes, which allowed for indeterminate sentences for women but not for men. Others focused on the unequal treatment of girls and women in training schools and prisons (Burkhart, 1976; Rodgers, 1972; Singer, 1973).

In this early phase, scholars challenged the "separate spheres" assumptions then operating explicitly in law, criminological theory and research, and justice practices. Separate spheres is a set of ideas about the respective places of men and women in the social order that emerged in the first quarter of the nineteenth century in the United States, as well as in other countries undergoing capitalist industrialization. This ideology placed men in the public sphere (paid workplace, politics, law) and women in the private sphere (household, family life); it characterized gender relations for white, middle-class, married heterosexual couples. Woman's place as mother and wife conferred her status (albeit limited) as the moral guardian of the home and the culture, but man's place as father, husband, and paid worker conferred his status as creator and formal arbiter of morality and culture.

First- and second-wave feminists challenged the separate spheres ideology in different ways, reflecting their historical circumstances. At the risk of oversimplifying, it can be said that first-wave feminists embraced women's capacities as mothers and moral guardians of the home to make the public sphere more accountable to women's interests. In the process, however, those feminists became involved in crusades for moral and social purity that resulted in unprecedented state involvement in the lives of young women. In efforts to raise the age of consent and to limit or eliminate prostitution, for example, reform-minded women unwittingly assisted the state in incarcerating large numbers of girls and young women for "immoral behavior" in the years just before and during World War I (Bland, 1985; Musheno and Seeley, 1986; Rosen, 1982; Schlossman and Wallach, 1978).

Second-wave feminists, especially during the 1960s and early 1970s, denounced the domestic or private sphere as oppressive to women and sought to achieve equality with men in the public sphere. In this intellectual context, feminists challenged gender-based laws and legal practices formulated from separate spheres thinking. Early feminist critiques of criminology and criminal law were similarly motivated, but as we shall see, such analyses and strategies for change omitted more subtle questions of equality and difference now being raised by feminists.

The problematic and limiting aspects of an essentially liberal feminist response to the separate spheres ideology became clear with the appearance of two books analyzing women's arrest trends in the 1960s and early 1970s. Adler's (1975) *Sisters in Crime* and Simon's (1975) *Women and Crime* proposed ideas about women's criminality that were troubling to feminists because they were largely an outgrowth of the unexamined assumption that the emancipation of women resided solely in achieving legal and social equality with men in the public sphere. Although the books differed in tone and reached somewhat different conclusions, they touched a raw nerve by linking women's crime to the women's movement and to the goal of equality with men in the public sphere.

Women's Emancipation and Crime

The merits and flaws of Simon's, but more especially Adler's, analyses of women and crime have been discussed extensively. It is superfluous to catalog here the critiques and empirical tests of their ideas because others have done so (see, e.g., Chapman, 1980; Datesman and Scarpitti, 1980b; Giordano, Kerbel, and Dudley, 1981; Gora, 1982; Heidensohn, 1985; Miller, 1986; Smart, 1979; Steffensmeier, 1978, 1980). Our interest is in Adler's and Simon's conception of the role of gender in crime causation. In the process we will demonstrate why the issues they raised continue to be discussed by criminologists today.

Both Adler's and Simon's analyses assumed that female criminality had been kept in check by women's limited aspirations and opportunities. They argued that social circumstances, not biology, explained gender differences in crime. For Adler, the lifting of restrictions on women's behavior gave women the opportunity to act like men—that is, to be as violent, greedy, and crime-prone as men. Simon took a more qualified view because she read the statistical evidence more accurately. Having found no changes in women's share of arrests for violent crime, she reasoned that their increasing share of arrests for property crime (especially larceny, fraud, and embezzlement) might be explained by their increasing opportunities in the workplace (or public sphere) to commit crime. Moreover, she wondered whether the ideology of equality for men and for women might make police and court officials more interested in treating men and women the same.

Adler has been faulted extensively for claiming a link between feminist goals of emancipation for women and increases in female crime. In characterizing female crime as the "darker side" (1975:3) of women's liberation, reflecting feminist attitudes of female offenders, Adler assumed that low-income women somehow were seeking equality with their male counterparts, as though crime in some sense was a desirable occupation. Simon has been criticized for assuming that increases in female crime were due to new workplace opportunities for some women, not to increasing economic immizeration for other women. Critics took Adler and Simon to task by pointing out that occupational structures had changed little, that arrested or imprisoned women held traditional (not feminist) views of work and family life, and that careful analyses of arrest data failed to support their claims.

On a broader scale, the challenges to Adler and Simon have been limited to questions of whether the trends they described were actually occurring. Little has been said about the limitations of the liberal feminist perspective on gender that informed their work. This perspective typically ignores class and race differences among women and defines gender either as the possession of masculine or feminine attitudes or as role differences between men and women. Such a view assumes that when women become less feminine in outlook or enter roles occupied previously by men, they will begin to think and act like men. This line of thinking continues to dominate research on gender differences in crime and delinquency.

By contrast, a radical or socialist feminist views gender as constructed by power relations, not simply by roles (see Lopata and Thorne, 1978, for a critique of applying role theory to gender). These feminist perspectives consider the impact of patriarchy (a social structure of men's control over women's labor and sexuality), and they assume that both roles and attitudes are embedded in this larger structure. Although radical and socialist feminists differ in regard to the role played by class and race, both call for placing men's and women's criminality in its patriarchal social context, just as Marxist criminologies seek to place criminal behavior in its class context.

Debate over women's emancipation and crime has not been fruitful, but important questions for criminology are latent in this and related debates. What is the relationship between crime and women's changing social and economic situation? What happens when some women enter positions, circumstances, or social arenas previously occupied only by men? How do gender relations shape the patterns of men's and women's crime? Adler and Simon, their critics, and others have presupposed the answers to these questions in the absence of appropriate empirical inquiry or an understanding that different feminist perspectives on gender will yield different interpretations.

During this period, however, second-wave feminist scholarship was just gaining momentum, and criminologists were only dimly aware of the dimensions of the problem they had encountered. Lacking theoretical guidance, they focused on a compelling empirical deficit: Little was known about women's crime or gender differences in crime. For that matter, little was known about girls' or women's experience in any facet of the juvenile or criminal justice systems—whether as offenders, victims, or workers. Therefore, filling these empirical gaps was a major task.

Approaches to Building Theories of Gender and Crime

Theories of gender and crime can be built in several ways, and criminologists are taking three tacks. Some are focusing on the generalizability problem, while others are interested in the gender ratio problem. Still others want to bracket both problems, regarding each as premature for an accurate understanding of gender and crime.

The Generalizability Problem

Do theories of men's crime apply to women? Can the logic of such theories be modified to include women? In addressing the generalizability problem, scholars have tested theories derived from all-male samples to see if they apply to girls or women (e.g., Cernkovich and Giordano, 1979; Datesman and Scarpitti, 1975; Figueira-McDonough and Selo, 1980; Giordano, 1978; Warren, 1982; Zeitz, 1981). Others have borrowed elements from existing theories (e.g., Moyer, 1985, on conflict theory) or have recast the logic of a theory altogether (e.g., Schur, 1984, on labeling). According to Smith and Paternoster's (1987) review of the large body of studies taking this approach, the available evidence is limited, mixed, and inconclusive. More studies will likely confirm a consistent, logical answer to the question, "Do theories of men's crime apply to women?" The answer is, "yes and no": The truth lies in this equivocation.

The Gender Ratio Problem

The gender ratio problem poses the following questions: Why are women less likely than men to be involved in crime? Conversely, why are men more crime-prone than women? What explains gender differences in rates of arrest and in variable types of criminal activity? In contrast to the gender composition of generalizability scholars, almost all gender ratio scholars seem to be men. Their approach is to develop new theoretical formulations by drawing primarily from statistical evidence, secondary sources, elements of existing theory (e.g., social control, conflict, Marxist), and at times from feminist theory. Box (1983), Gove (1985), Hagan, Simpson, and Gillis (1987), Harris (1977), Messerschmidt (1986), Steffensmeier (1983), and Wilson and Herrnstein (1985) have offered ideas on this issue. Heidensohn (1985) is one of the few female criminologists to take this route.

Juxtaposing the Generalizability and Gender Ratio Problems

Much of the confusion and debate that surround the building of theories of gender and crime can be resolved when scholars realize that they are on different tracks in addressing the generalizability and gender ratio problems. Members of each camp seem to be unaware of the other's aims or assumptions; but when the two are juxtaposed, their logic and their limitations are revealed. Analogous developments have taken place in building theories of gender and the labor market; some of that literature is thus sketched below to clarify problems in developing theories of gender and crime.

A model of occupational status attainment, outlined by Blau and Duncan (1967) and using an all-male sample, was applied subsequently to samples of women. This research suggested that the same variables predicted occupational status for men and for women (see Sokoloff's 1980 review); the implication was that the processes of intergenerational occupational mobility were the same for men and women. Those taking a more structural approach to the labor market soon raised this question, however: How was it that the "same" processes produced such distinctive distributions of men and women in the paid occupational structure (job segregation) and caused such marked differences in men's and women's wages? That query inspired a rethinking of the structural and organizational contexts of men's and women's work (paid and unpaid), which now commands the attention of many sociologists and economists.

The gender and labor market literature today is several steps ahead of that for gender and crime, but similarities at different stages are clear. Generalizability scholars are not concerned with gender differences in rates of arrest or in arrests for particular crimes (or in rates and types of delinquent acts). Instead they want to know whether the same processes (or variables) describe intragender variability in crime and delinquency. Setting aside the mixed research findings, they (like status attainment theorists) confront a vexing question. Even if (for the sake of argument) the same processes or variables explain intragender variability in crime and delinquency or in its detection, why do such similar processes produce a distinctive, gender-based structure to crime or delinquency? Moreover, what does it mean to develop a gender-neutral theory of crime, as some scholars now advocate, when neither the social order nor the structure of crime is gender-neutral?[4]

Smith and Paternoster (1987) proposed developing a gender-neutral theory of crime because gender-specific theories of the past (meaning theories of *female* criminality) held sexist and stereotypic assumptions of female behavior. (Note that theories of male crime are assumed to be universal and are not construed as gender-specific.) When Smith and Paternoster then considered the gender ratio problem, they suggested that the volume of criminal deviance may reflect "*differential exposure* to factors that precipitate deviant behavior among both males and females" (1987:156). Their surmise begs the question of *how* gender relations structure "differential exposure" and "factors," and seemingly denies the existence of gender relations.

Like structural analysts of gender and the labor market, gender ratio criminologists take the position that patterns of men's and women's crime are sufficiently different to warrant new theoretical formulations. Focusing on intergender variability in rates of arrest or in arrests for particular crimes, several theorists offer these starting points: the power relations both between and among men and women, the control and commodification of female sexuality, sources of informal social control, and the greater enforcement of conformity in girls' and women's lives. In contrast to generalizability scholars, gender ratio scholars assume that different (or gender-specific) variables predict intergender variability in crime or delinquency.

In the wake of arguments developed by gender ratio scholars, those who pursue the generalizability problem may begin to rethink concepts or variables, or they may abandon their enterprise as too limiting. That change may require some time, however, because the contributions of the gender ratio scholars to date are also limited or provisional. Although they acknowledge that crime (like the occupational order) is gendered, many display only a primitive understanding of what this fact means, and all face problems of slim evidence (save statistical distributions) from which to develop sound propositions about female crime or gender differences in crime.

Bracketing the Two Problems

Many feminist criminologists tend for the present to bracket the generalizability and the gender ratio problems. They are skeptical of previous representations of girls' or women's lives and want a better understanding of their social worlds. Moreover, they are unimpressed with theoretical arguments derived from questionable evidence and having little sensitivity to women's (or men's) realities. Like criminologists of the past (from the 1930s to the 1960s), they seek to understand crime at close range, whether through biographical case studies, autobiographical accounts, participant observation, or interviews (e.g., Alder, 1986; Bell, 1987; Campbell, 1984; Carlen, 1983, 1985; Carlen and Worrall, 1987; Chesney-Lind and Rodriguez, 1983; Délacoste and Alexander, 1987; Miller, 1986; Rosenbaum, 1981). For this group of scholars, the quality and the depth of evidence are insufficient to address the generalizability or gender ratio problems. Perhaps more important, the ways in which questions are framed and results are interpreted by many (though not all) of those pursuing the generalizability or gender ratio problems remain tied to masculinist perspectives, ignoring the insights from feminist scholarship.

Controlling Men's Violence Toward Women

The victimization (and survivorship) of women is a large and growing part of criminology and is of central interest to feminists in and outside criminology. The relatively high feminist visibility in this area may lead criminologists to regard it as the only relevant site for feminist inquiry in criminology. Not so; the more one reads the literature on victimization—the physical and sexual abuse of children, women, and men—the more difficult it becomes to separate victimization from offending, especially in the case of women

(Browne, 1987; Chesney-Lind, forthcoming; Chesney-Lind and Rodriguez, 1983; McCormack, Janus, and Burgess, 1986; Silbert and Pines, 1981).

In research on physical abuse and sexual violence by men against women, these major themes and findings are seen:

♦ Rape and violence—especially between intimates—are far more prevalent than imagined previously.

♦ Police, court officials, juries, and members of the general public do not take victims of rape or violence seriously, especially when victim-offender relations involve intimates or acquaintances.

♦ Myths about rape and intimate violence are prevalent. They appear in the work of criminologists, in criminal justice practices, and in the minds of members of the general public.

♦ Whereas female victims feel stigma and shame, male offenders often do not view their behavior as wrong.

♦ Strategies for change include empowering women via speakouts, marches, shelters and centers, and legal advocacy; and changing men's behavior via counseling, presumptive arrest for domestic violence, and more active prosecution and tougher sanctions for rape.

Although feminists of all types agree that men's rape and battery of women require urgent attention, scholars and activists have different views on the causes and the malleability of men's sexual and physical aggression. Pornography (and its links to men's sexual violence) and prostitution (and its links to pornography) are prominent in the dissensus. We turn to these debates and their implications for criminal justice policy.

Causes of Men's Violence Toward Women

Radical feminists tend to construct men's nature as rapacious, violent, and oriented toward the control of women (see, e.g., Brownmiller, 1975; Dworkin, 1987; MacKinnon, 1982, 1983, 1987; Rich, 1980). Both rape and intimate violence are the result and the linchpin of patriarchal systems, in which women's bodies and minds are subject to men's dominion. Marxist and socialist feminists (e.g., Hooks, 1984; Klein, 1982; Messerschmidt, 1986; Schwendinger and Schwendinger, 1983) differ from radical feminists on one key point: They believe that men's nature cannot be described in universalistic (or biologically based) terms but is a product of history and culture and is related to other systems of domination such as classism, racism, and imperialism. In contrast, liberal feminists offer no theory of causes; but, like Marxist and socialist feminists, they envision the possibility that men's socially structured violent nature can change. What role, then, should the state play in controlling men's violence and protecting women from such violence? Feminist responses are contradictory, and the dilemmas are pro-found.

Questioning the Role of the State

PORNOGRAPHY

Differences among feminists over the causes of men's violence and the state's role in controlling it are nowhere so clear as in the pornography issue. Part of the debate concerns the effect of pornography on increasing or caus-ing men's sexual violence toward women. Research ethics preclude an an-swer, but clinical evidence to date shows that pornography with violent content increases aggression, whereas pornography without violent content diminishes aggression (see Baron and Straus, 1987:468). Such evidence hardly settles the matter either for antipornography or for anticensorship feminists. At issue are different views of men's sexuality and the causes of men's violence, with radical feminists initiating the antipornography move-ment. Also at issue is whether state officials can be trusted to render the judgments that antipornography activists seek via the proposed civil rem-edy (Waring, 1986). Finally, anticensorship feminists see greater harm for women and sexual minorities in efforts to suppress the many forms of com-mercialized pornography.

PROSTITUTION

Debates among and between feminists and sex-trade workers (Bell, 1987; Délacoste and Alexander, 1987) reveal differences in how women view sexu-ality and sexual power, as well as problems in relying on a male-dominated state to protect women. These differences are often submerged in a coalition of civil liberties groups, women's groups, and sex-trade workers' organiza-tions who reject state regulation *or* criminalization of prostitution. In advo-cating the decriminalization of prostitution and a range of issues associated with prostitutes' right to work, the concerned groups achieve a short-term solution: Women can make a living and are not singled out as criminals in a commercial activity that men control, use, and profit from. Nevertheless, the institution of prostitution remains intact, and with it this feminist dilemma: Will support for some women's right to work perpetuate an institution that ultimately objectifies women and exploits them sexually, may foster vio-lence against women, and may harm female prostitutes? Today, however, as in the past, the state's stance on vigorous enforcement of prostitution and other related ordinances depends on how prostitution harms men via sexu-ally transmitted diseases, rather than on the institution's impact on women (Alexander, 1987; Bland, 1985; Daly, 1988; Walkowitz, 1980).

In juxtaposing prostitution and pornography, one sees that contradictions and dilemmas for feminists who campaign for redress against men's violence toward women (often by seeking an expanded role for the state in protecting women) while simultaneously advocating women's economic and sexual freedom. Similar dilemmas arise in controlling intimate violence.

INTIMATE VIOLENCE AND RAPE

State criminal laws for the arrest and prosecution of spouse (or intimate) abuse and rape have changed significantly in a short period of time (see reviews by Bienen, 1980; Lerman, 1980). Civil remedies such as the temporary restraining order to protect battered women are more readily available than in the past. These legal changes are a symbolic victory for many feminists, who see in them the state's accommodation to their demands for protection against men's violence. Yet the effect of new laws and programs on changing police and court practices seems far less impressive. Officials' resistance and organizational inertia are common themes; program success can be short-lived (Berk, Loseke, Berk, and Rauma, 1980; Berk, Rauma, Loseke, and Berk, 1982; Crites, 1987; Grau, Fagan, and Wexler, 1984; Quarm and Schwartz, 1984; Spencer, 1987). Some scholars think legal reforms may serve a deterrent and educative function over the long term, and thus that it may be unreasonable to expect immediate change in men's violence or in the state's response (Osborne, 1984).

A thread of hope hangs on the promise of presumptive arrest as a method of reducing intimate (or spouse) violence. Sherman and Berk's (1984) study in Minneapolis found that arrest may deter men from future assaults on their mates, more so than the police actions of ordering the suspect to leave the premises or giving the suspect advice. This study's findings were diffused quickly and were embraced by many feminists as evidence that intimate abuse would be reduced by a tougher state stance. A program of field experiments in six other American cities is currently under way; it may reveal more about the wisdom and the special deterrent effect of presumptive arrest for intimate violence.[5]

We wear our criminologist hats in questioning feminist (or nonfeminist) optimism in a presumptive arrest policy. Certainly, a get-tough, "lock 'em up" response offers women short-term protection and retributive justice, but it is part of a more general incarceral "solution" to crime that has arisen in the last decade. Apart from short-term incapacitation, however, it is difficult to see how this or any other reactive policy can be effective in reducing violent crime. Other methods, aimed at the structural sources of men's violence toward women, must be pursued more strenuously. These include empowering women to leave destructive relationships, to be freed from continued predation by their mates, and to impugn the normative supports for men's sexual and physical violence.

Many people might argue that in the absence of presumptive arrest, men's violence toward women is condoned; thus, some state intervention is better than none. At the margins, a more active state role in controlling intimate violence may alleviate women's suffering and reduce spousal (or intimate) homicide, but there are disadvantages to state intervention. For example, will presumptive arrest of male suspects also lead to the arrest of women because the police are uncertain which is the batterer and which is the victim? Will a battered woman's ambivalence about arresting a mate be ignored? Will women be jailed for failing to testify against an abusive mate? We await studies of the implementation and effect of these policies over the next decade; perhaps our skepticism will prove unfounded. Like a handful of others (e.g., Carlen and Worrall, 1987:13), however, we suspect that such policies are shortsighted. Harris (1987:34) posed this issue as a dilemma of safety and protection for women, but it can be applied more broadly: "How can we respond effectively to people who inflict injury and hardship on others without employing the same script and the same means that they do?" That dilemma should be explored fully by the entire criminological community in contemplating the role of the state and its citizens in reducing crime.

Gender Equality in the Criminal Justice System

In the early days of second-wave feminism, calls for legal equality with men were apparent everywhere, and the early feminist critics of criminal law and justice practices reflected this ethos. Today feminist legal scholars are more skeptical of a legal equality model because the very structure of law continues to assume that men's lives are the norm, such that women's legal claims are construed as "special treatment." Alternatives to thinking about equality and difference have been proposed in view of women's social and economic subordinate status and gender differences in paid employment, sexuality, and parenthood; see, e.g., *International Journal of the Sociology of Law*, 1986; MacKinnon, 1987; Rhode, 1987; Vogel, forthcoming; *Wisconsin Women's Law Journal*, 1987. Feminist dissensus over what should be done partly reflects different perspectives on gender, but increasingly one finds that strategies for change reflect lessons learned from engaging in the legal process. As feminists have moved to change the law, so too has the law changed feminism.[6]

Questioning Equality Doctrine and the Equal Treatment Model

Feminist analyses of criminal justice practices are reflecting a similar shift by moving away from a liberal feminist conceptualization of gender discrimination as a problem of equal treatment. This recent change is more pronounced in British than in American criminology (related, no doubt, to the preponderance of statistical approaches in the United States). It is seen in studies and literature reviews by Allen (1987), Chesney-Lind (1986, 1987),

Daly (1987a, 1987b), Eaton (1983, 1985, 1986, 1987), Heidensohn (1986, 1987), Smart (1985), and Worrall (1987). Unlike previous statistical studies of gender-based disparities in court outcomes (for reviews see Nagel and Hagan, 1983; Parisi, 1982), more recent qualitative studies of legal processes analyze the interplay of gender, sexual and familial ideology, and social control in courtroom discourse and decision making at both the juvenile and the adult levels. This work addresses how gender relations structure decisions in the legal process, rather than whether men and women are treated "the same" in a statistical sense. Eaton (1986:15) summed up the limitations of analyzing sentencing as an equal treatment problem in this way: "The [discrimination] debate is conducted within the terms of legal rhetoric—'justice' and 'equality' mean 'equal treatment,' existing inequalities are to be ignored or discounted." Thus, just as feminist legal scholars are critiquing equality doctrine, feminist criminologists now are questioning how research on discrimination in the courts is conducted.

While feminist scholars are identifying the limitations of an equal treatment model in law or in research on legal practices, that model and the statistical evidence on which it is based form the centerpiece of sentencing reforms in the United States. Although these reforms are taking shape in different ways (Blumstein, Cohen, Martin, and Tonry, 1983; Shane-DuBow, Brown, and Olsen, 1985; Tonry, 1987), they aim to reduce sentencing disparity by punishing "like crimes" in the same way. A major problem is that sentencing reforms are designed to reduce race- and class-based disparities in sentencing men. Their application to female offenders may yield equality with a vengeance: a higher rate of incarceration and for longer periods of time than in the past.[7] Like reforms in divorce (Weitzman, 1985) and in child custody (Fineman, 1988), devised with liberal feminist definitions of equality, sentencing reform may also prove unjust and may ultimately work against women.

The limitations of current equality doctrine are also apparent for changing the prison (or jail) conditions of incarcerated women. Litigation based on equal protection arguments can improve conditions for women to some degree (e.g., training, educational, or work release programs), but such legal arguments are poorly suited to the specific health needs of women and to their relationships with children (Leonard, 1983; Resnik and Shaw, 1980). Indirectly they may also make it easier to build new facilities for female offenders than to consider alternatives to incarceration. Historical studies of the emergence of women's prisons in the United States suggest that separate spheres notions, which were applied to penal philosophy, may have offered somewhat better conditions of confinement for women (notably white, not black women; see Rafter, 1985) than an equality-with-men model (Freedman, 1981; Schweber, 1982). Therefore, equality defined as equal treatment of men and women, especially when men's experiences and behavior are taken as the norm, forestalls more fundamental change and in some instances may worsen women's circumstances.

Reflections

We are in a time of transition in which gender equality (or equality for other social groups), founded on legal principles of equal access to and due process in social institutions, offers a limited prospect for changing the panoply of inequalities in daily life. In the case of gender relations we cannot retreat to separate spheres, nor can we embrace equality doctrine uncritically. Criminologists, especially those involved in the formation of policy, should be aware that equal treatment is only one of several ways of redressing discrimination and of moving toward a more humane justice system.

Notes

1. First-wave feminism (termed "the woman movement") arose in the United States and in some European countries in conjunction with the movement to abolish slavery. Its beginning in the United States is typically marked by the Seneca Falls, New York, convention (1848), and its ending by the passage of the Nineteenth Amendment to the United States Constitution (granting women's suffrage), coupled with the falling-out among women activists over the Equal Rights Amendment proposed in the early 1920s. See DuBois (1981) for the nineteenth-century context, Cott (1987) for the early twentieth-century context when the term "feminist" was first used, Giddings (1984) for black women's social movement activity, Kelly-Gadol (1982) for "pro-woman" writers in the four centuries before the nineteenth century, and Kimmell (1987) for men's responses to feminism. Second-wave American feminism emerged in the mid-1960s in conjunction with the civil rights movement, the New Left, and a critical mass of professional women (see Evans, 1979; Hooks, 1981, 1984). It has not ended (but see Stacey, 1987, for an analysis of "postfeminist" consciousness). Note that the conventional dating of the first and second wave is rightly challenged by several scholars who find greater continuity in feminist consciousness and action (Cott, 1987; Delmar, 1986; Kelly-Gadol, 1982).
2. As we make clear later, the kind of feminist perspective we take is socialist feminist, which colors our commentary throughout this chapter.
3. It is uncertain who introduced the concept "male-stream" because citations vary. *The Feminist Dictionary* (Kramarae and Treichler, 1985:244) says "coined by Mary Daly," but does not say where.
4. The same question could be raised for other theories of crime, which take this position although they do not purport to be "class-neutral" or "race-neutral." They include varieties of social learning, social control, and rational choice theories. The generalizability problem is not confined to theories of gender and crime; it is also seen in efforts to apply theories of male juvenile offending to white-collar crime (e.g., Hirschi and Gottfredson, 1987).
5. For a conceptualization of the project and a sketch of start-up designs, see National Institute of Justice (1985 and 1988 respectively). In addition to Minneapolis, field experiments are being conducted in Omaha, Colorado Springs, Dade County (Florida), Atlanta, Charlotte, and Milwaukee. Cohn and Sherman (1987:1) reported the following policy changes from surveys taken in 1984, 1985, and 1986

of all police departments in American cities with a population of greater than 100,000. Of the 146 departments surveyed each year, the proportion saying that their preferred policy was arrest for minor domestic assault cases increased from 10 percent in 1984 to 31 percent in 1985 and to 46 percent in 1986.

6. This observation paraphrases a remark made by Martha Fineman at the Feminism and Legal Theory Conference, University of Wisconsin Law School, July 1988. Feminist analyses of law and strategies for change are prodigious; see Graycar (1987) for a summary of some themes. Majury (1987), Rights of Women, Family Law Subgroup (1985), and Schneider (1986) have illustrated dilemmas in legal strategy.

7. For example, California's determinate sentencing law may have had an impact on increasing the length of prison sentences for women (Blumstein et al., 1983, vol. 1:114, 213–14). To our knowledge, evidence on the impact of sentencing reform in changing the rates of incarceration for women is not yet available. We note, however, that the female share of the jail and prison population has increased in the last decade. Of those in jail, women were 6 percent in 1978 and 8 percent in 1986 (Bureau of Justice Statistics, 1987:5); of those in state and federal prisons, women were 4 percent in 1978 (Flanagan and McLeod, 1983:545) and 5 percent in 1987 (Bureau of Justice Statistics, 1988:3).

References

Abel, E., & Abel, E. K. (Eds.). (1983). *The signs reader: Women, gender, and scholarship*. Chicago: University of Chicago Press.

Adler, F. (1975). *Sisters in crime: The rise of the new female criminal*. New York: McGraw-Hill.

Alcoff, L. (1988). Cultural feminism versus post-structuralism. *Signs: Journal of Women in Culture and Society*, 13(3), 406–36.

Alder, C. (1986). "Unemployed women have got it heaps worse:" Exploring the implications of female youth unemployment. *Australian and New Zealand Journal of Criminology*, 19, 210–25.

Alexander, P. (1987). Prostitutes are being scapegoated for heterosexual AIDS. In F. Délacoste & P. Alexander (Eds.), *Sex work: Writings by women in the sex industry* (pp. 248–63). San Francisco: Cleis.

Allen, H. (1987). Rendering them harmless: The professional portrayal of women charged with serious violent crimes. In P. Carlen & A. Worrall (Eds.), *Gender, crime and justice* (pp. 81–94). Philadelphia: Open University Press.

Baron, L., & Straus, M. A. (1987). Four theories of rape: A macrosociological analysis. *Social Forces*, 34(5), 467–88.

Bell, L. (Ed.). (1987). *Good girls/bad girls: Feminists and sex trade workers face to face*. Seattle: Seal.

Berk, R. A., Loseke, D. R., Berk, S. F., & Rauma, D. (1980). Bringing the cops back in: A study of efforts to make the criminal justice system more responsive to incidents of family violence. *Social Science Research*, 9, 193–215.

Berk, R. A., Rauma, D., Loseke, D. R., & Berk, S. F. (1982). Throwing the cops back out: The decline of a local program to make the criminal justice system more responsive to incidents of family violence. *Social Science Research*, 11, 145–79.

Bertrand, M. A. (1969). Self-image and delinquency: A contribution to the study of female criminality and women's image. *Acta Criminologia: Études sur la Conduite Antisociale, 2* (January), 71–144.

Bienen, L. (1980). Rape III—Rape reform legislation. *Women's Rights Law Reporter, 6*(3), 170–213.

Bland, L. (1985). In the name of protection: The policing of women in the First World War. In J. Brophy & C. Smart (Eds.), *Women in law: Explorations in law, family, and sexuality* (pp. 23–49). Boston: Routledge & Kegan Paul.

Blau, P., & Duncan, O. D. (1967). *The American occupational structure.* New York: Wiley.

Blumstein, A., Cohen, J., Martin, S. E., & Tonry, M. H. (Eds.). (1983). *Research on sentencing: The search for reform,* vols. 1 & 2. Washington, D.C.: National Academy Press.

Bowles, G., & Klein, R. D. (Eds.). (1983). *Theories of women's studies.* Boston: Routledge & Kegan Paul.

Box, S. (1983). *Power, crime, and mystification.* New York: Tavistock.

Browne, A. (1987). *When battered women kill.* New York: Free Press.

Brownmiller, S. (1975). *Against our will: Men, women, and rape.* New York: Simon & Schuster.

Bureau of Justice Statistics, U.S. Department of Justice. (1987). Jail inmates 1986, NCJ-107123. Washington, D.C.: U.S. Government Printing Office.

Bureau of Justice Statistics, U.S. Department of Justice. (1988). Prisoners in 1987, NCJ-110331. Washington, D.C.: U.S. Government Printing Office.

Burkhart, K. W. (1976). *Women in prison.* New York: Popular Library.

Campbell, A. (1984). *The girls in the gang: A report from New York City.* New York: Blackwell.

Carlen, P. (1983). *Women's imprisonment: A study in social control.* Boston: Routledge & Kegan Paul.

Carlen, P. (Ed.). (1985). *Criminal women: Autobiographical accounts.* Cambridge, England: Polity.

Carlen, P., & Worrall, A. (Eds.). (1987). *Gender, crime and justice.* Philadelphia: Open University Press.

Carrigan, T., Connell, B., & Lee, J. (1985). Toward a new sociology of masculinity. *Theory and Society, 14,* 551–604.

Cernkovich, S. A., & Giordano, P. C. (1979). Delinquency, opportunity and gender. *Journal of Criminal Law and Criminology, 70* (Summer), 145–51.

Chapman, J. R. (1980). *Economic realities and the female offender.* Lexington, Mass. Lexington Books.

Chesney-Lind, M. (1973). Judicial enforcement in the female sex role: The family court and the female delinquent. *Issues in Criminology, 8*(2), 51–69.

Chesney-Lind, M. (1986). Women and crime: The female offender. *Signs: Journal of Women in Culture and Society, 12*(1), 78–96.

Chesney-Lind, M. (1987). Female offenders: Paternalism reexamined. In L. L. Crites & W. L. Hepperle (Eds.), *Women, the courts, and equality* (pp. 114–39). Newbury Park, Calif.: Sage.

Chesney-Lind, M., & Rodriguez, N. (1983). Women under lock and key. *The Prison Journal, 63,* 47–65.

Cohn, E. G., & Sherman, L. W. (1987). *Police policy on domestic violence, 1986: A national survey.* Washington, D.C.: Crime Control Institute.

Cott, N. (1987). *The grounding of modern feminism*. New Haven, Conn.: Yale University Press.

Crites, L. L. (1987). Wife abuse: The judicial record. In L. L. Crites & W. L. Hepperle (Eds.), *Women, the courts, and equality* (pp. 38–53). Newbury Park, Calif.: Sage.

Culley, M., & Portuges, C. (Eds.). (1985). *Gendered subjects: The dynamics of feminist teaching*. Boston: Routledge & Kegan Paul.

Daly, K. (1987a). Structure and practice of familial-based justice in a criminal court. *Law and Society Review, 21*(2), 267–90.

Daly, K. (1987b). Discrimination in the criminal courts: Family, gender, and the problem of equal treatment. *Social Forces, 66*(1), 152–75.

Daly, K. (1988). The social control of sexuality: A case study of the criminalization of prostitution in the Progressive era. In S. Spitzer & A. T. Scull (Eds.), *Research in law, deviance, and social control*, vol. 9 (pp. 171–206). Greenwich, Conn.: JAI.

Datesman, S. K., & Scarpitti, F. R. (1975). Female delinquency and broken homes: A reassessment. *Criminology, 13* (May), 33–55.

Datesman, S. K., & Scarpitti, F. R. (1980b). Women's crime and women's emancipation. In S. K. Datesman & F. R. Scarpitti (Eds.), *Women, crime, and justice* (pp. 355–76). New York: Oxford University Press.

Délacoste, F., & Alexander, P. (Eds.) (1987). *Sex work: Writings by women in the sex industry*. San Francisco: Cleis.

Delmar, R. (1986). What is feminism? In J. Mitchell & A. Oakley (Eds.), *What is feminism?* (pp. 8–33). New York: Pantheon.

DuBois, E. C. (1981). *Elizabeth Cady Stanton/Susan B. Anthony: Correspondence, writings, and speeches*. New York: Schocken.

DuBois, E. C., Kelly, G. P., Kennedy, E. L., Korsmeyer, C. W., & Robinson, L. S. (1985). *Feminist scholarship: Kindling in the groves of academe*. Urbana, Ill.: University of Illinois Press.

Dworkin, A. (1987). *Intercourse*. New York: Free Press.

Eaton, M. (1983). Mitigating circumstances: Familiar rhetoric. *International Journal of the Sociology of Law, 11*, 385–400.

Eaton, M. (1985). Documenting the defendant: Placing women in social inquiry reports. In J. Brophy & C. Smart (Eds.), *Women in law: Explorations in law, family, and sexuality* (pp. 117–38). Boston: Routledge & Kegan Paul.

Eaton, M. (1986). *Justice for women? Family, court and social control*. Philadelphia: Open University Press.

Eaton, M. (1987). The question of bail: Magistrates' responses to applications for bail on behalf of men and women defendants. In P. Carlen & A. Worrall (Eds.), *Gender, crime and justice* (pp. 95–107). Philadelphia: Open University Press.

Enloe, C. H. (1983). *Does khaki become you? The militarization of women's lives*. Boston: South End Press.

Enloe, C. H. (1987). Feminists thinking about war, militarism, and peace. In B. B. Hess & M. M. Feree (Eds.), *Analyzing gender* (pp. 526–47). Newbury Park, Calif.: Sage.

Evans, S. (1979). *Personal politics: The roots of women's liberation in the civil rights movement and the New Left*. New York: Knopf.

Figueira-McDonough, J., & Selo, E. (1980). A reformulation of the "equal opportunity" explanation of female delinquency. *Crime and Delinquency, 26*, 333–43.

Fineman, M. (1988). Dominant discourse, professional language, and legal change in child custody decisionmaking. *Harvard Law Review, 10*(4), 727–74.

Flanagan, T. J., & McLeod, M. (Eds.). (1983). *Sourcebook of criminal justice statistics— 1982.* Bureau of Justice Statistics, U.S. Department of Justice. Washington, D.C.: U.S. Government Printing Office.

Flax, J. (1987). Postmodernism and gender relations in feminist theory. *Signs: Journal of Women in Culture and Society, 12*(4), 621–43.

Freedman, E. B. (1981). *Their sisters' keepers: Women's prison reform in America, 1830– 1930.* Ann Arbor: University of Michigan Press.

Gelsthorpe, L., & Morris, A. (1988). Feminism and criminology in Britain. *British Journal of Criminology, 28*(2), 223–40.

Giddings, P. (1984). *When and where I enter: The impact of black women on race and sex in America.* New York: Morrow.

Giordano, P. C. (1978). Girls, guys and gangs: The changing social context of female delinquency. *Journal of Criminal Law and Criminology, 69* (Spring), 126–32.

Giordano, P. C., Kerbel, S., & Dudley, S. (1981). The economics of female criminality: An analysis of police blotters, 1890–1975. In L. H. Bowker (Ed.), *Women and crime in America* (pp. 65–82). New York: Macmillan.

Gora, J. (1982). *The new female criminal: Empirical reality or social myth.* New York: Praeger.

Gove, W. R. (1985). The effect of age and gender on deviant behavior: A biopsychoso-cial perspective. In A. S. Rossi (Ed.), *Gender and the life course* (pp. 115–44). New York: Aldine.

Grau, J., Fagan, J., & Wexler, S. (1984). Restraining orders for battered women: Issues of access and efficacy. *Women and Politics, 4*(3), 13–28.

Graycar, R. (1986). Yes, Virginia, there is a feminist legal literature: A survey of some recent publications. *Australian Journal of Law and Society, 3*, 105–35.

Griffin, J. T., & Hoffman, N. (Eds.). (1986). Teaching about women, race, and culture. *Women's Studies Quarterly, 14*(1–2).

Gross, E. (1986). What is feminist theory? In C. Pateman & E. Gross (Eds.), *Feminist challenges: Social and political theory* (pp. 190–204). Boston: Northeastern University Press.

Hagan, J., Simpson, J., & Gillis, A. R. (1987). Class in the household: A power-control theory of gender and delinquency. *American Journal of Sociology, 92*(4), 788–816.

Harding, S. (1986). *The science question in feminism.* Ithaca: Cornell University Press.

Harding, S., & Hintikka, M. (Eds.). (1983). *Discovering reality: Feminist perspectives on epistemology, metaphysics, methodology and philosophy of science.* Boston: Reidel.

Harris, A. R. (1977). Sex and theories of deviance: Toward a functional theory of deviant type-scripts. *American Sociological Review, 42*(1), 3–16.

Harris, M. K. (1987). Moving into the new millennium: Toward a feminist vision of justice. *The Prison Journal, 67*(2), 27–38.

Heidensohn, F. M. (1968). The deviance of women: A critique and an enquiry. *British Journal of Sociology, 19*(2), 160–76.

Heidensohn, F. M. (1985). *Women and crime: The life of the female offender.* New York: New York University Press.

Heidensohn, F. M. (1986). Models of justice: Portia or Persephone? Some thoughts on equality, fairness and gender in the field of criminal justice. *International Journal of the Sociology of Law, 14*, 287–98.

Heidensohn, F. M. (1987). Women and crime: Questions for criminology. In P. Carlen & A. Worrall (Eds.), *Gender, crime and justice* (pp. 16–27). Philadelphia: Open University Press.

Hirschi, T., & Gottfredson, M. R. (1987). Causes of white collar crime. *Criminology, 25*(4), 949–74.

Hooks, B. (1981). *Ain't I a woman?* Boston: South End.

Hooks, B. (1984). *Feminist theory: From margin to center.* Boston: South End.

Jaggar, A. M. (1983). *Feminist politics and human nature.* Totowa, N.J.: Rowman & Allenheld.

Jaggar, A. M., & Rothenberg, P. S. (Eds.). (1984). *Feminist frameworks: Alternative theoretical accounts of the relations between men and women* (2nd ed.). New York: McGraw-Hill.

Kelly-Gadol, J. (1977). Did women have a Renaissance? Reprinted 1987 in R. Bridenthal, C. Koonz, & S. Stuard (Eds.), *Becoming visible: Women in European history* (2nd ed.) (pp. 175–201). Boston: Houghton Mifflin.

Klein, D. (1973). The etiology of female crime: A review of the literature. *Issues in Criminology, 8,* 3–30.

Klein, D. (1982). The dark side of marriage: Battered wives and the domination of women. In N. H. Rafter & E. A. Stanko (Eds.), *Judge, lawyer, victim, thief* (pp. 83–107). Boston: Northeastern University Press.

Klein, R. D. (1987). The dynamics of the women's studies classroom: A review essay of the teaching practice of women's studies in higher education. *Women's Studies International Forum, 10*(2), 187–206.

Kramarae, C., & Treichler, P. A. (1985). *A feminist dictionary.* Boston: Pandora/Routledge & Kegan Paul.

Leonard, E. B. (1983). Judicial decisions and prison reform: The impact of litigation on women prisoners. *Social Problems, 31*(1), 45–58.

Lerman, L. G. (1980). Protection of battered women: A survey of state legislation. *Women's Rights Law Reporter, 6*(4), 271–84.

Lopata, H. Z., & Thorne, B. (1978). On the term "sex roles." *Signs: Journal of Women in Culture and Society, 3*(3), 718–21.

MacKinnon, C. A. (1982). Feminism, Marxism, method, and the state: An agenda for theory. *Signs: Journal of Women in Culture and Society, 7*(3), 515–44.

MacKinnon, C. A. (1983). Feminism, Marxism, method, and the state: Toward feminist jurisprudence. *Signs: Journal of Women in Culture and Society, 8*(4), 635–58.

MacKinnon, C. A. (1987). *Feminism unmodified: Discourses on life and law.* Cambridge, Mass.: Harvard University Press.

Majury, D. (1987). Strategizing in equality. *Wisconsin Women's Law Journal, 3,* 169–87.

McCormack, A., Janus, M.-K., & Burgess, A. W. (1986). Runaway youths and sexual victimization: Gender differences in an adolescent runaway population. *Child Abuse and Neglect, 10,* 387–95.

Messerschmidt, J. W. (1986). *Capitalism, patriarchy, and crime: Toward a socialist feminist criminology.* Totowa, N.J.: Rowman & Littlefield.

Miller, E. M. (1986). *Street woman.* Philadelphia: Temple University Press.

Millman, M. (1975). She did it all for love: A feminist view of the sociology of deviance. In M. Millman & R. M. Kanter (Eds.), *Another voice: Feminist perspectives on social life and social science* (pp. 251–79). Garden City, N.Y.: Anchor/Doubleday.

Mitchell, J., & Oakley, A. (Eds.). (1986). *What is feminism?* New York: Pantheon.

Morris, A. (1987). *Women, crime and criminal justice.* New York: Blackwell.

Moyer, I. L. (1985). Crime, conflict theory, and the patriarchal society. In I. L. Moyer (Ed.), *The changing roles of women in the criminal justice system* (pp. 1–29). Prospect Heights, Ill.: Waveland.

Musheno, M., & Seeley, K. (1986). Prostitution policy and the women's movement. *Contemporary Crises, 10,* 237–55.

Nagel, I. H., & Hagan, J. (1983). Gender and crime: Offense patterns and criminal court sanctions. In M. H. Tonry & N. Morris (Eds.), *Crime and justice: An annual review of research,* vol. 4 (pp. 91–144). Chicago: University of Chicago Press.

National Institute of Justice, U.S. Department of Justice. (1985). Replicating an experiment in special deterrence: Alternative police responses to spouse assault, Research solicitation.

National Institute of Justice, U.S. Department of Justice. (1988). Spouse assault replication program, start-up designs. Unpublished mimeo.

Osborne, J. A. (1984). Rape law reform: A new cosmetic for Canadian women. *Women and Politics, 4*(3), 49–64.

Parisi, N. (1982). Are females treated differently? A review of the theories and evidence on sentencing and parole decisions. In N. H. Rafter & E. A. Stanko (Eds.), *Judge, lawyer, victim, thief* (pp. 205–20). Boston: Northeastern University Press.

Pateman, C. (1986). The theoretical subversiveness of feminism. In C. Pateman & E. Gross (Eds.), *Feminist challenges: Social and political theory* (pp. 1–10). Boston: Northeastern University Press.

Quarm, D., & Schwartz, M. D. (1984). Domestic violence in criminal court: An examination of new legislation in Ohio. *Women and Politics, 4*(3), 29–46.

Rafter, N. H. (1985). *Partial justice: Women in state prisons, 1800–1935.* Boston: Northern University Press.

Reckless, W. C. (1961). *The crime problem* (3rd ed.). New York: Appleton-Century-Crofts.

Resnik, J., & Shaw, N. (1980). Prisoners of their sex: Health problems of incarcerated women. In I. Robbins (Ed.), *Prisoners' rights sourcebook: Theory, litigation and practice,* vol. 2 (pp. 319–413). New York: Clark Boardman.

Rhode, D. (1987). Justice, gender, and the justices. In L. L. Crites & W. L. Hepperle (Eds.), *Women, the courts, and equality* (pp. 13–34). Newbury Park, Calif.: Sage.

Rich, A. (1980). Compulsory heterosexuality and lesbian existence. *Signs: Journal of Women in Culture and Society, 5*(4), 631–60.

Rights of Women, Family Law Subgroup. (1985). Campaigning around family law: Politics and practice. In J. Brophy & C. Smart (Eds.), *Women in law: Explorations in law, family, and sexuality* (pp. 188–206). Boston: Routledge & Kegan Paul.

Rodgers, K. O. (1972). For her own protection . . . Conditions of incarceration for female juvenile offenders in the state of Connecticut. *Law and Society Review, 7*(2), 223–46.

Rosen, R. (1982). *The lost sisterhood: Prostitution in America, 1900–1918.* Baltimore: Johns Hopkins University Press.

Rosenbaum, M. (1981). *Women on heroin.* New Brunswick, N.J.: Rutgers University Press.

Schlossman, S., & Wallach, S. (1978). The crime of precocious sexuality: Female juvenile delinquency and the Progressive era. *Harvard Educational Review, 48*(1), 65–94.

Schneider, E. M. (1986). Describing and changing: Women's self-defense work and the problem of expert testimony on battering. *Women's Rights Law Reporter, 9*(3–4), 195–225.

Schur, E. M. (1984). *Labeling women deviant: Gender, stigma, and social control.* New York: Random House.

Schweber, C. (1982). The government's unique experiment in salvaging women criminals: Cooperation and conflict in the administration of a women's prison—The case of the federal industrial institution for women at Alderson. In N. H. Rafter & E. A. Stanko (Eds.), *Judge, lawyer, victim, thief* (pp. 277–303). Boston: Northeastern University Press.

Schweber, C., & Feinman, C. (Eds.). (1984). Criminal justice politics and women: The aftermath of legally mandated change. *Women and Politics, 4*(3). Reprint, Haworth (1985).

Schwendinger, J. R., & Schwendinger, H. (1983). *Rape and inequality.* Newbury Park, Calif.: Sage.

Shane-DuBow, S., Brown, A. P., & Olsen, E. (1985). *Sentencing reform in the United States: History, context, and effect.* National Institute of Justice, U.S. Department of Justice. Washington, D.C.: U.S. Government Printing Office.

Sherman, J. A., & Beck, E. T. (Eds.). (1979). *The prism of sex: Essays in the sociology of knowledge.* Madison: University of Wisconsin Press.

Sherman, L. A., & Berk, R. A. (1984). The specific deterrent effects of arrest for domestic violence. *American Sociological Review, 49*(2), 261–92.

Silbert, M., & Pines, A. M. (1981). Sexual child abuse as an antecedent to prostitution. *Child Abuse and Neglect, 5*, 407–11.

Simon, R. J. (1975). *Women and crime.* Lexington, Mass.: Lexington Books.

Singer, L. (1973). Women and the correctional process. *American Criminal Law Review, 11*(2), 295–308.

Smart, C. (1976). *Women, crime and criminology: A feminist critique.* Boston: Routledge & Kegan Paul.

Smart, C. (1979). The new female criminal: Reality or myth? *British Journal of Criminology, 19*(1), 50–59.

Smart, C. (1985). Legal subjects and sexual objects: Ideology, law and female sexuality. In J. Brophy & C. Smart (Eds.), *Women in law: Explorations in law, family and sexuality* (pp. 50–70). Boston: Routledge & Kegan Paul.

Smith, D. A., & Paternoster, R. (1987). The gender gap in theories of deviance: Issues and evidence. *Journal of Research in Crime and Delinquency, 24*(2), 140–72.

Sokoloff, N. J. (1980). *Between money and love: The dialectics of women's home and market work.* New York: Praeger.

Spencer, C. C. (1987). Sexual assault: The second victimization. In L. L. Crites & W. L. Hepperle (Eds.), *Women, the courts, and equality* (pp. 54–73). Newbury Park, Calif.: Sage.

Stacey, J. (1987). Sexism by a subtler name? Postindustrial conditions and postfeminist consciousness in the Silicon Valley. *Socialist Review, 17*(96), 7–28.

Stacey, J., & Thorne, B. (1985). The missing feminist revolution in sociology. *Social Problems, 32*(4), 301–16.

Stanley, L., & Wise, S. (1983). *Breaking out: Feminist consciousness and feminist research.* Boston: Routledge & Kegan Paul.

Steffensmeier, D. J. (1978). Crime and the contemporary woman: An analysis of changing levels of female property crime, 1960–75. *Social Forces, 57*(2), 566–84.

Steffensmeier, D. J. (1980). Sex differences in patterns of adult crime, 1965–77. *Social Forces, 58*(4), 1080–1109.

Steffensmeier, D. J. (1983). Organizational properties and sex-segregation in the underworld: Building a sociological theory of sex differences in crime. *Social Forces, 61*(4), 1010–32.

Temin, C. E. (1973). Discriminatory sentencing of women offenders. *American Criminal Law Review, 11*(2), 355–72.

Tonry, M. H. (1987). *Sentencing reform impacts.* National Institute of Justice, U.S. Department of Justice. Washington, D.C.: U.S. Government Printing Office.

Vogel, L. (forthcoming). Debating difference: The problem of special treatment of pregnancy in the workplace. *Feminist Studies.*

Walkowitz, J. R. (1980). *Prostitution and Victorian society: Women, class and the state.* New York: Cambridge University Press.

Waring, N. W. (1986). Coming to terms with pornography: Towards a feminist perspective on sex, censorship, and hysteria. In S. Spitzer & A. T. Scull (Eds.), *Research in law, deviance and social control,* vol. 8 (pp. 85–112). Greenwich, Conn.: JAI.

Warren, M. Q. (1982). Delinquency causation in female offenders. In N. H. Rafter & E. A. Stanko (Eds.), *Judge, lawyer, victim, thief* (pp. 181–202). Boston: Northeastern University Press.

Weitzman, L. J. (1985). *The divorce revolution: The unexpected social and economic consequences for women and children in America.* New York: Free Press.

Wilson, J. Q., & Herrnstein, R. J. (1985). *Crime and human nature.* New York: Simon & Schuster.

Wisconsin Women's Law Journal. (1987). Vol. 3. Papers from the 1986 Feminism and Legal Theory Conference, University of Wisconsin Law School, Madison.

Worrall, A. (1987). Sisters in law? Women defendants and women magistrates. In P. Carlen & A. Worrall (Eds.), *Gender, crime and justice* (pp. 108–24). Philadelphia: Open University Press.

Zietz, D. (1981). *Women who embezzle or defraud: A study of convicted felons.* New York: Praeger.

23

An Assensus Model of Justice

HERMAN BIANCHI

The aftermath of crime is often dramatic because our perception of it is usually connected with the problems of good and evil, right and wrong. Such a direct connection arouses emotions and makes us call for redress. This reaction is normal and human, and if in cases of violence the sequence of events is tense, that is natural. Not everyone is a stoic philosopher. In many discussions of crime control, unfortunately, the omission of the search for a definition of good and evil often affects the arguments in negative ways. In view of the importance of the matter and its often serious effects, we must first find out whether we can agree not only on the ways in which crimes in our society are usually defined but also on the ways in which their consequences are assessed.

We know from everyday experience that defining crime can create great difficulties. What you term execution, I might call homicide; the person you call a freedom fighter, I might call a terrorist; and what you call use, I might term theft. And the definitions of crime differ not only among persons but also in relation to time and place. Yesterday's crime may not be tomorrow's crime, and a crime here may not be a crime there. Regarding the problem of crime definition, we suffer apparently from one of the most elementary human deficiencies: lack of precise knowledge concerning good and evil, the primordial predicament of humankind. The biblical myth of what happened in the Garden of Eden was an attempt to give a religious explanation of this human incapacity. Man was created good and had, in consequence, knowledge of good but not of evil. In the Garden of Eden, humans succeeded in getting acquainted with evil, to our utter confusion ever since. We are too good to be entirely evil and too evil to be entirely good.

We have tried, of course, to work out legal definitions to help us. But these definitions are of only limited help. For words of law must be put into practice by statements of a court, and who would agree with all the verdicts pronounced by all the courts on this globe?

If it were easy to know good and evil, the definition of crime would not be so much of a problem. If it were easy to distinguish between right and wrong human performances, we would not labor in assessing the consequences of crime. But defining and assessing good and evil are thorny matters, and whatever the system of crime control, it is our duty to find a solution. We cannot simply shut our eyes and appease our conscience by thinking that law has solved most of the problems. Ignoring the definition of crime and refraining from the assessment of consequences would be worse. Society could not endure.

Since the beginning of human civilization, people surely have tried to find the right way in the thorny fields of good and evil by more or less successful definitions of norms and values. But that only put off a solution because norms and values themselves can be defined in endless ways.

Through centuries of trial and error, people in Western society have followed three roads in coping with the problem of defining crime, and on this basis we can distinguish three models for interpreting norms and values: the *consensus model*, the *dissensus model*, and the *assensus model*. From the viewpoint of sociolegal theory these three models are ideal types, meant to sensitize our thinking. In society they rarely, if ever, appear in pure form. This chapter will analyze them separately, in order to come to a better understanding of the problem of crime definition, the assessment of its consequences, and the arrangement of crime conflict and its resolution.

The Consensus Model

The consensus model presumes that there is basic agreement among the members of a society with regard to the interpretation of norms and values. Any conflict emerging from the generally accepted interpretation is considered such an unacceptable threat to an orderly society that strict rules are enacted for clearing away the conflict. This clearance is carried out by a stratified organization of administrators of justice, representing and personifying the assumed fundamental agreement.

The consensus model is in reality one of the boldest, most megalomaniac conceptions society has reached for social control. With fear of divergence and uncertainty so great, effective measures seem necessary to rule out all ambiguity once and for all. That applies to our present system of crime control. In the Age of Enlightenment, during which the bulk of our institutions of crime control originated, an excessive confidence in the abilities of legislators made people believe that courts had to do nothing but pronounce the words of the law. The law, however, does not clearly specify under what cultural circumstances human acts can be called crimes. Administrators of justice (and in some countries their helpers, the jurors) have for that reason been endowed with the monopoly of interpretation. The result is that a creature from outer space would be perplexed on our planet to see that person A kills person B and is invested with a medal of honor, whereas person C kills person D and is arrested, convicted, and executed.

The problem lies in the craft of our semantic skills and the vileness of our justificatory logic. Nobody denies that theft and violence ought to be considered unethical or immoral. Even a professional thief will admit that theft is objectionable when the thief is the victim. The most violent gangster and the most bellicose military commander will say that violence carried out against them is illicit, though considering their own identical acts to be acceptable. Politics is even more frightening, because there the ends are so often thought to justify the means. The military computes death rates in "limited" nuclear wars, the administrators of justice desecrate convicted human beings by using them as "deterrents" in national anticrime crusades, and the most massive war acts are called surgical bombings. Our skill for putting violent words in sheep's clothing is overwhelming; think of ethnic cleansing.

With the wide divergence in ethical matters, the rulers of Western society have thought it necessary to appease their people. To avoid troublesome questions, crime controllers have invented the consensus model, which assumes that most of us agree on moral and ethical matters. This model implies that fear of anomie is not justified, that we don't need to panic. Once the model is generally accepted and immense moral and political power is turned over to police, courts, and prison administrators, no ethical problem exists, for these officials are presumed to personify the consensus. They speak our words and express our thoughts, so we are expected to accept their judgment without further discussion, for now justice is being done.

In the consensus model we are expected not only to agree on norms and values and their interpretation; we are also assumed to agree that conflicts are unwelcome, noxious occurrences, threatening our social existence and our society, so that harsh measures must be taken against those who thus jeopardize the social balance. Unchecked conflicts might lead to anarchy. It is understandable that in a crime control system relying so evidently on punitive measures, a well-empowered but otherwise well-controlled body should administer these firm and often harsh operations.

As a matter of course, if one thinks war is the ultimate way of solving international political problems, it is not a bad idea to institute a standing army and to establish it in a securely organized and well-controlled setting. If one adheres to the opinion that a war against crime implemented by a repressive system is the best way of coping with criminality, it seems appropriate to set up a standing, safely organized, and well-controlled body for criminal justice administration. The painful disadvantage of standing organizations, however, is that sooner or later they need to take action to prove themselves. Still, it seems a logical and watertight way of arguing. But is it a correct way of applying logic? Yes, if one accepts the premise.

It becomes a socially and ethically unacceptable argument if the premise is incorrect. And because the overall results of the repressive system are so blatantly unsatisfactory, one should have grave doubts about it. Criminality has never decreased as a result of repression; when it has decreased, the decrease was the result of political and economic factors and not because of the efficient administration of repressive justice.

Analyzing the consensus model a bit further, we find that the assumption of a firm consensus in society is not based on reliable research. It is rather an ancient, stereotyped way of thinking. Even in modern times, courts have rarely ordered sociological research regarding the normative values that they pretend to interpret in agreement with all people. In truth, this presumed consensus in the interpretation of norms runs counter to everyday experience. But in the consensus model such reservations are of no importance. For the model has become a persistent, quasi-metaphysical dogma and a logical axiom, not requiring further evidence. It is simply needed, not so much to maintain peace in society—for the model does not work and we have to live under an anomic system—but rather to give peace of mind to all those who find their work in the administration of justice. They would have sleepless nights if they thought their own work did not express the moral needs of the whole society.

What is the origin of this dogma, and why was it formulated? Since the Age of Enlightenment the consensus model has constituted a part of the dogma of the existence of a "social contract," the belief in some general agreement among citizens to cooperate for social benefits, e.g., by sacrificing some individual freedom in exchange for state protection.

In the course of the eighteenth century, as we have seen, trust in people's ability to resolve their own conflicts in a eunomic system of law gradually gave way to an exclusive system of state monopoly. Settlement of disputes was thus gradually taken out of the hands of the citizens, who in the course of several centuries unlearned little by little how to cope with their own conflicts. Their natural skills atrophied. The monopolized repressive system of crime control resulted in so much power being put into the hands of punitive controllers, and the abuses were so outrageous, that normal citizens could not as a matter of course be entrusted with such an intricate exercise of power. It seemed quite logical to allow a bureaucracy of more or less professional administrators of punishment to do the job. In the view of those who believed in the social contract, the citizens were quite happy to be relieved of the duty of resolving conflicts.

The consensus model assumes that the system of crime control is governed by strict rules and that criminal trials indeed solve the conflicts brought to them. But everyone knows that trials, like wars, do not solve conflicts, since they affect neither the cause nor the administered solution. Every war generates the germ of the next conflict, and every conviction implemented by the repressive system generates the germ of a new crime. But any such supposition is taboo in a consensus system; dogmatic doctrines are not supposed to be challenged. Many criminologists and well-informed lawyers may pronounce their doubts about its effectiveness, but the consensus model seems to stand firm.

On still closer scrutiny, the consensus model appears to be based on another assumption, rarely unveiled but as a matter of fact strongly felt by all participants. In order to serve the assumption of a social contract, our cultural system is believed to be composed of two layers: an upper culture and numerous subcultures underneath. This conception is a rather stereotyped construction of social reality. It can be compared to a similar conception with regard to language. Language likewise is believed to consist of two layers. At the top is the general civilized language, the received speech of cultivated, educated, well-bred, and civilized people. The people speaking that variety of a language are considered to be right-thinking and right-minded, having the right opinions about norms and values. They therefore are entitled to occupy the powerful positions, where morals are devised. In short, they are the moral entrepreneurs. The members of this culture are so self-assured that they often see themselves simply as *the* culture. But not everyone happens to speak, behave, believe, and act according to the norms and values of the upper culture. Daily experience shows that many groups construct different realities, acting apparently according to norm interpretations more or less at variance from those of the upper culture. How is this problem to be solved?

In a consensus model the solution seems easy. According to this model the concept of an upper culture is badly needed in order to weigh the variances of subcultures. Upper culture thus is believed to function as a sort of train schedule through which we get not only information about the departure and arrival times of trains but also about how far the trains are deviating from the schedule. A consensus model likewise needs an assumed upper culture in order to assess and control deviance.

In itself such a pattern of normative interpretation appears quite acceptable, but only if the upper culture is indeed a fair guide for the assessment of subcultural deviance. If all members of society without exception considered the upper culture as their own, supporting and helping them to shape their lives—if they experienced it as eunomic, serving all of them—it would be excellent. But reality is different. In general it is a subculture, not the upper culture, that provides people with eunomie. People experience eunomie if they can take part in the interpretation of norms and values, not if such an interpretation is imposed on them. But in a consensus model the division of upper culture and subculture unfortunately generates anomie.

The upper culture serves in reality as a subculture to those who actually have the power of moral enterprise. These powerful people experience eunomie because they know the ins and outs of their own culture. They seem amazed that members of other cultures become bewildered when strange moral interpretations are forced on them. If representatives of the upper culture could acknowledge that their interpretations are in fact subcultural, things might be better. But they cannot, not in a consensus model.

In particular, the dispensers of justice behave like members of a subculture. They rarely explain their particular interpretations of norms, unfairly taking for granted that "of course" everyone knows what they mean. Since this pretended upper culture serves as just another subculture, though endowed with the power of enforcement, it contributes in large measure to alienation in society.

Eunomie can arise only when people partake in interpretations of morals concerning their own conflicts. Countries with the jury system should not be misled by the illusion of democracy assumed in this remarkable institution. A jury system of whatever kind by no means contributes to eunomie, since it is in all respects part of a punitive system and shares its anomic features. Jury verdicts do not settle disputes between parties or open the way to reconciliation and redress. A jury simply contributes to the repressive expulsion of offenders from society, to alienation of offenders and victims from their own conflicts, and as such it generates as much anomie as do repressive crime control systems without juries. If a jury were a body of persons sworn to render solidarity to conflicting parties in dispute settlement, to accused and plaintiff alike, it might be marvelous. But the jury doesn't. The jury has been, since its very beginning, a lost opportunity. In the United States one even gets the impression that juries are intentionally selected to reinforce subcultural or racial tensions and thus to intensify anomie.

A consensus model is not only the determining principle of an anomic system; it is also its sting. Not only does it constitute the chief ingredient for the punitive model; it also produces the justification needed for disciplining mere deviance. When a consensus model is prevalent, the dispensers of justice create punishable deviance by labeling it as such, largely for the maintenance and continuation of their pain-inflicting bureaucracy.

The consensus model unfortunately has found support in structural functionalism. This sociological syndrome sees society as operating like a living organism. Consensus, according to this theory, is a pressing need of society, a necessity for the maintenance of the whole system and by implication for law and order. Any kind of conflict, any kind of deviance, might in principle constitute a danger for the social system. Therefore, a workable social system provides itself with a servomechanism to prevent conflicts from arising; if they do nevertheless arise, a built-in and well-constructed institution becomes operative to eliminate conflicts and to make deviance innocuous. When social reality is interpreted according to a model of structural functionalism, survival of society is the highest pursuable value—and not just any society or a better one but rather the existing one. Any official action is justifiable as long as the system is kept hobbling.

We find several varieties of this kind of social interpretation in modern criminology. One is the so-called theory of social engineering, which holds that the maintenance of society should be realized, if possible, by decent and efficient means. Conflict should be prevented by effective servomechanisms that keep society in continuous balance by due measures at timely moments. Usually, it is assumed, moderate measures of adjustment, if applied at the right moment, will produce a greater effect than harsh punitive arrangements badly administered and perhaps not accepted or internalized by society.

This sort of thinking does not seem unreasonable and is welcome to some. But social engineering is still very far from generating eunomic crime control. Under some circumstances, social engineering might even hamper eunomie, as long as it maintains a basically anomic system. Anomie does not become less objectionable if maintained by methods that should serve a better end.

We have an example in history: the "enlightened" princes of the eighteenth century. They wanted to keep their power upright by applying moderate, decent, but effective means and not by what they saw as the stupid harshness of their predecessors. But they remained authoritarian rulers. It might be argued that they contributed to the emergence of democratic movements in the nineteenth and twentieth centuries, but that is a matter of historical interpretation. Respectable methods of social engineering, if applied in a eunomic model, might indeed contribute eventually to the emergence of eunomie. But social engineering is not eunomie in itself, and it leads to eunomie only if certain conditions are fulfilled.

Another example is the concept of due process. It implies that fairness is offered by law and codes of criminal procedure, if only the requirements of the law are duly adopted. According to this concept, offenders get sufficient chance to defend themselves and to obtain fair trials if their lawyers and legal aid providers are willing to demand strict application of all the legal requisites.

The idea of due process is alluring, enchanting almost, if the legislator's original intentions had been to grant fair eunomic trials to everyone. But fair legislation, usually prepared by jurist-clerks, is not intended for all citizens, only for those who comply with certain conditions. These conditions include acceptance of the consensus model, for the decisions are made by the court and not by the conflicting parties; overall agreement of all justiciable participants to the consensus based on the existing procedural rules; their willingness and ability to speak the language of their prosecutors; and the means to afford lawyers who can get the court to observe all the legal technicalities. If offenders do not meet these conditions, no lawyer can help them. Thus, due process, being the precise application of a wrong system of conflict control, does not lead to eunomie.

Due process may nonetheless have a favorable effect in the long run, for it may awaken people's interest in the necessity of rules, particularly rules of procedure. But it will help only if concerned parties—accused and plaintiffs—learn again to settle their own disputes, if need be by rules and procedures. Eunomie is based on rules known by and observable by the parties concerned.

It may be useful here to reflect on the remarkable expression "to take the law into one's own hands." Where does the negative connotation of this expression come from? After all, it seems quite reasonable for people to take the law into their own hands. It is their law; it is everyone's law, and not just the repressive system's law. In reality it is the punitive administrators who take the law into their own hands, as if it were their property, while excluding the parties concerned. It is evident, of course, that the negative meaning of the expression originates from the simple fact that under a professionalized punitive system the concerned parties lose their skill in the proper use of the law. It would be better if the legal system taught people how to take the law into their own hands and to apply the law for a proper and fair solution of their conflicts. That would generate eunomie.

The Dissensus Model

A dissensus model, in contrast to a consensus model, claims that regarding the interpretation of norms and values, the members of society never did and never will agree. Any assumption of such agreement distorts reality. Given dissensus, conflict is conceived quite positively as an effective and necessary means for setting up discussions on the interpretation of norms and values, for contesting normative repression, and for safeguarding value-related interests. While the consensus model embraces the proud but careless assumption of general knowledge about good and evil, about right and wrong, the existence of such comfortable knowledge is disputed in a dissensus model.

Dissensus stems from an entirely different conception of culture. According to a dissensus model, all culture is entirely and exclusively built up of subcultures. Members of a society who call their own subculture the upper culture, or simply "culture," can do so only because, as a "top" culture, they are endowed with power to enforce their interpretation of norms on "bottom" subcultures. There are subcultures with and without such potentialities. According to a dissensus model, the subdued and oppressed bottom cultures should confront the powerful top cultures: This is the eternal struggle between top dogs and underdogs. Whereas power plays the important part in a consensus model, confrontation of power comes to the fore in a dissensus model.

From the viewpoint of social mechanics, the dissensus model is quite interesting. It shows a continuous tendency either toward a consensus model or toward an assensus model; otherwise it might end up in a sociocultural deadlock. If one of the disputing parties in subcultural disputes acquires sufficient power, it will try to enforce its interpretation on the others and thereby reach the status of consensus model. A dissensus model is a small-scale civil war, violent or nonviolent, between subcultures. Victory by either party leads to a consensus model. If the dissensus model tends toward an assensus model, parties come to some sort of fragile agreement that can be disturbed at any moment when old suspicions return.

If a dissensus model continues for a long time, it has a tendency to end in stalemate, for parties disputing along the lines of dissensus will try to organize themselves for the sake of survival. But then they will follow the destiny of all organizations: They will build up a bureaucracy, and all bureaucracy tends to perpetuate itself for nothing except the guarantee of jobs for the faithful.

A dissensus model in our culture is in fact more familiar than a consensus model, the latter being used only in anomic and repressive crime control. The dissensus model is most common in international affairs. It is particularly cherished by rulers of superpowers. When the cold war was still going on, the superpowers often claimed to be champions of political values such as democracy and human rights. Their discussions usually had a propagandistic intent that allowed them to depict the opponent as evil and lacking all credibility. In a dissensus model one needs an enemy. This model is less common among nations on friendly terms with one another.

In many degrees of fierceness we find the dissensus model in our sociocultural system: in labor, housing, and armament, particularly nuclear arms. The means used in a politicized dissensus model are strikes, demonstrations, squatting, siege, occupation of buildings, barricades, etc.; these actions are meant to force the other side to discuss and negotiate. In recent times, ancient means of violent dissensus enforcement—such as hijacking, piracy, kidnapping, and hostage taking—have reappeared. They indicate a serious escalation of dissent. In a dissensus model the risk of escalation is always present, and sometimes even intended.

The ultimate aim of a dissensus model is civil war and eventual imposition of a consensus model by the victors. Citizens become fed up with aggressive dissensus and are, in their longing for peace, willing to submit themselves again to a political consensus model. But that will not last long either, except in the case of a dictatorship.

A dissensus model has been tried recently in the procedures of repressive criminal justice. Terrorists in particular have tried to use the model for their purposes. They have often succeeded in turning their trials into political dissensus arenas. They committed their crimes for political reasons, often using the same semantic tricks as their repressive opponents: They called homicide a coincidental casualty in wartime, or murder a popular execution, or bank robbery a confiscation or redistribution of wealth. Human semantic ingenuity is infinite. But semantic objections should be addressed to both controllers and terrorists.

The mischievous aspect of the whole thing is that in both models—consensus and dissensus—the participants seem to care nothing about the follow-up of crime. In a consensus model the administrators of justice inflict pain without much consideration for offenders or society, and they ignore the victims (plaintiffs). Justice in their narrow view is just retaliation for the crimes they have labeled as evil. Terrorists are by no means held responsible, nor are they concerned about the evil outcome of their actions.

Dispensers of justice, whether they are public prosecutors, police, courts, or juries, pretend to have clean hands. As soon as the thorny subject of the follow-up of their pretended justice is raised, they look like children of innocence. It is not different with terrorists. I know of only one occasion when terrorists, during trial, spoke about innocent victims and offered to redress some of the hurt they had done to innocent people. They did so out of free will, not because the court demanded it. Punitive courts never demand responsibility and liability.

Does the dissensus model deserve serious consideration in matters of crime control and criminal procedures? Experience so far has proved far from favorable. The dissensus model is based entirely on political views; it stands or falls by politicization. It implies that crimes should be explained predominantly in political terms. Even if we grant that more criminality can be explained in political terms than many dispensers of today's repressive system are willing to admit, a crime is a crime. In a consensus model, politicization of crime is taboo. In a dissensus model, however, things move to the other extreme: Most crime is considered political protest or the forgivable consequence of political action.

A dissensus model applied in criminal cases tends to be cleared away by semantic ingenuity. Even if all crime is called political action, the negative results of the crime are there, and they need redress. Political or not, anyone committing a crime must be held responsible and liable.

The Assensus Model

The assensus model recognizes that full agreement with regard to the interpretation of norms and values among members of a society does not exist, has never existed, will never exist, and can therefore not be pretended either. In light of the human incapacity to make final judgments in matters of right and wrong, interpretations of norms and values must be made in a never-ending and open process of discussion.

In an assensus model, emerging conflicts are transposed into dispute settlements between the parties directly involved. In crime cases, a reconciliatory redress in the postcrime situation is a mandatory subject of discussion.

The assensus model is not a relativization of matters of good and evil. It is most certainly not laxity in what is most important in human relations. On the contrary, in an assensus model the problems of right and wrong are taken so seriously that one is aware of our incapacity to pronounce final statements about them. In an assensus model one is suspicious of all final judgments: Do not judge lest thou be judged. Most evil is the result of aggressive counteraction against evil. Just as most aggression is counteraggression, most violence is counterviolence, most punishment is countercrime, and most evil is counterevil. The original evil is abused to justify counterevil. But counterevil is as much evil as the original evil. It can come to a halt only if we stop applying evil, aggression, violence, and punishment, whether it be an original or a counteraction.

The fundamental principles of the assensus model have never been better analyzed than by Cardinal Newman. In *An Essay in Aid of a Grammar of Assent* he was engaged with the problems of faith and doctrine. He had a very practical and empirical mind, and that is why he wanted to establish the groundwork for human competence in ethical and religious affairs. In judgment, he argued, rules a twofold sentiment. One is the notional assent, which is purely conceptual, infertile, and often misleading. It is a kind of perceiving of reality that obstructs real cognition. The other is real assent, the positive and substantial accord to understanding and sensibility. Real assent involves the essentials of human existence; it needs the whole person.

All assent may have to be part of a long process, but in the case of real assent, interaction and adjustment are needed for it to come about. Assent is subtle and cannot be forced. It is generated by being with others as much as being by oneself. A community has to live with truth, to meditate on it, come to an affection with it, and learn to give it reverence. In the *Grammar*, Newman uses what he calls the illative sense of meaning, a motion toward or into meaning. As an inference he states: I can prove Christian faith to my own satisfaction, but I can never force it upon someone else; assent is a body of grounds in their totality, although I cannot know all the grounds except by half-articulate experience.

Newman was a forerunner of the existentialism of the twentieth century or, as far as the social sciences are concerned, of interactionism. All perception, all cognition, is always part of an interactionist process: We are incapable of any competence if we do not engage ourselves with other people as much as with ourselves. Cognition demands interaction, and interaction generates cognition.

Assensus is likewise the ground principle of the way in which Jewish people through the centuries have been dealing with Torah. Torah does not allow final judgment; it implies rather general directives, indications, road signs, invocations to discussion. Dealing with Torah is like taking a meal. We need food to stay alive, but taking food is also one of the major patterns of social interaction. We need sex, but having sex is likewise a major social interaction. Eating and having sex take place in our cultures in ceremonials and rituals, in old institutions as much as in arranged sceneries and playgrounds, but their social settings are as important as their biological ones, if not more so.

So it is with law. Finding law, equity, and justice is a major pattern of social interaction. And the support of social interaction produced in the process of assessing law and justice is as important as the law itself. Is not the law there for us, instead of us being there for the law? Without social interaction in a reasonable and fair setting, there will be no justice. But what is a reasonable setting? The answer is not difficult: A reasonable setting exists when all parties directly concerned can interact.

In Jewish tradition, Torah interpretation usually occurred in a *bethmidrash*, a house of learning. This term speaks volumes, for Torah is not applied but is learned; Torah is not imposed but is pursued in an open and neverending process. Some people are more learned in the law than others, but everyone is expected to take part.

We find a similar pattern of social interaction in non-Jewish traditions. In antiquity, justice was often discussed at the forum, the marketplace. All people concerned could take part in discussions about law, equity, and justice. That is the way to find justice, to pursue equity, and to arrange the problems of crime control.

We can see the assensus model all around us, in all our social patterns, all our interactions. Except in the present crime control system, it is omnipresent in the legal system; for the assensus model is nothing out of the ordinary. Unlike consensus and dissensus, assensus is the ground principle of our culture and our legal system. We practice the law when we shop, drive, discuss politics, vote, and settle neighborhood disputes. Though reactionaries might argue that people in modern society have unlearned to partake in law-and-justice interactions, the contrary is true. People are still as capable and eager in law interactions and discussions as they have ever been, notwithstanding the complexity of modern legislation.

Why has social interaction concerning crime control been taken out of our hands? Why is the modern criminal courtroom so alien? If juries would hold their discussions in the presence of offenders and victims, defendants and plaintiffs, then justice might be obtainable. It is a sickening delusion to speak of justice in the absence of the major parties. It is difficult to understand how an otherwise democratic culture such as ours could ever develop the ritual of criminal procedure that we now have. It contravenes all patterns of human experience regarding social life.

It is no better in the courtrooms of Europe where juries are either unknown or where just a few laymen take part in repressive decisions. The defendant may always be present in the courtroom, but the inequality in power between defendant and public prosecutor is so vast as to make justice unobtainable.

It is not that administrators of justice are unwilling or of bad character. "The senators are usually fine but the senate is awful," as the Romans used to say. The structures of criminal trial as we know them today, after erroneous development over several centuries, are unfit to generate justice of any kind. So many excellent representatives of the judiciary who could do a better job have no workable structures at their disposal.

Yet the assensus model is not all paradise. The great peril, always alluring, is power. People generate many mock justifications to defend their use of power. They argue that the only way to control power is to use counterpower, forgetting that the original abuser of power had used the same argument. So they are doing nothing but stepping into an escalation process. When the state received almost unlimited power, a monopoly of violence, using power against power, making the offender powerless, the result was not a balance of power, not even a control of power. The result was rather an overpowering force, so that normal human interaction was out of the question.

There can never be justice when the offender is made powerless. Justice does not endure powerless persons. Of course we are not justifying the offender. There is no apology for crime or criminal. But overpowering the offender does not result in justice.

References

Abel, R. (Ed.). (1982). *The politics of informal justice*. New York: Academic Press.

Armstrong, T. E. (1988). *Japanese consensus methods and their relevance to Canada*. Kingston, Ontario: Industrial Relations Centre, Queen's University at Kingston.

Atkinson, D. (1971). *Orthodox consensus and radical alternative: A study in sociological theory*. London: Heinemann.

Aubert, V. (1963). Competition and dissensus: Two types of conflict resolution. *Journal of Conflict Resolution, 7*, 26–42.

Bau, P. (1964). *Exchange of power in social life*. London: Wiley.

Beran, H. (1987). *The consent theory of political obligation*. London: Croom Helm.

Bernard, T. J. (1983). *The consensus-conflict debate: Form and content in social theories*. New York: Columbia University Press.

Center for the Study of Democratic Institutions. (1963). *Natural law and modern society*. Cleveland: World.

Clastres, P. (1974). *La société contre l'état*. Paris: Editions de Minuit.

Franks, C. E. S. (1989). *Dissent and the state*. Toronto: Oxford University Press.

Gurvitch, G. (1962). *Dialectique et sociologie*. Paris: Presses Universitaires de France.

Herzog, D. (1989). *Happy slaves: A critique of consent theory*. Chicago: University of Chicago Press.

Hodges, H. (1971). *Conflict and consensus: An introduction to sociology*. New York: Harper & Row.

Le Goff, J., & Nora, P. (1974). *Faire l'histoire*. 3 vols. Paris: Gallimard.

Lipset, S. M. (1985). *Consensus and conflict: Essays in political sociology*. New Brunswick: Transaction Books.

Partridge, P. (1970). *Consent and consensus*. New York: Macmillan.

Pepin, J. (1976). *Saint Augustin et la dialectique*. Villanova, Pa.: Augustinian Institute, Villanova University.

Pepinsky, H. (1976). *Crime and conflict: A study of law and society.* London: Martin Robertson.

Pepinsky, H. (1980). *Crime control strategies: An introduction to the study of crime.* New York: Oxford University Press.

Pepinsky, H. (1991). *The geometry of violence and democracy.* Bloomington: Indiana University Press.

Quinney, R. (1977). *The problem of crime: A critical introduction to criminology.* New York: Harper.

Roodenburg, H. (1990). *Onder censuur: De kerkelijke tucht in de gereformeerde gemeente van Amsterdam, 1578–1700.* Hilversum: Verloren.

Rossi, I. (1983). *From the sociology of symbols to the sociology of signs: Toward a dialectical sociology.* New York: Columbia University Press.

Sandywell, B. (1975). *Problems of reflexivity and dialectics in sociological inquiry.* London: Routledge & Kegan Paul.

Siegrist, J. (1970). *Das Consensus-Modell: Studien zur Interaktions theorie und zur kognitiven Sozialisation.* Stuttgart: Ferdinand Enke.

Taylor, I., Walton, P., & Young, J. (1973). *The new criminology: For a social theory of deviance.* London: Routledge & Kegan Paul.

Taylor, I., Walton, P., & Young, J. (Eds.). (1975). *Critical criminology.* London: Routledge & Kegan Paul.

Wheeler, H. (Ed.). (1973). *Beyond the punitive society: Operant conditioning, social and political aspects.* San Francisco: W. H. Freeman.

24

A Communitarian Theory of Social Order

PETER CORDELLA

Social order in a given society is achieved and maintained through the establishment of sources of willing conformity and the use of mechanisms of social control. The social consciousness associated with different unity patterns creates a sense of willing conformity "by socializing individuals into an understanding of why the established way of doing things is the right way of doing them" (Michalowski, 1985:51). In situations where willing conformity is not sufficient to keep an individual from transgressing the norms, society must use either informal or formal mechanisms of control to maintain social order. Criminologists have generally understood these variables of social order to be inversely related. Most criminological theory has been based on the assumption that as societies have become more complex, the sources of willing conformity have decreased in number and diminished in effectiveness, thereby necessitating greater use of mechanisms of social control, especially formal ones such as criminal law (Sherman, 1993; Michalowski, 1985; Zehr, 1976). As a result, criminology has focused its inquiry almost exclusively on the question of control. With the exception of two well-known studies of societies with little crime (Clinard, 1973; Adler, 1983) almost no attention has been directed to the question of conformity. The lack of interest in the phenomenon of willing conformity can be traced to the widely held belief among criminologists that societies with high levels of willing conformity are characterized by extensive kinship ties and diffuse role structures. Criminologists have perceived such societies to be pathologically overcontrolled and largely irrelevant to the understanding of social order in modern, complex societies (Durkheim, 1933; Kraybill, 1989; Cronk, 1981; Macmurray, 1977).

The criminological critique of social order has suggested that with the increasing division of labor in society, the mutual social order of small-scale, simple societies has given way to the more rational, functional social order of present-day, complex societies. While such an observation of social order is generally true, it fails to take into account either the continued presence of mutual social order in important segments of contemporary society or its importance to the effectiveness of rational, functional social order both in terms of willing conformity and social control. Three distinct unity patterns, corresponding to the three types of social order, exist in every society: One is personally structured, one is organically structured, and one is atomistically structured. In any given society one or more of these unity patterns will become dominant as the other patterns become dependent.

Each of the unity patterns gives individuals an understanding of the nature of social relations and social order. An atomistic unity pattern, based on a rational understanding of social relations, conceives social order in terms of a calculus of coercion embodied in both criminal and civil law. An organic unity pattern, based on a functional understanding of social relations, conceives social order in terms of cooperation embodied in a sense of social obligation. A personal unity pattern, based on a mutualist understanding of social relations, conceives social order in terms of a communitarian ethos embodied in personal trust. Each of these unity patterns is characterized by a distinctive conception of morality that reflects the relational position of persons in different social settings. Morality in this case is defined in terms of Emile Durkheim's (1957) conception of social solidarity. Morality in the Durkheimian sense represents the totality of ties that bind each person to society. Morality makes a unitary aggregate of the mass of individuals. According to Durkheim, everything that is the source of solidarity, everything that forces one to take account of others, and everything that forces one to regulate one's conduct through some process other than the striving of one's ego is moral. For Durkheim morality consists of a state of dependency. This state of dependency may be personal (e.g., familial morality), functional (e.g., occupational morality), or societal (e.g., civic morality).

In an atomistic social setting the lack of either functional interdependence or consistent personal interaction necessitates a mechanical morality (i.e., law). Both order maintenance and conflict resolution in an atomistic setting are achieved through coercive regulation on the part of society and personal calculation on the part of the individual. Law acts mechanically in terms of the particular situation and the specific roles of the individuals involved. The legitimacy of law in an atomistic context is dependent more on its uniform and consistent application than on its content or effectiveness. In an organic social setting the state of dependence among coparticipants necessitates a social morality (i.e., obligation). Order maintenance and conflict resolution in an organic setting are predicated on a social solidarity that is functionally determined. Social morality is limited to an institutional sphere of influence that assumes a free association among institutional members. As long as an institution meets the minimum functional expectations of its members, it will be able to maintain social order effectively by creating a sense of reciprocal cooperation. In a mutualist setting the trust among persons in a relational position generates a personal morality (i.e., communitarianism). Order maintenance and conflict resolution in a mutualist setting are predicated on a sense of concern for others for their own sake. Personal morality is conciliatory in nature, and social harmony is its primary goal. In mutualist settings where trust is central to social interaction, persons can base their actions on considerations other than self-interested and/or functional ones.

The relative balance among unity patterns has been shown to correlate both with a society's level of willing conformity and with the effectiveness of its mechanisms of social control. In their analysis of institutional anomie, Messner and Rosenfeld (1996) have pointed out that to achieve and maintain social order, all institutional patterns of behavior (described above as unity patterns) must be integrated and interrelated to some degree. Because actual social systems are never perfectly integrated, tensions and contradictions within social structures and among social institutions are inevitable. Such normal tensions and contradictions are the source of social problems such as deviance and crime. However, when unity patterns are highly imbalanced, a society will experience abnormally high rates of deviance and crime. Messner and Rosenfeld suggested that the exceptionally high rate of crime in the United States compared with other industrialized and developmentally advanced societies is the result of "cultural contradictions that become particularly acute as a result of a fundamental imbalance in the institutional structure of American society" (1996:143).

The fundamental imbalance to which Messner and Rosenfeld referred is between the macro-level economic structure of American society, which is characterized by an atomistic unity pattern, and mid-level institutional structures, which are characterized by an organic unity pattern. The dominance of the atomistic unity pattern, with its self-interested frame of reference and its rationally calculating approach to social relations, contributes to abnormally high rates of crime by undermining institutional control over the members of society. Because of their organic orientation, social institutions instill in their members a sense of social obligation, which acts to inhibit the deviant impulses of individual members. Social institutions, through socialization and informal mechanisms of control (e.g., ostracism, gossip, etc.), are the primary source of social control in society. In the United States, the dominance of the economically inspired atomistic unity pattern has substantially weakened institutional social control by devaluing all noneconomic (as opposed to economic) social patterns and functions and forcing the subordination of noneconomic roles (e.g., parenting, teaching, friendship, etc.) to economic roles when conflicts arise (Messner and Rosenfeld, 1996). The more social institutions become estranged from their primary mandate of creating social solidarity, the more individual members lose sight of their social obligations. The resulting alienation from social institutions makes it more likely that individuals will deviate. Although self-interested calculations inhibit the deviant impulses of the economically well integrated (because the risk to material and human capital far outweighs the benefit derived from the deviant act), economically marginal individuals will be less inhibited by either the limited risk to their economic well-being or decreasingly relevant social institutions.

Unity Patterns and Willing Conformity

The institutional-anomie theory explains how the imbalance of unity patterns, specifically the imbalance between atomistic and organic unity patterns, diminishes the social control capacity of intermediate institutions. It does not, however, explain the effect of the imbalance of unity patterns on the capacity of social groups to generate willing conformity. Willing conformity, unlike a mechanism of social control, is associated with personal rather than organic unity patterns. Levels of willing conformity in a particular society or social group are determined by the relative presence or absence of personal unity patterns in relation to both atomistic *and* organic unity patterns. Although low levels of deviance and crime can be attributed primarily to either willing conformity or social control in a given social situation, it is also important to note that high levels of willing conformity among members of a social group increase the effectiveness of the group's social control mechanisms. John Braithwaite's analysis of crime, shame, and reintegration suggests that the best place to see *reintegrative* shaming is in a loving family that epitomizes the personal unity pattern. Within such a personal unity pattern, punishment is not "administered within a framework of disharmony and fundamentally irreconcilable interests (as is the case in atomistic or organic contexts), it is imposed within a framework of reconcilable and mutually supportive interests" (Braithwaite, 1994:56). Reintegrative shaming is possible only within the framework of a personal unity pattern, because punishment cannot be reintegrative unless its intent is mutually motivated. In other words, the punishment must be intended to benefit the transgressor as well as the group by allowing him or her to regain full status within the group through showing remorse, accepting responsibility, and making amends. This interactive process restores the transgressor and the group to their original social statuses, thus restoring the trust and mutualist characteristic of willing conformity.

Personal unity patterns are not characteristic of most intermediate institutions. The majority of intermediate institutions are predicated on a functional unity pattern, the primary exception being the family. Personal unity patterns are often found outside institutional frameworks, because the bureaucratic nature of most institutions is designed to limit the personal. Bureaucratic institutions, whatever their specific functions may be, are structured to maintain equal access to all potential clients or members to achieve their stated goal, by definition limiting consideration of the personal. As bureaucracies become more functionally efficient through the extension of the "formal" aspects of interaction, individuals become further removed from personal unity patterns. Unlike organic unity patterns, personal unity patterns require not simply a compatibility of means but also a compatibility of ends (Macmurray, 1977; Hauerwas, 1981). In a personal unity pattern, "our intentions must not be merely possible they must be compossible with those of all others" (Macmurray, 1977:32). "Compossibility" is what distinguishes communitarianism from cooperation. The goal of the latter is strictly functional; individuals come together to commit to a goal out of self-interest. It is a unity of functions, not persons; therefore "the system of cooperation . . . has in itself no reference to justice. Its regulative principle is sheer efficiency . . . the demand for justice in this cooperation is imposed upon it to safeguard the individual rights of all participants and to prevent the sacrifice of freedom to mere efficiency. Justice is a negative and external principle" (Macmurray, 1977:33).

The cooperation that characterizes organic unity patterns requires a rational integration of functions whereby power is concentrated "in the hands of those persons or groups that exercise superior function" (Macmurray, 1977:33). When an incompatibility of intentions arises between those who are deemed to exercise superior functions and those who are not, "those who have superior power will achieve freedom at the expense of their functional inferiors" (Macmurray, 1977:33). Like the economic inequality inherent in atomistic unity patterns, the functional inequality inherent in organic unity patterns militates against the establishment and maintenance of willing conformity. In either an atomistic or organic context, justice is predicated on the mitigation of the concentration of power (either materially or functionally). Justice is therefore external to the lives of the individuals involved in conflict (including crime) because it imposes compossibility; and it is negative because it does so by applying a rule that does not alter the fear-inspired, self-interested motives of the individuals or the group. Individuals in an organic unity pattern are united not as persons but as functions structured to achieve a common purpose. If its structure breaks down or its common purpose disappears, the organic unity pattern loses its legitimacy. For example, when an intermediate institution such as public education is no longer able to fulfill its common purpose for an expanding number of lower-income individuals, it loses its legitimacy as a source of social control for these individuals. If we view all intermediate institutions, including family and religion, in terms of organic unity alone (as most criminologists have done), we should expect less effective informal social control as a result of the general decline of legitimacy among intermediate institutions in contemporary society. Such an analysis, however, ignores the potential of some intermediate institutions and noninstitutional social groups to use their capacity for personal unity to generate willing conformity.

Personal unity patterns, unlike organic unity patterns, are not based on a common purpose; rather, they are constituted by a common life. The common purposes that occur in the context of the personal express rather than constitute the unity of association. Common purposes may change or disappear, but the association remains because its principle of unity is personal. Its unity is one of persons as persons. Personal unity does not express itself in terms of functional differentiation or a division of labor. Unlike cooperative unities, personal unities do not and cannot involve the functional subordination of one person to another. Personal unity is predicated on two basic principles. The first is equality. Although natural and functional differences between individuals do exist and cannot be ignored, personal equality overrides them. "It means that any two human beings whatever their individual differences can recognize and treat one another as equals" (Macmurray, 1977:51). The second principle of personal unity is freedom. It cannot be imposed. It must begin with and remain a free activity between equal persons and it must be mutual and unconstrained. Only in personal unity can someone express his or her whole self. In the context of a cooperative unity individuals can express only their functional identity (e.g., teacher-student, landlord-tenant, manager-employee, etc.), thus playing a part, being other than their complete selves. The inner strength required to limit oneself to a functional identity represents the negative nature of freedom. It is a denial of one's true nature as a person. Only in personal unity, because of its basis in trust, do the constitutive principles of freedom and equality come together (Macmurray, 1974).

The trust and mutuality that characterize personal unity patterns and are conspicuously absent from organic or atomistic unity patterns are established through a communicative process. Braithwaite pointed out that, while all intermediate institutions are characterized by interdependence, only in the personal unity patterns of a communitarian context is this interdependence characterized by trust and mutual obligation (Braithwaite, 1994). In communitarianism interdependence is defined in terms of mutual loyalty rather than individual convenience. Braithwaite suggested that communitarianism is established and maintained through sustained personal interaction among the members of a social group. The sense of mutuality and trust is engendered in an extended series of communicative interactions among all members of the group, regardless of material and functional differences among them. Such a communicative process creates a flexible and adaptive normative system. In the context of personal unity, law (as well as justice and equity) is a pattern of social interaction rather than a theoretical concept (Bianchi, 1994a). Communicative law, according to Herman Bianchi, "does not allow final judgement, it implies rather general directives, indications, road signs, invocations to discussions" (1994a:85). Communicative law requires real assent generated through a continuous process of interaction and adjustment among all persons in the community. Real assent involves the essentials of personal unity: trust and mutuality. It requires the participation of whole individuals, not simply their functional identities. Because communicative law is dependent on direct personal involvement, it must remain in the hands of those directly involved rather than being transferred to functional (i.e., bureaucratic) specialists. In the context of personal unity, perception and cognition of law are always part of an interactionist process. From the standpoint of the communicative conception of law, much of the failure of contemporary crime control can be traced to the shift from community-based conflict resolution to bureaucracy-based criminal processing. By redefining conflict as crime and shifting responsibility from the community to the state, we have increased the probability of stigmatizing offenders, thereby decreasing their prospects of reintegration (Braithwaite, 1994; Pepinsky, 1976).

A communicative system of law reflects a life-affirming model of justice (Bianchi, 1994). Societies with a life-affirming model of justice combine the two functions of justice, order maintenance and conflict resolution, into one unified system of law, whereas more repressive systems of justice tend to separate them into criminal and civil realms. Bianchi used Martin Buber's description of *tsedakah* (justice): "the incessant diligence to make people experience the genuine substantiation of confirmed truths, right and duties" as the definition of a life-affirming system of law. Bianchi argued that Emile Durkheim employed just such an understanding of law in his theory of the two laws of penal evolution (1994). Such a reinterpretation of Durkheim's classical theory requires a fundamental reassessment of the concept of anomie, which has served as the foundation of the sociological explanation of crime and its control. Traditionally, anomie has been defined as a state of normlessness, an absence of rules. Anomie has generally been perceived to be a temporary state, which receded as normative boundaries were reestablished or new boundaries were created. It has long been assumed that the establishment of normative boundaries in societies characterized by mechanical solidarity (i.e., simple societies) was accomplished through the application of penal law, whereas the establishment of normative boundaries in societies characterized by organic solidarity (i.e., complex societies) was accomplished through the application of restitutive law.

By defining societies in terms of unity patterns rather than structural complexity, it is possible to view law as an integral element of all social interaction rather than as a specialized process reserved only for serious conflict and crime. This more expansive understanding conceives of law as a cohesive discussion rather than as a disruptive edict. The communicative conception of law encourages people—law in hand—to discuss the main problems of their social life. By engaging in such a discourse, members of a society or group keep alive the sense that law unites rather than separates them. According to this conception of law, simple societies with mechanical rules were structured in such a way as to allow people to participate in the experi-

ence of their rules. These rules were not general or theoretical but specifically life-supporting. Such rules are more likely to exist in personal unity
patterns than in organic or atomistic unity patterns (Kirkpatrick, 1994; Bianchi, 1994). Anomie is not a lack of norms but a lack of the supportive qualities of norms—such as reconciliation, compensation, education, and
reintegration. The rise of anomie can be traced to increasing bureaucratization. In a bureaucratic setting the function of participation in the legal system is served organically by specialized institutions. As a result people can
no longer enjoy personal legal experience. The decreasing use of normal
(i.e., communicative/interactive) abilities to cope with conflicts has led to
alienation and anomie (Bianchi, 1994).

The way in which crime is defined determines whether a society's legal
system will be communicative or bureaucratic. The definition of crime in a
given society is determined by one of three models for interpreting norms
and values: the consensus model, the dissensus model, or the assensus
model (Bianchi, 1994). In the consensus model norms and values are seen as
the embodiment of society's will; any normative transgression is perceived
to be a threat to the general will and is therefore defined as a crime that
requires punitive action to maintain social solidarity. Conversely, the dissensus model views values and norms as representing the interests of the powerful in society; any definition of crime must therefore be viewed as a
political act designed to maintain the existing power imbalance. The weaknesses of the consensus model are its inability to incorporate changing circumstances as a variable in determining criminality and its transference of
participation in law from the people in general to a specialized bureaucracy.
In the case of the dissensus model, even if crime is politically defined, the
negative results of crime for the victim and society exist and must be redressed (Bianchi, 1994; DeKeseredy and Schwartz, 1991; Pepinsky, 1990). In
the assensus model proposed by Bianchi, conflicts are transposed into dispute settlements between the parties directly involved. In the case of crime,
reconciliatory redress in the postcrime negotiations is a mandatory element
of the discussion. While the reestablishment of such a communicative system of law within the context of modern society is an important objective in
terms of achieving greater overall social order, its feasibility depends on the
expansion of the personal realm. For communicative law to reestablish itself,
mutualist considerations must become as important as material and functional considerations.

Communicative Law in Three Societies

Communicative law is the underlying process for achieving and maintaining
social order in societies that are defined primarily in terms of personal unity,
such as Old Order Anabaptists (e.g., Hutterites, Amish, Mennonites). It is
present to a lesser extent in societies such as Japan that are defined by or-

ganic unity patterns, and it is also present, although in continued decline, in atomistically defined societies such as contemporary America. Ironically, societies like the Old Order Anabaptists, which sociologists and criminologists have characterized as legally rigid and inflexible and socially overcontrolled, actually use a more fluid system of social order than do organic or atomistic societies. The fluidity of the system is a direct result of its interactive nature. In the case of Old Order communities, social order is synonymous with the concept of *Gelassenheit*, the actualization of the mutualist model of community. Accordingly, Gelassenheit is less a philosophy or theory than a way of life. It is not based on a set of laws adjudicated through a system of justice; rather, it is based on one principle that is internalized by all members and guides all their personal actions. That one principle is "yieldedness." In all relations persons yield to others for their own sake. By yielding, persons establish an atmosphere of trust in which fear and self-interest are subordinated to mutuality. Without an atmosphere of mutuality and trust, communicative law is not possible.

The yielding spirit of Gelassenheit does not, however, preclude individual expression. On the contrary, by subordinating fear and creating an atmosphere of trust, a person is able to be fully himself or herself. There are no preconceived expectations to limit the self. The only expectation is yieldedness, and membership in the community is based solely on acceptance of the principle of Gelassenheit. Even the expulsion or isolation of a member is carried out in the hope of the eventual reintegration of that member—not for what he or she can functionally offer the community but for the member's own sake. In turn, the transgressing member is required to act toward others for their own sake. Through Gelassenheit all social life, including law, is order by the personal. As a consequence, law must be responsive to the personal.

The tendency of organic unity patterns to specialize and separate functions generally undermines mutuality by promoting superiority and subordination, with such functional differentiation ultimately leading to personal differentiation. However, some societies defined by organic unity patterns are still strongly influenced by mutualist considerations. In Japan, for example, despite the preponderance of organic unity patterns, the primary cultural value is *wa*, or harmony. The Japanese notion of harmony is a direct result of the basic living conditions of Japan (Wagatsuma and Rosett, 1986). Population density in Japan has led to the development of a hybrid unity pattern that emphasizes both functional cooperation and personal interaction "in which the interest of the individual becomes best served when he or she seeks the welfare of the group. Wa involves both a basic respect for the rights of others and a willingness to subordinate one's personal wishes when they conflict with common interests" (Westermann and Burfeind, 1991:38). The harmony of Japanese life is maintained through reverence for and loyalty to tradition. This tradition manifests itself through the communicative process of extensive social interaction. Guided by wa, these extensive patterns of social interaction contribute directly to the high level of willing conformity present in Japanese society. Willing conformity among the Japanese is directly attributable to the sense of group relatedness produced by the communicative process. Group relatedness has also been extremely important to the development of informal social control processes in Japan. Group relatedness itself is a product of consistent social interaction that develops strong feelings of dependency and a need for affiliation. *Amae*, which defines the Japanese attitude of dependency toward the group, requires more than a functional awareness of and commitment to group membership. The concept of the group in Japanese society is so powerful that the concept of self is derived from one's group membership. The incentives to remain a member of the group in good standing are so powerful, especially in the cases of family and work, that it is difficult for most Japanese even to contemplate any type of deviance or crime, however minor, for fear that it will jeopardize their group identity. Amae, like Gelassenheit, requires a subordination of the self. "The most important feature of the self in Japan is its dissolution into the group" (Masatsugu, 1982:62). For the Japanese this dissolution of self is an act of will, a form of self-control or self-discipline. Unlike Gelassenheit, in amae self-surrender is directed not toward a generalized other but toward a specific group.

Willing conformity in Japanese society is achieved through a reciprocal arrangement in which individuals commit themselves to the group to the point of accepting the group identity as their own; in return the group provides a sense of unconditional acceptance, recognition, and belonging that gives the person's life meaning and purpose. In other words, the group is life-affirming. The meaning and purpose of life are conveyed through an extensive, interactive, communicative process among members that reflects the social rather than the functional identity of the group. The communicative processes within a group such as work include more than occupational interactions. For example, conflict resolution is considered an integral element of any Japanese workplace. Conflicts of all types, including crimes that involve coworkers, are likely to be resolved in the context of the workplace rather than being transferred to a specialized legal bureaucracy to be processed criminally or civilly. The Japanese have retained a belief in the community ownership of conflict so essential to communicative law (Christie, 1977). The Japanese sense of collective responsibility is manifested in the commitment of the group to the ownership of its own conflict. By retaining ownership of conflict, groups are able to convey to the individual disputants their own responsibility for the resolution of the conflict. Disputants are not only allowed but encouraged to be actively involved in the process of resolution (Hulsman, 1986). The restorative nature of communicative law necessitates the use of such interactive processes as negotiation, apology, and forgiveness by both the disputants (i.e., offender and victim) and the broader community. Because processes such as negotiation, apology, and forgiveness are essentially symbolic speech acts, they must be carried out face-to-face. The Japanese recognize that such processes cannot be effectively executed through a bureaucratic intermediary such as a criminal court. The interactive, as opposed to bureaucratic, conflict resolution practiced by the Japanese actually strengthens willing conformity by allowing persons to participate directly in the definition of conflict, the negotiation of a settlement, and the reestablishment of normative boundaries, thereby providing them with an opportunity to shape the identity of the group in some small but significant way. Participation in the conflict resolution process in Japan increases the commitment of those involved to fulfill the terms of the agreement, while at the same time enhancing their sense of group identity (Westermann and Burfeind, 1991; Masatsugu, 1982). The fact that conflict resolution in Japan is considered part of everyday interaction rather than a separate process contributes to its effectiveness. Its embeddedness within the larger personal/organic unity pattern enhances its reintegrative capacity.

The Japanese experience demonstrates the importance of the presence of communitarian structures, such as group relatedness and collective responsibility, in establishing willing conformity and promoting reintegration (Braithwaite, 1994; Westermann and Burfeind, 1991). The relative lack of such communitarian structures in contemporary American society makes willing conformity less likely and reintegration more difficult. The strong presence of atomistic unity patterns in the United States today has shifted the orientation of social interaction from cultural reinforcement to rational calculation. The interdependencies of contemporary American life are rational rather than personal. They are perceived as isolated exchange relationships of convenience rather than culturally significant personal obligations (Braithwaite, 1994). A communitarian society, on the other hand, "combines a dense network of personal interdependencies with strong cultural commitments to mutuality of obligation" (Braithwaite, 1994:85). The shift from communitarianism to individualism in Western societies—and especially in the United States—is both ideological and structural. The ideology of individualism, which encourages personal autonomy at the expense of group identification, weakens the capacities of intermediate institutions to produce willing conformity and sanction transgressors. The ideology of individualism defines group affiliation and participation in terms of individual material interest. Social institutions and groups become a means to an end rather than an end in themselves. Membership in social institutions and groups becomes much less stable, with persons accepting membership only for as long as it serves their individual interests.

Unstable membership reduces the ability of the institution or group to socialize new members effectively, because it disrupts the normal patterns of social interaction through which individuals learn both personal and functional expectations for themselves and for others. Socialization is a process that is more interactive than educative. Through effective socialization, people learn not only what they should do but also why they should do it. Understanding why normative actions are the right actions forms the basis of willing conformity. Without normative understanding, conformity is not willing but either calculated or coerced. In an atomistic unity pattern, individuals conform either because they believe it is in their best interest to do so or because they feel powerless to do otherwise. Calculated conformity is an adequate way of maintaining order among those who are economically embedded. However, for those individuals with limited human capital and few material resources, conformity does not translate into continued material prosperity. Nor do deviance and crime represent a serious material risk for the economically marginal. As a result, even substantial formal sanctions (e.g., imprisonment) are relatively ineffective in deterring individuals who are not embedded in the economic mainstream. Recent empirical evidence suggests that the deterrent effect of formal sanctions is enhanced in cases where individuals are embedded in intermediate institutions such as the family, the military, and work (Sherman, 1993; Sampson and Laub, 1994). Institutional embeddedness may be either economically or mutually motivated. As the number of economically marginal individuals expands, it becomes increasingly important to understand and promote mutually motivated institutional commitment (Kirkpatrick, 1985).

The realization of a more mutually motivated sense of social relations will require an ideological reorientation of the political-economic structure of Western societies from individualism to communitarianism. The economic cooperation that determines the social structure and guides social relations in the West is fundamentally different from the mutuality found among Old Order communities or in Japanese institutions. Without mutuality as its dominant intention, economic cooperation transforms work from a personal to a functional action. Because the economic sphere dominates all aspects of social life in the West, the shift from the personal to the functional has affected virtually all social relations. The economic integration of society determines for the most part what forms of personal life are possible. Therefore, it is not possible to extend the personal unity pattern without transforming existing political and economic life as a whole. For the transformation to take place, "economic activity in general and work in particular have to be subordinated and adjusted to the personal life of society as a whole and to the personal lives of all its members" (Macmurray, 1961:186). The organic unity patterns (including all intermediate institutions) must be transformed from an institutional means to a self-interested end to an end in itself—a mutual end. Mutuality must become the overarching motivation behind all functional as well as personal relations.

Only by extending the personal can Western societies reverse the trends of declining willing conformity and decreasing effectiveness of informal and formal mechanisms of social control. Only by extending the personal can nonprimitive approaches to crime control, such as dispute settlement, become fully integrated into the legal process (Quinney and Pepinsky, 1991). And only by extending personal unity patterns will we truly be able to realize the possibility of a communitarian system of law in the West that promotes willing conformity as the primary means of achieving and maintaining social order.

References

Adler, F. (1983). *Nations not obsessed with crime*. Colorado: F. B. Rothman.

Bianchi, H. (1994a). *Justice as sanctuary*. Bloomington: Indiana University Press.

Bianchi, H. (1994b). Abolition: Assensus and sanctuary. In A. Duff & D. Garland (Eds.), *A reader on punishment*. New York: Oxford University Press.

Black, D. (1976). *The behavior of law*. New York: Academic Press.

Braithwaite, J. (1994). *Crime, shame and reintegration*. New York: Cambridge University Press.

Christie, N. (1977). Conflict as property. *British Journal of Criminology, 17*, 1–15.

Christie, N. (1981). *Limits to pain*. Oslo: Universitetsforlaget.

Clinard, M. (1978). *Cities with little crime*. Cambridge, England: Cambridge University Press.

Cronk, S. (1981). Gelassenheit: The rights of the redemptive process in Old Order Amish and Old Order Mennonite communities. *The Mennonite Quarterly Review, 55*, 1.

DeKeseredy, W., & Schwartz, M. (1991). British and U.S. left realism: A critical comparison. *International Journal of Offender Therapy and Comparative Criminology, 35*, 3.

Durkheim, E. (1933). *The division of labor in society*. New York: Free Press.

Durkheim, E. (1957). *Professional ethics and civic morals*. London: Routledge & Kegan Paul.

Hauerwas, S. (1981). *Community of character*. Notre Dame, Ind.: Notre Dame University Press.

Hostetler, J. (1974). *Hutterite society*. Baltimore: Johns Hopkins University Press.

Hostetler, J. (1980). *Amish society* (3rd ed.). Baltimore: Johns Hopkins University Press.

Hulsman, L. (1986). Critical criminology and the concept of crime. *Contemporary Crises, 10*, 63–80.

Kirkpatrick, F. (1985). *Community: A trinity of models*. Washington, D.C.: Georgetown Press.

Kraybill, D. (1989). *The riddle of Amish culture*. Baltimore: Johns Hopkins University Press.

Macmurray, J. (1961). *Persons in relation*. New York: Harper & Brothers.

Macmurray, J. (1974). *Freedom in the modern world*. London: Faber & Faber.

Macmurray, J. (1977). *Conditions of freedom*. Toronto: Mission Press.

Masatsugu, M. (1982). *The modern samurai society: Duty and dependence in contemporary Japan*. New York: American Management Association.

Messner, S., & Rosenfeld, R. (1996). An institutional-anomie theory of the social distribution of crime. In P. Cordella & L. Siegel (Eds.), *Readings in contemporary criminological theory*. Boston: Northeastern University Press.

Michalowski, R. (1985). *Order, law and crime*. New York: Random House.

Pepinsky, H. (1976). *Crime and conflict: A study of law and society*. London: Martin Robertson.

Pepinsky, H. (1980). *Crime control strategies: An introduction to the study of crime*. New York: Oxford University Press.

Quinney, R., & Pepinsky, H. (1991). *Criminology as peacemaking*. Bloomington: Indiana University Press.

Sampson, R., & Laub, J. (1993). *Crime in the making: Pathways and turning points through life*. Cambridge, Mass.: Harvard University Press.

Sherman, L. (1993). Defiance, deterrence and irrelevance: A theory of criminal sanction. *Journal of Research in Crime and Delinquency, 30,* 445–473.

Wagatsuma, H., & Rosett, A. (1986). The implications of apology: Law and culture in Japan and the United States. *Law and Society Review, 20,* 461–507.

Westermann, T., & Burfeind, J. (1991). *Crime and justice in two societies: Japan and the United States*. Belmont, Calif.: Wadsworth.

Zehr, H. (1976). *Crime and the development of modern society*. London: Croom Helm.

Contributors

ROBERT AGNEW is Associate Professor of Sociology at Emory University in Atlanta. Professor Agnew has written extensively on strain theory, including "Stability and Change in Crime Over the Life Course: A Strain Theory Explanation" in *Advances in Criminological Theory: Developmental Theories of Crime and Delinquency*, edited by Terence Thornberry.

HERMAN BIANCHI is retired Professor of Criminology and former Dean of the Law School at the Free University of Amsterdam. Among his many publications are *Ethics of Punishing* and *Position and Subject Matter of Criminology*.

JOHN BRAITHWAITE is Professional Fellow of Law at the Australian National University in Canberra, Australia. Professor Braithwaite has written extensively on crime, social class, and corporate criminality, including *Corporate Crime in the Pharmaceutical Industry*.

MEDA CHESNEY-LIND is Director of the Women's Study Program at the University of Hawaii-Manoa. Professor Chesney-Lind has recently coauthored with Randall Shelden *Girls, Delinquency and Juvenile Justice*.

PETER CORDELLA is Associate Professor and Chair in the Criminal Justice Department at Saint Anselm College in Manchester, New Hampshire. Professor Cordella's publications on restorative justice include "Reconciliation and the Mutualist Model of Community" in *Criminology as Peacemaking*, edited by Harold Pepinsky and Richard Quinney.

KATHLEEN DALY is Associate Professor of Sociology at the University of Michigan. Professor Daly has recently published an analysis of gender discrimination against women prisoners entitled *Gender, Crime & Punishment*.

WALTER S. DEKESEREDY is Associate Professor of Sociology and Anthropology at Carleton University in Ottawa. Professor DeKeseredy coauthored with Martin Schwartz a critical criminological text entitled *Contemporary Criminology* (1996).

LEE ELLIS is Associate Professor of Sociology at Minot State College in Minot, North Dakota. Professor Ellis has written on the link between biology and antisocial behavior, including *Crime in Biological, Social and Moral Contexts,* coedited with Harry Hoffman.

DAVID P. FARRINGTON is Professor of Psychological Criminology at the Institute of Criminology at Cambridge University. Among Professor Farrington's many publications on crime causation and prevention is the recently published *Building a Safer Society: Strategic Approaches to Crime Prevention,* coedited with Michael Tonry.

MARCUS FELSON is Associate Professor of Sociology and Senior Research Associate in the Social Science Research Institute at the University of Southern California. Professor Felson has written extensively on the routine activities approach to crime control, including *Crime & Everyday Life: Insights and Implications for Society.*

MICHAEL R. GOTTFREDSON is Professor of Management and Policy in the Law and Psychology Program at the University of Arizona. Professor Gottfredson has recently coedited with Travis Hirschi *The Generality of Deviance.*

The late RICHARD J. HERRNSTEIN was Edgar Pierce Professor of Psychology at Harvard University, where he did research on human motivational and learning processes. His books include *IQ in the Meritocracy* and *The Bell Curve: Intelligence and Class Structure in America,* coauthored with Charles Murray.

TRAVIS HIRSCHI is Regents Professor of Sociology at the University of Arizona. Among Professor Hirschi's many research publications are the criminological classic *Causes of Delinquency* and the recently published *Delinquency Research: An Appraisal of Analytic Methods,* coauthored with Hanan Selvin.

LEEANN IOVANNI was most recently Assistant Professor of Criminology at Indiana University of Pennsylvania. Professor Iovanni has recently coauthored with Susan Miller "Determinants of Perceived Risk of Formal Sanctions for Courtship Violence," which appeared in *Justice Quarterly* (1994).

JOHN H. LAUB is Professor in the College of Criminal Justice at Northeastern University in Boston. Professor Laub is coauthor with Robert Sampson of the critically acclaimed *Crime in the Making: Pathways and Turning Points Through Life.*

MICHAEL J. LYNCH is Associate Professor of Criminology at Florida State University. Professor Lynch's work on Marxist thought and crime includes *A Primer in Radical Criminology,* coedited with Byron Groves.

STEVEN F. MESSNER is Professor of Sociology, University at Albany, SUNY. Professor Messner recently coauthored with Richard Rosenfeld a contemporary analysis of social structure and anomie entitled *Crime and the American Dream* (1994).

TERRIE E. MOFFITT is Professor of Psychology at the University of Wisconsin–Madison. Professor Moffitt has coedited with S. A. Mednick and Steven Stack *Biological Contributions to Crime Causation.*

RAYMOND PATERNOSTER is Professor of Criminal Justice and Criminology at the University of Maryland. Among Professor Paternoster's most recent work is "General Strain Theory of Delinquency: A Replication and Extension" in the *Journal of Research in Crime and Delinquency* (1994), coauthored with Paul Mazerolle.

NICOLE HAHN RAFTER is Professor at the College of Criminal Justice at Northeastern University in Boston. Professor Rafter has recently coedited with Frances Heidensohn *International Feminist Perspectives in Criminology: Engendering a Discipline.*

RICHARD ROSENFELD is Associate Professor of Criminology and Criminal Justice at the University of Missouri–St. Louis. Professor Rosenfeld has coauthored with Steven Messner *Crime and the American Dream* (1994).

MARTIN D. SCHWARTZ is Professor and Chair of the Department of Sociology at Ohio University in Athens, Ohio. Professor Schwartz has coauthored with Walter DeKeseredy a critical criminological text entitled *Contemporary Criminology* (1996).

LARRY SIEGEL is Professor of Criminal Justice at the University of Massachusetts at Lowell. Professor Siegel's books include *Criminology* and *Introduction to Criminal Justice,* coauthored with Joseph Senna.

SALLY S. SIMPSON is Associate Professor of Criminal Justice and Criminology at the University of Maryland. Professor Simpson's most recent work includes "Doing Gender: Sorting Out the Caste and Crime Conundrum," which appeared in *Criminology* (1995).

MARK C. STAFFORD is Associate Professor of Rural Sociology at Washington State University. Professor Stafford's publications include "The Influence of Delinquent Peers: What They Think and What They Do," coauthored with Mark Warr, which appeared in *Criminology* (1991).

RODNEY STARK is Professor of Sociology at the University of Washington. Professor Stark has recently written *Criminology: An Introduction Using Microcase.*

TERENCE P. THORNBERRY is Professor in the School of Criminal Justice, University at Albany, SUNY. Professor Thornberry has published extensively on the subject of integrated theory, including the recently published *Developmental Theories of Crime and Delinquency.*

BRYAN VILA is Assistant Professor in the Criminology, Law and Society Program at the University of California–Irvine. Professor Vila has also authored with Lawrence Cohen "Crime as Strategy: Testing an Evolutionary Ecological Theory of Expropriative Crime," which appeared in the *American Journal of Sociology* (1993).

MARK WARR is Associate Professor of Sociology at the University of Texas at Austin. Among Professor Warr's publications is "The Influence of Delinquent Peers: What They Think and What They Do," coauthored with Mark Stafford, which appeared in *Criminology* (1991).

JAMES Q. WILSON is Collins Professor of Management at the University of California at Los Angeles. Professor Wilson has written on the subject of social order, including the recently published *Good Order: Right Answers to Contemporary Questions.*

Acknowledgments

"A Reconceptualization of General and Specific Deterrence" by Mark C. Stafford and Mark Warr. *Journal of Research on Crime and Delinquency 30* (May 1993), pp. 123–135. Copyright © 1993 by Sage Publications. Reprinted with permission of Sage Publications.

"Crime, Shame, and Reintegration" was excerpted from "Summary of the Theory" pp. 98–106 in *Crime, Shame and Reintegration* by John Braithwaite. Copyright 1994 by Cambridge University Press. Reprinted with permission of Cambridge University Press.

"Criminal Anthropology in the United States" by Nicole Hahn Rafter. *Criminology 30* (November 1992), pp. 525–545. Reprinted in abridged form with permission of the American Society of Criminology.

"The Neuropsychology of Conduct Disorder" by Terrie E. Moffitt. *Development and Psychopathology 5* (1993), pp. 135–151. Copyright 1993 by Cambridge University Press. Reprinted with permission of Cambridge University Press.

"Deviant Places: A Theory of the Ecology of Crime" by Rodney Stark. *Criminology 25* (November 1987), pp. 893–909. Reprinted with permission of the American Society of Criminology.

"Foundation for a General Strain Theory of Crime and Delinquency" by Robert Agnew. *Criminology 30* (February 1992), pp. 47–87. Reprinted with permission of the American Society of Criminology.

"The Labeling Perspective and Delinquency: An Elaboration of the Theory and an Assessment of the Evidence" by Raymond Paternoster and Leeann

Iovanni. *Justice Quarterly 6* (September 1985), pp. 359–394. Copyright © 1985 by Academy of Criminal Justice Sciences. Reprinted with permission of the Academy of Criminal Justice Sciences.

"The Nature of Criminality: Low Self-Control" by Michael R. Gottfredson and Travis Hirschi was excerpted from "The Nature of Criminality: Low Self-Control" pp. 85–100 in *A General Theory of Crime* by Michael Gottfredson and Travis Hirschi. Reprinted with the permission of the publishers, Stanford University Press. Copyright © 1990 by the Board of Trustees of the Leland Stanford Junior University.

"Crime as Choice" by James Q. Wilson and Richard J. Herrnstein was excerpted from "Crime and Its Explanation" pp. 43–65 in *Crime and Human Nature* by James Q. Wilson and Richard J. Herrnstein. Copyright 1985 by Simon and Schuster. Reprinted with permission of Simon Schuster.

"Toward an Interactional Theory of Delinquency" by Terence P. Thornberry. *Criminology 25* (November 1987), pp. 863–891. Reprinted with permission of the American Society of Criminology.

"Crime in the Making: Pathways and Turning Points Through Life" by John H. Laub was originally presented as the Thirtieth Annual Robert D. Klein University Lecture at Northeastern University. Reprinted with permission of the Board of Trustees of Northeastern University.

"The Explanation and Prevention of Youthful Offending" by David P. Farrington was excerpted from "The Explanation and Prevention of Youthful Offending" pp. 68–148 in *Delinquency and Crime: Current Theories,* edited by J. D. Hawkins. Copyright 1996 by Cambridge University Press. Reprinted with permission of Cambridge University Press.

"A Genergal Paradigm of Criminality" by Bryan Vila. *Criminology 32* (August 1994), pp. 311–359. Reprinted with permission of the American Society of Criminology.

"British and U.S. Left Realism: A Critical Comparison" by Walter S. DeKeseredy and Martin D. Schwartz. *International Journal of Offender Therapy and Comparative Criminology 35:3* (Fall 1991), pp. 248–262. Reprinted with permission of Guilford Press.

"Feminist Theory, Crime, and Justice" by Sally S. Simpson. *Criminology 27* (November 1989), pp. 605–631. Reprinted with permission of the American Society of Criminology.

Index